DIVOR
SHERI

Fifth Edition

S. A. Bennett, LL.B.
Advocate

W. GREEN/Sweet & Maxwell
EDINBURGH
1997

First published, 1984
Reprinted, 1984
Second edition, 1987
Third edition, 1991
Fourth edition, 1994
Fifth edition, 1997

© 1997
W. GREEN & SON LTD

No natural forests were destroyed to make this product;
only farmed timber was used and replanted

ISBN 0 414 01177 5

A CIP catalogue record for this book is available from the British Library

Typeset by LBJ Enterprises Ltd, Chilcompton and Aldermaston
Printed and bound in Great Britain by Redwood Books, Trowbridge, Wiltshire

To the memory of my beloved parents

ACKNOWLEDGMENT

I wish to thank David Nicol of Messrs Allan McDougall & Co., S.S.C. for expertly reviewing the text in draft, once again.

Edinburgh,   S. A. Bennett
July, 1997

FOREWORD

Sheriff Principal Graham Cox, Q.C.

This is the fifth edition of a book which first reached our bookshelves in 1984. I cannot recall any other work which has gone through so many editions in so short a time. Yet such is the pace of change in this area of the law that each succeeding edition has not merely been justified, but essential. Since the last edition in 1994 for example there has been enacted and brought into force the Children (Scotland) Act 1995. This has required the author to substantially rewrite Chapter 6 which he has done in a masterly fashion faithful to his familiar style which is precise and concise. Not only does he bring us up to date with this new and most important piece of legislation, but he has also incorporated such judicial decisions as there are pertaining to it. The new legislation relating to pensions has also been incorporated into Chapter 7, the simplicity of the title "MONEY", belying the complexities which lie within its pages. In Appendix V there is helpfully reproduced the Divorce Etc. (Pensions) (Scotland) Regulations 1996.

The author deserves not only our warm congratulations on the speed with which he has produced this new edition, but also our thanks for yet again providing us with an up-to-date compact statement of the law. It will, I am sure, be much appreciated by students, practitioners and sheriffs alike.

Airdrie,   Graham Cox
July 31, 1997

CONTENTS

Acknowledgment vii
Foreword ix
Table of Cases xiii
Table of Statutes xxi
Table of Conventions xxv
Table of Statutory Instruments xxvii
Table of Ordinary Cause Rules xxix
Table of Forms xxxi

1. **PROCEDURE PECULIAR TO DIVORCE** 1
   Citation and intimation 1
   Proof 7
   Defended actions 9
   Simplified procedure 11

2. **MISCELLANEOUS TOPICS** 14
   Reconciliation 14
   Proof of marriage 14
   Jurisdiction 15
   Concurrent proceedings 18
   Mental disorder 22

3. **THE MERITS** 25
   Adultery 28
   Behaviour 29
   Desertion 31
   Two-year and five-year actions 32

4. **PROTECTIVE MEASURES** 36
   Accommodation address 36
   Matrimonial interdicts 36
   Powers of arrest 39
   Interim exclusion orders 41
   Orders restricting removal of children 46
   Orders relating to avoidance transactions 46
   Inhibition and arrestment on the dependence 47

5. PROPERTY ORDERS 49
   Orders regulating occupancy rights 49
   Orders dispensing with consent to dealing 51
   Orders transferring tenancy 53

6. CHILDREN 55
   Jurisdiction of the court 55
   Duties of the court 56
   Powers of the court 60

7. MONEY 71
   Orders made before the granting of decree 71
   Orders made upon the granting of decree 74
   Orders made after the granting of decree 94

Appendix I: *Specimen Craves and associated Pleas-in-Law*   97
Appendix II: *Specimen Writs*   106
Appendix III: *Court Practice re Divorce Affidavits*   130
Appendix IV: *Ordinary Cause Forms relative to Divorce*
                 Actions   135
Appendix V: *The Divorce etc. (Pensions) (Scotland)*
                 Regulations 1996   172
Appendix VI: *Table of Matrimonial Property and Resources*   179
Appendix VII: *Reported Cases involving Principles B to E* ...   181

Index   191

TABLE OF CASES

A.B. *v.* C.B., 1937 S.C. 408 22
Abusaif *v.* Abusaif, 1984 S.L.T. 90 68
Adams *v.* Adams (No. 1), 1997 S.L.T. 144 .... 83, 184
Adams *v.* Adams (No. 2), 1997 S.L.T. 150 84
Adamson *v.* Adamson 1996 G.W.D. 1–3 61
Anderson *v.* Anderson, 1989 S.C.L.R. 475 .... 68, 89
Anderson *v.* Anderson, 1991 S.L.T. (Sh.Ct.) 11 .... 82, 90
Anderson *v.* Anderson, 1993 G.W.D. 35–2258 43
Anthony *v.* Anthony, 1996 G.W.D. 11–671 44
Aranda *v.* Aranda, 1990 S.L.T. (Sh.Ct.) 101 13
Armitage *v.* Armitage, 1993 S.C.L.R. 173 42
Assar *v.* Assar, 1994 G.W.D. 2–102 44
Atkinson *v.* Atkinson, 1988 S.C.L.R. 396 .... 91, 185, 187

BAILEY *v.* BAILEY, 1987 S.C.L.R. 1 38
Bannon *v.* Bannon, 1993 S.L.T. 999 .... 75, 83
Barclay *v.* Barclay, 1991 S.C.L.R. 205 .... 91, 186, 188
Barr *v.* Barr, 1939 S.C. 696 25
Begg *v.* Begg, 1987 S.C.L.R. 704 72
Bell *v.* Bell, 1983 S.L.T. 224 .... 41, 44
Bell *v.* Bell, 1988 S.C.L.R. 457 .... 75, 91, 187
Bird *v.* Bird, 1931 S.C. 371 28
Birmingham City Council *v.* H (a minor) [1994] 2 A.C. 212 57
Bisset *v.* Bisset, 1993 S.C.L.R. 284 72
Bolton *v.* Bolton, 1995 G.W.D. 14–799 .... 80, 93, 189
Bowman *v.* Bowman, Lord Grieve, February 24, 1984, unreported 44
Boyd *v.* Boyd, 1978 S.L.T. (Notes) 55 35
Boyle *v.* Boyle, 1977 S.L.T. (Notes) 69 .... 34, 45
Boyle *v.* Boyle, 1986 S.L.T. 656 45
Britton *v.* Central Regional Council, 1986 S.L.T. 207 64
Brixey *v.* Lynas, 1996 S.L.T. 908 58
Brooks *v.* Brooks, 1993 S.L.T. 184 83
Brown *v.* Brown, 1948 S.C. 5 68
Brown *v.* Brown, 1985 S.L.T. 376 .... 43, 44
Brown *v.* Brown, 1996 G.W.D. 29–1753 81
Brunton *v.* Brunton, 1986 S.L.T. 49 72
Buchan *v.* Buchan, 1992 S.C.L.R. 766 80
Buchanan *v.* Buchanan, 1989 G.W.D. 26–1166 82
Buckle *v.* Buckle, 1995 S.C.L.R. 590 .... 75, 91, 186, 189
Buczynska *v.* Buczynski, 1989 S.L.T. 558 .... 78, 79, 82, 83
Budge *v.* Budge, 1990 S.L.T. 319 82
Burnett *v.* Burnett, 1958 S.C. 1 32
Byrne *v.* Ross, 1993 S.L.T. 307 39

C *v.* C (a minor: custody appeal) [1991] 1 F.L.R. 223 58
C. *v.* S. 1989 S.L.T. 168 60
Calder Chemicals Ltd *v.* Brunton, 1984 S.L.T. (Sh.Ct.) 96 38
Caldwell *v.* Caldwell, 1983 S.L.T. 610 68
Cameron *v.* Cameron, 1996 S.C.L.R. 552 5
Cameron *v.* Cameron, 1996 S.L.T. 306 18

Carpenter v. Carpenter, 1990 S.L.T. (Sh.Ct.) 68 83
Celso v. Celso, 1992 S.C.L.R. 175 68
City of Edinburgh District Council v. Davis, 1987 S.L.T. (Sh.Ct.) 33 15
Clokie v. Clokie, 1993 G.W.D. 16–1059 82
Colagiacomo v. Cologiacomo, 1983 S.L.T. 559 .... 44, 45
Colville v. Colville, 1988 S.L.T. (Sh.Ct.) 23 13
Cooper v. Cooper, 1987 S.L.T. (Sh.Ct.) 37 27
Cooper v. Cooper, 1989 S.C.L.R. 347 83
Cosh v. Cosh, 1979 S.L.T. (Notes) 72 63
Coster v. Coster, 1992 S.C.L.R. 210 .... 44, 45
Crockett v. Crockett, 1992 S.C.L.R. 591 (O.H.) 81, 82, 83, 179
Crockett v. Crockett, Extra Division, June 30, 1993, unreported 84
Crosbie v. Crosbie, 1996 S.L.T. (Sh.Ct.) 86 .... 83, 92

Daley v. Daley, 1988 G.W.D. 3–118 91
Dalgleish v. Robinson, 1991 S.C.L.R. 892 61
Davidson v. Davidson, 1989 S.L.T. 466 89
Davidson v. Davidson, 1993 G.W.D. 31–2000 .... 82, 83, 182, 188
De Dampierre v. De Dampierre [1988] A.C. 92 22
Demarco v. Demarco, 1990 S.C.L.R. 635 .... 73, 92, 94
DeWinton v. DeWinton, 1996 G.W.D. 29–1752 .... 86, 113
DeWinton v. DeWinton (No. 2), 1997 G.W.D. 2–58 85
Dever v. Dever, 1988 S.C.L.R. 352 .... 91, 184
Dickson v. Dickson, 1990 S.L.T. (Sh.Ct.) 80 72
Dickson v. Dickson, 1990 S.C.L.R. 692 18
Donnelly v. Donnelly, 1991 S.L.T. (Sh.Ct.) 9 .... 9, 35
Dorrian v. Dorrian, 1991 S.C.L.R. 661 75
Doughton v. Doughton, 1958 S.L.T. (Notes) 34 36
Duncan v. Duncan, 1986 S.L.T. 17 32
Dunnett v. Dunnett, 1990 S.C.L.R. 135 9
Dunsmore v. Dunsmore, 1986 S.L.T. (Sh.Ct.) 9 51

Edgar v. Edgar (Porter v. Porter), 1990 S.L.T. (Sh.Ct.) 82 32
Edmond v. Edmond , 1971 S.L.T. (Notes) 8 33
Ellerby v. Ellerby, 1991 S.C.L.R. 608 91

F (specific issue: child interview), Re [1995] 1 F.L.R. 819 63
Farley v. Farley, 1991 S.L.T. 74 25
Farrell v. Farrell, 1990 S.C.L.R. 717 .... 82, 83
Ferguson v. Maclennan Salmon Co. Ltd., 1990 S.L.T. 428 85
Findlay v. Findlay, 1991 S.L.T. 457 30
Finlayson v. Finlayson's Extrx., 1986 S.L.T. 19 95
Fleming v. Fleming, 1993 G.W.D. 9–621 .... 80, 83
Forbes v. Forbes, 1994 S.L.T. 16 39
Fraser v. McFayden (1940) 56 Sh.Ct. Rep. 66 16
Fyfe v. Fyfe, 1987 S.L.T. (Sh.Ct.) 38 51

Gallacher v. Gallacher, 1934 S.C. 339 27
Geddes v. Geddes, 1993 S.L.T. 494 93
Gibson v. Gibson, 1970 S.L.T. (Notes) 60 22
Gibson v. Gibson, 1990 G.W.D. 4–213 80

Gillon v. Gillon (No. 1), 1994 S.L.T. 978 90
Gillon v. Gillon (No. 2) 1994 S.L.T. 984; 1994 S.C. 162 89
Gillon v. Gillon (No. 3), 1995 S.L.T. 678 90
Gover v. Gover, 1969 S.L.T. (Notes) 78 58
Gracie v. Gracie, 1997 S.L.T. (Sh.Ct.) 15 .... 75, 93
Gray v. Gray, 1991 S.C.L.R. 422 .... 88, 186
Gray v. Gray, 1991 G.W.D. 8–477 30
Gribb v. Gribb, 1992 S.C.L.R. 776 16
Gribb v. Gribb, 1994 S.L.T. (Sh.Ct.) 43 .... 91, 188
Gribb v. Gribb, 1996 S.L.T. 719 91
Gribben v. Gribben, 1976 S.L.T. 266 .... 38, 39
Grimes v. Grimes, 1995 S.C.L.R. 268 11
Gulline v. Gulline, 1992 S.L.T. (Sh.Ct.) 71 75
Gunn v. Gunn, 1955 S.L.T. (Notes) 69 38

H and others (prohibited steps order), Re [1995] 4 All E.R. 110 63
HG (specific issue order: sterilisation), Re [1993] 1 F.L.R. 587 63
Hall v. Hall, 1987 S.L.T. (Sh.Ct.) 15 52
Hannah v. Hannah, 1988 S.L.T. 82 61
Harris v. Harris, 1988 S.L.T. 101 47
Harris v. Martin, 1995 S.C.L.R. 580 66
Hastie v. Hastie, 1985 S.L.T. 146 30
Haughan v. Haughan, 1996 S.C.L.R. 170 .... 88, 91, 189
Henderson v. Henderson, 1991 G.W.D. 31–1864 72
Hernandez-Cimorra v. Hernandez-Cimorra, 1992 S.C.L.R. 611 47
Horn v. Horn, 1935 S.L.T. 589 17
Horton v. Horton, 1992 S.L.T. (Sh.Ct.) 37 89
Hulme v. Hulme, 1990 S.L.T. (Sh.Ct.) 25 72
Hunter v. Hunter (1900) 2 F. 774 28
Hunter v. Hunter 1979 S.L.T. (Notes) 2 8
Hutchinson v. Goodale, 1940 S.L.T. (Sh.Ct.) 24 16

J v. C [1970] A.C. 668 58
Jacques v. Jacques, (I.H.) 1995 S.C. 327 92
Jacques v. Jacques, (H.L.) 1997 S.L.T. 459; 1997 S.C.L.R. 108 .... 74, 82, 83
Jesner v. Jesner, 1992 S.L.T. 999 .... 82, 181
Johnstone v. Johnstone, 1990 S.L.T. (Sh.Ct.) 79 .... 91, 188
Jongejan v. Jongejan, 1993 S.L.T. 595 89

KAVANAGH v. KAVANAGH, 1989 S.L.T. 134 72
Kelly v. Kelly, 1992 G.W.D. 36–2130 .... 75, 91, 182, 186, 188
Kerr v. Kerr, 1995 S.C.L.R. 1130 71
Kerrigan v. Kerrigan, 1988 S.C.L.R. 603 .... 82, 181
Knox v. Knox, 1993 S.C.L.R. 381 30

LATTER v. LATTER, 1990 S.L.T. 805 .... 77, 80, 81, 83
Lawrence v. Lawrence, 1992 S.C.L.R. 199 73
Lawson v. Lawson, 1996 S.L.T. (Sh.Ct.) 83 81
Leslie v. Leslie, 1983 S.L.T. 186 47
Leslie v. Leslie, 1987 S.L.T. 232 47
Lewis v. Lewis, 1993 S.C.L.R. 32 92

Little v. Little, 1989 S.C.L.R. 613 (O.H.) 83, 181
Little v. Little, 1990 S.L.T. 785; 1991 S.C.L.R. 47 (I.H.) 74, 75, 83, 84
Little v. Little, Lord Cameron of Lochbroom, May 24, 1990, unreported .. 92, 94
Longmuir v. Longmuir, 1985 S.L.T. (Sh.Ct.) 33 51
Louden v. Louden, 1994 S.L.T. 381 .... 81, 91, 182, 186
Luckwell v. Luckwell, 1992 G.W.D. 34–2005 182

McAFEE v. McAFEE, 1990 S.C.L.R. 805 90
McAfee v. McAfee, 1993 G.W.D. 28–1782 90
McBain v. McIntyre, 1996 S.C.L.R. 181 63
McBride v. McBride, 1995 S.C.L.R. 1021 60
McCafferty v. McCafferty, 1986 S.L.T. 650 .... 43, 44
MacClue v. MacClue, 1994 S.C.L.R. 933 .... 73, 92
McColl v. McColl, 1993 S.L.T. 617 72
McConnell v. McConnell, 1993 G.W.D. 34–2185 .... 80, 81, 91, 94, 186
McCormick v. McCormick, 1994 S.C.L.R. 958 80
McCormick v. McCormick, 1994 G.W.D. 35–2078 .... 91, 92, 182, 184
McCulloch v. McCulloch, 1987 G.W.D. 19–738 30
McCulloch v. McCulloch, 1990 S.L.T. (Sh.Ct.) 63 9
McDevitt v. McDevitt, 1988 S.C.L.R. 206 91
Macdonald v. Macdonald, 1985 S.L.T. 244 59
Macdonald v. Macdonald, 1993 S.C.L.R. 132 (O.H.) 182, 184
Macdonald v. Macdonald 1995 S.L.T. 72 (O.H.) 84, 92
Macdonald v. Macdonald, 1994 G.W.D. 7–404 (I.H.) 84
McEwan v. McEwan, 1997 S.L.T. 118 75
McGeach v. McGeach, 1996 G.W.D. 29–1751 72
McGeachie v. McGeachie, 1989 S.C.L.R. 99 72
McGowan v. McGowan, 1986 S.L.T. 112 53
McGuire v. McGuire's Curator Bonis, 1991 S.L.T. (Sh.Ct.) 76 83
McInnes v. McInnes, 1990 S.C.L.R. 327 8
MacInnes v. MacInnes, 1993 S.L.T. 1108 71
MacIntyre v. MacIntyre, 1962 S.L.T. (Notes) 70 67
McIver v. McIver, 1996 S.L.T. 733 39
Mackay v. Mackay, 1946 S.C. 78 27
McKechnie v. McKechnie, 1990 S.L.T. (Sh.Ct.) 75 68
McKenna v. McKenna, 1984 S.L.T. (Sh.Ct.) 92 .... 37, 38,
McKenzie v. McKenzie, 1991 S.L.T. 461 .... 81, 91, 188
McKeown v. McKeown, 1988 S.C.L.R. 355 .... 73, 92, 94
Mackin v. Mackin, 1991 S.L.T. (Sh.Ct.) 22 .... 74, 81, 90, 91
Maclachlan v. Maclachlan, 1997 G.W.D. 8–339 .... 86, 184
MacLean v. MacLean, 1996 G.W.D. 22–1278 .... 82, 93
Maclellan v. Maclellan, 1988 S.C.L.R. 399 79
MacLure v. MacLure, 1911 S.C. 200 38
MacNaught v. MacNaught, 1996 S.C.L.R. 151 76
McNeill v. McNeill, 1960 S.C. 30 16
MacQueen v. MacQueen, 1992 G.W.D. 28–1653 .... 73, 83
MacRitchie v. MacRitchie, 1994 S.L.T. (Sh.Ct.) 72 79
McVinnie v. McVinnie (No. 2) 1997 S.L.T. (Sh.Ct.) 12 .... 77, 183
Main v. Main, 1988 G.W.D. 24–1036 91
Mather v. Mather, 1987 S.L.T. 565 45
Matheson v. Matheson, 1995 S.L.T. 765 48
Matthews v. Matthews, 1985 S.L.T. (Sh.Ct.) 68 32
Mathieson v. Mathieson, 1986 S.L.T. (Sh.Ct.) 2 43
Mazur v. Mazur, 1990 G.W.D. 35–2017 38

Millar *v.* Millar, 1990 S.C.L.R. 666 .... 88, 183, 185
Millar *v.* Millar, 1991 S.C.L.R. 649 43
Miller *v.* Miller, 1995 G.W.D. 23–1248 182
Mills *v.* Mills, 1990 S.C.L.R. 213 91
Milne *v.* Milne, 1994 G.W.D. 11–666 .... 82, 83
Mitchell *v.* Mitchell, 1992 S.C.L.R. 553 61
Mitchell *v.* Mitchell, 1993 S.L.T. 123 22
Mitchell *v.* Mitchell, 1994 S.C. 601; 1995 S.L.T. 426 79
Monkman *v.* Monkman, 1988 S.L.T. (Sh.Ct.) 37 .... 86, 91, 183
Morris *v.* Morris, 1993 S.C.L.R. 144 18
Morrison *v.* Morrison, 1989 S.C.L.R. 574 183
Morton *v.* Morton, 1996 G.W.D. 22–1276 38
Muir *v.* Muir, 1989 S.L.T. (Sh.Ct.) 20 .... 83, 91, 181, 183, 185, 187
Muir *v.* Muir, 1993 G.W.D. 39–2593 74
Munro *v.* Munro, 1986 S.L.T. 72 72
Murdoch *v.* Murdoch, 1973 S.L.T. (Notes) 13 .... 37, 38
Murley *v.* Murley, 1995 S.C.L.R. 1138 94
Murphy *v.* Murphy, 1992 S.C.L.R. 62 50
Murphy *v.* Murphy, 1996 S.L.T. (Sh.Ct.) 91 83
Murray *v.* Murray, 1993 G.W.D. 16–1058 .... 186, 188

Nasir *v.* Nasir, 1993 G.W.D. 30–1909 .... 40, 45
Nelson *v.* Nelson, 1988 S.L.T. (Sh.Ct.) 26 .... 42, 44
Nelson *v.* Nelson, 1993 S.C.L.R. 149 73
Nolan *v.* Nolan, 1979 S.L.T. 293 35
Norris *v.* Norris, 1992 S.L.T. (Sh.Ct.) 51 13
Nottinghamshire C.C. *v.* P. [1993] 3 All E.R. 815 63

O *v.* O 1995 S.L.T. 238 .... 57, 66, 67
Oliver *v.* Oliver, 1989 S.L.T. (Sh.Ct.) 1 44
O'Neill *v.* O'Neill, 1987 S.L.T. (Sh.Ct.) 26 52
Orr *v.* Orr, 1989 G.W.D. 12–506 44

P (a minor) (education), Re [1992] 1 F.L.R. 316 63
Park *v.* Park, 1988 S.C.L.R. 584 .... 82, 91, 185
Patterson *v.* Patterson, 1994 S.C.L.R. 166 66
Peacock *v.* Peacock, 1994 S.L.T. 40 .... 74, 83
Perkins *v.* Perkins, Glasgow Sheriff Court, December 11, 1984, unreported 52
Petrie *v.* Petrie, 1988 S.C.L.R. 390 .... 83, 87, 91, 178, 181, 184
Phillip *v.* Phillip, 1988 S.C.L.R. 427 82
Porter *v.* Porter (Edgar *v.* Edgar), 1990 S.L.T. (Sh.Ct.) 82 32
Pow *v.* Pow, 1987 S.L.T. 127 48
Proctor *v.* Proctor, 1994 G.W.D. 30–1814 184
Pryde *v.* Pryde, 1991 S.L.T. (Sh.Ct.) 26 .... 72, 78, 80

R (a minor) (blood transfusion) Re [1993] 2 F.L.R. 757 63
Rae *v.* Rae, 1991 S.L.T. 454 53
Ranaldi *v.* Ranaldi, 1994 S.L.T. (Sh.Ct.) 25 182
Reynolds *v.* Reynolds, 1991 S.C.L.R. 175 92
Richardson *v.* Richardson, 1991 S.L.T. (Sh.Ct.) 7 72
Rixson *v.* Rixson, 1990 S.L.T. (Sh.Ct.) 5 72

Robertson v. Robertson. 1989 S.C.L.R. 71 90
Robertson v. Robertson, 1996 G.W.D. 3–167 .... 39, 47
Robson v. Robson, 1973 S.L.T. (Notes) 4 68
Rodgers v. Rodgers (No. 2), 1994 G.W.D. 31–1869 77
Russell v. Russell, Lord Weir, February 18, 1986, unreported 53
Russell v. Russell, 1991 S.C.L.R. 429 5
Russell v. Russell, 1996 G.W.D. 15–895 .... 82, 85

SANDERSON v. McMANUS, 1997 G.W.D. 6–220 .... 58, 63
Sandison's Extrx. v. Sandison, 1984 S.L.T. 111 95
Savage v. Savage, 1993 G.W.D. 28–1779 .... 81, 91, 93, 188
Scott v. Scott, 1987 G.W.D. 17–647 .... 87, 91
Shand v. Shand, 1994 S.L.T. 387 75
Sheret v. Sheret, 1990 S.C.L.R. 799 .... 91, 183, 185
Shipton v. Shipton, 1992 S.C.L.R. 23 .... 81, 180, 181
Short v. Short, 1994 G.W.D. 21–1300 .... 82, 90
Simpson v. Bruce, 1984 S.L.T. (Sh.Ct.) 38 16
Sinclair v. Sinclair, 1986 S.L.T. (Sh.Ct.) 54 27
Singh v. Singh, 1988 S.C.L.R. 541 15
Skarpaas v. Skarpaas, 1991 S.L.T. (Sh.Ct.) 15 .... 83, 181
Skarpaas v. Skarpaas, 1993 S.L.T. 343 .... 79, 81
Smith v. Smith, 1989 S.L.T. 668 80
Smith v. Smith, 1992 G.W.D. 23–1324 78
Sochart v. Sochart, 1988 S.L.T. 799 89
Spence v. Spence, 1995 S.L.T. 335 17
Stancroft Securities Ltd v. McDowall, 1990 S.L.T. 746 48
Stein v. Stein, 1936 S.L.T. 103 36
Stephen v. Stephen 1995 S.C.L.R. 175 83
Stewart v. Stallard, 1995 S.C.L.R. 167 38
Stewart v. Stewart, 1987 S.L.T. (Sh.Ct.) 48 .... 28, 30
Stewart v. Stewart, 1990 S.C.L.R. 360 89
Stott v. Stott, 1987 G.W.D. 17–645 .... 184, 187
Symon v. Symon, 1991 S.C.L.R. 414 .... 83, 92

T AND E (proceedings: conflicting interests), Re [1995] 1 F.L.R. 581 57
Tahir v. Tahir, (No. 2), 1995 S.L.T. 451 .... 47, 93, 182
Tattersall v. Tattersall, 1983 S.L.T. 506 38
Taylor v. Taylor, 1988 S.C.L.R. 60 33
The Royal Bank of Scotland v. Mason, 1995 S.L.T. (Sh.Ct.) 32 9
Thirde v. Thirde, 1987 S.C.L.R. 335 91
Thom v. Thom, 1990 S.C.L.R. 800 48
Thomson v. Thomson, (1887) 14 R. 634 22
Thomson v. Thomson, 1955 S.L.T. (Sh.Ct.) 99 28
Thomson v. Thomson, 1979 S.L.T. (Sh.Ct.) 11 68
Thomson v. Thomson, 1991 S.L.T. 126 .... 91, 185
Toye v. Toye, 1992 S.C.L.R. 95 .... 91, 181, 184
Tyrell v. Tyrell, 1990 S.L.T. 406 .... 80, 91, 181, 185, 187

WALKER v. WALKER, 1991 S.L.T. 157; 1990 S.C.L.R. 687 77
Walker v. Walker, 1994 G.W.D. 8–496 94
Walker v. Walker, 1995 S.L.T. 375 95
Walker v. Walker and Harrison, [1981] N2 Recent Law 257 57

Wallis *v.* Wallis (I.H.) 1992 S.L.T. 676; 1993 S.C.L.R. 7 .... 80, 82
Wallis *v.* Wallis (H.L.) 1993 S.L.T. 1348 .... 74, 77, 80
Ward *v.* Ward, 1983 S.L.T. 472 .... 41, 44
Waugh *v.* Waugh, 1992 S.L.T. (Sh.Ct.) 17 13
Webster *v.* Webster, 1992 G.W.D. 25–1432 82
Welsh *v.* Welsh, 1987 S.L.T. (Sh.Ct.) 30 38
Welsh *v.* Welsh, 1994 S.L.T. 828 .... 93, 182
White *v.* White, 1947 S.L.T. (Notes) 51 28
White *v.* White, 1990 G.W.D. 12–162 28
White *v.* White, 1990 G.W.D. 12–616 183
White *v.* White, 1992 S.C.L.R. 769 82
Whitecross *v.* Whitecross, 1977 S.L.T. 255 67
Whittome *v.* Whittome (No. 1), 1993 S.C.L.R. 137; 1994 S.L.T. 114 ...... 78, 80
Whittome *v.* Whittome (No. 2), 1994 S.L.T. 130 84
Williamson *v.* Williamson, 1989 S.L.T. 866 73
Wilson *v.* Wilson, 1939 S.C. 102 26
Wilson *v.* Wilson, 1981 S.L.T. 101 48
Wilson *v.* Wilson, Lord Wylie, January 10, 1986, unreported 53
Wilson *v.* Wilson, 1993 G.W.D. 38–2521 .... 83, 186
Wiseman *v.* Wiseman, 1989 S.C.L.R. 757 71
Worth *v.* Worth, 1994 S.L.T. (Sh.Ct.) 54 90

YOUNG *v.* YOUNG (No. 2), 1991 S.L.T. 869 90

TABLE OF STATUTES

1835 Statutory Declarations
       Act 131
1853 Evidence (Scotland) Act—
       s.3 27
1874 Evidence Further Amend-
       ment (Scotland) Act—
       s.2 . . . . 25, 27
1880 Married Women's Policies
       of   Assurance
       (Scotland) Act—
       s.2 93
1907 Sheriff Courts (Scotland)
       Act 39
       s.38B(1), (2) 3
1949 Law Reform (Miscellaneous
       Provisions) Act—
       s.7(2) 28
1958 Matrimonial Proceedings
       (Children) Act 133
       s.8(2) 133
       s.11(1), (4) 67
       s.12 170
1960 Mental Health (Scotland)
       Act—
       s.6 134
1968 Law Reform (Miscellaneous
       Provisions) (Scotland)
       Act—
       s.10 31
       s.11 26
1971 Rent (Scotland) Act—
       s.3 53
       Misuse of Drugs Act 70
       Sheriff Courts (Scotland)
       Act—
       s.32(j) 59
       Form F9 59
1972 Administration of Justice
       (Scotland) Act—
       s.1(1) 73
       Matrimonial Proceedings
       (Polygamous) Marriages
       Act—
       s.2(2) 4
1973 Guardianship Act—
       s.11(1)(b) 170
       Domicile and Matrimonial
       Proceedings Act 18
       s.4 17
       s.8(2) 15
       s.8(2)(b)(ii) 16
       s.8(3),(4) 16

1973 Domicile and Matrimonial
       Proceedings Act—cont.
       s.10(1),(1A) 55
       Sched. 3 . . . . 18, 19
       para. 3(2) 20
       para. 4(a), 7 19
       para. 8 20
       para. 9(1) 19, 21
       para. 9(2) 21
       para. 9(4) 19
       para. 10(1) 21, 22
       para. 10(2) 21
       para. 11(1), (2)(a), (b) . . 20
       para. 11(2)(c) 20
       para. 11(3),(4) 21
1975 Children Act—
       s.47 165
1976 Divorce (Scotland) Act—
       s.1(1) 25
       s.1(2) 25, 34
       s.1(2)(a) 3, 28
       s.1(2)(b) 29, 30, 31
       s.1(2)(c) 31
       s.1(2)(d),(e)   11, 23, 26, 32,
                        134, 159, 162
       s.1(3) 29
       s.1(5) 35
       s.1(6) 27
       s.2 14
       s.2(1) 14
       s.2(2) 29
       s.2(3) 32
       s.2(4) 33
       s.3(1),(2) 26
       s.5 71
       s.5(6) 34
       s.13(2) 32
       Sexual Offences (Scotland)
       Act—
       s.2A–C 70
1981 Matrimonial Homes
       (Family Protection)
       (Scotland) Act 10, 49,
                                148
       s.1(1),(1A) 41
       s.1(2) 50
       s.1(3) 41
       s.2(1)(e) 49
       s.2(3) 49
       s.2(4)(a),(b) 49
       s.2(5)(b) 49
       s.3(1) 6, 49

1981 Matrimonial Homes (Family Protection) (Scotland) Act—*cont.*
s.3(2) 6, 49
s.3(3) 44, 49, 50, 51, 53
s.3(4) 50
s.3(5) 50
s.4 6
s.4(1) 41
s.4(2) 43
s.4(3) 43, 44
s.4(4)(a)–(c) 45
s.4(6) 41, 42
s.5–6(3)(a)(i) 51
s.5(1)(a) 41
s.7 .... 6, 51
s.7(1) 51
s.7(1)(a)–(d) 52
s.7(2),(3) 52
s.13 6
s.13(1) 53
s.13(2) 53
s.13(3)–(4) 53
s.13(5) 54
s.13(7) 53
s.13(9)–(11) 53
s.14(2) 37
s.14(2)(d)–(3) 51
s.15(1)(a) 39
s.15(1)(b) 40
s.15(2) 40, 41
s.15(3), (4) 39, 40
s.18 6
s.22 .... 42, 43
s.35(3)(a)–37(1) 46
1982 Civil Jurisdiction and Judgments Act—
ss.44–46 16
Sched. 9, para. 1 16
1983 Divorce Jurisdiction, Court Fees and Legal Aid (Scotland) Act—
Sched. 1, para. 18 15
1984 Mental Health (Scotland) Act—
s.1(2) 22, 26
s.1(3) 22
1985 Child Abduction and Custody Act 18
s.23(2) 46
Law Reform (Miscellaneous Provisions) (Scotland) Act—
s.13(2), (3) 41
s.13(5),(10) 42

1985 Family Law (Scotland) Act .. 35, 51, 71, 157, 160, 163, 164, 172
s.4 72
s.5(1) 60
s.5(1A) 61
s.5(4) 61
s.6 73
s.6(1)(b) 71
s.6(2),(3) 71
s.6(4) 73
s.8 .... 146, 149
s.8(1) 74, 92
s.8(1)(a) 76, 94
s.8(1)(aa) 6, 77,94
s.8(1)(ba) 6, 76, 77, 94
s.8(1)(b) 94
s.8(2) 72, 77, 91, 93, 94, 102, 103, 128
s.8(2)(b) 77
s.8(3) 74
s.9 .... 77, 91, 93, 94
s.9(1) 77
s.9(1)(a) 101, 127, 184
s.9(1)(b) 86
s.9(1)(d) 102, 128, 184, 185, 186, 187, 188, 189
s.9(1)(e) .. 88, 103, 184, 187, 188, 189
s.9(2) 85
s.10 75
s.10(1) 77, 82
s.10(2) 80
s.10(3) 78, 173
s.10(3)(a) 93
s.10(4) 79, 173
s.10(5) 79, 173, 174
s.10(5A) 75
s.10(6) 82, 83
s.10(6)(a)–(c) 82
s.10(6)(b) 84
s.10(6)(d) 83, 84
s.10(6)(e) 83
s.10(7) 78
s.10(8) 172
s.10(8)(a) 81
s.10(8)(b) 81
s.10(10) 79, 172, 173
s.10(10)(b),(c) 81
s.10(11) 75, 81, 173
s.11 61
s.11(2) 62, 86
s.11(2)(a) 86
s.11(3) 86
s.11(4) 87

1985 Family Law (Scotland) Act—*cont.*

s.11(5) 88
s.11(6) 86, 87, 88
s.11(7) 85
s.11(7)(a) 85, 86, 87, 88
s.11(7)(b) 87, 88
s.11(13) 61
s.12 77
s.12(1) 74
s.12(1)(b) 74, 94
s.12(2) 75, 83
s.12(3) 75, 7ᴜ, 83
s.12(4) 95
s.12A 83, 149, 173
s.12A(1) 75, 76
s.12A(2) ... 74, 75, 176–178
s.12A(3) 74, 176–178
s.12A(3)(a),(b),(c) 76
s.12A(4)(a) 75
s.12A(4)(b) 75, 76
s.12A(6)(a) 175
s.12A(7) 95, 176, 178
s.12A(8) 172
s.12A(10) 172
s.13 77
s.13(1)(a) 90
s.13(1)(b) 90, 94
s.13(1)(c) 94, 95
s.13(2) 55, 91
s.13(3) 90
s.13(4) 55, 90
s.13(4)(a)–(c),(6) 95
s.13(5) 55, 94
s.13(7)(a) 90
s.13(7)(b) 90
s.14 .... 77, 92, 94
s.14(1) 72, 94, 95
s.14(2) 74, 91
s.14(2)(d) 92
s.14(2)(j) 93
s.14(3) 94
s.14(4) 73, 95
s.14(5) 92
s.15 77
s.15(1) 76
s.15(2) 61, 76
s.16(1)(a) 91, 95
s.16(1)(b) 10, 89, 90
s.16(2)(a) 91
s.16(2)(b) 88
s.16(3) 10, 91
s.16(4) 90
s.16(5) 89

1985 Family Law (Scotland) Act—*cont.*

s.18 .... 10, 16, 47
s.18(1)–(4) 47
s.19(1),(2) 48
s.20 .... 71, 73
s.25 81
s.27(1) 71, 73
s.27(2) 78
s.28(3) 71
Sched. 1, para. 11 53

1986 Family Law Act—
s.11 56
s.11(1) 69
s.12(1),(3) 56
s.13(6),(7) 56
s.13(4) 69
s.14(1),(2) 56
s.15(1)–(3) 69
s.26 69
s.33(1) 67
s.33(2) 68
s.35(3) 46
s.54 56

1987 Housing (Scotland) Act ... 53
1988 Civil Evidence (Scotland) Act—
s.1 39
s.1(1) 14
s.8 134
s.8(1) 7
s.8(3),(4) 25

1989 Children Act—
s.1(3) 57
1990 Law Reform (Miscellaneous Provisions) (Scotland) Act—
s.64(a),(b) 40
Sched. 8, para. 34 74
Sched. 9 74
1991 Age of Legal Capacity (Scotland) Act—
s.7 17
Child Support Act 60
s.4(10) 60
s.7(10) 60
s.8 60
s.8(3A) 60
1993 Pension Schemes Act 172
s.1 .... 79, 193
s.94(1)(a) 173
s.94(1)(b) 174
s.95(1) 174

1995 Children (Scotland) Act—
s.1(1) 61
s.1(1)(a),(b),(d) 63
s.1(2) 61
s.1(3) 21
s.2(1) 62
s.2(1)(b),(d) 63
s.2(2),(3) 62
s.2(4) 21
s.2(7) 62
s.3(4) 62, 64
s.3(5) 62
s.6(1) 5
s.11   62, 64, 65, 67–69, 141,
157, 160, 163, 164, 166, 167
s.11(1) 57, 58, 61
s.11(1)(a),(b) 62
s.11(2) 63
s.11(2)(g),(h) 62
s.11(3)(a)(i),(ii) 64
s.11(3)(b) 64
s.11(5) 64
s.11(7)(a) 57, 58
s.11(7)(b) 59
s.11(8) 60
s.11(9),(10) 59
s.11(11) 64
s.12(2) 57
s.12(4) 56
s.25 70

1995 Children   (Scotland)
Act—*cont.*
s.52(2) 69
s.52(3) 70
s.54 61
s.54(1) 69, 70
s.54(3) 70
s.68 70
s.69 70
s.70 62
s.86 70
Sched. 4, para. 9 67
Sched. 4,
para. 20(2)(a),(b) 55
Sched. 4, para. 30 43
Sched. 4, para. 41(4) 69
Civil   Evidence   (Family
Mediation) (Scotland)
Act—
ss.1, 2 66
Pensions Act 172
s.124 172
s.167(1) 74
s.167(2)(a) 79
s.167(2)(b) 81
s.167(3) 75, 76
s.180(1) 75
1996 Family Law Act—
s.17 80
s.17(b) 75

TABLE OF CONVENTIONS

United Nations Convention on the
  Rights of the Child—
    Article 9(3) 63
    Article 12 . . . . 5, 59

TABLE OF STATUTORY INSTRUMENTS

(**bold** denotes page S.I. reproduced on)

1986 Occupational Pension Schemes (Disclosure of Information) Regulations (S.I. 1986 No. 1046)—
Reg. 6 174
Reg. 6(7) 175
Sched. 2 174
Sched. 2, para. 8, 9 175
1987 Personal Pensions Schemes (Disclosure of Information) Regulations (S.I. 1987 No. 1110)—
Sched. 2, para. 2(a),(b) ....
174, 175

1989 Evidence in Divorce Actions (Scotland) Order (S.I. 1989 No. 582)—
paras. 2(1), 3 25
1996 Divorce, etc. (Pensions) (Scotland) Regulations (S.I. 1996 No. 1676) .. 75, **172**
Regs. 3, 4 81
1996 Pensions Act 1995 (Commencement No. 6) Order (S.I. 1996 No. 1843)—

TABLE OF ORDINARY CAUSE RULES

3.1(6) 1, 34
5.3(2) ... 135–140, 145–150, 152, 157, 160, 169
5.6 1
9.6(3) 10, 65
33.1(1) 1
33.1(3) 19
33.2 19
33.2(2)(a),(b) 19
33.2(3) 20
33.3(1)(a) 65
33.3(2) 65
33.4 7
33.5 .... 61, 90
33.6(2),(3),(5) 61
33.7 .... 3, 7, 65
33.7(1) 65
33.7(1)(a) 1, 3, 135
33.7(1)(b) 4, 29, 136
33.7(1)(c) 4, 22, 23, 137
33.7(1)(d) 4, 138
33.7(1)(e) 4, 64
33.7(1)(e)(i) 139
33.7(1)(e)(ii) 139
33.7(1)(e)(iii) 140
33.7(1)(f) 5, 64, 141
33.7(1)(g) 5, 64, 142
33.7(1)(h) 5, 64, 143
33.7(1)(i) 6, 146
33.7(1)(j) 6, 47
33.7(1)(k) 6, 53, 148
33.7(1)(l) 6, 149
33.7(3) 6
33.7(4) 5, 142
33.7(5) 3, 6, 64, 65
33.7(6) 1, 3, 7
33.7(7) 3, 5, 64, 65
33.8 .... 3, 30
33.8(1),(2) 30
33.8(3) 30, 150
33.9(a) 15
33.9(b) 15, 65
33.10 .... 1, 151
33.11(1) 1, 152, 166
33.11(2) 1, 154
33.12(2) 142
33.12(3) 3, 5, 142
33.13 .... 1, 23
33.13(1)(a) 152
33.13(1)(c) 155
33.13(1)(d) 156
33.13(2) 23, 156

33.13(3) 23
33.13(4) 23
33.14 .... 33, 152
33.14(1) 23
33.14(1)(a)(i) 33, 157, 159
33.14(1)(a)(ii) 160, 162
33.14(1)(b)(i) 34, 163
33.14(1)(b)(ii) 164
33.14(2) 33, 34
33.15(1) 3
33.15(2) 5, 29, 47, 50, 53, 56
33.15(3) 3, 7, 65
33.16 .... 7, 23
33.16(2)–(7) 23, 34
33.16(8),(9) 24
33.17 20
33.18 33
33.18(1) 33, 159, 162
33.18(2) 34
33.19 59
33.19(1),(2) 59
33.19(1)(a)(ii) 165
33.19(2)(i) 165
33.19(3) 68
33.20 59
33.20(1),(2) 59
33.21(2)–(6) 67
33.22 66
33.22A(1) 66
33.22A(1)(a),(b) 65
33.22A(2)–(3) 66
33.22A(4) 65, 66
33.22A(5) 10, 66
33.22A(6) 66
33.23 68
33.24(1)(a),(b) 46
33.24(2),(3) 46
33.25 .... 2, 63
33.26 .... 9, 68
33.26(c) 88
33.27 .... 9, 44
33.28 .... 7, 168
33.28(1),(2),(3) 8
33.29(1) 8
33.29(2) 9
33.29(1)(b) 168
33.33 2
33.34 10
33.34(1) 10
33.34(1)(b)(ii) 77
33.34(1)(c)(iii) 40, 42, 50, 53, 65

33.34(2) 10
33.34(2)(a) 166
33.34(2)(b) 77
33.34(2)(b)(i) 40, 42, 50, 53, 65
33.34(3) 7
33.35, 36 10
33.37 11
33.37(1)–(4) 11
33.37(2)(a) 8
33.39(1) 60
33.39(1)(a) 10, 63, 65
33.39(1)(b) 65
33.39(2)(a) 63, 65
33.39(2)(b) 10, 60, 63
33.40(c) 169
33.41 170
33.43(a) 60
33.43(a)(i) 61
33.43(b) 64, 65
33.44(1)(a) 69
33.44(2) 69
33.45(1) 60
33.45(2) 60, 61
33.46 60
33.48(1)(a) 10, 46, 53, 77, 90
33.48(2)(a) 77
33.48(2)(b) 10, 90
33.48(2)(c) 10, 46
33.49(1),(2) 73

33.49(1)(a),(b) 71
33.50 . . . . 71, 72
33.51 94
33.51(1)(a)(ii) 94
33.51(2) 95
33.52 91
33.52(b) 46
33.53(1),(2) 46
33.64(1)(c) 169
33.64(2) 170
33.67(1)(b) 40, 42, 50
33.69(1)(a) 50
33.69(1)(b) 42
33.69(1)(d) 40
33.69(2) 2, 42, 50
33.69(2)(a) 40
33.70(1)(a) 41, 51, 56
33.70(1)(b) 41, 51
33.70(2) 2, 46
33.70(2)(a) 41
33.72(1) 40, 41, 171
33.72(2) 41, 168, 171
33.73(1)–(3) 12
33.74 . . . . 11, 12
33.75–77 12
33.78(1),(4) 12
33.78(2) 13
33.79 13
33.81, 82 13

TABLE OF FORMS
(**bold** denotes page form reproduced on)

F1 . . . . 3, **135**	F18 . . . . 23, **156**
F2 . . . . 4, **136**	F19 . . . . 33, **157**, 159
F3 . . . . 4, **137**	F20 . . . . 33, 157, **159**
F4 . . . . 4, **138**	F21 . . . . **160**, 162
F5 . . . . 4, **139**	F22 . . . . 160, **162**
F6 . . . . **140**	F23 . . . . 34, **163**
F7 . . . . 5, **141**	F24 . . . . **164**
F8 . . . . 3, 5, **142**	F25 . . . . **165**
F9 . . . . 5, 59, **143**, 167	F26 . . . . 1, 10, 65, 141, 152, 157, 160,
F10 . . . . 6, **146**	163, 164, **166**
F11 . . . . **147**	F27 . . . . 8, **168**
F12 . . . . 6, **148**	F28 . . . . **169**
F12A 6, **149**	F29 . . . . **170**
F13 . . . . 30, **150**	F30 . . . . 40, 41, **171**
F14 . . . . 1, **151**	
F15 . . . . 1, 23, **152**	G3 2
F16 . . . . 1, **154**	G4 2
F17 . . . . 23, **155**	G5 24

CHAPTER 1

PROCEDURE PECULIAR TO DIVORCE[1]

THE ordinary cause rules include special provisions applicable to actions of divorce. Some of these rules are drawn to the attention of practitioners under the relevant subject heading (*e.g.* mental disorder). Others are mentioned in this chapter.

CITATION AND INTIMATION

Citation

Except where the address of the defender is not known to the pursuer and cannot reasonably be ascertained, citation of the defender requires to be in Form F15, which must be attached to a copy of the initial writ and warrant of citation in Form F14 and must have appended to it a notice of intention to defend in Form F26.[2] The certificate of citation requires to be in Form F16 which must be attached to the initial writ.[3]

Where the address of the defender is not known to the pursuer and cannot reasonably be ascertained, citation of the defender is effected in accordance with rule 5.6,[4] which provides as follows:

"(1) Where the address of a person to be cited or served with a document is not known and cannot reasonably be ascertained, the sheriff shall grant warrant for citation or service upon that person—

---

[1] For the purpose of this Chapter, "divorce" is taken to include other family actions (as defined in r.33.1(1)), as appropriate.

[2] rr.33.10 and 33.11(1). As to service in cases of mental disorder of defender, see r.33.13 (set forth in Chap. 2, n.52). As to designation of a defender who is temporarily in custody, *cf.* Court of Session Practice Note, July 23, 1952.

[3] r.33.11(2).

[4] r.5.6 applies to all ordinary causes. In actions of divorce and other family actions, there is the additional requirement of intimation in terms of rr.33.7(1)(*a*) and (6) (as to which, see text accompanying nn.10 and 28 *infra*). The pursuer must also aver in the condescendence what steps have been taken to ascertain the defender's present whereabouts—r.3.1(6). See also Chap. 2, n.6.

   (a) by the publication of an advertisement in Form G3
      in a specified newspaper circulating in the area of the
      last known address of that person, or

   (b) by displaying on the walls of court a copy of the
      instance and crave of the initial writ, the warrant of
      citation and a notice in Form G4;

and the period of notice fixed by the sheriff shall run from
the date of publication of the advertisement or display on the
walls of court, as the case may be.

(2) Where service requires to be executed under paragraph
(1), the pursuer shall lodge a service copy of the initial writ
and a copy of any warrant of citation with the sheriff clerk
from whom they may be uplifted by the person for whom
they are intended.

(3) Where a person has been cited or served in accordance
with paragraph (1) and, after the cause has commenced, his
address becomes known, the sheriff may allow the initial writ
to be amended subject to such conditions as to re-service,
intimation, expenses or transfer of the cause as he thinks fit.

(4) Where advertisement in a newspaper is required for the
purpose of citation or service under this rule, a copy of the
newspaper containing the advertisement shall be lodged with
the sheriff clerk by the pursuer.

(5) Where display on the walls of court is required under
paragraph (1)(b), the pursuer shall supply to the sheriff clerk
for that purpose a certified copy of the instance and crave of
the initial writ and any warrant of citation."

Intimation

The sheriff may, at any time, (i) order intimation of an action[5] to
be made to such person as he thinks fit; (ii) postpone intimation,
where he considers that such postponement is appropriate and, in
that case, make such order in respect of postponement of intimation as he thinks fit; or (iii) dispense with intimation, where he

---

[5] Intimation of motions and other matters falls to be made in terms of, *e.g.* rr.33.25,
33.69(2) and 33.70(2). (The requirement to intimate motions does not apply in an
action of divorce where no notice of intention to defend has been lodged or
insofar as it proceeds as undefended—r.33.33.)

considers that such dispensation is appropriate.[6] A crave[7] or motion[8] to dispense with intimation may be granted by him.

Rule 33.7(1) requires the pursuer to include in the initial writ[9] a crave for a warrant for intimation—

    (a) in an action where the address of the defender is not known to the pursuer and cannot reasonably be ascertained, to—

        (i) every child of the marriage between the parties who has reached the age of 16 years, and

        (ii) one of the next-of-kin of the defender who has reached that age,

    unless the address of such a person is not known to the pursuer and cannot reasonably be ascertained, and a notice of intimation in Form F1 shall be attached to the copy of the initial writ intimated to any such person[10];

    (b) in an action where the pursuer alleges that the defender has committed adultery[11] with another person, to that person, unless—

        (i) that person is not named in the initial writ and, if the adultery is relied on for the purposes of section 1(2)(a) of the Divorce (Scotland) Act 1976 (irretrievable breakdown of marriage by reason of adultery), the initial writ contains an averment that his or her identity is not known to the pursuer and cannot reasonably be ascertained, or

---

[6] r.33.15(1). In terms of r.33.12(3) the sheriff may, if he thinks fit, order intimation to a local authority (such intimation requiring to be in Form F8). Whenever he considers it necessary for the proper disposal of an action of divorce, the sheriff must direct that the action be brought to the notice of the Lord Advocate in order that he may determine whether he should enter appearance therein—Sheriff Courts (Scotland) Act 1907, s.38B(1). (No expenses are claimable by or against the Lord Advocate in any action in which he has entered appearance under that section—Sheriff Courts (Scotland) Act 1907, s.38B(2).)

[7] r.33.7(5), applicable to pursuers (see text accompanying n.26 *infra*) and r.33.15(3), applicable to any party (see text accompanying nn.25 and 26). See also r.33.7(7), n.18 *infra*.

[8] r.33.7(6), applicable to any party (see text accompanying n.28 *infra*). See also r.33.8 (see Chap. 3, n.33).

[9] In the event that the pursuer makes a crave or averment which, had it been made in the initial writ, would have required a warrant for intimation under r.33.7, she requires to include a crave in her writ for a warrant for intimation or to dispense with such intimation; and r.33.7, with the necessary modifications, applies to such a crave as it applies to a crave under that rule—r.33.15(3).

[10] r.33.7(1)(a).

[11] In the event that the pursuer alleges an "improper association" (namely sodomy, incest or any homosexual relationship) between the defender and another named person, r.33.8 applies (Chap. 3, n.33).

(ii) the pursuer alleges that the defender has been guilty
of rape upon or incest with that named person,
and a notice of intimation in Form F2 shall be attached to
the copy of the initial writ intimated to any such person[12];

(c) in an action where the defender is a person who is
suffering from a mental disorder, to—

(i) those persons mentioned in sub-paragraph (a)(i) and
(ii), *supra*, unless the address of such person is not
known to the pursuer and cannot reasonably be
ascertained, and

(ii) the *curator bonis* to the defender, if one has been
appointed,
and a notice of intimation in Form F3 shall be attached to
the copy of the initial writ intimated to any such person[13];

(d) in an action relating to a marriage which was entered into
under a law which permits polygamy where—

(i) one of the decrees specified in section 2(2) of the
Matrimonial Proceedings (Polygamous Marriages)
Act 1972 is sought, and

(ii) either party to the marriage in question has any
spouse additional to the other party,
to any such additional spouse, and a notice of intimation
in Form F4 shall be attached to the initial writ intimated
to any such person[14];

(e) in an action where the sheriff may make a section 11 order
in respect of a child—

(i) who is in the care of a local authority, to that
authority and a notice of intimation in Form F5 shall
be attached to the initial writ intimated to that
authority;

(ii) who, being a child of one party to the marriage, has
been accepted as a child of the family by the other
party to the marriage and who is liable to be
maintained by a third party, to that third party, and a
notice of intimation in Form F5 shall be attached to
the initial writ intimated by that third party; or

(iii) in respect of whom a third party in fact exercises care
or control, to that third party, and a notice of
intimation in Form F6 shall be attached to the initial
writ intimated to that third party[15];

---

[12] r.33.7(1)(*b*).
[13] r.33.7(1)(*c*).
[14] r.33.7(1)(*d*).
[15] r.33.7(1)(*e*).

(f) in an action where the pursuer craves a section 11 order, to any parent or guardian of the child who is not a party to the action, and a notice of intimation in Form F7 shall be attached to the initial writ intimated to any such parent or guardian[16];

(g) in an action where the pursuer craves a residence order in respect of a child and the pursuer is—

   (i) not a parent of that child, and

   (ii) resident in Scotland when the initial writ is lodged, to the local authority within which area the pursuer resides, and a notice of intimation in Form F8 shall be attached to the initial writ intimated to that authority[17];

(h) in an action which includes a crave for a section 11 order, to the child to whom such an order would relate if not a party to the action, and a notice of intimation in Form F9 shall be intimated to that child[18];

---

[16] r.33.7(1)(*f*).

[17] r.33.7(1)(*g*). Rule 33.7(4) requires a pursuer not resident in Scotland when the initial writ is lodged for warranting who craves a residence order in respect of a child of which he or she is not a parent to include a crave for an order for intimation in Form F8 to such local authority as the sheriff thinks fit. Note that r.33.12(3) bestows upon the sheriff a general discretionary power to order intimation to a local authority (in Form F8).

[18] r.33.7(1)(*h*), subject to r.33.(7)(7), which provides that where a pursuer considers that to order such intimation is inappropriate, he or she must (a) include a crave in the initial writ to dispense with intimation to that child, and (b) include in the initial writ averments setting out the reasons why such intimation is inappropriate, and the sheriff may dispense with such intimation or make such other order as he or she thinks fit. One such reason would be the belief that the child is not "capable of forming his or her own views" (*cf.* U.N. Convention on the Rights of the Child, Art. 12, reproduced in Chap. 6, n.22), applicable where the child suffers a sufficient degree of intellectual impairment or is not of sufficient age or maturity to form a view. In the latter regard, a child of 12 years or more may be presumed to be of sufficient age and maturity (Children (Scotland) Act 1995, s.6(1)). It is a matter of judgment as to whether any particular child is capable of forming his or her own views (*cf. e.g. Cameron v. Cameron*, 1996 S.C.L.R. 552 (child of seven held not to have attained an age and degree of maturity at which it was appropriate to take account of her views) and *Russell v. Russell*, 1991 S.C.L.R. 429 (negative feelings of child of six taken into account)). In terms of r.33.15(2), where the sheriff is considering whether to make a s.11 order by virtue of s.12 of the Act (as to which, see Chap. 6, text accompanying nn.7–10), he requires to order intimation in Form F9 to the child to whom the order would relate unless intimation has already been given or the sheriff considers that the child is not of sufficient age or maturity to express [*sic*] his views. (As to procedure thereafter, see Chap. 6, text accompanying nn.25–30.) Note that the initial writ itself does not fall to be intimated in terms of either r.33.7(1)(h) or r.33.15(2).

    (i) in an action where the pursuer makes an application for an order under section 8(1)(aa) of the Family Law (Scotland) Act 1985 (transfer of property) and—

        (i) the consent of a third party to such a transfer is necessary by virtue of an obligation, enactment or rule of law, or

        (ii) the property is subject to a security,

    to the third party or creditor, as the case may be, and a notice of intimation in Form F10 shall be attached to the initial writ intimated to any such person[19];

    (j) in an action where the pursuer makes an application for an order under section 18 of the 1985 Act (which relates to avoidance transactions), to—

        (i) any third party in whose favour the transfer of, or transaction involving, the property is to be or was made, and

        (ii) any other person having an interest in the transfer of, or transaction involving, the property,

    and a notice of intimation in Form F11 shall be attached to the initial writ intimated to any such person[20];

    (k) in an action where the pursuer makes an application for an order under the Matrimonial Homes (Family Protection) (Scotland) Act 1981, where the application is under section 3(1), 3(2), 4, 7, 13 or 18 of that Act, and the entitled spouse is a tenant or occupies the matrimonial home by permission of a third party, to the landlord or the third party, as the case may be, and a notice of intimation in Form F12 shall be attached to the initial writ intimated to any such person[21]; and

    (l) in an action where the pursuer makes an application for an order under section 8(1)(ba) of the Family Law (Scotland) Act 1985, to the trustees or managers of the pension scheme, and a notice of intimation in Form F12A shall be attached to the initial writ intimated to any such person.[22]

Each notice of intimation must be on a period of notice of 21 days unless the sheriff otherwise orders; but the sheriff cannot order a period of notice of less than two days.[23]

Where a defender intends to make an application for a section 11 order which, had it been made in an initial writ, would have

---

[19] r.13.7(1)(*i*).
[20] r.13.7(1)(*j*).
[21] r.13.7(1)(*k*).
[22] r.33.7(1)(*l*).
[23] r.33.7(3).

required a warrant for intimation under rule 33.7, he must include a crave in his notice of intention to defend for a warrant for intimation or to dispense with such intimation.[24]

Where a party makes a crave or averment which, had it been made in an initial writ, would have required a warrant for intimation under rule 33.7, that party must include a crave in his writ for a warrant for intimation or to dispense with such intimation.[25]

Where the address of a person mentioned in paragraphs (b), (d), (e), (f), (h), (i), (j), (k) or (l) *supra* is not known and cannot reasonably be ascertained, there must be included in the writ of the party concerned a crave to dispense with intimation; and the sheriff may grant that crave or make such other order as he thinks fit.[26]

Where the identity or address of any person in respect of whom a warrant for intimation requires to be applied for is not known and cannot reasonably be ascertained, the party required to apply for the warrant must include in his pleadings an averment of that fact and averments setting out what steps have been taken to ascertain the identity or address, as the case may be, of that person.[27]

Where the identity or address of a person to whom intimation is required becomes known during the course of the action, the party who would have been required to insert a warrant for intimation to that person must lodge a motion for a warrant for intimation to that person or to dispense with such intimation.[28]

PROOF

The requirement of proof

In an action of divorce, whether or not appearance has been entered for the defender, no decree or judgment in favour of the pursuer may be pronounced until the grounds of action have been established by evidence.[29]

---

[24] r.33.34(3), also providing that r.33.7, with the necessary modifications, applies to a crave for a warrant under r.33.34(3) as it applies to a crave for a warrant under that rule.

[25] r.33.15(3), also providing that r.33.7, with the necessary modifications, applies to a crave for a warrant under r.33.15(3) as it applies to a crave for a warrant under that rule.

[26] rr.33.7(5) (pursuer) and 33.15(3) (any party).

[27] r.33.4.

[28] r.33.7(6).

[29] Civil Evidence (Scotland) Act 1988, s.8(1).

As a consequence of this requirement of proof, default by the defender in an action of divorce entitles the sheriff only to allow the case to proceed as undefended.[30]

Affidavits

In actions to which rule 33.28 applies, evidence requires to be given by affidavit,[31] unless the sheriff otherwise directs.[32] The rule applies to: (a) actions in which no notice of intention to defend has been lodged; (b) an action in which a curator *ad litem* has been appointed under rule 33.16 where the curator *ad litem* to the defender has lodged a minute intimating that he does not intend to lodge defences; (c) any action which proceeds at any stage as undefended where the sheriff so directs; and (d) the merits of an action which is undefended on the merits where the sheriff so directs, notwithstanding that the action is defended on an ancillary matter.[33] Where the rule applies, unless the sheriff otherwise directs, evidence relating to the welfare of a child must be given by affidavit, at least one affidavit being emitted by a person other than a parent or party to the action.[34]

In an action to which rule 33.28 applies, the pursuer must at any time after the expiry of the period for lodging a notice of intention to defend: (a) lodge in process the affidavit evidence; and (b) endorse a minute in Form F27 on the initial writ.[35]

A minute in Form F27 is as follows:

> "(*Insert name of solicitor for the pursuer*) having considered the evidence contained in the affidavits and the other documents all as specified in the Schedule hereto and being satisfied that upon the evidence a motion for decree (in terms

---

[30] r.33.37(2)(*a*).

[31] The applicable Practice Note or Act of Court relative to divorce affidavits should be consulted before affidavit evidence is presented to the court (see App. III). An affidavit sworn prior to the raising of the action is admissible only insofar as it relates to events which occurred before the action was raised (*McInnes v. McInnes*, 1990 S.C.L.R. 327). Rule 33.28(4) provides that evidence in the form of a written statement bearing to be the professional opinion of a duly qualified medical practitioner, which has been signed by him and lodged in process, shall be admissible in place of parole evidence by him.

[32] r.33.28(2). Note that at any proof in an undefended action, it is not necessary to record the evidence—r.33.32.

[33] r.33.28(1).

[34] r.33.28(3). Where a child is in the care of a local authority it is sufficient to tender evidence of that fact by affidavit from a person qualified to speak to that fact (*Hunter v. Hunter*, 1979 S.L.T. (Notes) 2).

[35] r.33.29(1).

of the crave(s)[36] of the initial writ) [*or in such restricted terms as may be appropriate*][37] may properly be made, moves the court accordingly.

> In respect whereof
> Signed
> Solicitor for the pursuer (*add designation and business address*)

SCHEDULE
(*Number and specify documents[38] considered*)."

The sheriff may at any time after the pursuer has complied with the foregoing,[39] without requiring the appearance of parties, grant decree in terms of the motion for decree; or may remit the cause for such further procedure, including proof by parole evidence, as he thinks fit.[40]

The sheriff may accept evidence by affidavit at any hearing for an order or interim order.[41]

DEFENDED ACTIONS

Part 3 of Chapter 33 of the ordinary cause rules comprises rules applicable to actions of divorce which are defended.

---

[36] Note that r.33.26 entitles the sheriff to grant decree in respect of those parts of a joint minute in relation to which he could otherwise make an order, whether or not such a decree would include a matter for which there was no crave.

[37] Illustrations of "restricted terms" are as follows:
   (i) . . . for decree in terms of the first, third and fourth craves of the initial writ
   . . .
   (ii) . . . for decree in terms of the first crave and the joint minute no. 10 of process . . .
   (iii) . . . for decree in terms of the first and second craves, and, in relation to the third crave (for a periodical allowance) for the sum craved or for such other sum as the court thinks fit . . .

[38] Such documents include affidavits, the parties' marriage certificate and the birth certificate of any child of the family as well as any notice of consent or joint minute and any extract decree or conviction, photograph, medical report or other production relevant to the case. Each witness should docquet any production relative to his or her evidence and refer to that production by its process number in his or her affidavit. The pursuer should identify the defender's signature on any document signed by him (*e.g.* joint minute, notice of consent).

[39] Subject to the rule of law that an action falls if no procedure has followed within a year and a day of the expiry of the period of notice—*McCulloch v. McCulloch*, 1990 S.L.T. (Sh.Ct.) 63 and *Dunnett v. Dunnett*, 1990 S.C.L.R. 135 (*cf. Donnelly v. Donnelly*, 1991 S.L.T. (Sh.Ct.) 9 (rule of law inapplicable where action defended for a time) and *The Royal Bank of Scotland plc v. Mason*, 1995 S.L.T. (Sh.Ct.) 32 (rule of law inapplicable where motion enrolled for decree in absence, albeit unsuccessfully)).

[40] r.33.29(2).

[41] r.33.27.

Rule 33.34 makes provision regarding notices of intention to defend and defences, applying[42] where the defender seeks—

(a) to oppose any crave in the initial writ;
(b) to make a claim for—
    (i) aliment[43];
    (ii) an order for financial provision[44]; or
    (iii) a section 11 order[45];
(c) an order—
    (i) under section 16(1)(b) or (3) of the Family Law (Scotland) Act 1985 (setting aside or varying agreement as to financial provision)[46];
    (ii) under section 18 of the 1985 Act (which relates to avoidance provisions)[47]; or
    (iii) under the Matrimonial Homes (Family Protection) (Scotland) Act 1981; or
(d) to challenge the jurisdiction of the court.

In such an action, the defender must—

(a) lodge a notice of intention to defend in Form F26 before the expiry of the period of notice; and
(b) make any claim or seek any order, as above referred to, in those defences by setting out in his defences—
    (i) craves;
    (ii) averments in the answers to the condescendence in support of those craves; and
    (iii) appropriate pleas-in-law.[48]

Notwithstanding abandonment by a pursuer, the court may allow a defender to pursue an order or claim sought in his defences; and the proceedings in relation to that order or claim shall continue in dependence as if a separate cause.[49]

Parties to a defended action of divorce require, except on cause shown, to attend in person at the options hearing.[50] Failure by a

---

[42] r.33.34(1).
[43] Also provided for by r.33.39(1)(*a*) and (2)(*b*).
[44] Also provided for by r.33.48(1)(*a*) and (2)(*a*).
[45] Also provided for by r.33.39(1)(*a*) and (2)(*a*). But see r.9.6(3), mentioned in n.48 *infra*.
[46] Also provided for by r.33.48(1)(*a*) and (2)(*b*).
[47] Also provided for by r.33.48(1)(*a*) and (2)(*c*).
[48] r.33.34(2). But see r.9.6(3) (in divorce action neither crave nor averments need be made in defences which relate to a s.11 order).
[49] r.33.35.
[50] r.33.36. The parties are similarly obliged to attend any child welfare hearing (along with any child who has indicated his or her wish to attend)—r.33.22A(5). As to such hearings, see Chap. 6, text accompanying nn.57–62.

party to attend, however, attracts no sanction provided that he or she is represented at the diet.[51]

Provision is made by rule 33.37 for the granting of decree by default, the rule applying[52] in an action in which the defender has lodged a notice of intention to defend where a party fails—

(a) to lodge, or intimate the lodging of, any production or part of process;

(b) to implement an order of the sheriff within a specified period, or

(c) to appear or be represented at any diet.

Where a party has so failed, and is thereby in default, the sheriff may—

(i) allow the action to proceed as undefended under Part 2 of Chapter 33 of the rules; or

(ii) grant decree of absolvitor; or

(iii) dismiss the action or any claim made or order sought; and

(iv) award expenses.[53]

Where no party appears at a diet, the sheriff may dismiss the action.[54]

The sheriff may, on cause shown, prorogate the time for lodging any production or part of process, or for intimating or implementing any order.[55]

SIMPLIFIED PROCEDURE

Simplified divorce applications (namely applications for divorce by a party to a marriage made in the manner prescribed by rule 33.74) may be made if, but only if—

(a) the applicant relies on the facts set out in section 1(2)(d) (no cohabitation for two years with consent of defender to decree), or section 1(2)(e) (no cohabitation for five years) of the Divorce (Scotland) Act 1976;

(b) in an application under section 1(2)(d) of the 1976 Act, the other party consents to decree of divorce being granted;

---

[51] *Grimes v. Grimes*, 1995 S.C.L.R. 268.
[52] r.33.37(1).
[53] r.33.37(2).
[54] r.33.37(3).
[55] r.33.37(4).

    (c) no other proceedings are pending in any court which could have the effect of bringing the marriage to an end;

    (d) there are no children of the marriage under the age of 16 years;

    (e) neither party to the marriage applies for an order for financial provision on divorce; and

    (f) neither party to the marriage suffers from mental disorder.[56]

If an application ceases to be one to which the foregoing applies at any time before the final decree, it is deemed to be abandoned and must be dismissed.[57]

Rule 33.74 provides that:

> "(1) A simplified divorce application in which the facts set out in section 1(2)(d) . . . are relied on shall be made in Form F31 and shall only be of effect if—(a) it is signed by the applicant[58]; and (b) the form of consent in Part 2 of Form F32 is signed by the party to the marriage giving consent.
>
>   (2) A simplified divorce application in which the facts set out in section 1(2)(e) . . . are relied on shall be made in Form F33 and shall only be of effect if it is signed by the applicant."

It is the duty of the sheriff clerk to cite any person and intimate any document in connection with a simplified divorce application[59] and such requires to be done in accordance with rules 33.76 and 33.77.

Any person on whom service or intimation of a simplified divorce application has been made may give notice by letter sent to the sheriff clerk that he challenges the jurisdiction of the court[60] or opposes the grant of decree of divorce and giving the reasons for his opposition to the application[61]; and in that event, the sheriff

---

[56] r.33.73(1) and (3).

[57] r.33.73(2).

[58] The applicant requires also to send an extract or certified copy of the marriage certificate and the appropriate fee—r.33.75.

[59] r.33.76(2).

[60] The sending of such a letter does not imply acceptance of the jurisdiction of the court—r.33.78(4).

[61] r.33.78(1).

must dismiss the application unless he is satisfied that the reasons given for the opposition are frivolous.[62]

Parole evidence cannot be given in a simplified divorce application.[63]

Any appeal against an interlocutor granting decree of divorce in terms of the simplified divorce application may be made, within 14 days after the date of decree, by sending a letter to the court giving reasons for the appeal.[64]

Any application to the court after decree of divorce has been granted in a simplified divorce application which could have been made if it had been made in an action of divorce requires to be made by minute.[65]

---

[62] r.33.78(2). As to "frivolous", see *Waugh v. Waugh*, 1992 S.L.T. (Sh.Ct.) 17. An application was dismissed where a question arose as to the validity of the marriage in *Aranda v. Aranda*, 1990 S.L.T. (Sh.Ct.) 101.

[63] r.33.79.

[64] r.33.81. As to "reasons for the appeal," see *Colville v. Colville*, 1988 S.L.T. (Sh.Ct) 23 and *Norris v. Norris*, 1992 S.L.T. (Sh.Ct.) 51.

[65] r.33.82. See Chap. 7 (second) n.31.

CHAPTER 2

MISCELLANEOUS TOPICS

MISCELLANEOUS topics of significance in divorce law and practice are considered in this chapter.

RECONCILIATION

One of the aims of the Divorce (Scotland) Act 1976, according to its long title, is "to facilitate reconcilation of the parties in consistorial causes".

Section 2 of the Act contains certain provisions for the encouragement of reconciliation between spouses.[1] The court is empowered by that provision in appropriate cases to continue any pending action of divorce for such period as it thinks proper to enable attempts to be made to effect reconciliation (and any cohabitation during this period is disregarded for the purposes of that action).[2] Practitioners have been enjoined by a Court of Session Practice Note,[3] to:

> "try to identify, at as early a stage as possible, those cases in which the parties might benefit from the expert advice and guidance of a marriage counsellor, and in those cases [to] encourage the parties to seek such advice and guidance."

PROOF OF MARRIAGE

As a prerequisite to obtaining decree of divorce, the pursuer must aver and prove the parties' marriage. It is sufficient for the pursuer to give evidence of the date and place of the marriage ceremony,[4]

---

[1] Those provisions affecting the merits of divorce actions are noticed in Chap. 3, text accompanying nn.28, 39, and 44.
[2] s.2(1).
[3] March 11, 1977.
[4] Civil Evidence (Scotland) Act 1988, s.1(1).

14

at least where the marriage is undisputed.[5] However, unless the sheriff otherwise directs, a warrant for citation will not be granted without there being produced with the initial writ an extract[6] of the relevant entry in the register of marriages or an equivalent document.[7] Such a direction, it is thought, would be justified where a warrant is required as a matter of urgency (and an undertaking to lodge the certificate within a certain period of time is given) or where it is impossible to obtain relevant documentation and it is intended to prove the marriage by parole or affidavit evidence.

JURISDICTION

A sheriff court has jurisdiction by virtue of section 8(2) of the Domicile and Matrimonial Proceedings Act 1973[8] to entertain an action for divorce if (and only if[9])

    (a) either party to the marriage in question—
          (i) is *domiciled* in Scotland at the date when the action is begun,[10] or
        (ii) was *habitually resident* there throughout the period of one year ending with that date;

    and

    (b) either party to the marriage—

---

[5] If the marriage is disputed certain statutory provisions may fall to be applied (as to which, see Clive, *The Law of Husband and Wife in Scotland* (3rd ed., 1992) (hereinafter 'Clive'), pp. 448–451).
[6] Where the defender's whereabouts are unknown, a recently issued certificate should be produced (see 1950 S.L.T. (News) 11) unless the parties were married in Scotland, in which event a letter from General Register Office stating that the parties are not already divorced should be lodged (see 1984 S.L.T. (News) 100).
[7] r.33.9(*a*). The same applies where a s.11 order is craved, in respect of birth certificates—r.33.9(*b*).
[8] As amended by the Divorce Jurisdiction, Court Fees and Legal Aid (Scotland) Act 1983, Sched. 1, para. 18.
[9] Prorogation, for example, is not a ground of jurisdiction in actions of divorce— *Singh v. Singh*, 1988 S.C.L.R. 541.
[10] *cf. City of Edinburgh District Council v. Davis*, 1987 S.L.T. (Sh.Ct.) 33 (action "raised" when citation of defender effected).

    (i) was resident in the sheriffdom[11] for a period of 40
        days ending with that date,[12] or
   (ii) was resident in the sheriffdom for a period of not
        less than 40 days ending not more than 40 days
        before the said date and has no known residence in
        Scotland at that date.[13]

A sheriff court also has jurisdiction to entertain an action of
divorce begun at a time when a similar action is pending in relation
to the marriage in respect of which the court has jurisdiction.[14] The
foregoing provisions are without prejudice to any sheriff court's
jurisdiction to entertain an action of divorce remitted to it in
pursuance of any enactment or rule of court.[15]

There remains to be considered the meaning of the terms
"domicile" and "habitual residence".

Domicile

As the following quotation[16] indicates, "domicile"[17] is a term not
readily defined:

"the concept of domicile is a complicated one, and it is
possible merely to state the circumstances in which Scots law
will impute to a person a domicile within a particular
country. In epitome, the common law of Scotland imputes to
a legitimate child at his birth the domicile of his father and to
an illegitimate or posthumous child the domicile of his
mother. This is his domicile of origin . . . [Until he attains the

---

[11] There seems to be nothing as a matter of law to require the raising of the action
in the *sheriff court district* in which the party was resident. As a matter of practice,
however, special cause must be shown to obtain warrant for citation from any
court within a sheriffdom other than that in which the cause would normally fall
to be dealt, namely the court within the district of which the relevant party was
resident (see *Simpson v. Bruce*, 1984 S.L.T. (Sh.Ct.) 38).
[12] Residence within the sheriffdom thereafter cannot be taken into account in
determining whether or not there is jurisdiction—*McNeill v. McNeill*, 1960 S.C.
30.
[13] There would appear to be no room to interpret s.8(2)(b)(ii) in anything other
than a literal fashion: *cf. McNeill; Fraser v. Macfadyen* (1940) 56 Sh.Ct.Rep. 66;
and *Hutchinson v. Goodale*, 1940 S.L.T. (Sh.Ct.) 24.
[14] 1973 Act, s.8(3).
[15] 1973 Act, s.8(4). An example of an action of divorce remitted to the sheriff court
is *Gribb v. Gribb*, 1992 S.C.L.R. 776.
[16] Anton, *Private International Law* (2nd ed., 1990), p. 125.
[17] "Domicile" is separately defined for the purposes of the Civil Jurisdiction and
Judgments Act 1982 by ss.44–46 of that Act. By virtue of Sched. 9, para. 1
thereof, the 1982 Act does not govern jurisdiction in actions of divorce.

age of 16 years] his domicile changes with that of the person upon whom he is dependent.[18] [Thereafter][19] his existing domicile continues to be attributed to him unless and until he resides in a different country, with the intention of residing there permanently. If these elements of fact and intention concur, he is then attributed a domicile in that country, called a domicile of choice.[20] Scots law will continue to infer that he is domiciled in the country of choice either until he leaves that country with the settled intention of abandoning it as a home, when he is deemed to revert to his domicile of origin, or until he acquires a domicile of choice in another country."

Facts from which domicile may be inferred should be averred.[21]

---

[18] By virtue of s.4 of the 1973 Act, when his parents are alive but living apart, a child's dependent domicile shall be that of his mother if (a) he then has his home with her and has no home with his father; or (b) he has at any time had her domicile by virtue of para. (*a*) and has not since had a home with his father; and if his mother then dies and he has not since had a home with his father the child has the domicile which she last had before she died. The Scottish Law Commission in their *Report on Family Law* (Scot. Law Com. No. 135, 1992) propose the following enactment relative to the domicile of children:

"45—(1) A child is domiciled in the country with which he or she is for the time being most closely connected.

(2) Where the child's parents are domiciled in the same country and the child has his or her home with either or both of them, it is to be presumed, unless the contrary is shown, that the child is most closely connected with that country.

(3) Where the child's parents are not domiciled in the same country and the child has his or her home with one of them, but not with the other, it is to be presumed, unless the contrary is shown, that the child is most closely connected with the country in which the parent with whom the child has his or her home is domiciled.

(4) The rule laid down by the foregoing provisions of this section apply to times before this Act comes into force but only for the purpose of determining where at any time after this Act comes into force a child is domiciled.

(5) Where those rules apply, they do so in place of the corresponding rules of the common law and section 4 of the Domicile and Matrimonial Proceedings Act 1973 and section 9(1)(a) of the Law Reform (Parent and Child) (Scotland) Act 1986.

(6) In this section—
'child' means a person who has not attained the age of 16 years;
'country' includes territory and means, in relation to a person whose domicile at a particular time is in question, a country which has its own system of law at that time."

[19] By virtue of s.7 of the Age of Legal Capacity (Scotland) Act 1991, the time at which a person first becomes capable of having an independent domicile is the date at which he attains the age of 16 years.

[20] Whether or not a husband had acquired a domicile of choice in Spain was the issue in *Spence v. Spence*, 1995 S.L.T. 335.

[21] *Horn v. Horn*, 1935 S.L.T. 589.

Habitual residence

The term "habitual residence" in the context of the 1973 Act[22] was considered in *Morris v. Morris*[23] wherein the sheriff principal observed:

> "Habitual residence has not been defined. At the end of the day it is a question of fact. Without seeking to lay down any definition I would consider that it encompasses the idea of where the person normally lives."

In the Scottish Law Commission's report[24] on which the 1973 Act was based there is averred a justification for use of that particular term:

> "to indicate that it is not enough for a person to make his occasional residence within the territory but that, on the other hand, residence which in substance is stable should not be ignored because the person in question occasionally interrupts it to go elsewhere for purposes of business or recreation."

CONCURRENT PROCEEDINGS[25]

Where more than one legal system has jurisdiction to divorce the parties to a marriage, complex rules are required to avoid conflicts of jurisdiction.

These rules are to be found in Schedule 3 to the Domicile and Matrimonial Proceedings Act 1973. Broadly speaking, they require the parties to certain Scottish actions (including actions of divorce) to tell the court about any proceedings continuing outwith Scotland which are in respect of the marriage or capable of affecting its

---

[22] "Habitual residence" in the context of the Child Abduction and Custody Act 1985 was considered by the Inner House in *Dickson v. Dickson*, 1990 S.C.L.R. 692 and in *Cameron v. Cameron*, 1996 S.L.T. 306. In *Dickson* the First Division's view was that "a habitual residence is one which is being enjoyed voluntarily for the time being and with the settled intention that it should continue for some time . . . A person can, we think, have only one habitual residence at any one time" (at p.703B). In *Cameron* the Second Division differed from that view only to the extent that it was not satisfied that in all cases the residence had to be voluntarily adopted before there could be habitual residence.

[23] 1993 S.C.L.R. 144 at p. 145.

[24] *Report on Jurisdiction in Consistorial Cases affecting Matrimonial Status* (Scot. Law Com. No. 25, 1972), at para. 71.

[25] See Chap. 6, text accompanying nn.55 and 56, regarding concurrent proceedings concerning children.

validity or subsistence (hereinafter referred to as "concurrent proceedings"); and they make provision, discussed *infra*, regarding mandatory and discretionary sists by the Scottish court where there are concurrent proceedings elsewhere.

This duty on parties to inform the court of any concurrent proceedings subsists while the action is pending and until proof in the action has begun.[26] Failure of a person to perform this duty prolongs the time within which the court has a discretion to sist the cause (which discretion would otherwise cease to be exercisable at the beginning of the proof).[27]

Ordinary cause rule 33.2 provides the machinery whereby each party may discharge this duty.

The pursuer must state in the condescendence of the initial writ whether to her knowledge any proceedings are continuing[28] in Scotland or in any other country which are in respect of the marriage to which the initial writ relates or are capable of affecting its validity or subsistence.[29]

Where such proceedings are continuing, the pursuer must also state:

(a) the court, tribunal or authority before which they have been commmenced;
(b) the date of commencement;
(c) the names of the parties;
(d) the date or expected date of any proof (or its equivalent) in the proceedings; and
(e) such other facts as may be relevant to the question of whether or not the action before the sheriff should be sisted under Schedule 3 to the 1973 Act (discussed *infra*).[30]

Where such proceedings are continuing; the action before the sheriff is defended; and either (i) the initial writ does not contain the statement anent those proceedings above referred to, or (ii) the particulars mentioned in (a) to (e) above are incomplete or incorrect, any defences or minute, as the case may be, lodged by

---

[26] Sched. 3, para. 7. Neither the taking of evidence on commission nor a separate proof relating to any preliminary plea is to be regarded as part of the proof in the action: Sched. 3, para. 4(a); *quaere* when proof could be said to begin where evidence is submitted in the form of affidavits.

[27] para. 9(1) and (4); there is no other sanction in respect of such failure: para. 9(4).

[28] Proceedings are "continuing" at any time after they have commenced and before they have been finally disposed of—r.33.1.(3).

[29] r.33.2(2)(*a*).

[30] r.33.2(2)(*b*).

any person to the action must include that statement and, where appropriate, the further or correct particulars.[31]

Mandatory sists

Where before the beginning of the proof in a continuing divorce action it appears to the court, on the application[32] of a party to the marriage, that proceedings in respect of that marriage for divorce or nullity of marriage are continuing in a related jurisdiction (*i.e.* another country within the United Kingdom[33]) and certain other conditions are satisfied, the court *must* sist the action.[34]

These other conditions are that it appears to the court:

(1) that the parties to the marriage have resided together after the marriage was contracted;
(2) that the place where they resided together when the action in the Scots court was begun (or, if they did not then reside together, where they last resided together before that date) is in that related jurisdiction; and
(3) that either party was habitually resident in that related jurisdiction throughout the year ending with the date on which they last resided together before the action in the Scots court was begun.

Where an action has been sisted by reference to proceedings in a related jurisdiction, the Scots court loses the power to make a "relevant order" in that action, namely an interim order relating to aliment or children.[35] Any such order already made ceases to have effect three months from the date of the sisting of the action (unless the order or the sist has by then been recalled).[36] These provisions are subject to the court's power to make, or extend the duration of, a relevant order if the court considers such to be necessary "as a matter of necessity and urgency."[37]

If at the time of the sisting of the Scots action there is in force, or if therafter there comes into force, in the proceedings elsewhere an order in relation to any of certain specified matters, that order

---

[31] r.33.2(3).
[32] Application must be made by written motion—r.33.17.
[33] Namely, England, Wales, Northern Ireland, Jersey, Guernsey (including Alderney and Sark) and the Isle of Man—para. 3(2).
[34] para. 8.
[35] para. 11(2)(a); "relevant order" is defined in para. 11(1).
[36] para. 11(2)(b).
[37] para. 11(2)(c).

supersedes any similar order in the Scots action that has been, or might be, made.[38] These matters are periodical payments for a spouse, periodical payments for a child, arrangements to be made concerning with whom a child is to live, contact with a child, and any other matter relating to parental responsibilities within the meaning of section 1(3) of the Children (Scotland) Act 1995 or parental rights within the meaning of section 2(4) of that Act.

These provisions have no effect on the power of the court to make relevant orders once the sist has been recalled; to vary or recall relevant orders still in force; or to enforce any relevant order as respects any period when it is or was in force.[39]

The court may on the application of a party to the action recall a mandatory sist if it appears to the court that the proceedings elsewhere are sisted or concluded or that the prosecution of them has been unreasonably delayed.[40] Once the sist has been recalled, the rule on mandatory sists has no further application.[41]

Discretionary sists

Where before the beginning of the proof[42] in a continuing divorce action it appears to the court that there are concurrent proceedings in another jurisdiction (*i.e.* outwith the United Kingdom) the court *may* sist the action.[43]

Its discretion to do so is to be exercised if it appears to the court that the balance of fairness (including convenience) as between the parties to the marriage is such that it is appropriate for those other proceedings to be disposed of before further steps are taken in the Scots action.[44] In considering the balance of fairness and convenience, the court requires to have regard to all factors appearing to be relevant, including the convenience of witnesses and any delay or expense which may result from the proceedings being sisted, or not being sisted.[45] It has been held that the proper initial approach to the question of the balance of fairness (including convenience) is to consider the overall connection of the marriage with the jurisdictions in question; and if the overall connection of the

---

[38] para. 11(3), including any order judged to be necessary as a matter of necessity and urgency.
[39] para. 11(4).
[40] para. 10(1). As to the mode of application, see n.32 *supra*.
[41] para. 10(2).
[42] See n.26 *supra*.
[43] para. 9(1).
[44] *ibid*.
[45] para. 9(2).

marriage is prima facie with Scotland, the court would only be entitled to grant the sist if it were to take the view that there were, nevertheless, other circumstances by reason of which justice required that a sist should be granted.[46]

The court may on the application of a party to the action recall a discretionary sist if it appears to the court that the proceedings elsewhere are sisted or concluded or that the prosecution of them has been unreasonably delayed.[47]

MENTAL DISORDER

Mentally disordered pursuer

An insane person cannot competently pursue an action of divorce.[48] Mental disorder falling short of insanity does not of itself preclude the raising of an action of divorce; the pursuer must however have the capacity to give instructions for the raising and prosecution of the action.[49] A preliminary proof as to the pursuer's mental condition is competent; the onus on the defender to establish incapacity is a heavy one.[50]

Mentally disordered defender

In an action where the defender is a person who is suffering from a mental disorder,[51] intimation requires to be made in accordance with rule 33.7(1)(c); and where the defender is also

---

[46] *Mitchell v. Mitchell*, 1993 S.L.T. 123. See also *De Dampierre v. De Dampierre* [1988] A.C. 92.

[47] para. 10(1). As to the mode of application, see n.32 supra.

[48] *Thomson v. Thomson* (1887) 14 R. 634.

[49] *Gibson v. Gibson*, 1970 S.L.T. (Notes) 60.

[50] *AB v. CB*, 1937 S.C. 408.

[51] "Mental disorder" is defined by the Mental Health (Scotland) Act 1984 as "mental illness or mental handicap, however caused or manifested" (s.1(2)). By virtue of s.1(3), no person is to be treated as suffering from mental disorder by reason only of promiscuity or other immoral conduct, sexual deviancy or dependence on alcohol or drugs.

resident in a hospital or other similar institution, citation requires to be effected in accordance with rule 33.13.[52]

Rule 33.16 applies where it appears to the court that the defender is suffering from a mental disorder. In that event, the sheriff must:

(a) appoint a curator *ad litem* to the defender;
(b) where the facts set out in section 1(2)(d) of the Divorce (Scotland) Act 1976 (no cohabitation for two years with consent of defender to decree) are relied on—
    (i) make an order for intimation of the ground of the action to the Mental Welfare Commission for Scotland; and
    (ii) include in such an order a requirement that the Commission sends to the sheriff clerk a report indicating whether in its opinion the defender is capable of deciding whether or not to give consent to the granting of decree.[53]

Within seven days after the appointment of a curator *ad litem*, the pursuer must send to him—

(a) a copy of the initial writ and any defences (including any adjustments and amendments) lodged; and

---

[52] As to r.33.7(1)(c), see Chap. 1 (text accompanying n.13). Rule 33.13 requires citation to be executed by registered post or the first class recorded delivery service addressed to the medical officer in charge of that hospital or institution; and there requires to be included with the copy of the initial writ—
  (a) a citation in Form F15;
  (b) any notice required by r.33.14(1) (see Chap. 3, nn.45 and 53 and accompanying text).
  (c) a request in Form F17;
  (d) a form of certificate in Form F18 requesting the medical officer to—
    (i) deliver and explain the initial writ, citation and any notice or form of notice of consent required under r.33.14(1) personally to the defender; or
    (ii) certify that such delivery or explanation would be dangerous to the health or mental condition of the defender; and
  (e) a stamped envelope addressed for return of that certificate to the pursuer or his solicitor, if he has one.
The medical officer must send the certificate in Form F18 duly completed to the pursuer or his solicitor, as the case may be, and that certificate must be attached to the certificate of citation (r.33.13(2) and (3)).
Where such a certificate bears that the initial writ has not been delivered to the defender, the sheriff may, at any time before decree
  (a) order such further medical inquiry, and
  (b) make such order for further service or intimation as he thinks fit (r.33.13 (4)).
[53] r.33.16(2).

    (b) a copy of any notice in Form G5 sent to him by the sheriff clerk.[54]

On receipt of a report from the Commission, the sheriff clerk must—

    (a) lodge the report in process; and
    (b) intimate that this has been done to—
        (i) the pursuer;
        (ii) the solicitor for the defender, if known; and
        (iii) the curator *ad litem*.[55]

The curator *ad litem* requires to lodge in process within 14 days after the report of the Commission has been lodged in process or, where no such report is required, within 21 days after the date of his appointment, one of the following:

    (a) a notice of intention to defend;
    (b) defences to the action;
    (c) a minute adopting defences already lodged; or
    (d) a minute stating that the curator *ad litem* does not intend to lodge defences.[56]

Notwithstanding that he has lodged a minute stating that he does not intend to lodge defences, a curator *ad litem* may appear at any stage of the action to protect the interests of the defender.[57]

If, at any time, it appears to the curator *ad litem* that the defender is not suffering from mental disorder, he may report that fact to the court and seek his own discharge.[58]

The pursuer is responsible, in the first instance, for payment of the fees and outlays of the curator *ad litem* incurred during the period from his appointment until—

    (a) he lodges a minute stating that he does not intend to lodge defences;
    (b) he decides to instruct the lodging of defences or a minute adopting defences already lodged; or
    (c) being satisfied after investigation that the defender is not suffering from mental disorder, he is discharged.[59]

The effect of mental disorder on the use of affidavit procedure and the simplified procedure is noted in Chapter 1.[60]

---

[54] r.33.16(3).
[55] r.33.16(4).
[56] r.33.16(5) and (6).
[57] r.33.16(7).
[58] r.33.16(8).
[59] r.33.16(9).
[60] See Chap. 1, text accompanying nn.33 and 56.

CHAPTER 3

THE MERITS

IN an action for divorce the court may upon an application by the pursuer[1] grant decree of divorce, if, but only if, it is established in accordance with section 1(2) of the Divorce (Scotland) Act 1976 that the marriage has broken down irretrievably.[2] There are five ways of establishing irretrievable breakdown, each of which is considered in turn. Some general rules relating to proof of the merits of a divorce action are considered first.

Sufficiency of evidence

Some specialties regarding sufficiency of evidence in divorce actions require mention:

(a) subject to section 8(4) of the Civil Evidence (Scotland) Act 1988 (as to which, see (b) *infra*), the evidence in an action of divorce establishing the grounds of action must consist of or include evidence other than that of a party to the marriage.[3] The evidence of the parties, therefore, whilst admissible,[4] is always insufficient (except in cases falling within (b)).

(b) by virtue of section 8(4) of the Civil Evidence (Scotland) Act 1988 and the Evidence in Divorce Actions (Scotland) Order 1989,[5] the foregoing requirement of evidence other than that of a party to the marriage does not apply to actions of divorce in which—

    (i) the action is undefended[6];

---

[1] There is no provision in the ordinary cause rules for a defender to apply for decree of divorce (*cf. Farley v. Farley*, 1991 S.L.T. 74).

[2] 1976 Act, s.1(1).

[3] Civil Evidence (Scotland) Act 1988, s.8(3).

[4] Evidence Further Amendment (Scotland) Act 1874, s.2. Note that failure by the defender to lodge defences is not a fact upon which the pursuer may found (*Barr v. Barr*, 1939 S.C. 696).

[5] S.I. 1989 No. 582, paras. 2(1) and 3.

[6] For the purpose of the Order, an action is treated as undefended when the defender has not entered appearance or, having entered appearance, has not lodged defences or has withdrawn them—para. 2(2).

(ii) the action is brought in reliance on the facts set out in section 1(2)(d) or (e) of the Divorce (Scotland) Act 1976;

(iii) there are no children of the marriage under the age of 16 years;

(iv) neither party applies for an order for financial provision on divorce; and

(v) neither party suffers from mental disorder within the meaning of section 1(2) of the Mental Health (Scotland) Act 1984 (*i.e.* mental illness or mental handicap, however caused or manifested).

(c) by virtue of section 3(1) of the Divorce (Scotland) Act 1976, where a decree of separation has been granted in respect of facts which are the same, or substantially the same, as those averred in support of an action for divorce, an extract of that decree lodged in process may be treated as sufficient proof of the facts upon which such decree was granted.

The foregoing does not entitle the court to grant decree of divorce without receiving evidence from the pursuer,[7] for:

> "Past conduct that has become spent will not do . . . There must in every case be a live cause of action. It follows that, while past conduct may suffice, every action must be subject to all such bars, impediments, and defences as are open in all actions of divorce under the existing law."[8]

The pursuer must therefore, in addition to lodging a certified copy initial writ and extract decree of separation, update by way of affidavit or parole evidence the contents thereof (usually by narrating that the parties have neither lived together nor had marital relations since the date upon which decree of separation was granted).

Section 3(1) is not applicable to actions of divorce for adultery (which are separately provided for[9]) and is necessarily of limited value, if any, in relation to two- and five-year actions.[10]

---

[7] 1976 Act, s.3(2).

[8] *per* the Lord Justice-Clerk in *Wilson v. Wilson*, 1939 S.C. 102 at p. 107.

[9] Law Reform (Miscellaneous Provisions) (Scotland) Act 1968, s.11.

[10] This is because the relevant period of the parties' non-cohabitation in these cases is that immediately preceding the bringing of the action of divorce; in two-year cases there is the added complication that the defender must consent to the granting of decree of divorce.

Burden and standard of proof

The onus of proving irretrievable breakdown of the marriage is of course on the pursuer. It is not for her to prove the absence of any defence to divorce, but:

> "Divorce procedure . . . is not purely adversarial. The court can take note of bars to divorce even if not pleaded and is entitled to require full information to be laid before it, where that can reasonably be done, to enable it to discharge its functions. It is not reasonable to expect the pursuer to negate *lenocinium* and collusion. It is, however, reasonable enough to expect the pursuer to say whether there has been cohabitation between the parties after adultery or after the expiry of the two-year period in a divorce for desertion. It is also reasonable enough to expect the pursuer in a five years case to provide information about the financial position of the parties so far as known to him."[11]

The standard of proof required to establish irretrievable breakdown is proof on the balance of probability.[12]

Competency and compellability of witnesses

The rules of competency and compellability of witnesses apply to actions of divorce as to other causes, with the exception that the privilege attached to communications between spouses during the marriage has not in practice been applied in relation to the merits of divorce.[13] (On the other hand, there has been no relaxation in practice of the statutory protection[14] afforded to all witnesses against any question tending to show that he or she has been guilty

---

[11] Clive, pp. 443 and 444. In its *Report on Family Law* (Scots Law Com. No. 135, 1992) the Scottish Law Commission proposes an amendment to the Divorce (Scotland) Act 1976 as follows:

"8A. In an action for divorce the court shall not grant decree of divorce if it is satisfied that (whether or not through the collusion of the parties) the pursuer has put forward a false case or the defender has withheld a good defence."

[12] 1976 Act, s.1(6).

[13] Evidence (Scotland) Act 1853, s.3, not applied in *Gallacher v. Gallacher*, 1934 S.C. 339, and *Mackay v. Mackay*, 1946 S.C. 78.

[14] Evidence Further Amendment (Scotland) Act 1874, s.2. It has been held that where a witness admits adultery on oath by way of an affidavit, such affidavit should disclose *in gremio* that the witness has been warned of his or her right to refuse to answer any question tending to show guilt of adultery—*Cooper v. Cooper*, 1987 S.L.T. (Sh.Ct.) 37 (*cf. Sinclair v. Sinclair*, 1986 S.L.T. (Sh.Ct.) 54).

of adultery.) The parties to an action of divorce are competent and probably compellable witnesses.[15] Neither can be compelled in any proceedings to give evidence that marital intercourse did or did not take place between them during any period.[16]

Although it may not strictly be a matter of competency or compellability, the attention of practitioners is drawn to judicial dicta stressing that it is undesirable for the defender to avoid giving evidence in a defended divorce action.[17]

ADULTERY

Irretrievable breakdown is established if:

> "since the date of the marriage the defender has committed adultery" (1976 Act, s.1(2)(a)).

Adultery is:

> "voluntary sexual intercourse between a married person and a person of the opposite sex, not being the marriage partner."[18]

Thus one act of adultery is sufficient. How the offended spouse responds to it or perceives it is immaterial.[19] Whether or not the marriage partners were cohabiting at the time is irrelevant. Good faith (*e.g.* committing adultery in the genuine belief that the marriage partner is dead) is not a defence.[20]

Adminicles of evidence relevant to proof of adultery include admissions of adultery,[21] "opportunity plus",[22] diaries and letters,[23] fathering or mothering a child by a third party[24] and other sexual behaviour.[25]

---

[15] Clive, p. 446.
[16] Law Reform (Miscellaneous Provisions) Act 1949, s.7(2).
[17] *Bird v. Bird*, 1931 S.C. 371 at pp. 374 and 375, and *White v. White*, 1947 S.L.T. (Notes) 51; see also *Thomson v. Thomson*, 1955 S.L.T. (Sh.Ct.) 99.
[18] Clive, p. 402, referring to monogamous marriages. As to adultery and polygamy, see Clive, p. 403.
[19] *Stewart v. Stewart*, 1987 S.L.T. (Sh.Ct.) 48 at p. 50.
[20] *Hunter v. Hunter* (1900) 2 F. 774.
[21] See Clive, p. 455.
[22] *ibid*. p. 463 and *White v. White*, 1990 G.W.D. 12–612.
[23] *ibid*. pp. 455–458.
[24] *ibid*. pp. 458–462.
[25] *ibid*. pp. 462–464.

Irretrievable breakdown is not to be taken to be established if the adultery has been connived at in such a way as to raise the defence of *lenocinium*.[26] The essence of this defence is:

"that a spouse who has actively promoted, or who is art and part in, the other spouse's adultery cannot found on that adultery as a ground of divorce."[27]

Irretrievable breakdown is also not to be taken to be established if the adultery has been condoned by the pursuer's cohabitation with the defender in the knowledge or belief that the defender has committed the adultery; and adultery will not be held to have been so condoned by reason only of the fact that after the commission of the adultery the pursuer has continued or resumed cohabitation with the defender, provided that the pursuer has not cohabited with the defender at any time after the end of the period of three months from the date on which cohabitation was continued or resumed with the aforesaid knowledge or belief.[28]

Intimation of an adultery action and of an adultery allegation falls to be made in accordance with rules 33.7(1)(b) and 33.15(2), respectively.[29]

BEHAVIOUR

Irretrievable breakdown is established if:

"since the date of the marriage the defender has at any time behaved (whether or not as a result of mental abnormality and whether such behaviour has been active or passive) in such a way that the pursuer cannot reasonably be expected to cohabit with the defender" (1976 Act, s.1(2)(b)).

The question as to whether the pursuer can reasonably be expected to cohabit with the defender is a question as to the position at the date of proof and the court is entitled to take into account the pursuer's circumstances at that date and the changes

---

[26] 1976 Act, s.1(3). The Scottish Law Commission in its *Report on Family Law* (Scot. Law Com. No. 135, 1992) proposes that s.1(3) be amended so as to read that irretrievable breakdown is not to be taken to be established if the adultery has been "actively promoted or encouraged by the pursuer."
[27] Clive, p. 433. Examples of this bar to divorce are putting one's wife out to prostitution, indulging in wife-swapping and encouraging one's wife to commit adultery in order to obtain evidence for a divorce.
[28] 1976 Act, ss.1(3) and 2(2).
[29] See Chap. 1, text accompanying nn.11, 12 and 25.

that will have occurred in the parties' lives since they separated.[30]
Irretrievable breakdown is however only to be taken to be established where the fact that the pursuer cannot reasonably be
expected to cohabit with the defender flows, in a causal sense, from
the nature of the relevant behaviour of the defender.[31]

Whereas

> "adultery is based on objective fact and affords a ground for
> divorce however the offended spouse responds to it or
> perceives it . . . in relation to s.1(2)(b) of the 1976 Act, the
> effective question is how the offended spouse could reason-
> ably be expected to react to specific behaviour on the part of
> the other spouse".[32]

The more obvious examples of behaviour establishing irretrievable breakdown include habitual abuse of alcohol or drugs, violence directed at the pursuer (including attempted and threatened
violence), and extra-marital sexual activity (including sodomy,
incest or any homosexual relationship,[33] bestiality and other inde-
cent behaviour, adultery and, depending on the circumstances,
behaviour with other members of the opposite sex falling short of
adultery[34]). Relevant conduct may be persistent, or cumulative, or
(exceptionally) neither:

> ". . . conduct on the part of a defender, by word or act, may
> be of such a nature that even if there is no risk of a repetition
> it is so destructive of a marriage relationship as to make it
> unreasonable to expect the pursuer to cohabit with the
> defender".[35]

---

[30] *Findlay v. Findlay*, 1991 S.L.T. 457.

[31] *Findlay, supra*. See also *Knox v. Knox*, 1993 S.C.L.R. 381.

[32] *Stewart v. Stewart*, 1987 S.L.T. (Sh.Ct.) 48 at p. 50 (admission of extra-marital
"association" after persistent late homecoming justified divorce). See also
McCulloch v. McCulloch, 1987 G.W.D. 19–738.

[33] Where the pursuer alleges sodomy, incest or any homosexual relationship
between the defender and another named person, r.33.8 applies. Rule 33.8(1)
requires the pursuer, immediately after expiry of the period of notice, to lodge a
motion for an order for intimation to that person or to dispense with such
intimation. In terms of r.33.8(2), the sheriff in determining the motion may
(a) make such order for intimation as he thinks fit; or (b) dispense with
intimation; and (c) where he dispenses with intimation, order that the name of
that person be deleted from the condescendence of the initial writ. Where
intimation is ordered, a copy of the initial writ and an intimation in Form F13
must be intimated to the named person (r.33.8(3)).

[34] *Stewart, supra*.

[35] *Hastie v. Hastie*, 1985 S.L.T. 146 at p. 148 (false accusations of infidelity and of an
incestuous association) (*cf. Gray v. Gray*, 1991 G.W.D. 8–477).

Where the defender has been convicted of a criminal offence upon which the pursuer wishes to found (*e.g.* assault upon her), she may rely upon section 10 of the Law Reform (Miscellaneous Provisions) (Scotland) Act 1968 to establish the commission of the offence. It is improper, it is considered, to aver that a person has been convicted of a criminal offence without first having had sight of an extract conviction.

DESERTION

Irretrievable breakdown is established if:

"the defender has wilfully and without reasonable cause deserted the pursuer, and during a continuous period of two years immediately succeeding the defender's desertion—

(i) there has been no cohabitation between the parties, and

(ii) the pursuer has not refused a genuine and reasonable offer by the defender to adhere." (1976 Act, s.1(2)(c)).

This provision may be broken down into its component parts as follows:

(a) The defender has wilfully deserted the pursuer.
This entails the defender's withdrawal from cohabitation with the intention of ending the married life, while the pursuer is willing to continue it.[36]

(b) The desertion was without reasonable cause.
Adultery committed by the pursuer provides "reasonable cause" for the defender to desert, as does behaviour on her part falling within section 1(2)(b). There is a question as to whether the conduct founded on by the defender requires to have been known to him at the time of desertion in order to provide "reasonable cause".[37]

(c) During a continuous period of two years immediately succeeding the defender's desertion there has been no cohabitation between the parties.[38]

---

[36] See, generally, Clive, pp. 415–420.
[37] Fully discussed by Clive, pp. 420–423.
[38] The action must be brought after the expiry of that period (n.41 *infra*). As to "cohabitation" and the statutory provision affecting the assessment of whether or not the two-year period has been continuous, see nn.42–44 *infra* and accompanying text.

If, after the expiry of the two-year period, the pursuer has resumed cohabitation with the defender and has cohabited with the defender at any time after the end of the period of three months from the date on which cohabitation was resumed as aforesaid, irretrievable breakdown will not be taken to have been established.[39]

(d) During the aforesaid two-year period the pursuer has not refused a genuine and reasonable offer by the defender to adhere.

Whether an offer is "genuine and reasonable" will turn on the facts of the particular case; the defender will generally be well-advised not to attach conditions to the offer.[40]

TWO-YEAR AND FIVE-YEAR ACTIONS

Irretrievable breakdown is established if:

"there has been no cohabitation between the parties at any time during a continuous period of two years after the date of the marriage and immediately preceding the bringing of the action[41] and the defender consents to the granting of decree of divorce" (1976 Act, s.1(2)(d));

or:

"there has been no cohabitation between the parties at any time during a continuous period of five years after the date of the marriage and immediately preceding the bringing of the action" (1976 Act, s.1(2)(e)).

In both actions, accordingly, it must be averred and proved that the parties have not cohabited for the requisite period of time.

---

[39] 1976 Act, s.2(3).
[40] See, *e.g. Burnett v. Burnett*, 1958 S.C. 1 and earlier cases cited by Clive at p. 424.
[41] An action raised before the expiry of the requisite period of non-cohabitation is "manifestly groundless"—*Matthews v. Matthews*, 1985 S.L.T. (Sh.Ct.) 68. Conversion of an action, whether for divorce or for separation, to a two-year or five-year action by amendment after the expiry of the requisite period of non-cohabitation is competent—*Duncan v. Duncan*, 1986 S.L.T. 17; *Edgar v. Edgar*, 1990 S.L.T. (Sh.Ct.) 82 (*cf. Porter v. Porter*, 1990 S.L.T. (Sh.Ct.) 82).

Section 13(2) of the 1976 Act provides that:

"the parties to a marriage shall be held to cohabit with one another only when they are in fact living together as man and wife; and 'cohabitation' shall be construed accordingly."[42]

In considering whether or not a period of non-cohabitation has been continuous no account is to be taken of any period (or periods) not exceeding six months[43] in all during which the parties cohabited with one another, any such period (or periods) however not counting as part of the period of non-cohabitation.[44]

Two-year actions

Ordinary cause rules 33.14 and 33.18 provide the machinery for the giving and the withdrawal of consent to the granting of decree of divorce.

The pursuer requires to attach to the copy initial writ served upon the defender a notice in Form F19 and a notice of consent in Form F20.[45] The defender thereafter indicates to the court his consent by giving notice in writing in Form F20 to the sheriff clerk.[46] The evidence of one witness is sufficient for the purpose of

---

[42] The expression "in fact living together as man and wife" is considered in detail by Clive at pp. 429–431. At p. 429 he suggests: "Whether a couple are in fact living together as man and wife is, manifestly, a question of fact . . . The question must be approached by applying the statutory words directly to the circumstances of each case. Various factors will be important—the amount and nature of time spent together, living under the same roof, sleeping together, having sexual intercourse together, eating together, having a social life and other leisure activities together, supporting each other, talking to each other, loving each other, sharing resources, sharing household and child-rearing tasks and so on—but, with one apparent exception, none will be conclusive on its own. The one apparent exception is total physical separation for the two- or five-year period. It is only an apparent exception because this factor cannot exist on its own: it necessarily involves an absence of most other relevant factors."
[43] According to Clive, this must mean six *lunar* months (*i.e.* 24 weeks) rather than six *calendar* months (p. 431).
[44] 1976 Act, s.2(4) (applicable to desertion, two-year and five-year cases); if a pursuer intends to found on this provision, that intention should be made clear upon averment—*Edmond v. Edmond*, 1971 S.L.T. (Notes) 8 at p. 9.
[45] r.33.14(1)(*a*)(i). The certificate of citation must state which notice or form has been attached in the initial writ—r.33.14(2). See also Chap. 1, n.2 and accompanying text.
[46] r.33.18(1). The defender is free to deliver the notice of consent personally or have an intermediary (*e.g.* the pursuer's solicitor) deliver it—*Taylor v. Taylor*, 1988 S.C.L.R. 60. Where a defender sought to indicate his consent in oral evidence, decree was refused in *Rodgers v. Rodgers*, 1994 S.C.L.R. 750.

establishing that the signature on the notice of consent is that of the defender.[47]

The defender is entitled to withdraw his consent at any time and for any reason. Where the initial writ contains an averment that the defender consents to the grant of decree, he may give notice in writing to the court that he has not consented to decree being granted or that he withdraws any consent which he has already given.[48] Where he does so, the sheriff clerk must intimate the terms of the letter to the pursuer who is required within 14 days after the date of the intimation, if none of the other facts mentioned in section 1(2) of the Divorce (Scotland) Act 1976 is averred in the initial writ, to lodge a motion for the action to be sisted.[49] If no such motion is lodged, the pursuer shall be deemed to have abandoned the action and the action must be dismissed.[50] If the motion is granted and the sist is not recalled or renewed within a period of six months from the date of the interlocutor granting the sist, the pursuer is deemed to have abandoned the action and the action must be dismissed.[51] In any case where the defender has not given or has withdrawn his consent, it is incompetent or at least inappropriate, it seems, for the court to pronounce any interlocutor in the process, save as already mentioned.[52]

Five-year actions

The pursuer in a five-year case requires to send with the copy initial writ served upon the defender a notice as nearly as may be in terms of Form F23.[53]

Where the defender's address is unknown in a five-year case, the pursuer must satisfy the court that all reasonable steps have been taken to ascertain it.[54] Averments setting out what steps have been taken should be made.[55]

---

[47] r.33.18(2). It has been held that where a lengthy period of time has elapsed since the date of the defender's signature the sheriff has a discretion as to whether or not to treat the consent form as valid—*Donnelly v. Donnelly*, 1991 S.L.T. (Sh.Ct.) 9.

[48] r.33.18(3).

[49] r.33.18(4) and (5).

[50] r.33.18(6).

[51] r.33.18(7).

[52] See *Boyle v. Boyle*, 1977 S.L.T. (Notes) 69.

[53] r.33.14(1)(*b*)(i). The certificate of citation must state which notice or form has been attached to the initial writ—r.33.14(2). See also Chap. 1, n.2 and accompanying text.

[54] 1976 Act, s.5(6). *cf.* Chap. 1, n.4 and accompanying text, and Chap. 2, n.6.

[55] r.3.1(6).

Nothwithstanding that irretrievable breakdown has been established in a five-year case, the court is not bound to grant decree if in the opinion of the court the grant of decree of divorce would result in grave financial hardship to the defender.[56] "Hardship" is defined as including the loss of the chance of acquiring any benefit.[57] In order to enable the court to exercise its discretion in the area, the pursuer in any five-year case should narrate the whole financial circumstances of both parties, whether or not a financial claim is to be made.[58]

---

[56] 1976 Act. s.1(5). See *e.g. Nolan v. Nolan*, 1979 S.L.T. 293 and *Boyd v. Boyd*, 1978 S.L.T. (Notes) 55. The Scottish Law Commission in its *Report on Family Law* (Scot. Law Com. No. 135, 1992) proposes the repeal of this subsection, which rests uneasily with the court's powers in the Family Law (Scotland) Act 1985 for the ordering of financial provision (see, especially, Chap. 7, text accompanying n.97).

[57] *ibid.*

[58] See text accompanying n.11 *supra*.

CHAPTER 4

PROTECTIVE MEASURES

IN this chapter various measures for the protection of a party's position in an action of divorce are discussed. These range in importance and effect from the accommodation address to matrimonial interdicts and interim exclusion orders.

ACCOMMODATION ADDRESS

Where the pursuer does not wish to disclose her whereabouts to the defender, she may be designed as care of her solicitors in the instance of the initial writ. Use of an accommodation address is however a privilege, for, when a party's true address is not given, he is not properly designed, and accordingly the initial writ is not properly framed.[1]

There are circumstances in which the court will allow the use of an accommodation address (*e.g.* where there would otherwise be a risk of molestation); facts to justify the privilege must however be fully stated in the initial writ.[2] Application may be made to the court by motion to ordain a party using an accommodation address to reveal his or her true address.[3]

MATRIMONIAL INTERDICTS

An interdict is a matrimonial interdict (to which a power of arrest may be attached[4]) if it is:

"an interdict including an interim interdict which—
  (*a*) restrains or prohibits any conduct of one spouse towards the other spouse or a child of the family, or

---

[1] *Doughton v. Doughton*, 1958 S.L.T. (Notes) 34.
[2] *ibid.*
[3] As in *Stein v. Stein*, 1936 S.L.T. 103.
[4] Powers of arrest are dealt with in this chapter, *infra*.

(*b*) prohibits a spouse from entering or remaining in a
matrimonial home or in a specified area in the
vicinity of the matrimonial home."[5]

The phrase "matrimonial interdict" itself has no content unless
applied to an interdict in specific terms; and such interdict, to be
classed a "matrimonial interdict", must fall within the category of
interdict above-mentioned.[6] A matrimonial interdict may have a
common law or a statutory basis.[7] If the former, the terms of the
interdict must be no wider than are necessary to curb the illegal
actings complained of, and so precise and clear that the person
interdicted is left in no doubt what he is forbidden to do[8]; must be
sharply defined and related specifically to the particular risks which

---

[5] Matrimonial Homes (Family Protection), (Scotland) Act 1981, s.14(2). In its
Report on Family Law (Scot. Law Com. No. 135, 1992) the Scottish Law
Commission proposes the repeal of s.14 and its substitution by the following:
   "14.(1) The court may, on the application of a spouse, grant an interdict, or an
interim interdict, (to be known as a 'matrimonial interdict') which—
   (a) restrains or prohibits any conduct of the non-applicant spouse towards
      the applicant spouse or a child of the family;
      or
   (b) subject to subsection (2) below, prohibits the non-applicant spouse from
      entering or remaining in—
      (i) the matrimonial home;
      (ii) any other home or other premises occupied by the applicant
         spouse;
      (iii) any place of work, or the school attended by any child in the care,
         of the applicant spouse; or
      (iv) a specified area in the vicinity of any such home, premises, place of
         work or school.
   (2) If the non-applicant spouse is entitled, or permitted by a third party, to
occupy the matrimonial home, or has occupancy rights in it, the court shall
not grant a matrimonial interdict prohibiting that spouse from entering, or
remaining in, that home or a specified area in its vicinity unless the interdict
is ancillary to an exclusion order or (as the case may be) to a refusal by the
court of leave to exercise occupancy rights in the circumstances mentioned in
section 1(3) of this Act.
   (3) In the foregoing provisions of this section . . .—
'applicant spouse' means the spouse who applied for the interdict;
'non-applicant spouse' shall be construed accordingly;
'spouse' includes former spouse.
   (4) It shall be competent for the court to entertain an application for a
matrimonial interdict, whether or not the spouses concerned are living
together as husband and wife."
[6] *McKenna v. McKenna*, 1984 S.L.T. (Sh.Ct.) 92 at p. 95.
[7] As to the latter, see Interim Exclusion Orders, *infra*.
[8] *Murdoch v. Murdoch*, 1973 S.L.T. (Notes) 13 at p. 13. In *McKenna, supra*, it was
considered reasonable to protect the pursuer against the possibility that the
defender would seek him out at his home.

justify its grant[9]; must not be so framed as to prevent the exercise of undoubted legal rights[10]; and must be justified by the applicant's pleadings.[11]

Where there is no information of a wrong actually being committed by the defender against the pursuer, there must be reasonable apprehension that the defender may, in the future, do the illegal acts which the pursuer seeks to have him restrained from doing in her crave.[12] The court must be "satisfied that the pursuer, unless interdict is granted, is likely to be exposed, without other adequate protection, to conduct on the part of the defender which will put her at risk or in fear, alarm, or distress."[12a]

In any application for perpetual interdict, whether or not the action is defended, it is the duty of the court to exercise a sound judicial discretion in deciding whether interdict should be granted; and such grant can only be made on strong or at least reasonable grounds.[13] It is competent for a sheriff to grant a matrimonial interdict preventing the commission of an unlawful act outwith his territorial jurisdiction.[14]

Breach of interdict

When an interim interdict in a divorce process is claimed to have been breached, a minute may be lodged containing detailed averments in support of a crave for the court to ordain the defender to appear at the bar to explain his actings.[15] A breach of interdict constitutes a contempt of court which may lead to

---

[9] *Murdoch, supra.*

[10] *Tattersall v. Tattersall*, 1983 S.L.T. 506, wherein the legal rights in question were those of the tenant in respect of possession of the property. An interdict at common law against a non-entitled spouse seeking to enter the matrimonial home without leave of the court would, it is thought, be competent (*cf. MacLure v. MacLure*, 1911 S.C. 200). An interdict at common law against an entitled spouse seeking to prevent a non-entitled spouse from continuing to occupy the matrimonial home is competent (*Mazur v. Mazur*, 1990 G.W.D. 35–2017). An interdict at common law preventing removal of furniture and plenishings from the matrimonial home has been held to be competent (*Welsh v. Welsh*, 1987 S.L.T. (Sh.Ct.) 30).

[11] See, *e.g. McKenna, supra.*

[12] *Bailey v. Bailey*, 1987 S.C.L.R. 1 at p. 4.

[12a] *Murdoch, supra.*

[13] *Bailey, supra.* (see also *Gunn v. Gunn*, 1955 S.L.T. (Notes) 69 and *Morton v. Morton*, 1996 G.W.D. 22–1276).

[14] *McKenna, supra.* (*cf. Calder Chemicals Ltd v. Brunton*, 1984 S.L.T. (Sh.Ct.) 96).

[15] See *Gribben v. Gribben*, 1976 S.L.T. 266. Note that an interim interdict ceases to be operative when the action ceases to be pending (*Stewart v. Stallard*, 1995 S.C.L.R. 167).

punishment, and it is necessary in the interests of fairness that the alleged contempt should be clearly and distinctly averred and that the proceedings for contempt be confined to the averments.[16]

Such a minute may only be presented with the concurrence of the procurator fiscal concerned with any criminal proceedings which may be taken as a result of the actings in question.[17] It is understood that consent will not be forthcoming if the matter is to be the subject of such proceedings. If the alleged breach is denied, answers may be ordered and a proof held. The standard of proof is proof beyond reasonable doubt.[18] Proceedings for breach of interdict are civil proceedings to which section 1 of the Civil Evidence (Scotland) Act 1988 applies.[19] If the breach is admitted or proved, the defender is liable to punishment by fine or imprisonment.[20]

Where perpetual interdict is claimed to have been breached, procedure is by way of initial writ.[21] Proceedings taken by way of initial writ for breach of interdict are civil proceedings to which the appeal provisions of the Sheriff Courts (Scotland) Act 1907 apply.[22]

POWERS OF ARREST

A power of arrest entitles a police officer to arrest without warrant a spouse whom he has reasonable cause to suspect is in breach of a matrimonial interdict.[23] The court must attach a power of arrest, when asked, where the matrimonial interdict is ancillary to an exclusion order, or an interim exclusion order.[24] The court must also do so, when asked, in relation to any other matrimonial interdict, subject to two provisos:

---

[16] *Byrne v. Ross*, 1993 S.L.T. 307.
[17] *Gribben, supra.* Once the procurator fiscal has indicated that he does not intend to intervene, it is not necessary to intimate any adjustments or amendments to the minute regarding other incidents which are all part of the same course of conduct—*Byrne*, at p. 310.
[18] *Gribben, supra.*
[19] *Byrne, supra.*
[20] See Dobie, *Sheriff Court Practice*, p. 509. *cf. Robertson v. Robertson*, 1996 G.W.D. 3–167. In *Forbes v. Forbes*, 1994 S.L.T. 16 the Inner House observed that it is proper not to call on the minuter in hearing submissions as to penalty, except with respect to matters of competency.
[21] *e.g. Forbes, supra.*
[22] *Maciver v. Maciver*, 1996 S.L.T. 733.
[23] 1981 Act, s.15(3). Police powers and procedure following arrest are governed by ss.16 and 17 of the Act.
[24] 1981 Act, s.15(1)(a).

(1) the non-applicant spouse must have had the opportunity of being heard by or represented before the court[25]; and

(2) the court need not do so where it appears to the court that in all the circumstances of the case such a power is unnecessary.[26]

An application for an order attaching a power of arrest, if made after the application for matrimonial interdict, must be made by motion intimated to the non-applicant spouse.[27]

A power of arrest has no effect unless and until the interdict together with the attached power of arrest is served on the non-applicant spouse.[28] The applicant spouse requires as soon as possible after such service on the non-applicant spouse to ensure that there is delivered to the chief constable of the police area in which the matrimonial home is situated (and also to his counterpart in the police area in which the applicant spouse resides, if different) the following:

(i) a copy of the application for the interdict;

(ii) a copy of the interlocutor granting the interdict; and

(iii) a certificate of service of the interdict[29];

and, where the application to attach the power of arrest to the interdict was made after the interdict was granted,

(i) a copy of the application to attach the power of arrest to the interdict;

(ii) a copy of the interlocutor granting that application; and

(iii) a certificate of service of the interdict together with the attached power of arrest[30];

and must thereafter lodge in process a certificate of delivery in Form F30.[31]

---

[25] As to intimation of the application if made separately from the application for matrimonial interdict, see n.27 *infra* and accompanying text.

[26] 1981 Act, s.15(1)(*b*). In *Nasir v. Nasir*, 1993 G.W.D. 30–1909 the Lord Ordinary held that a power of arrest was not appropriate where there was no allegation of actual physical assaults. In its *Report on Family Law* (Scot. Law Com. No. 135, 1992) the Scottish Law Commission proposes substituting for the words "it appears to the court" the words "the court is satisfied by the non-applicant spouse".

[27] r.33.69(1)(*d*) and (2)(*a*). Otherwise, the application is made by a crave in the initial writ or defences—rr.33.67(1)(*b*) and 33.34(1)(*c*)(iii) and (2)(*b*)(i).

[28] 1981 Act, s.15(2), as amended by the Law Reform (Miscellaneous Provisions) (Scotland) Act 1990, s.64(a).

[29] 1981 Act, s.15(4).

[30] *ibid.* s.15(4), as amended by the Law Reform (Miscellaneous Provisions) (Scotland) Act 1990, s.64(b).

[31] r.33.72(1).

Unless previously recalled, a power of arrest ceases to have effect upon the termination of the marriage.[32] Where the power of arrest ceases to have effect by reason of variation or recall of the matrimonial interdict, the spouse who applied for the variation or recall must carry out the procedure above referred to with respect to a copy of the application for variation or recall and of the interlocutor granting the application, and must thereafter lodge in process a certificate of delivery in Form F30.[33] The foregoing must also be done where the power of arrest ceases to have effect by reason of decree of divorce being granted, the procedure being carried out by the applicant spouse.[34]

Application to the sheriff for recall of a power of arrest requires to be made by minute intimated to the other spouse.[35]

INTERIM EXCLUSION ORDERS[36]

Where there is an entitled and a non-entitled spouse,[37] or where both spouses are entitled, or permitted by a third party, to occupy a

---

[32] 1981 Act, s.15(2). In its *Report on Family Law* (Scot. Law Com. No. 135, 1992) the Scottish Law Commission proposes amending s.15(2) so as to provide that a power of arrest ceases to have effect on the expiry of a period of three years commencing with the date on which the power was granted unless it has been recalled or, on cause shown, renewed within that period.

[33] r.33.72(1).

[34] r.33.72(2).

[35] r.33.70(1)(*b*) and (2)(*a*).

[36] "Interim exclusion order" is not a term found in the 1981 Act; it is used here to denote an interim order granted in terms of s.4(6) of the Act. Since exclusion orders cease to have effect upon termination of the marriage (1981 Act, s.5(1)(a)), it seems appropriate when discussing the exclusion of a party to a divorce action from a matrimonial home to concentrate upon such orders *ad interim*. Different considerations apply in respect of the court's power, on or after granting decree of divorce, to grant an incidental order excluding a party to the marriage from occupation of a matrimonial home (as to which, see Chap. 7 (second) n.21 and accompanying text). The tests applicable to the making of exclusion orders (text accompanying nn.42 to 46) apply also to the making of interim exclusion orders (*Bell v. Bell*, 1983 S.L.T. 224 and *Ward v. Ward*, 1983 S.L.T. 472).

[37] A "non-entitled spouse" is a spouse who, apart from the provisions of the 1981 Act, is not entitled, or permitted by a third party, to occupy a matrimonial home; such a spouse has the right (a) if in occupation, to continue to occupy the matrimonial home, together with any child of the family, and (b) if not in occupation, with leave of the court to enter into and occupy the matrimonial home, together with any child of the family—1981 Act, s.1(1), (1A) and (3), as amended by the Law Reform (Miscellaneous Provisions) (Scotland) Act 1985, s.13(2) and (3). In its *Report on Family Law* (Scot. Law Com. No. 135, 1992), the Scottish Law Commission proposes an amendment to s.1 so as to add

matrimonial home,[38] either spouse, whether or not in occupation at the time of the application, may apply to the court for an order (an "exclusion order") suspending the occupancy rights of the other spouse in a matrimonial home.[39] Application for an interim exclusion order requires to be made by motion.[40] An interim order may only be made if the non-applicant spouse has been afforded an opportunity of being heard by or represented before the court.[41] The court requires to make the order—

---

the following subsection:

"(7) If an entitled spouse and a non-entitled spouse have been living apart from each other for a continuous period of two years and the non-entitled spouse has not occupied the matrimonial home at any time during that period, the occupancy rights of the non-entitled spouse in the home shall be extinguished at the end of that period."

[38] "Matrimonial home" means any house, caravan, houseboat or other structure, which has been provided or has been made available by one or both of the spouses as, or has become, a family residence and includes any garden or other ground or building attached to, and usually occupied with, or otherwise required for the amenity or convenience of, the house, caravan, houseboat or other structure but does not include a residence provided or made available by one spouse for that spouse to reside in, whether with any child of the family or not, separately from the other spouse—1981 Act, s.22, as amended by the Law Reform (Miscellaneous Provisions) (Scotland) Act 1985, s.13(10). In its *Report on Family Law* (Scot. Law Com. No. 135, 1992) the Scottish Law Commission proposes amending the definition of "matrimonial home" so as to mean:

"any house, caravan, houseboat or other structure which has been provided or has been made available by one or both of the spouses as, or has become, a family residence and includes any garden or other ground or building usually occupied with, or otherwise required for the amenity or convenience of, the house, caravan, houseboat or other structure but does not include a residence provided or made available by anyone for one spouse to reside in, whether with any child of the family or not, separately from the other spouse and if the tenancy of a matrimonial home is transferred from one spouse to the other by agreement or under any enactment in order that the home may become the residence of the transferee separately from the other spouse, the residence shall not be a matrimonial home after the transfer."

[39] 1981 Act, s.4(1), as amended by the Law Reform (Miscellaneous Provisions) (Scotland) Act 1985, s.13(5).

[40] r.33.69(1)(*b*). In terms of s.4(6), an interim exclusion order may be made by the court "pending the making of an exclusion order". It seems, therefore, that the final order should be craved (in the initial writ or the defences, as the case may be—rr.33.67(1)(*b*), 33.34(1)(*c*)(iii) and 33.34(2)(*b*)(i)) on the footing that decree may be sought in the event that divorce is not granted.

[41] 1981 Act, s.4(6). Failure to intimate the motion for an interim exclusion order to the non-applicant spouse precludes the sheriff from granting it (*Nelson v. Nelson*, 1988 S.L.T. (Sh.Ct.) 26). The non-applicant spouse should ordinarily be given an opportunity to lodge affidavits (*Armitage v. Armitage*, 1993 S.C.L.R. 173). Rule 33.69(2) requires intimation of the motion also to be given, where the entitled spouse is a tenant or occupies the matrimonial home by the permission of a third party, to the landlord or third party, as the case may be; and, in any event, to any other person to whom intimation is required by the sheriff to be made.

"if it appears to the court that the making of the order is necessary for the protection of the applicant or any child of the family[42] from any conduct or threatened or reasonably apprehended conduct[43] of the non-applicant spouse which is or would be injurious to the physical or mental health of the applicant or child."[44]

The court must not however make the order:

"If it appears to the court that the making of the order would be unjustified or unreasonble . . . having regard to all the circumstances of the case including . . ."[45]

(*a*) the conduct of the spouses in relation to each other and otherwise;

(*b*) the respective needs and financial resources of the spouses;

(*c*) the needs of any child of the family;

(*d*) the extent (if any) to which the matrimonial home is used in connection with a trade, business or profession of either spouse . . .

(*e*) whether the entitled spouse offers or has offered to make available to the non-entitled spouse any suitable alternative accommodation; and

(*f*) where the matrimonial home is or is part of an agricultural holding . . . or is let, or is a home in respect of which possession of which is given, to the non-applicant spouse or to both spouses by an employer as an incident of employment, subject to a requirement of residence [therein] . . . that requirement and the likely consequences of the exclusion of

---

[42] "Child of the family" includes any child or grandchild of either spouse, and any person who has been brought up or treated by either spouse as if he or she were a child of that spouse, whatever the age of such a child, grandchild or person may be—1981 Act, s.22, as amended by the Children (Scotland) Act 1995, Sched. 4, para. 30.

[43] As to "conduct" see *Matheson v. Matheson*, 1986 S.L.T. (Sh.Ct.) 2 and *Anderson v. Anderson*, 1993 G.W.D. 35–2258. The fact that the parties are not at the time of the motion living together is not a bar to the obtaining of an order (*Brown v. Brown*, 1985 S.L.T. 376), even where they have been separated for a lengthy period (*Millar v. Millar*, 1991 S.C.L.R. 649); but see n.37, *supra*.

[44] 1981 Act, s.4(2). The court does not require, before granting an interim exclusion order, to be satisfied that the applicant spouse would be in immediate danger of suffering irreparable harm (*McCafferty v. McCafferty*, 1986 S.L.T. 650 at p. 652).

[45] 1981 Act, s.4(3).

the non-applicant spouse from the matrimonial home."[46]

The court has a discretion as to whether or not to make an interim exclusion order; an appellate court could only interfere with any decision taken in exercise of this discretion if it were to be satisfied that the judge of first instance had misdirected himself and had erred in law, or, if he had applied the correct test, that he had reached an unwarranted conclusion.[47] If it appears to the court that an interim interdict (with or without the attachment of a power of arrest, as the case may be) is providing or would provide adequate protection to the applicant spouse, an interim exclusion order will not be granted.[48] The court cannot be satisfied that the making of the order is necessary on the basis of *ex parte* statements alone— there must be sufficient material for the court to be satisfied on a prima facie basis that the pursuer required the protection of such an order.[49] Appropriate "material" includes the following:

(i) Affidavits[50];
(ii) Extract convictions (where relevant);
(iii) Medical reports.

---

[46] 1981 Act, ss.3(3) and 4(3).

[47] *McCafferty v. McCafferty*, 1986 S.L.T. 650. See also *Bell v. Bell*, 1983 S.L.T. 224, *Brown v. Brown*, 1985 S.L.T. 376, and *Coster v. Coster*, 1992 S.C.L.R. 210. An appeal can competently be taken without leave of the sheriff against the award of an interim exclusion order where an ancillary interim interdict has also been granted (*Oliver v. Oliver*, 1989 S.L.T. (Sh.Ct.) 1) even where leave to appeal that award has been refused by the sheriff (*Anthony v. Anthony*, 1996 G.W.D. 11–671). Failure by the defender to lodge a notice of intention to defend does not mean that he has no locus to appeal (*Nelson v. Nelson*, 1983 S.L.T. (Sh.Ct.) 26). An interim exclusion order is an exception to the general rule that the effect of an appeal is to sist execution on a decree (*Orr v. Orr*, 1989 G.W.D. 12–506).

[48] *Bell, supra*. If the sheriff has applied the correct test and taken into account all relevant factors in granting an interim exclusion order, failure on his part to state that an interim matrimonial interdict preventing molestation would be insufficient to protect the applicant spouse would seem not to justify recall of the order by the appellate court: *Brown, supra* (*cf. Colagiacomo v. Colagiacomo*, 1983 S.L.T. 559 at p. 561). See also *Ward v. Ward*, 1983 S.L.T. 472 for an illustration of circumstances in which means other than an interim exclusion order would be unlikely to secure the desired degree of protection (drink-related course of conduct over a long period).

[49] *Ward, supra*, at p. 475. The court in *Ward* relied on material presented in an independent report ordered by the court in connection with a dispute between the parties over custody of their children. Alternatively the court may order a preliminary proof, as was done in *Bowman v. Bowman* (Lord Grieve, February 24, 1984, unreported) and *Assar v. Assar*, 1994 G.W.D. 2–102 (on minute and answers).

[50] r.33.27.

What quantity and quality of material is sufficient will depend on the circumstances of each case.[51]

In making an interim exclusion order the court *must*, on the application of the applicant spouse:

(i) grant an interdict prohibiting the non-applicant spouse from entering the matrimonial home without the express permission of the applicant[52];

(ii) grant a warrant for the summary ejection of the non-applicant spouse from the matrimonial home, unless the non-applicant spouse satisfies the court that it is unnecessary to grant such a warrant[53]; and

(iii) grant an interdict prohibiting the removal by the non-applicant spouse, except with the written consent of the applicant or by a further order of the court, of any furniture and plenishings in the matrimonial home, unless the non-applicant spouse satisfies the court that it is unnecessary to grant such an interdict.[54]

In making an interim exclusion order the court *may*:

(a) grant an interdict prohibiting the non-applicant spouse from entering or remaining in a specified area in the vicinity of the matrimonial home[55];

(b) where the warrant for the summary ejection of the non-applicant spouse has been granted in his or her absence, give directions as to the preservation of the non-applicant spouse's goods and effects which remain in the matrimonial home[56];

(c) on the application of either spouse, make the interim exclusion order, or the warrant or interdict mentioned in (i), (ii), (iii) or (a) *supra*, subject to such terms and conditions as the court may prescribe[57]; and

---

[51] See, *e.g. Colagiacomo v. Colagiacomo*, 1983 S.L.T. 559; *Boyle v. Boyle*, 1986 S.L.T. 656; *Coster v. Coster*, 1992 S.C.L.R. 210; and *Nasir v. Nasir*, 1993 G.W.D. 30–1909.

[52] 1981 Act, s.4(4)(b).

[53] *ibid.* s.4(4)(a). See, *e.g. Mather v. Mather*, 1987 S.L.T. 565 (interim exclusion order granted but suspended for three months to allow husband to find alternative accommodation).

[54] *ibid.* s.4(4)(c). "Furniture and plenishings" means any article situated in a matrimonial home which (a) is owned or hired by either spouse or is being acquired by either spouse under a hire-purchase agreement or conditional sale agreement; and (b) is reasonably necessary to enable the home to be used as a family residence, but does not include any vehicle, caravan, houseboat or other structure as is mentioned in the definition of "matrimonial home" (n.38, *supra*).

[55] *ibid.* s.4(5)(a).

[56] *ibid.* s.4(5)(b).

[57] *ibid.* s.4(5)(c).

46 Divorce in the Sheriff Court

(d) on the application of either spouse, make such other order as it may consider necessary for the proper enforcement of any of the foregoing orders ((i) to (iii) and (a) to (c) inclusive).[58]

Applications for variation or recall of any order suspending occupancy rights require to be made by minute intimated: (a) to the other spouse; (b) where the entitled spouse is a tenant or occupies the matrimonial home by the permission of a third party, to the landlord or third party, as the case may be; and (c) to any other person to whom intimation is ordered by the sheriff to be made.[59]

ORDERS RESTRICTING REMOVAL OF CHILDREN

Section 35(3) of the Family Law Act 1986 enables the court in a divorce action to grant interdict or interim interdict prohibiting the removal of a child from the United Kingdom or any part thereof,[60] or out of the control of the person in whose care the child is.[61] The court may order the surrender of any United Kingdom passport issued to or containing particulars of the child.[62]

ORDERS RELATING TO AVOIDANCE TRANSACTIONS

Where an application for an order for financial provision, or for variation or recall of such order, has been made in a divorce action, the party making the claim may, not later than one year from the date of the disposal of the claim, apply[63] to the court for an order—

---

[58] 1981 Act, s.4(5)(d).
[59] r.33.70(1)(a) and (2).
[60] Any such interdict or interim interdict automatically has effect in the rest of the United Kingdom—s.36.
[61] s.35(3)(a) enables the order to be made at any time after the commencement of the proceedings, being proceedings in connection with which the court would have jurisdiction to make an order under Pt. 1 of the Act relative to the child. Proceedings are held to commence when the warrant of citation is signed—s.35(5)(b). The order may be applied for by any party to the proceedings, the guardian of the child concerned, and any other person who has or wishes to obtain the care of the child—s.35(4). An application by a party to the action requires to be made by motion (r.33.24(1)(a)) and by any other person by minute (r.33.24(1)(b)). The application need not be served or intimated (r.33.24(2)). As to applications under s.23(2) of the Child Abduction and Custody Act 1985, see r.33.24(3).
[62] s.37(1).
[63] Application must be made by a crave in the initial writ or defences, as the case may be, except that an application after final decree requires to be made by minute in the process of the action to which the application relates—rr.33.48(1)(a) and (2)(c) and 33.52(b) or r.33.53(1) and (2).

(i) setting aside[64] or varying any transfer of, or transaction involving, property effected by the other party not more than five years before the date of the making of the claim; or

(ii) interdicting the other party from effecting any such transfer or transaction.[65]

If the court is satisfed that the transfer or transaction had the effect of, or is likely to have the effect of, defeating in whole or in part the applicant's claim, it may make the order applied for or such other order as it thinks fit.[66] The court may include in the order such terms and conditions as it thinks fit and may make any ancillary order which it considers expedient to ensure that the order is effective.[67]

The order must not prejudice any rights of a third party in or to the property where that third party:

(a) has in good faith acquired the property or any of it or any rights in relation to it for value; or

(b) derives title to such property or rights from any person who has done so.[68]

Intimation therefore requires to be given in accordance with rules 33.7(1)(j) and 33.15(2).[69]

INHIBITION AND ARRESTMENT ON THE DEPENDENCE

Circumstances may arise in actions of divorce where a financial claim is being made by one spouse against the other in which some security for the claim would be desirable. Inhibition and arrestment on the dependence of the action may be very effective remedies for this purpose. They have been described by the Scottish Law Commission as follows:

---

[64] The power to "set aside" a transaction implies a power to reduce a writing or deed by which the transaction is effected—*Hernandez-Cimorra v. Hernandez-Cimorra*, 1992 S.C.L.R. 611. (*cf. Harris v. Harris*, 1988 S.L.T. 101). A letter purporting to acknowledge a loan was set aside in *Tahir v. Tahir (No. 2)*, 1995 S.L.T. 451.

[65] Family Law (Scotland) Act 1985, s.18(1). (*Cf. Robertson v. Robertson*, 1996 G.W.D. 3—167.)

[66] *ibid.* s.18(2). In *Tahir, supra*, the Lord Ordinary reduced a sheriff court decree in order to give effect to the setting aside of a fictitious borrowing transaction.

[67] *ibid.* s.18(4).

[68] *ibid.* s.18(3). (As to onus, *cf. Leslie v. Leslie*, 1983 S.L.T. 186 and 1987 S.L.T. 232.)

[69] See Chap. 1, text accompanying nn.20 and 25.

"Inhibition is a procedure whereby the defender in an action can be prevented, pending the disposal of the action, from disposing of his heritable property. Arrestment on the dependence is a procedure whereby a third party holding moveable property for the defender or owing money to the defender can be prevented from parting with the property or money pending the disposal of the action."[70]

Where a claim for aliment or for an order for financial provision has been made, the sheriff has power, on cause shown,[71] to grant warrant for arrestment on the dependence of the action in which the claim is made and, if he or she thinks fit, to limit the arrestment to any particular property or to funds not exceeding a specified value.[72]

Application for a warrant for inhibition requires to be made to the Court of Session, that court having power, on cause shown, to grant such warrant and, if it thinks fit, to limit the inhibition to any particular property.[73] Inhibition has been judicially observed to be a more effective and more suitable method of protection than interdict against the disposal of a heritable property.[74]

---

[70] *Report on Aliment and Financial Provision* (Scot. Law Com. No. 67, 1981), para. 3–152.

[71] Such would include where the defender is verging on insolvency (as to which, see *Pow v. Pow*, 1987 S.L.T. 127), or is outside Scotland, or is about to decamp, or is depleting his assets to defeat the pursuer's claim—Scot. Law Com., *loc. cit.* Warrant to arrest on the dependence was recalled in *Matheson v. Matheson*, 1995 S.L.T. 765 on the basis that arrestments interfering with the legitimate business operations of the defender unduly hampered and frustrated his ordinary trading activities without legitimate advantage to the pursuer, the recall being subject to full disclosure of the transactions entered into and of the application of all sums thus realised.

[72] Family Law (Scotland) Act 1985, s.19(1) and (2). As to intimation of applications for such warrant, cf. *Stancroft Securities Ltd v. McDowall*, 1990 S.L.T. 746.

[73] 1985 Act, s.19(1) and (2). In terms of R.C.S. 59.1(5) an application for letters of inhibition falls to be made to the Lord Ordinary, whose decision thereon is final and not subject to review. For an illustration of circumstances in which the court's power would not be exercised, see *Thom v. Thom*, 1990 S.C.L.R. 800.

[74] *Wilson v. Wilson*, 1981 S.L.T. 101 at p. 102.

CHAPTER 5

PROPERTY ORDERS

THE sheriff is empowered by statute[1] to make various orders, described herein as "property orders", relative to a matrimonial home.[2] The more important of these (excepting exclusion orders and related remedies[3]) are discussed in this chapter.[4]

ORDERS REGULATING OCCUPANCY RIGHTS

The Matrimonial Homes (Family Protection) (Scotland) Act 1981[5] provides for the granting of certain orders concerning spouses' occupancy rights[6] as follows:

  (i) declaring the occupancy rights of the applicant spouse;
 (ii) enforcing the occupancy rights of the applicant spouse;
(iii) restricting the occupancy rights of the non-applicant spouse;
 (iv) regulating the exercise by either spouse of his or her occupancy rights;
  (v) protecting the occupancy rights of the applicant spouse in relation to the other spouse; and
 (vi) granting to a spouse with occupancy rights the possession or use of furniture and plenishings in a matrimonial home owned, hired or being acquired by the other spouse.[7]

---

[1] The Matrimonial Homes (Family Protection) (Scotland) Act 1981 and the Family Law (Scotland) Act 1985.

[2] Orders introduced by the 1985 Act relative to *any* property of the parties are noted in Chap. 7.

[3] As to which, see Chap. 4.

[4] Orders under the 1981 Act, s.2(1)(e) and (4)(a) (authorisation of non-entitled spouse to carry out non-essential repairs and improvements to matrimonial home) and s.2(3), (4)(b) and (5)(b) (apportionment between spouses of certain expenditure relating to matrimonial home) are not discussed herein.

[5] 1981 Act, s.3(3).

[6] Occupancy rights are those enjoyed by a non-entitled spouse (a) if in occupation, to continue to occupy the matrimonial home; (b) if not in occupation, to enter and occupy the matrimonial home, together with any child of the family — 1981 Act, s.1(1) and (1A).

[7] 1981 Act, s.3(1) and (2).

An order in category (i) must be granted if it appears to the court that the application relates to a matrimonial home.[8] The court may make such order relating to an application[9] within the remaining categories as appears to it to be just and reasonable having regard to all the circumstances of the case, including the matters specified in paragraphs (a) to (e) of section 3(3),[10] except that no such order may be made if it appears that the effect of the order would be to exclude the non-applicant spouse from the matrimonial home.[11]

Since the granting of decree of divorce automatically terminates occupancy rights,[12] the criteria for the making of interim orders regulating such rights are of greater practical significance for present purposes. These criteria are "necessity" and "expediency", the court being empowered to make such interim order as it may consider necessary or expedient in relation to—

(a) the residence of either spouse in the home to which the application relates;

(b) the personal effects of either spouse or of any child of the family; or

(c) the furniture and plenishings.[13]

An interim order may only be made if the non-applicant spouse has had an opportunity of being heard by or represented before the court.[14] Application for an interim order must be made by motion.[15] The court may vary or recall an order

---

[8] 1981 Act, s.3(3), subject to s.1(2) (as to which, see *Murphy v. Murphy,* 1992 S.C.L.R. 62). Such an order is accordingly appropriately craved where there is any question as to whether or not any particular property is a matrimonial home.

[9] An application by a pursuer or a defender must be made by a crave in the initial writ or in defences, as the case may be (rr.33.67(1)(*b*) and 33.34(1)(*c*)(iii) and (2)(*b*)(i)), intimated in accordance with rr.37(1)(*k*) and 33.15(2) (see Chap. 1, text accompanying nn.21 and 25).

[10] Paras. (a) to (e) of s.3(3) are set forth in Chap. 4, part of text accompanying n.46).

[11] 1981 Act, s.3(5).

[12] This is implicit in the scheme of the Act; subject to s.18, only "spouses" may have occupancy rights (*cf.* s.1).

[13] 1981 Act, s.3(4).

[14] *ibid.*

[15] r.33.69(1)(*a*). Intimation of the motion requires to be made to the non-applicant spouse and if the entitled spouse is a tenant or occupies the matrimonial home by the permission of a third party to the landlord or third party, as the case may be—r.33.69(2). In terms of the 1981 Act, s.3(4) an interim order may be made by the court "pending the making of [a property] order". It seems, therefore, that the final order should be craved (in the initial writ or the defences, as the case may be—rr.33.67(1)(*b*), 33.34(1)(*c*)(iii) and 33.34(2)(*b*)(i)) on the footing that decree may be sought in the event that divorce is not granted.

regulating occupancy rights upon an application therefor made by minute.[16]

The Family Law (Scotland) Act 1985 empowers the sheriff, on or after the granting of decree of divorce, to make an incidental order regulating the occupation of the matrimonial home or the use of furniture and plenishings therein or regulating liability, as between the parties, for outgoings in respect of the matrimonial home or furniture or plenishings therein.[17]

ORDERS DISPENSING WITH CONSENT TO DEALING

A non-entitled spouse's occupancy rights are unaffected by any dealing (*e.g.* sale) by the entitled spouse relating to a matrimonial home, except where *inter alia* the non-entitled spouse gives consent thereto.[18] Because occupancy rights depend on there being a subsisting marriage, an entitled spouse with time to await an application for and the granting of decree of divorce need not concern himself to seek that consent. Where however consent is more urgently required and is not forthcoming, the entitled spouse may apply[19] for an order dispensing with the non-entitled spouse's consent to a "dealing which has taken place or a proposed dealing".[20]

---

[16] 1981 Act, s.5 and r.33.70(1)(*a*). Intimation requires to be made in accordance with the preceding footnote.

[17] s.14(2)(d) and (e) and (3) (as to which, see Chap. 7 (second) nn.21 and 22 and accompanying text).

[18] 1981 Act, s.6(1) and (3)(a)(i); other exceptions are to be seen in s.6(3).

[19] Application is by motion intimated to the other spouse and any other person to whom intimation is ordered to be made—r.33.(1)(*c*) and (2)(*a*) and (*c*). As to procedure where relevant and material facts are disputed, see *Longmuir v. Longmuir,* 1985 S.L.T. (Sh.Ct.) 33 at p. 36.

[20] 1981 Act, s.7(1). " 'A proposed dealing' requires that a stage of negotiations has been reached in which proposals in regard to price and other conditions are being discussed" (*per* the Sheriff Principal in *Fyfe v. Fyfe,* 1987 S.L.T. (Sh.Ct.) 38 at p. 41). See also *Dunsmore v. Dunsmore,* 1986 S.L.T. (Sh.Ct.) 9 at p. 10. In its *Report on Family Law* (Scot. Law Com. No. 135, 1992) the Scottish Law Commission proposes adding the following subsections to s.7:

"(3A) Notwithstanding that negotiations have not yet been started or concluded in relation to a proposed dealing, the court may make an order under subsection (1) above but subject to the dealing consisting of—

    (a) a sale which is for a price not less than an amount specified in the order and which is concluded within such time after the making of the order as may be specified therein;

    (b) the grant of a heritable security for a loan of not more than an amount specified in the order and to be executed within such time

Such an order may be granted if the consent has been unreasonably withheld.[21] The onus is on the applicant spouse to show that consent is being unreasonably withheld.[22] The court in considering whether to make the order must have regard to all the circumstances of the case, including the matters specified in paragraphs (a) to (e) of section 3(3) of the 1981 Act,[23] except that consent is taken to have been unreasonably withheld where it appears to the court that—

(a) the non-entitled spouse has led the entitled spouse to believe that such consent would be given and that the non-entitled spouse would not be prejudiced by any change in the circumstances of the case since such apparent consent was given, or

(b) that the entitled spouse has, having taken all reasonable steps to do so, been unable to obtain an answer to a request for consent.[24]

In considering circumstances in which consent might be deemed to have been withheld unreasonably, it has been suggested that:

"a wife who refuses consent to a sale because she does not want to move to a new home on her husband obtaining employment elsewhere would no doubt be regarded as unreasonable. It would be otherwise if the sale was simply to raise money and no alternative accommodation was offered to her."[25]

---

after the making of the order as may be specified therein.

(3B) If the court declines to make an order under this section, it may make occupation of the matrimonial home by the non-entitled spouse subject to the non-entitled spouse making payment or payments to the owner of the home, and subject to such other conditions, in respect of the occupancy as the court may specify."

[21] 1981 Act, s.7(1)(a); it may also be granted if consent cannot be given by reason of physical or mental disability or where the non-entitled spouse cannot be found after reasonable steps have been taken to trace him or her, or where he or she is under legal disability by reason of nonage (1981 Act, s.7(1)(b)-(d)).

[22] *Hall v. Hall,* 1987 S.L.T. (Sh.Ct.) 15.

[23] 1981 Act, s.7(3). (Paras. (a) to (e) are set forth in Chap. 4, part of text accompany n.46).

[24] *ibid.* s.7(2).

[25] Nichols and Meston, *The Matrimonial Homes (Family Protection) (Scotland) Act 1981,* p. 50. *cf. Hall supra, Perkins v. Perkins,* Glasgow Sheriff Court, December 11, 1984, unreported, (consent held to be withheld unreasonably where non-applicant spouse had not lived in the matrimonial home for two years and had own accommodation and was withholding consent because of disagreement as to how proceeds of sale should be divided) and *O'Neill v. O'Neill,* 1987 S.L.T. (Sh.Ct.) 26 (consent held to be withheld unreasonably where purpose of withholding not to protect occupancy rights but to attempt to force the other spouse into certain actings in exchange).

An application for such an order will be refused where a transfer of property order relative to the matrimonial home is craved by the non-applicant spouse.[26]

ORDERS TRANSFERRING TENANCY[27]

A sheriff in an action for divorce may, on granting decree or within such period as he may specify on granting decree, make an order:

  (i) transferring the tenancy of a matrimonial home to a non-entitled spouse,[28] or
  (ii) where the spouses are joint or common tenants of a matrimonial home, vesting the tenancy in one spouse only.[29]

In either case, the court may provide for payment by the applicant spouse to the other of such compensation as seems just and reasonable in all the circumstances of the case.[30]

The court is required in determining whether or not to grant the order to have regard to all the circumstances of the case, including the matters specified in paragraphs (a) to (e) of section 3(3) of the Act and the suitability of the applicant to become the tenant (or sole tenant, as the case may be) and his or her capacity to perform the obligations under the lease.[31]

The applicant spouse must serve a copy of the application on the landlord who must have an opportunity of being heard by the court before the order may be granted.[32]

---

[26] *Rae v. Rae,* 1991 S.L.T. 454.
[27] Applications for these are not competent where the tenancy is a service tenancy, a lease of a farm, croft or similar holding, a long lease or a tenancy-at-will—1981 Act, s.13(7). Note also that "tenancy" includes subtenancy, statutory tenancy as defined in s.3 of the Rent (Scotland) Act 1971 and statutory assured tenancy as defined in s.16(1) of the Housing (Scotland) Act 1988—s.22.
[28] 1981 Act, s.13(1) and (2) (as amended by the Family Law (Scotland) Act 1985, Sched. 1, para. 11).
[29] *ibid.* s.13(9) and (10).
[30] *ibid.* s.13(1) and (9); where the matrimonial home is a secure tenancy within the meaning of Part 3 of the Housing (Scotland) Act 1987, no account is to be taken, in assessing the amount of any compensation to be awarded under subs. (1) or (9) of the loss, by virtue of the transfer of the tenancy of the home, of a right to purchase the home under Part 1 of that Act—s.13(11).
[31] *ibid.* s.13(3). For an illustration of circumstances justifying the granting of an order under s.13, see *McGowan v. McGowan,* 1986 S.L.T. 112. For illustrations of circumstances justifying the refusing of the order, see *Wilson v. Wilson,* Lord Wylie, January 10, 1986, unreported, and *Russell v. Russell,* Lord Weir, February 18, 1986, unreported.
[32] *ibid.* s.13(4). Intimation of the application (which is made by a crave in the initial writ or in defences—rr.33.48(1)(*a*) and (2)(*d*) and 33.34(1)(*c*)(iii) and (2)(*b*)(i)) requires to be made to the landlord in accordance with rr.33.7(1)(*k*) and 33.15(2) (see Chap. 1, text accompanying nn.21 and 25).

The effect of the order is to vest the tenancy (or sole tenancy, as the case may be) in the applicant spouse without intimation to the landlord, subject to all the liabilities under the lease, other than any arrears of rent for the period before the making of the order.[33] The importance of the order lies in the fact that a spouse without a right of tenancy or incidental order entitling his or her occupation is liable to ejection once the marriage is terminated by divorce.[34]

---

[33] 1981 Act, s.13(5); these remain the non-applicant spouse's responsibility.
[34] See nn.12 and 17 and accompanying text, *supra.*

Chapter 6

CHILDREN

The subject of children in the context of divorce law and practice is discussed in this chapter; and the jurisdiction, duties and powers of the court in this connection are considered in turn.

JURISDICTION OF THE COURT

Where an application is competently made to a sheriff court for the making, variation or recall of an order which is ancillary or collateral to an action of divorce and which relates to children, as a general rule if the court has jurisdiction to entertain the action it has jurisdiction to entertain the application.[1]

The court does not, however, have jurisdiction to entertain such an application after the dismissal of the action or after decree of absolvitor is granted therein, unless the application was made on or before such dismissal or the granting of the decree of absolvitor[2]; nor does the court have jurisdiction to entertain an application for variation of such an order in an action where the court has refused to grant the principal remedy sought in the action if, on the date of the application, matrimonial proceedings in respect of the marriage are continuing in another court in the United Kingdom.[3]

A court which has such jurisdiction may make an order declining the same if (a) it appears to the court with respect to the child in question that but for certain statutory provisions, another court in Scotland would have jurisdiction to entertain such an application or a court in another part of the United Kingdom would have jurisdiction to make an order or an order varying the order; and

---

[1] Domicile and Matrimonial Proceedings Act 1973, s.10(1) and (1A), as amended and inserted, respectively, by para. 20(2)(a) and para. 20(2)(b) of Sched. 4 to the Children (Scotland) Act 1995.

[2] Family Law Act 1986, s.13(2).

[3] *ibid.* s.13(4), not applicable if the court in which the other proceedings are continuing has made one of the orders referred to in s.13(5) (orders declining jurisdiction or staying proceedings for recorded purpose of enabling proceedings to be taken in Scotland or, as the case may be, in another court in Scotland) and that order is in force—s.13(5).

(b) the court considers that it would be more appropriate for such matters to be determined in that other court or part.[4]

A court which has such jurisdiction may refuse the application in any case where the matter in question has already been determined in other proceedings,[5] or may sist the proceedings on such application at any stage where it appears to the court (a) that proceedings with respect to the matters to which the application relates are continuing outside Scotland or in another court in Scotland; or (b) that it would be more appropriate for those matters to be determined in proceedings outside Scotland or in another court in Scotland, and that such proceedings are likely to be taken there.[6]

DUTIES OF THE COURT

Restrictions on decrees affecting children

In any action for divorce where a child of the family[7] has not reached the age of 16 years,[8] the court is bound to consider (in the light of such information as is before the court as to the arrangements which have been or are proposed to be made for the upbringing of that child) whether to exercise with respect to him certain statutory powers.[9] In all such actions in which there is any such child, therefore, the pursuer should include averments in the initial writ anent the arrangements made or proposed for the child whether or not he or she is seeking any order from the court.

Where the court is of the opinion that (a) the circumstances of the case require or are likely to require it to exercise any such

---

[4] 1986 Act, s.13(6), listing the relevant statutory provisions (which exclude jurisdiction in independent proceedings where matrimonial proceedings are continuing elsewhere). The court may recall an order declining jurisdiction—s.13(7).

[5] *ibid.* s.14(1).

[6] *ibid.* s.14(2).

[7] "Child of the family", in relation to the parties to a marriage means (a) a child of both of them; or (b) any other child, not being a child who is placed with them as foster-parents by a local authority or voluntary organisation, who has been treated by both of them as a child of the family—Children (Scotland) Act 1995, s.12(4).

[8] 1986 Act, s.12(3). The *punctum temporis* is the date when the question first arises as to whether the court should give such consideration as is mentioned in the provision (*ibid.*).

[9] *ibid.*, s.12(1). The powers are those conferred by ss.11 and 54 of the Act (to make, respectively, section 11 orders and references to the Principal Reporter). As to the sheriff's duty to order intimation to the child when so considering, see r.33.15(2), considered in Chap. 1, n.18.

power with respect to the child concerned; (b) it is not in a position to exercise that power without giving further consideration to the case; and (c) there are exceptional circumstances which make it desirable in the interests of that child that it should not grant decree in the action until it is in a position to exercise such power, it must postpone its decision on the granting of decree in the action until it is in such a position.[10]

The welfare principle

In considering whether or not to make a statutory order[11] with respect to a child and what order to make, the court must regard the *welfare* of the child concerned[12] as *its paramount consideration*.[13]

The term "welfare" is not statutorily defined but has been judicially explained as follows:

> "'Welfare' is an all encompassing word. It includes material welfare, both in the sense of adequacy of resources to provide a pleasant home and a comfortable standard of living and in the sense of adequacy of care to ensure that good health and due personal pride are maintained. However, while material considerations have their place they are secondary matters. More important are the stability and the security, the loving and understanding care and guidance, the warm and compassionate relationships, that are essential for the full development of the child's own character, personality and talents."[14]

---

[10] 1995 Act, s.12(2).

[11] The order in question is that under s.11(1) of the 1995 Act, considered *infra* (text accompanying nn.34–41).

[12] *cf. Birmingham City Council v. H (A Minor)* [1994] 2 A.C. 212 (regard not to be had to welfare of 15-year-old mother in application for contact with baby). Where sibling children with competing interests are the subject of an application in the same set of proceedings, and it is impossible to achieve what is in the paramount interests of each child, the court may require to balance the children's interests and achieve the situation of least detriment to all the children—see *Re T and E (Proceedings: Conflicting Interests)* [1995] 1 F.L.R. 581 at p. 587.

[13] 1995 Act, s.11(7)(a). It is not normally appropriate, where the welfare of children is involved, to dispose of an application solely on the pleadings, and the court will not dispose of the matter, except on a point of law only, without conducting some kind of inquiry into the facts—*O v. O*, 1995 S.L.T. 238.

[14] *per* Hardie Boys J. in *Walker v. Walker and Harrison*, noted in [1981] NZ Recent Law 257. See also the statutory list of relevant factors in the equivalent English legislation, the Children Act 1989, s.1(3), which includes the following: (a) the ascertainable wishes and feelings of the child concerned considered in the light of his age and understanding; (b) his physical, emotional and educational needs; (c) the likely effect on him of any change in his circumstances; (d) his age, sex,

What is in the best interests of any particular child is essentially a question of fact; and since cases vary infinitely on their facts, case law assumes a lesser significance in this area. Worthy of particular note, however, are the judicial expressions of (1) a general preference that the mother should have custody of the very young child[15] (2) the need for close and anxious attention to the possible effects on the child of any change to existing arrangements[16]; and (3) the desirability of placing very great and usually decisive weight on the wishes of the teenage child.[17]

The *paramountcy* formulation connotes:

"... a process whereby, when all the facts, relationships, claims and wishes of parents, risks, choices, and other circumstances are taken into account and weighed, the course to be followed will be that which is most in the interests of the child's welfare as that term has now to be understood. That is the ... paramount consideration because it rules on or determines the course to be followed."[18]

The minimum intervention principle

In considering whether or not to make a statutory order[19] with respect to a child and what order to make, the court must not make any such order unless it considers that it would be better for the child if the order were made, rather than that no order be made at all.[20]

Views of the child

In considering whether or not to make a statutory order[21] with respect to a child and what order to make, the court, taking

---

background and any characteristics of his which the court considers relevant; (e) any harm which he has suffered or is at risk of suffering; and (f) how capable each of his parents, and any other person in relation to whom the court considers the question to be relevant, is of meeting his needs.

[15] *Brixey v. Lynas,* 1996 S.L.T. 908.
[16] *J v. C* [1970] A.C. 668 at p. 715.
[17] *Gover v. Gover,* 1969 S.L.T. (Notes) 78. And see n.22 *infra.*
[18] *per* Lord MacDermott in *J v. C, supra,* at p.710, under reference to the formulation "its first and paramount consideration", thought to amount to the same thing in *C v. C (A Minor: Custody Appeal)* [1991] 1 F.L.R. 223 at p. 230; and see now *Sanderson v. McManus,* 1997 S.L.T. 629.
[19] The order in question is that under the 1995 Act, s.11(1), considered *infra* (text accompanying nn.34–41).
[20] 1995 Act, s.11(7)(a), giving effect to the recommendation of the Scottish Law Commission that the provision was needed to discourage unnecessary orders relating to children (*Report on Family Law* (Scot. Law Com. No. 135, 1992), para. 5.18).
[21] The order in question is that under the 1995 Act, s.11(1), considered *infra* (text accompanying nn.34–41).

account of the child's age and maturity, must so far as practicable (1) give him or her an opportunity to indicate whether he or she wishes to express his or her views; (2) if he or she does so wish, give him or her an opportunity to express them; and (3) have regard to such views as he or she may express.[22] A child who is 12 years of age or more is presumed to be of sufficient age and maturity to form a view for the purposes of the foregoing.[23]

The rules of court governing intimation of divorce actions to children have been considered *supra*.[24] Where a child has returned to the sheriff clerk Form F9 or otherwise indicated to the court a wish to express views on a matter affecting him or her, the sheriff requires to order such steps to be taken as he or she considers appropriate to ascertain the views of that child.[25] The child is not required to be represented in the proceedings if he or she does not wish to be.[26] He or she may express his or her views personally to the sheriff, orally or in writing.[27] Alternatively, somebody else, who need not be an advocate or a solicitor, may do so on his or her behalf,[28] and the sheriff may appoint somebody for the purpose of recording the views of the child in writing.[29] The sheriff may direct that such views, and any written views, given by a child be sealed in an envelope marked "Views of the child—confidential"; be kept in the court process without being recorded in the inventory of process; be available to a sheriff only; not be opened by any person other than a sheriff; and not form a borrowable part of the process.[30]

---

[22] 1995 Act, s.11(7)(b), and r.33.19. This provision gives effect to Art. 12 of the United Nations Convention on the Rights of the Child, which provides:
"1. States Parties shall assure to the child who is capable of forming his or her own views the right to express those views freely in all matters affecting the child, the views of the child being given due weight in accordance with the age and maturity of the child.
2. For this purpose, the child shall in particular be provided the opportunity to be heard in any judicial and administrative proceedings affecting the child, either directly, or through a representative or an appropriate body, in a manner consistent with the procedural rules of national law."
[23] *ibid.* s.11(10). See Chap. 1, text accompanying n.18, with regard to younger children.
[24] See Chap. 1, n.18 and accompanying text.
[25] r.33.19(1) and (2).
[26] 1995 Act, s.11(9).
[27] r.33.20. Note that an interview cannot be substituted for a proof—*Macdonald v. Macdonald*, 1985 S.L.T. 244.
[28] Sheriff Courts (Scotland) Act 1971, s.32(j) and Form F9.
[29] r.33.20(1).
[30] r.33.20(2).

Third party rights

The court must, notwithstanding its duties, endeavour to ensure that any order which it makes, or any determination by it not to make an order, does not adversely affect the position of a person who has, in good faith and for value, acquired any property of the child concerned, or any right or interest in such property.[31]

POWERS OF THE COURT

The court's powers in connection with the children in divorce actions are wide and include[32] (in addition to certain restricted powers to make provision for the maintenance of children[33])

---

[31] 1995 Act, s.11(8).

[32] See Chap. 4 as to the power of the court to prevent the removal of children. Note that the court has a statutory power in relation to court proceedings to restrict publicity concerning a person under the age of 17 years (see *C v. S*, 1989 S.L.T. 168).

[33] The court's powers to make provision for the maintenance of children have been very largely curtailed by the Child Support Act 1991. The residual role of the court in this respect, prescribed by s.8 of the Act is, broadly, confined to: (a) revoking maintenance orders (subs.(3)); (b) making maintenance orders giving effect to written agreements (subs.(5)); (c) making top up maintenance orders (subs.(6)); (d) making maintenance orders requiring payees to meet some or all of the expenses incurred in connection with the provision of instruction at an educational establishment or training for a trade, profession or vocation (subs.(7)); (e) making certain maintenance orders in relation to disabled children (subs. (8) and (9)); and (f) making maintenance orders against a person with care of the child (subs.(10)). An adult training centre attended by a handicapped child was held to be an educational establishment for the purposes of s.8(7) in *McBride v. McBride*, 1995 S.C.L.R. 1021. Applications for aliment require to be made by a crave in the initial writ or defences, as the case may be or, where the applicant is a third party, by minute (r.33.39(1) and (2)(*b*)), unless made after decree (in which case the application is made by minute in the original process— r.33.45(1)). Applications for interim aliment in either case are made by motion (rr.33.43(*a*) and 33.45(2)). An application may be made by a person over 18 years for aliment or interim aliment in terms of r.33.46. The court's powers to vary an order after decree are restricted to the circumstances described in s.8(3A), namely to cases where s.4(10) or s.7(10) prevents the making of an application for a maintenance assessment (written maintenance agreement made before April 5, 1993 or maintenance order in force, or benefit being paid to parent of child) and no application has been made for a maintenance assessment or such an application has been made but no maintenance assessment has been made in response to it. The powers are exercisable upon a material change of circumstances (Family Law (Scotland) Act 1985, s.5(1)) and may be sought to be invoked by way of minute lodged in the original process (r.33.45(1)). The making of a maintenance assessment with respect to a child for whom the decree of aliment was granted constitutes a material change of circumstances for the

powers to make orders[34] in relation to parental responsibilities[35] and parental rights[36] under section 11(1) of the Children (Scotland) Act 1995[37] and to make a reference to the Principal Reporter under section 54 of that Act.

---

purposes of s.5(1) (s.5(1A)). Where such a minute has been lodged, any party may lodge a motion for an interim order which may be made pending the determination of the application (r.33.45(2)). The court has power to backdate a variation, in terms of s.5(2) of the 1985 Act, to the date of the application for variation or, on special cause shown, to a date prior to that (see, *e.g. Hannah v. Hannah,* 1988 S.L.T. 82; *Dalgleish v. Robinson,* 1991 S.C.L.R. 892; *Mitchell v. Mitchell,* 1992 S.C.L.R. 553; and *Adamson v. Adamson,* 1996 G.W.D. 1–3), and in that event to order any sums paid under the decree to be repaid (1985 Act, s.5(4)). (As to variation of an order for interim aliment in a depending action, see Chap. 7, text accompanying nn.10–12 and r.33.43(*a*)(i)). In any action in which an order for aliment is sought, or is sought to be varied or recalled, the pleadings of the applicant must include an averment stating whether and, if so, when and by whom, a maintenance order has been granted in favour of or against that party or of any other person in respect of whom the order is sought (r.33.5). See also r.33.6(2) with respect to applications for top up maintenance orders; r.33.6(3) in relation to applications not covered by the Child Support Act 1991; and r.33.6(5) with regard to actions involving parties in respect of whom a decision has been made in any application, review or appeal under the 1991 Act relating to any child of those parties.

[34] "Orders" includes interim orders and orders varying or discharging orders—1995 Act, s.11(13). Where, before s.11 of the Act came into force (namely November 1, 1996), there has been final decree in a cause in which, as respects a child, an order for custody or access, or an order which is analogous to a section 11 order, has been made, any application on or after that date for variation or recall of the order shall proceed as if the order had been made under that section—s.15(2). (Otherwise, no provision in Pt. 1 of the Act affects any legal proceedings commenced, or any application made to a court, before that date—s.15(2)).

[35] "Parental responsibilities" are the following which a parent has in relation to his or her child—

"(a) to safeguard and promote the child's health, development and welfare;

(b) to provide, in a manner appropriate to the stage of development of the child—(i) direction; (ii) guidance, to the child;

(c) if the child is not living with the parent, to maintain personal relations and direct contact with the child on a regular basis; and

(d) to act as the child's legal representative, but only in so far as compliance with [the foregoing] is practicable and in the interests of the child."

—1995 Act s.1(1). "Child" means, for the purposes of (a), (b)(i), (c) and (d) above, a person under the age of 16 years; and for the purposes of (b)(ii), a person under the age of 18 years—s.1(2). As to statutory provisions common to parental responsibilities and parental rights, see n.36 *infra.*

[36] "Parental rights" are the following, which a parent has in order to enable him to fulfil his parental responsibilities in relation to his child—

"(a) to have the child living with him or otherwise to regulate the child's residence;

Section 11 orders

In terms of section 11(2) of the Act, the court may make such order in relation to parental responsibilities or parental rights under subsection (1) as it thinks fit; and without prejudice to the generality of that subsection may, in particular, so make any of the following orders[38]:

"(a) an order depriving a person of some or all of his parental responsibilities or parental rights in relation to a child;
(b) an order—
    (i) imposing upon a person (provided he is at least sixteen years of age or is a parent of the child) such responsibilities; and
    (ii) giving that person such rights;
(c) an order regulating the arrangements as to—
    (i) with whom; or
    (ii) if with different persons alternately or periodically, with whom during what periods, a child under the

---

(b) to control, direct or guide, in a manner appropriate to the stage of development of the child, the child's upbringing;
(c) if the child is not living with him, to maintain personal relations and direct contact with the child on a regular basis; and
(d) to act as the child's legal representative."
—1995 Act, s.2(1). "Child" means a person under the age of 16 years—s.2(7). Where two or more persons have a parental right as respects a child, each of them may exercise that right without the consent of the other or, as the case may be, of any of the others, unless any decree or deed conferring the right, or regulating its exercise, otherwise provides—s.2(2). Without prejudice to any court order, no person is entitled to remove a child habitually resident in Scotland from, or to retain any such child outwith, the United Kingdom without the consent of any person (whether or not a parent of the child) who for the time being has and is exercising in relation to him a right mentioned in (a) or (c) above; except that, where both the child's parents are persons so described, the consent required for his removal or retention must be that of them both—s.2(3). The fact that a person has parental responsibilities or parental rights in relation to a child does not entitle that person to act in any way which would be incompatible with any court order relating to the child or the child's property, or with any supervision requirement made under s.70 of the Act—s.3(4). A person who has parental responsibilities or parental rights in relation to a child cannot abdicate those responsibilities or rights to anyone else, but may arrange for some or all of them to be fulfilled or exercised on his behalf; and without prejudice to that generality any such arrangement may be made with a person who already has parental responsibilities or parental rights in relation to the child concerned—s.3(5)

[37] 1995 Act, s.11(1)(a) and (b).
[38] Orders in terms of s.11(2)(g) and (h) of the Act, relating to children's property and guardianship, are not considered herein.

age of sixteen years is to live (any such order being known as a "residence order")[39];

(d) an order regulating the arrangements for maintaining personal relations and direct contact between a child under that age and a person with whom the child is not, or will not be, living (any such order being known as a "contact order")[40]

(e) an order regulating any specific question which has arisen, or may arise, in connection with [*inter alia* parental responsibilities or parental rights] (any such order being known as a 'specific issue order')[41];

(f) an interdict prohibiting the taking of any step of a kind specified in the fulfilment of parental responsibilities or

---

[39] A residence order is intended to regulate where a child is to make his home; and so a contact order is the appropriate order to regulate overnight or longer stays— *McBain v. McIntyre,* 1996 S.C.L.R. 181. Where the court makes a residence order which requires that a child live with a person who, immediately before the order is made, does not have in relation to the child all the parental responsibilities mentioned in s.1(1)(a), (b) and (d) of the 1995 Act, and the parental rights mentioned in s.2(1)(b) and (d) of the Act, that person shall, subject to the provisions of the order and of any other order made under subs.(1), have the relevant responsibilities and rights while the residence order remains in force— s.11(12).

[40] *Quaere* what form an order would take preventing contact altogether (*cf. Nottinghamshire C.C. v. P.* [1993] 3 All E.R. 815 and *Re H and Others (Prohibited Steps Order)* [1995] 4 All E.R. 110). In this regard, the right of the child enshrined in Art. 9(3) of the U.N. Convention on the Rights of the Child to personal relations and direct contact with both parents on a regular basis requires to be borne in mind, albeit in the context no doubt of the welfare principle (*cf. Sanderson v. McManus,* 1997 S.L.T. 629). As to the responsibility of the parent with whom the child lives to help make contact orders work, see *e.g. Cosh v. Cosh,* 1979 S.L.T. (Notes) 72 at p. 73. Where the sheriff at his or her own instance or on the motion of a party is considering making a contact order or interim contact order subject to supervision by the social work department of a local authority, he or she must ordain the party moving for such an order to intimate to the chief executive of that local authority (where not already a party to the action and represented at the hearing at which the issue arises)—(a) the terms of any relevant motion; (b) the intention of the sheriff to order that the contact order be supervised by the social work department of that local authority; and (c) that the local authority shall, within such period as the sheriff has determined—(i) notify the sheriff clerk whether it intends to make representations to the sheriff; and (ii) where it intends to make representations in writing, to do so within that period—r.33.25.

[41] There does not have to be a dispute between the parties in order for the court to have power to make a specific issue order; it is sufficient that there is a question to be answered—*Re H.G. (Specific Issue Order: Sterilisation)* [1993] 1 F.L.R. 587. For other examples of such an order, see *Re R (A Minor) (Blood Transfusion)* [1993] 2 F.L.R. 757 and *Re F (Specific Issue: Child Interview)* [1995] 1 F.L.R. 819; and *cf. Re P (A Minor) (Education)* [1992] 1 F.L.R. 316.

the exercise of parental rights relating to a child or in the administration of a child's property".

A section 11 order has the effect of depriving a person of a parental responsibility or parental right only in so far as the order expressly so provides and only to the extent necessary to give effect to the order.[42] The fact that a person has parental responsibilities or parental rights in relation to a child, however, does not entitle that person to act in any way which would be incompatible with any court order relating to the child.[43]

A section 11 order is essentially discretionary and is thus subject to review only if it can be shown that the judge of first instance had exercised his discretion upon a wrong principle or that, his decision being so plainly wrong, he must have exercised his discretion wrongly.[44]

An order may be made (1) upon an application by any person who has parental responsibilities or parental rights in relation to the child in question[45] or who, not having, and never having had, parental responsibilities or parental rights in relation to the child, claims an interest[46]; or (2) in the absence of any application, where the court (even if it declines to make any other order) considers that it should be made.[47]

Application to the court for a section 11 order is made by the pursuer by a crave in the initial writ,[48] accompanied by any appropriate crave for warrant for intimation or to dispense with intimation.[49] Such an application falls to be made by a defender by

---

[42] 1995 Act, s.11(11).
[43] *ibid.* s.3(4).
[44] *cf. Britton v. Central Regional Council,* 1986 S.L.T. 207 at p. 208.
[45] 1995 Act, s.11(3)(a)(ii).
[46] *ibid.* s.11(3)(a)(i). Such a person would include, *e.g.* the child's step-parent and, by virtue of s.11(5) of the Act, the child itself (but not a local authority).
[47] *ibid.* s.11(3)(b).
[48] r.33.39(1)(*a*) and (2)(*a*). Application by a party in an action depending before the court for, or for variation of, a residence order or a contact order must be made by motion—r.33.43(*b*).
[49] r.33.7(1)(*e*) (intimation where child in care of local authority or third party or liable to be maintained by third party), r.33.7(1)(*f*) (intimation where s.11 order craved and parent not party to the action), r.33.7(1)(*g*) (intimation where residence order craved and pursuer is not parent and is resident in Scotland) and r.33.7(1)(*h*) (intimation to child where s.11 order craved); and r.33.7(5) (intimation dispensed with where address unknown) and r.33.7(7) (intimation dispensed with where inappropriate for child). These rules are reproduced in Chap. 1 (text accompanying nn.15–18 and 26).

a crave in the defences,[50] so accompanied,[51] or simply by completing Form F26 (notice of intention to defend in a family action) so as to indicate a wish to obtain a section 11 order.[52] Application for a section 11 order by a person other than the pursuer or defender is made by minute in the cause.[53]

Unless the sheriff on cause shown otherwise directs, a warrant for citation cannot be granted in a divorce action which includes a crave for a section 11 order without there being produced with the initial writ an extract of the relevant entry in the register of births or equivalent document.[54]

A party who makes an application for a section 11 order in respect of a child must include in his or her pleadings averments giving particulars of any other proceedings known to him or her, whether in Scotland or elsewhere and whether concluded or not, which relate to the child in respect of whom the section 11 order is sought.[55] Where such other proceedings are continuing or have taken place, and the averments of the applicant do not contain particulars of the other proceedings, or contain particulars which are incomplete or incorrect, any defences or minute, as the case may be, lodged by any party to the action must include such particulars or such further or correct particulars as are known to him or her.[56]

Where (a) on the lodging of a notice of intention to defend in a divorce action in which the initial writ seeks or includes a crave for a section 11 order, a defender wishes to oppose any such crave or order, or seeks the same order as that craved by the pursuer; (b) on the lodging of a notice of intention to defend in a divorce action, the defender seeks a section 11 order which is not craved by the pursuer; or (c) in any other circumstances in a divorce action, the sheriff considers that a child welfare hearing should be fixed and makes an order (whether at his own instance or on the motion of a party) that

---

[50] rr.33.34(1)(*b*)(iii) and (2)(*b*)(i), and 33.39(1)(*a*) and (2).(a). Contrast these provisions with r.9.6(3) (in divorce action neither crave nor averments need be made in defences which relate to s.11 order). See also r.33.43(*b*), mentioned in n.48 *supra*.

[51] r. 33.15(3) (party making crave which would have required warrant under r.33.7 if sought in initial writ required to include crave for warrant or to dispense with such intimation in his writ).

[52] r.33.22A(1)(*a*) and (*b*) and (4), and r.9.6(3).

[53] r.33.39(1)(*b*) and (2)(*a*). See also r.33.43(*b*), mentioned in n.48 *supra;* rr.33.7(1)(*e*)–(*h*), (5) and (7), mentioned in n.49 *supra;* and r.33.15(3), mentioned in n.51 *supra.*

[54] r.33.9(*b*).

[55] r.33.3(1)(*a*), implementing s.39 of the Family Law Act 1986.

[56] r.33.3(2).

such a hearing be fixed, the sheriff clerk requires to fix a date and time for a child welfare hearing on the first suitable court date occurring not sooner than 21 days after the lodging of such notice of intention to defend, unless the sheriff directs the hearing to be held on an earlier date.[57] On fixing the date for the child welfare hearing, the sheriff clerk must intimate that date in Form F41 to the parties,[58] whose right to make any other application to the court whether by motion or otherwise is unaffected thereby.[59] At the child welfare hearing (which may be held in private), the sheriff must seek to secure the expeditious resolution of disputes in relation to the child by ascertaining from the parties the matters in dispute and any information relevant to that dispute, and may (a) order such steps to be taken, or (b) make such order, if any, or (c) order further procedure, as he thinks fit.[60] All parties (including a child who has indicated his or her wish to attend) must, except on cause shown, attend the child welfare hearing *personally*.[61] It is the duty of the parties to provide the sheriff with sufficient information to enable him to conduct the child welfare hearing.[62]

In any divorce action in which an order in relation to parental responsibilities or parental rights is in issue, the sheriff may, at any stage of the action,[63] where he considers it appropriate to do so, refer that issue to a mediator accredited to a specified family mediation organisation.[64] In general, no information as to what occurred during family mediation is admissible as evidence in any civil proceedings.[65]

Where the court is considering any question relating to the care and upbringing of a child, it may, without prejudice to its power to appoint any other person,[66] not being an officer of the local authority

---

[57] r.33.22A(1).
[58] r.33.22A(2).
[59] r.33.22A(3).
[60] r.33.22A(4).
[61] r.33.22A(5).
[62] r.33.22A(6).
[63] Reference to a mediator may be made after proof (*Harris v. Martin*, 1995 S.C.L.R. 580) but is not a competent disposal as a final order of the court (*Patterson v. Patterson*, 1994 S.C.L.R. 166).
[64] r.33.22.
[65] Civil Evidence (Family Mediation) (Scotland) Act 1995, s.1, subject to s.2 (exceptions, *e.g.* as to contracts and where every participant agrees on admissibility).
[66] Such a person may be an advocate or a solicitor. Such appointment may most appropriately be made in cases of particular urgency, cases involving parties living in different local authority areas and cases where the local authority has already been extensively involved (*cf. O v. O*, 1995 S.L.T. 238 at p. 241).

for the purpose, appoint an appropriate local authority to investigate
and report to the court on all the circumstances of the child and on
the proposed arrangements for the care and upbringing of the
child.[67] On making an appointment for such purpose, whether of a
local authority or another person, the sheriff requires to direct that
the party who sought the appointment or, where the court makes the
appointment of its own motion, the pursuer or minuter (as the case
may be) must (a) instruct the local authority or reporter, and (b) be
responsible, in the first instance, for the fees and outlays of the local
authority or reporter appointed.[68] The party who sought the appointment or, where the sheriff makes the appointment of his own
motion, the pursuer or minuter (as the case may be) is required,
within seven days after the date of the appointment, to intimate the
name and address of the local authority or reporter to any local
authority to which intimation of the action has been made.[69] On
completion of his report, the local authority or reporter, as the case
may be, is required to send it, with a copy of it for each party, to the
sheriff clerk who must upon receipt send a copy to each party.[70]
Where a local authority or reporter has been appointed, an application for a section 11 order in respect of the child concerned cannot
be determined until the report has been lodged.[71]

Where in proceedings for or relating to a section 11 order in
respect of a child there is not available to the court adequate
information as to where the child is, the court may order any person
who it has reason to believe may have relevant information to
disclose it to the court.[72] Application for the order requires to be
made by motion; and the sheriff may ordain the person against
whom the order has been made to appear before him or to lodge an

[67] Matrimonial Proceedings (Children) Act 1958, s.11(1), as amended by the
Children (Scotland) Act 1995, Sched. 4, para. 9. If on consideration of the report
the court, either *ex proprio motu* or on the application of any person concerned,
considers it expedient to do so, it may require the person who furnished the
report to appear and to be examined on oath regarding any matter dealt with in
the report, and such person may be examined or cross-examined accordingly—
1958 Act, s.11(4). A report may be of assistance to the court in considering any
oral evidence which it may hear before disposing of the application on a
consideration of all the evidence—*O v. O, supra; MacIntyre v. MacIntyre,* 1962
S.L.T. (Notes) 70. (*per contra Whitecross v. Whitecross,* 1977 S.L.T. 225 at p. 227
(social work report not evidence)).
[68] r.33.21(2).
[69] r.33.21(3).
[70] r.33.21(4) and (5).
[71] r.33.21(6).
[72] Family Law Act 1986, s.33(1). *Cf. Abusaif v. Abusaif,* 1984 S.L.T. 90.

affidavit.[73] A person cannot be excused from complying with such an order by reason that to do so may incriminate him or his spouse of an offence; but a statement or admission made in compliance with the order is not admissible in evidence against either of them in proceedings for any offence other than perjury.[74]

To enforce section 11 orders the court may grant such orders as an order for delivery[75] or for sheriff officers to search for and take possession of a child.[76] Wilful failure to make a child available for the purposes of a contact order may be punishable as a contempt of court. A party alleged to be in breach of an interim order may be ordained to appear at the bar to answer the charge and, in the event of denial, minute and answers may be ordered.[77] Procedure in relation to a final order is by way of ordinary action commenced by initial writ.[78] If the court is satisfied that the order or interim order has been breached, it may impose a penalty of imprisonment or a fine, or may admonish the party in breach.[79] Where any parties have reached agreement in relation to a section 11 order, a joint minute may be entered into expressing that agreement; and, subject to rule 33.19(3) (no order before views of child expressed), the sheriff may grant decree in respect of those parts of the joint minute in relation to which he could otherwise make an order, whether or not such a decree would include a matter for which there was no crave.[80] No agreement can however bind the court.[81]

A section 11 order relating to parental responsibilities or parental rights ceases to have effect where a relevant order made outwith Scotland comes into force, so far as it makes provision for any matter for which the same or different provision is made by that

---

[73] r.33.23.
[74] 1986 Act, s.33(2).
[75] *cf. Brown v. Brown*, 1948 S.C. 5 and *Thomson v. Thomson*, 1979 S.L.T. (Sh.Ct.) 11. As to the power of the court to make an order for the delivery of a child by one parent to the other parent other than in implementation of a s.11 order, see the Family Law Act 1986, s.17(1).
[76] *cf. Caldwell v. Caldwell*, 1983 S.L.T. 610.
[77] *Johnston v. Johnston*, 1996 S.L.T. 499.
[78] *Celso v. Celso*, 1992 S.C.L.R. 175.
[79] *Macphail, Sheriff Court Practice*, para. 22–152. Note that the standard of proof is proof beyond reasonable doubt (*Johnston, supra*).
[80] r.33.26.
[81] *Robson v. Robson*, 1973 S.L.T. (Notes) 4: *Anderson v. Anderson*, 1989 S.C.L.R. 475; *McKechnie v. McKechnie*, 1990 S.L.T. (Sh.Ct.) 75.

order,[82] or in any event once the child reaches the age of 16 years.[83] Where a section 11 order made by a court in Scotland ceases by virtue of the coming into force of a relevant order to have effect so far as it makes provision for any matter, that court has no power to vary it so as to make provision for that matter.[84] Otherwise, the court may vary,[85] or recall, any section 11 order made by it notwithstanding that it would no longer have jurisdiction to make the original order.[86]

Application after final decree for, or for the variation or recall of, a section 11 order requires to be made by minute in the process of the action to which the application relates.[87] Where a minute has been lodged, any party may apply by motion for any interim order which may be made pending the determination of the application.[88]

Reference to the Principal Reporter

In terms of section 54(1) of the Children (Scotland) Act 1995, where it appears to the court that any of certain statutory conditions is satisfied with respect to a child, it may refer the matter to the Principal Reporter, specifying the condition.

The statutory conditions are those set forth in section 52(2), namely that the child:

"(a) is beyond the control of any relevant person;
 (b) is falling into bad association or is exposed to moral danger;
 (c) is likely (i) to suffer unnecessarily; or (ii) be impaired in his health or development, due to a lack of parental care;
 (d) is a child in respect of whom any of the offences mentioned in Schedule 1 to the Criminal Procedure (Scotland) Act 1975 (offences against children to which special provisions apply) has been committed;

---

[82] 1986 Act, s.15(1), as amended by the Children (Scotland) Act 1995, Sched. 4, para. 41(4), the relevant orders being an order under Part 1 of the 1986 Act, or an order varying such an order, competently made by another court in any part of the United Kingdom with respect to the child in question; or an order relating to the parental responsibilities or parental rights in relation to that child which is made outside the United Kingdom and recognised in Scotland by virtue of s.26 of the 1986 Act.
[83] In the unlikely case of an order in relation to the parental responsibility to provide guidance to the child (s.1(1)(b)(ii)), the order would cease to have effect on the child's eighteenth birthday—s.1(2)(b).
[84] 1986 Act, s.15(2).
[85] An order varying an original order means any order made with respect to the same child as the original order was made—s.15(3).
[86] s.15(2), subject to ss.11(1) and 13(4) of the 1986 Act.
[87] r.33.44(1)(a).
[88] r.33.44(2).

(e) is, or is likely to become, a member of the same household as a child in respect of whom any of the offences referred to in para. (d) above has been committed;

(f) is, or is likely to become, a member of the same household as a person who has committed any of the offences referred to in para. (d) above;

(g) is, or is likely to become, a member of the same household as a person in respect of whom an offence under sections 2A to 2C of the Sexual Offences (Scotland) Act 1976 (incest and intercourse with a child by step-parent or person in position of trust) has been committed by a member of that household;

(h) has failed to attend school regularly without reasonable excuse;

(i) [*not applicable*];

(j) has misused alcohol or any drug, whether or not a controlled drug within the meaning of the Misuse of Drugs Act 1971;

(k) has misused a volatile substance by deliberately inhaling its vapour, other than for medicinal purposes;

(l) is being provided with accommodation by a local authority under section 25, or is the subject of a parental responsibilities order obtained under section 86, of the Act and, in either case, his behaviour is such that special measures are necessary for his adequate supervision in his interest or in the interest of others."

Where the court has referred a matter to the Principal Reporter under section 54(1) he must—

(a) make such investigation as he thinks appropriate; and

(b) if he considers that compulsory measures of supervision[89] are necessary, arrange a children's hearing to consider the case of the child under section 69 of the Act; and section 54(1) applies as if the condition specified by the court thereunder were a ground of referral established in accordance with section 68 of the Act.[90]

---

[89] "Supervision" in relation to compulsory measures of supervision may include measures taken for the protection, guidance, treatment or control of the child— 1995 Act, s.52(3).

[90] 1995 Act, s.54(3).

CHAPTER 7

MONEY

THE subject of money in the context of divorce law and practice (excepting maintenance for children) is discussed in this chapter; and the court's powers to make orders relative to the subject under the Family Law (Scotland) Act 1985[1] before, upon, and after the granting of divorce are examined.

ORDERS MADE BEFORE THE GRANTING OF DECREE

Interim aliment orders

Either party to an action of divorce may claim interim aliment.[2] Application must be made by motion.[3] Whether or not the claim is disputed, the court may award the sum claimed or any lesser sum or may refuse to make an award.[4] An award of interim aliment must consist of an award of periodical payments payable only until the date of the disposal of the action or such earlier date as the court may specify.[5]

The court may order either party to provide details of his resources,[6] and may reasonably expect the parties to produce documentary evidence of their respective net[7] incomes at any

---

[1] In actions brought before September 1, 1986 (the date of commencement of the Family Law (Scotland) Act 1985) s.5 of the Divorce (Scotland) Act 1976 continues to operate—1985 Act, s.28(3). Material relative to the continued operation of s.5 may be located in the previous edition of this text (Chap. 7, n.1).

[2] s.6(1)(b).

[3] r.33.50. A crave for interim aliment is therefore inappropriate (compare, e.g. r.33.49(1)(a) and r.33.49(1)(b)). For a contrary view, see Kerr v. Kerr, 1995 S.C.L.R. 1130.

[4] s.6(2).

[5] s.6(3).

[6] s.20, considered infra. "Resources" means present and foreseeable resources—s.27(1). Both the benefit of a company car and payment by the company of pension contributions constitute resources which ought to be taken into account, at least to the extent that the recipient's cash income is thereby not subject to such outlays (Semple v. Semple, 1995 S.C.L.R. 569).

[7] As in Wiseman v. Wiseman, 1989 S.C.L.R. 757 and Pryde v. Pryde, 1991 S.L.T. (Sh.Ct.) 26. But see MacInnes v. MacInnes, 1993 S.L.T. 1108.

hearing on a claim for interim aliment. In deciding what award of interim aliment if any to make, the court may have regard to considerations applicable in determining the amount to award in respect of a claim for aliment, namely needs, earning capacity and general circumstances.[8]

Awards of interim aliment are within the discretion of the sheriff and an appellate court could only interfere with any decision taken in exercise of this discretion if it were to be satisfied that the judge of first instance had erred in law, or that he had failed to notice a relevant factor, or that he had arrived at a wholly unreasonable decision.[9]

An award of interim aliment may be varied or recalled by an order of the court[10] but no such variation or recall can be backdated.[11] It has been held that variation of an award of interim aliment is competent without a change of circumstances having been established, there requiring only to be a sufficient reason to justify a variation.[12]

Incidental orders

An incidental order may be made under section 8(2) of the Act before, as well as on or after, the granting or refusal of decree of divorce.[13] The orders which fall within the definition of an incidental order and the considerations applicable to the making thereof

---

[8] *McGeachie v. McGeachie*, 1989 S.C.L.R. 99 ("While it is true that the criteria set out in s.4 of the 1985 Act do not by virtue of the Act apply to interim aliment awards . . . these criteria are consistent with pre-existing law and practice in relation to the determination of interim aliment . . . [N]eeds, earning capacity and general circumstances are all proper elements to consider when awarding interim aliment." (*per* the Sheriff Principal at p. 100)). As to 'needs' see now *McGeoch v. McGeoch*, 1996 G.W.D. 29–1751. *Quaere* whether, and if so when, a spouse could reasonably expect to be alimented when cohabiting with a third party (*cf.* *Brunton v. Brunton*, 1986 S.L.T. 49 and *Kavanagh v. Kavanagh*, 1989 S.L.T. 134). See also *Munro v. Munro*, 1986 S.L.T. 72 and *Henderson v. Henderson*, 1991 G.W.D. 31–1864 (relevance of paying spouse's cohabitant's earnings).
[9] *Begg v. Begg*, 1987 S.C.L.R. 704 at p. 705. An appeal without leave of the sheriff against an award of interim aliment or the refusal of an application for interim aliment is incompetent (*Rixson v. Rixson*, 1990 S.L.T. (Sh.Ct.) 5, *Hulme v. Hulme*, 1990 S.L.T. (Sh.Ct.) 25, *Dickson v. Dickson*, 1990 S.L.T. (Sh.Ct.) 80 and *Richardson v. Richardson*, 1991 S.L.T. (Sh.Ct.) 7).
[10] 1985 Act, s.6(4). The provisions of s.6 apply to an award so varied and the claim therefor as they applied to the original award and the claim therefor—*ibid.* Application for variation or recall must be made by motion—r.33.50.
[11] *McColl v. McColl*, 1993 S.L.T. 617.
[12] *Bisset v. Bisset*, 1993 S.C.L.R. 284.
[13] 1985 Act, s.14(1), excepting the orders specified in the text accompanying (second) nn.21 and 22 *infra*. For illustrations of circumstances in which incidental

are detailed *infra*. An incidental order may be varied or recalled by subsequent order on cause shown.[14]

Orders for provision of details of resources

By virtue of section 20 of the Act, the court may order either party to provide details of his resources.[15] The power may be exercised even where there is no suggestion that the party called upon to provide details is in some way concealing some resource.[16] If the party so called upon fails to provide details of his present and foreseeable resources he will be in contempt of an order of court.[17] Section 20 does not however give the court power to conduct an inquiry as to the extent of the disclosure.[18] In order to fulfil his obligation, the party ordered must provide a figure for the value of each item of property but does not require to produce documentation vouching the figure.[19] The sheriff is entitled to seek clarification of matters in any list of resources and may appoint the solicitor for the party concerned to appear personally before him.[20] It remains for the party claiming a specific financial provision to formulate and prove the entitlement.[21]

---

orders sought *pendente lite* were refused as premature, see *McKeown v. McKeown*, 1988 S.C.L.R. 355 and *Demarco v. Demarco*, 1990 S.C.L.R. 635. A motion for an incidental order for the sale of the jointly owned matrimonial home by a party not craving any financial provision was refused as incompetent in *MacClue v. MacClue*, 1994 S.C.L.R. 933. Application may be made by motion, except that the sheriff is not bound to determine such a motion if he considers that the application should properly be by a crave in the initial writ or defences, as the case may be—r.33.49(1).

[14] 1985 Act, s.14(4). Application in a depending action for such variation or recall must be made by minute in the process of the action to which the application relates—r.33.49(2).

[15] "Resources" means present and foreseeable resources—s.27(1). Note that the power is additional to the power of the court to grant commission and diligence *inter alia* for the recovery of documents relative to a party's financial position (Administration of Justice (Scotland) Act 1972, s.1(1)).

[16] *Lawrence v. Lawrence*, 1992 S.C.L.R. 199.

[17] *Nelson v. Nelson*, 1993 S.C.L.R. 149.

[18] *ibid.*

[19] *ibid.*

[20] *ibid.*

[21] *Williamson v. Williamson*, 1989 S.L.T. 866 at p. 867. Once documents have been submitted in terms of s.20, however, the matter is properly before the court—*MacQueen v. MacQueen*, 1992 G.W.D. 28–1653.

ORDERS MADE UPON THE GRANTING OF DECREE

In terms of section 8(1) of the Act[22]:

> "In an action for divorce, either party to the marriage may apply to the court for one or more of the following orders—
>
>   (a) an order for the payment of a capital sum to him by the other party to the marriage [capital sum order];
>
>   (aa) an order for the transfer of property to him by the other party to the marriage [transfer of property order][23];
>
>   (b) an order for the payment of a periodical allowance to him by the other party to the marriage [periodical allowance order];
>
>   (ba) an order under section 12A(2) or (3) of this Act [pension lump sum order];
>
>   (c) an incidental order within the meaning of section 14(2) of this Act [incidental order]."

Any such order, defined in the Act as "an order for financial provision",[24] is essentially discretionary and is thus subject to review by an appellate court only if it can be shown that the judge of first instance misdirected himself in law or failed to take into account a relevant and material factor or reached a result which is manifestly inequitable or plainly wrong.[25] The considerations applicable to the various orders for financial provision are now considered in turn.

Capital sum, pension lump sum and transfer of property orders

A capital sum order or a transfer of property order may be made either (a) on granting decree of divorce, or (b) within such period as the court on granting decree of divorce may specify.[26] The court

---

[22] As amended by the Law Reform (Miscellaneous Provisions) (Scotland) Act 1990, Sched. 8, para. 34 and Sched. 9 and the Pensions Act 1995, s.167(1).

[23] A transfer of property order subject to a balancing payment was made in *Wallis v. Wallis*, 1993 S.L.T. 1348. Note that in *Muir v. Muir*, 1993 G.W.D. 39–2593 a transfer of property order was made to the applicant spouse without her requiring to make a balancing payment (notwithstanding that such a payment would have been equitable) because the non-applicant spouse had omitted to crave such payment.

[24] 1985 Act, s.8(3).

[25] *Little v. Little*, 1990 S.L.T. 785 at p. 787, approved by the House of Lords in *Jacques v. Jacques*, 1997 S.L.T. 459. See also *Peacock v. Peacock*, 1994 S.L.T. 40.

[26] 1985 Act, s.12(1). The only way in which the court can give effect to s.12(1)(b) is to order a proof on a specified day; adjournment of that diet has no effect on the court's power to make the orders—*Mackin v. Mackin*, 1991 S.L.T. (Sh.Ct.) 22.

may stipulate that the order will come into effect at a specified future date.[27]

The court, on making a capital sum order, may order that the capital sum will be payable by instalments.[28]

The court, on making an order for payment of a capital sum, may make an order in certain circumstances[29] requiring the trustees or managers of a pension scheme to pay the whole or part of a pension lump sum payable to the liable party, when it becomes due, to the other party to the marriage as a payment in or towards discharge of the liability under the capital sum order.[30] Such an

---

[27] 1985 Act, s.12(2). See *e.g. Little, supra* (payment postponed in part until after expected date of sale of matrimonial home), *Dorrian v. Dorrian*, 1991 S.C.L.R. 661, *Gulline v. Gulline*, 1992 S.L.T. (Sh.Ct.) 71, *Bannon v. Bannon*, 1993 S.L.T. 999 and *Gracie v. Gracie*, 1997 S.L.T. (Sh.Ct.) 15 (payment postponed in full or in part until date of vesting of pension entitlement) and *Shand v. Shand*, 1994 S.L.T. 387 (payment postponed until likely date of conclusion of defender's sequestration).

[28] *ibid.* s.12(3). "Instalment payments may well be appropriate when the capital asset concerned is an income-generating asset. Where there is no such capital asset, for the court to require capital to be created by payment of instalments arising out of income would be quite wrong and contrary to the intention of the Act. To do so would merely be to establish a requirement to pay a periodical allowance for a very extended period but under another name." (*Dorrian, supra,* at p. 663D). A capital sum payable by instalments was awarded in, *e.g. Bell v. Bell,* 1988 S.C.L.R. 457, *Kelly v. Kelly,* 1992 G.W.D. 36–2130, *Buckle v. Buckle,* 1995 S.C.L.R. 590, *Gracie, supra* and *McEwan v. McEwan,* 1997 S.L.T. 118 (proportion only).

[29] The relevant circumstances are those where—(a) the matrimonial property within the meaning of s.10 of the Act includes any rights or interests in benefits under a pension scheme which the liable party has or may have (whether such benefits are payable to him or in respect of his death); and (b) those benefits include a lump sum payable to him or in respect of his death—s.12A(1), inserted by the Pension Act 1995, s.167(3). In the case of an unfunded pension scheme, the court may not make an order which would allow assets to be removed from the scheme earlier than would otherwise have been the case—s.10(5A), as inserted by the Family Law Act 1996, s.17(b). The order may only be made in actions raised after August 19, 1996—Pensions Act 1995, s.180(1) and S.I. 1996 No. 1843.

[30] 1985 Act, s.12A(1), (2) and (4)(b), inserted by the Pensions Act 1995, s.167(3). Any such payment also discharges so much of the trustees' or managers' liability to or in respect of the liable party as corresponds to the amount of the payment—s.12A(4)(a). The trustees or managers of the scheme (as defined by s.10(11)—as to which, see n.61 *infra*) can recover from the liable party the reasonable administrative expenses of complying with the pension lump sum order in accordance with reg. 10 of the Divorce etc. (Pensions) (Scotland) Regulations 1996 (reproduced in App. V). Where a pension lump sum order imposes any requirement on the trustees or managers of a pension scheme [the first scheme] and the liable party acquires transfer credits under another scheme [the new scheme] which are derived (directly or indirectly) from a transfer from the first

order, or a variant thereof,[31] may also be made where a pension lump sum is payable in respect of the death of the liable party.[32] Where an order under section 8(1)(ba) is applied for, intimation falls to be made to the trustees or managers of the pension scheme.[33] No such requirement to pay can be imposed except by order of the court proceeding upon a duly intimated application.

The court is bound not to make a transfer of property order if the consent of a third party which is necessary under any obligation, enactment or rule of law has not been obtained.[34] An order for the transfer of property subject to security cannot be made without the consent of the creditor unless he had had an opportunity of being heard by the court.[35] Where the consent of a third party to such a transfer is necessary by virtue of an obligation,

---

scheme of all his accrued rights under that scheme; and the trustees or managers of the new scheme have been given notice in accordance with the Regulations (as to which, see App. V), the order has effect as if it had been made in respect of the trustees or managers of the new scheme—s.12A(6). The court may, nonetheless, on an application by any person having an interest, vary a pension lump sum order by substituting for the trustees or managers specified in the order the trustees or managers of any other pension scheme under which any pension lump sum is payable to the liable party or in respect of his or her death (see (second) n.37 *infra*). As to the power of the court to recall a pension lump sum order, see (second) n.36 *infra*.

[31] If the trustees or managers of the pension scheme have power to determine the person to whom the sum, or any part of it, is to be paid, the court, on making the capital sum order, may make an order requiring them to pay the whole or part of that sum, when it becomes due, to the other party—s.12A(3)(a). If the liable party has power to nominate the person to whom the sum, or any part of it, is to be paid, the court, on making the capital sum order, may make an order requiring the liable party to nominate the other party in respect of the whole or part of that sum—s.12A(3)(b). In any other case, the court, on making the capital sum order, may make an order requiring the trustees or managers of the pension scheme in question to pay the whole or part of that sum, when it becomes due, to the other party instead of to the person to whom, apart from the order, it would be paid—s.12A(3)(c).

[32] 1985 Act, s.12A(1), (3) and (4)(b), inserted by the Pensions Act 1995, s.167(3). As to ancillary provisions, see n.31 *supra*.

[33] See Chap. 1, text accompanying n.22.

[34] 1985 Act, s.15(1). This provision will apply in a case of a property which is subject to a standard security which includes a condition requiring the consent of the security holder to a transfer of the property—*MacNaught v. MacNaught*, 1996 S.C.L.R. 151.

[35] *ibid.* s.15(2). This provision will apply in a case of a property which is subject to a standard security which does not include a condition requiring the consent of the security holder to a transfer of the property. It confers upon such a security holder a right, which he would not otherwise have, to appear and be heard by the court in divorce proceedings, and it allows the court, having afforded such an opportunity to the security holder, to make a transfer order even without his consent—*MacNaught, supra*.

enactment or rule of law, or the property is subject to a security, intimation must be made to the third party or creditor, as the case may be.[36]

Application for a capital sum, transfer of property[37] or pension lump sum order may be made by the pursuer by inserting a crave therefor in the initial writ; and by the defender by inserting a crave in the defences.[38]

Where an application for an order under section 8(1)(a), (aa) or (ba) has been made, the court must make such order, if any, as is:

"(a) justified by the principles set out in section 9 of [the] Act; and
(b) reasonable having regard to the resources of the parties."[39]

Section 9(1) specifies the principles which the court must apply in deciding what order for financial provision, if any, to make. These are:

"(a) the net value of the matrimonial property should be shared fairly between the parties to the marriage [Principle A];
(b) fair account should be taken of any economic advantage derived by either party from contributions by the other,

---

[36] See Chap. 1, text accompanying n.19.

[37] "a sufficient description of the property should be included in the order which is to be made under section [8(1)(aa)] to satisfy the requirement of the common law, which is to distinguish the subjects from all other lands. In most cases a brief description will be all that is needed. In more complex cases it may be necessary for a more detailed description to be given. The court will expect to be provided with sufficient information by the party who seeks the order to enable this to be done." (*per* the Lord President in *Walker v. Walker*, 1991 S.L.T. 157 at p. 160B–C). It is to be noted that the issue of whether a transfer of property order (i) is an order which itself transfers the property to the other spouse, or (ii) is no more than an order that the spouse having the title to the property should transfer it to the other (see 1986 S.L.T. (News) 97 and 1990 J.L.S. 52) has been decided by *Walker* in favour of the latter proposition. A crave for a transfer of property order requires to be framed accordingly (see App. I).

[38] rr.33.48(1)(*a*) and (2)(*a*), and 33.34(1)(*b*)(ii) and (2)(*b*).

[39] 1985 Act, s.8(2), subject to ss.12–15 of the Act, noted *infra*. Section 8(2) sets out two criteria, but does not in terms direct the court to consider one in advance of, or in isolation from, the other—*McVinnie v. McVinnie (No. 2)*, 1997 S.L.T. (Sh.Ct.) 12 at p. 14. They are cumulative with the result that unless both are satisfied the court has no power to make an order (*Wallis v. Wallis*, 1993 S.L.T. 1348 at p. 1352F). Accordingly, s.8(2)(b) does not entitle the court to award any greater amount by way of a capital sum beyond what is justified by the principles set forth in the Act but "can only operate to cut down any sum, otherwise justified, having regard to the current resources of the parties" (*Latter v. Latter*, 1990 S.L.T. 805 at p. 807—see *e.g. Rodgers v. Rodgers (No. 2)*, 1994 G.W.D. 31–1869).

and of any economic disadvantage suffered by either party in the interests of the other party or the family [Principle B];

(c) any economic burden of caring, after divorce, for a child of the marriage under the age of 16 years should be shared fairly between the parties [Principle C];

(d) a party who has been dependent to a substantial degree on the financial support of the other party should be awarded such financial provision as is reasonable to enable him to adjust, over a period of not more than three years from the date of the decree of divorce, to the loss of that support on divorce [Principle D];

(e) a party who at the time of the divorce seems likely to suffer serious financial hardship as a result of the divorce should be awarded such financial provision as is reasonable to relieve him of hardship over a reasonable period [Principle E]."

The principles are at this juncture considered individually in relation to other provisions of the Act respecting their application.

Principle A. *The net value* of *the matrimonial property* should be *shared fairly* between the parties to the marriage.

(i) *The matrimonial property* is all the property[40] belonging to the parties or either of them at the relevant date[41] which was acquired by them or him (otherwise than by way of gift[42] or succession from a third party) either (a) before the marriage for use by them as a

---

[40] Such may be heritable *or* moveable property (*Petrie v. Petrie,* 1988 S.C.L.R. 390). As to the former, see *Smith v. Smith,* 1992 G.W.D. 23–1324.

[41] The "relevant date" is whichever is the earlier of (i) the date on which the parties ceased to cohabit; and (ii) the date of service of the summons (*sic*) in the action for divorce—s.10(3). (The Scottish Law Commission in its *Report on Family Law* (Scot. Law Com. No. 135, 1992) proposes an amendment to s.10(3) by adding after the word "summons" the words "or initial writ"). The parties to a marriage are held to cohabit with one another only when they are in fact living together as man and wife (s.27(2)), as to which see Chap. 3, n.42 and *Buczynska v. Buczynski,* 1989 S.L.T. 558. No account is to be taken of any cessation of cohabitation where the parties thereafter resumed cohabitation (except where the parties ceased to cohabit for a continuous period of 90 days or more before resuming cohabitation for a period or periods of less than 90 days in all)—s.10(7). As to s.10(7), see *Pryde v. Pryde,* 1991 S.L.T. (Sh.Ct.) 26.

[42] As to "gift", see *Whittome v. Whittome (No. 1),* 1993 S.C.L.R. 137; 1994 S.L.T. 114.

family home or as furniture or plenishings for such home[43] or (b) during the marriage but before the relevant date.[44] Property must fall within (a) or (b) to constitute matrimonial property.[45]

The proportion of any rights or interests of either party (a) under a life policy or similar arrangement; and (b) in any benefits under a pension scheme[46] which either party has or may have (including such benefits payable in respect of the death of either party), which is referable to the period between the date of the marriage and the relevant date is taken to form part of the matrimonial property.[47] A claim for damages in respect of an accident which occurred after the date of the marriage but before the relevant date has been held to be matrimonial property.[48] A claim for a refund in respect of income tax deducted after the date of the marriage but before the relevant date has been held to be matrimonial property.[49] Shares in a private company issued during the period between the date of the marriage and the relevant date and derived from a series of gifted shareholdings in five companies, which had become subsidiaries of the company following upon an

---

[43] In an action of divorce in which the parties had previously married and divorced one another, a matrimonial home acquired during the course of the first marriage for use by the parties as a family home was held to be matrimonial property (*Mitchell v. Mitchell*, 1994 S.C. 601; 1995 S.L.T. 426).

[44] 1985 Act, s.10(4).

[45] *Maclellan v. Maclellan*, 1988 S.C.L.R. 399 (croft tenancy acquired prior to marriage for use other than as family home not matrimonial property (but *cf. obiter dicta* in *Buczynska, supra,* at p. 560)).

[46] The phrase "benefits under a pension scheme" includes any benefits by way of pension, whether or not under a pension scheme—s.10(10). The phrase "pension scheme" means—(a) an occupational pension scheme or a personal pension scheme; (b) a retirement annuity contract; or (c) an annuity, or insurance policy, purchased or transferred for the purpose of giving effect to rights under an occupational or personal pension scheme—s.10(10). "Occupational pension scheme" is defined as any scheme or arrangement which is comprised in one or more instruments or agreements and which has, or is capable of having, effect in relation to one or more descriptions or categories of employments so as to provide benefits, in the form of pensions or otherwise, payable on termination of service, or on death or retirement, to or in respect of earners with qualifying service in an employment of any such description or category; and "personal pension scheme" is defined as any scheme or arrangement which is comprised in one or more instruments or agreements and which has, or is capable of having, effect so as to provide benefits, in the form of pensions or otherwise, payable on death or retirement to or in respect of earners who have made arrangements with the trustees or managers of the scheme for them to become members of it— Pension Schemes Act 1993, s.1, as applied by the 1985 Act, s.10(10).

[47] 1985 Act, s.10(5), as amended by the Pensions Act 1995, s.167(2)(a).

[48] *Skarpaas v. Skarpaas*, 1993 S.L.T. 343 (see also *Petrie v. Petrie*, 1988 S.C.L.R. 390).

[49] *MacRitchie v. MacRitchie*, 1994 S.L.T. (Sh.Ct.) 72.

overall reconstruction, have been held to be matrimonial property.[50] Shares in a private company allotted as a bonus issue during the period between the date of the marriage and the relevant date in respect of a gifted shareholding have been held not to be matrimonial property, as have the shares in the public company the registration and flotation of which resulted from the reorganisation of that same private company.[51] A matrimonial home bought in a party's name prior to the date of the marriage with funds given by that party's relatives to her solicitors prior to settlement has been held not to be matrimonial property.[52] A redundancy payment received after the relevant date has been held not to be matrimonial property.[53] A payment received upon leaving the army after the relevant date has been held not to be matrimonial property.[54]

(ii) *The net value* of the matrimonial property is the value[55] of the property at the relevant date after deduction of any debts,[56] outstanding[57] at that date, incurred by the parties or either of them (a) before the marriage so far as they relate to the matrimonial property, and (b) during the marriage, and (c) in the assets in respect of which either party has accrued rights to benefits under a pension scheme.[58] Any changes in value after the relevant date must be left out of account when calculating the value of the matrimonial property.[59]

The rights or interests of a party under a life policy may be valued on the basis of its surrender value or on the basis of its

---

[50] *Latter v. Latter,* 1990 S.L.T. 805.

[51] *Whittome v. Whittome (No. 1),* 1994 S.L.T. 114.

[52] *Latter, supra.*

[53] *Smith v. Smith,* 1989 S.L.T. 668 and *Tyrrell v. Tyrrell,* 1990 S.L.T. 406.

[54] *Gibson v. Gibson,* 1990 G.W.D. 4–213.

[55] Where the parties have not agreed the value of an item of matrimonial property, the court may only make a finding as to such value by reference to the evidence, which failing by selecting a figure falling within the parties' respective estimates— *Pryde v. Pryde,* 1991 S.L.T. (Sh.Ct.) 26 and *Fleming v. Fleming,* 1993 G.W.D. 9–621.

[56] *Quaere* whether capital gains tax exigible on a notional realisation of matrimonial property at the relevant date falls to be taken into account—see *Latter v. Latter,* 1990 S.L.T. 805 at p. 809 and *McConnell v. McConnell,* 1993 G.W.D. 34–2185; *per contra, Bolton v. Bolton,* 1995 G.W.D. 14–799. Any contingent tax liability that may emerge in the event of accrued interest due to a party being paid at some time in the future does not fall to be taken into account (*McConnell*).

[57] The income tax due on income earned up to the relevant date but not payable until after that date is not a debt outstanding at the relevant date (*McCormick v. McCormick,* 1994 S.C.L.R. 958, disapproving *Buchan v. Buchan,* 1992 S.C.L.R. 766).

[58] 1985 Act, s.10(2), as amended by the Family Law Act 1996, s.17.

[59] *Wallis v. Wallis,* 1992 S.L.T. 676 at p.679F and 1994 S.L.T. 1348 at p.1351L. For possible consequences of this, see the speech of Lord Keith of Kinkel at p. 1351F–L.

replacement value.[60] The rights or interests of a party in any benefits under a pension scheme fall to be valued as prescribed.[61] A claim for damages which is yet to be quantified and admitted may be valued on the basis that it will attract less if offered for sale in the market place than the amount awarded by the decree which is obtained at the end of the day.[62] A business may be valued on the basis of a break-up value or a forced sale or on the basis of a value as a going concern.[63] A house may be valued with a deduction for a penalty which would have been incurred by a hypothetical early sale at the relevant date.[64] Household contents may be valued on the basis of auction room prices or on a willing buyer/willing seller basis.[65] A debt due to a party to the marriage may be valued at less than its book value.[66] The court may derive assistance from a table of matrimonial property showing values.[67]

---

[60] "The surrender value is the amount which the insurance company is prepared to pay to the policy holder if he wishes to cease paying premiums. The replacement value is the amount of money which an individual would need to invest to replace the proceeds which might reasonably have been expected to arise from the policy." (*per* R. Watson & Sons, Consulting Actuaries, in "Watsons Comment," April 1990). There is no reported case indicating a judicial preference for one or other of these alternatives.

[61] 1985 Act, s.10(8)(*a*), inserted by the Pensions Act 1995, s.167(2)(b) and implemented by the Divorce etc. (Pensions) (Scotland) Regulations 1996, reg. 3 (valuation to be on "cash equivalent" basis, not available in general to members of schemes with less than two years' membership or to employees with less than one year until normal retirement age under the scheme or to members who have deferred retirement past normal retirement age or to retired members in receipt of pension, irrespective of their age). The trustees or managers of the pension scheme may be required to provide information as to the benefits' value and are entitled to recover the administrative expenses incurred by them in furnishing the information—s.10(8)(b), implemented by the 1996 Regulations, reg. 4. The 1996 Regulations are reproduced in App. V. Where the pension scheme is a retirement annuity contract or an annuity or insurance policy as described in s.10(10)(b) or (c) (see n.46 *supra*), the reference to trustees or managers should be read as a reference to the annuity provider and insurer, respectively—s.10(11).

[62] *Skarpaas v. Skarpaas,* 1993 S.L.T. 343. And see *Louden v. Louden,* 1994 S.L.T. 381.

[63] Businesses were valued on a going concern basis in *McKenzie v. McKenzie,* 1991 S.L.T. 461 and *Savage v. Savage,* 1993 G.W.D. 28–1779. The valuation of shares in private limited companies may present formidable difficulties—see *Latter v. Latter,* 1990 S.L.T. 805, *Crockett v. Crockett,* 1992 S.C.L.R. 591 *McConnell v. McConnell,* 1993 G.W.D. 34–2185 and *Brown v. Brown,* 1996 G.W.D. 29–1753.

[64] *Mackin v. Mackin,* 1991 S.L.T. (Sh.Ct.) 22 and *Lawson v. Lawson,* 1996 S.L.T. (Sh.Ct.) 83.

[65] Neither method may be held strictly apposite (*Latter, supra*). Note that there is a presumption of equal shares in household goods obtained in prospect of or during the marriage other than by gift or succession from a third party—1985 Act, s.25.

[66] See *Shipton v. Shipton,* 1992 S.C.L.R. 23.

[67] See *Crockett, supra* and App. VI.

(iii) The net value of the matrimonial property is taken to be *shared fairly* when it is shared equally or in such other proportions as are justified by special circumstances.[68]

Section 10(6) provides that "special circumstances", without prejudice to the generality of the words,[69] may include[70]:

(a) the terms of any agreement between the parties on the ownership or division of any of the matrimonial property[71];

(b) the source of the funds or assets used to acquire any of the matrimonial property where those funds or assets were not derived from the income or efforts of the parties during the marriage[72];

(c) any destruction or dissipation or alienation of property by either spouse[73];

(d) the nature of the matrimonial property, the use made of it (including use for business purposes or as a matrimonial

---

[68] 1985 Act, s.10(1).

[69] The words "special circumstances" do not have any technical meaning but refer to any circumstances which are special to the case—*Jacques v. Jacques,* 1997 S.L.T. 459 at p. 462D.

[70] See *Kerrigan v. Kerrigan,* 1988 S.C.L.R. 603 and *White v. White,* 1992 S.C.L.R. 769 (brevity of marriage held in each case to be a special circumstance), *Buczynska v. Buczynski,* 1989 S.L.T. 558 and *Wallis v. Wallis,* 1992 S.L.T. 676; 1993 S.L.T. 1348 (post-separation increase in value of matrimonial home held in each case not to be a special circumstance), *Farrell v. Farrell,* 1990 S.C.L.R. 717 (voluntary assumption of co-owning spouse's mortgage liability and low net value of matrimonial home held to be special circumstances), *Jesner v. Jesner,* 1992 S.L.T. 999 (husband's loss of household contents held to be a special circumstance), and *Wallis, supra* (mere fact of transfer of property into joint names held not to be a special circumstance). See also *Clokie v. Clokie,* 1993 G.W.D. 16–1059 (payment of entire price of a matrimonial home 21 years prior to separation a factor of less weight than if marriage had been of relatively short duration).

[71] 1985 Act, s.10(6)(a). See also *Anderson v. Anderson,* 1991 S.L.T. (Sh.Ct.) 11 and *Webster v. Webster,* 1992 G.W.D. 25–1432.

[72] *ibid.* s.10(6)(b); for relevant "sources" see, *e.g. Phillip v. Phillip,* 1988 S.C.L.R. 427 (pre-marriage house), *Kerrigan, supra* (pursuer's mother), *Buczynska, supra* (pursuer's mother), *Buchanan v. Buchanan,* 1989 G.W.D. 26–1166 (pre-marriage houses), *Budge v. Budge,* 1990 S.L.T. 319 (pre-marriage house), *Latter, supra* (defender's family), *Jesner, supra* (pre-marriage house and family trust); *Crockett v. Crockett,* 1992 S.C.L.R. 591 (O.H.) and Extra Division, June 30, 1993, unreported (I.H.) (defender's company); *Davidson v. Davidson,* 1993 G.W.D. 31–2000 (inheritance); *Milne v. Milne,* 1994 G.W.D. 11–666 (pursuer's family), and *Maclean v. Maclean,* 1996 G.W.D. 22–1278 (pursuer's mother).

[73] *ibid.* s.10(6)(c). And see *Park v. Park,* 1988 S.C.L.R. 584 (non-payment of mortgage not dissipation), *Short v. Short,* 1994 G.W.D. 21–1300 (encumbering matrimonial home by forging husband's signature was dissipation), and *Russell v. Russell,* 1996 G.W.D. 15–895 (failed business ventures not dissipation).

home) and the extent to which it is reasonable to expect it to be realised or divided or used as security[74];

(e) the actual or prospective liability for any expenses of valuation or transfer of property in connection with the divorce.[75]

It is for the court of first instance in each case to determine whether an event specified in section 10(6) amounts to special circumstances in the case in question and, if so, whether it justifies a division in proportions other than equal; the court is not required to effect an unequal division of the matrimonial property whenever special circumstances are found to exist.[76]

The court may adopt a global approach in assessing and dividing matrimonial property, or it may pursue a piecemeal approach, allowing it to divide a particular item from the rest to meet a special circumstance which bears on it primarily; there is room for

---

[74] 1985 Act, s.10(6)(d), applied in, *e.g. Petrie v. Petrie,* 1988 S.C.L.R. 390 (damages award), *Muir v. Muir,* 1989 S.L.T. (Sh.Ct.) 20 (pension), *Cooper v. Cooper,* 1989 S.C.L.R. 347 (matrimonial home), *Budge v. Budge,* 1990 S.L.T. 319 (matrimonial home/croft), *Carpenter v. Carpenter,* 1990 S.L.T. (Sh.Ct.) 68 (pension), *Little v. Little,* 1989 S.C.L.R. 613 (O.H.) and 1990 S.L.T. 785 (I.H.) (motor cars, matrimonial home, pension), *Farrell v. Farrell,* 1990 S.C.L.R. 717 (matrimonial home), *Skarpaas v. Skarpaas,* 1991 S.L.T. (Sh.Ct.) 15 (damages claim), *Symon v. Symon,* 1991 S.C.L.R. 414 (pension), *McGuire v. McGuire's Curator Bonis,* 1991 S.L.T. (Sh.Ct.) 76 (criminal injuries compensation award). *MacQueen v. MacQueen,* 1992 G.W.D. 28–1653 (pension), *Crockett v. Crockett,* 1992 S.C.L.R. 591 (O.H.) and Extra Division, June 30, 1993, unreported (I.H.) (pension and shares), *Fleming v. Fleming,* 1993 G.W.D. 9–621 (pension), *Milne v. Milne,* 1994 G.W.D. 11–666 (matrimonial home), *Wilson v. Wilson,* 1993 G.W.D. 38–2521 (pension), *Bannon v. Bannon,* 1993 S.L.T. 999 (pension), *Davidson v. Davidson,* 1993 G.W.D. 31–2000 (farm), *Peacock v. Peacock,* 1994 S.L.T. 40 (matrimonial home), *Stephen v. Stephen,* 1995 S.C.L.R. 175 (pension), *Crosbie v. Crosbie,* 1996 S.L.T. (Sh.Ct.) 86 (pension) and *Murphy v. Murphy,* 1996 S.L.T. (Sh.Ct.) 91 (matrimonial home and pension). Note that in the case of an interest in a pension scheme, the non-realisable nature of the asset and the deferred rights which it represents may be reflected in different ways: "In some cases an order for the transfer of the rights in such a scheme may be appropriate if those rights are assignable. In others, a discount may be appropriate, although this must depend very much upon the basis upon which the value has been arrived at in the first place. In others, an order for payment by instalments under section 12(3) may be the solution. In others, payment of the value may be deferred in whole or in part to a specified future date under section 12(2)" (*per* the Lord President in *Little v. Little,* 1990 S.L.T. 785 at p. 789D). See also now s.12A of the Act (*supra*). Note further that there may be cases where an equal and instant division of the full actuarial value of the interest is capable of being made by virtue of the availablity of other realisable assets (*Little, supra* at p. 788L, *Latter v. Latter,* 1990 S.L.T. 805, *Brooks v. Brooks,* 1993 S.L.T. 184).

[75] *ibid.* s.10(6)(e).

[76] *Jacques v. Jacques,* 1997 S.L.T. 459 at pp. 460L and 462P.

the scheme of the Act to be applied in different ways in different situations as a matter of discretion.[77] Subparagraphs (b) and (d) of section 10(6) might be thought to invite the latter approach: some items of matrimonial property might thus, for example, be treated differently from others according to their nature or the use to which they are put.[78]

The question of expenses is bound up intimately with the division of the matrimonial property and the effects of that division on the parties' resources.[79] The normal principle in petitory actions that expenses should follow success cannot be applied in its full rigour to cases involving such division, particularly where much trouble has been taken to achieve a fair division of the matrimonial property between the parties with the full co-operation of both sides.[80] The parties' conduct of the litigation rather than the result itself should, accordingly, be the principal criterion on which to proceed.[81] Factors which may be taken into account by the court in exercising its discretion as to expenses, therefore, include the reasonableness of the parties' claims, the extent to which they have co-operated in disclosing, and agreeing the value of, their respective assets, the offers they have made to settle, the extent to which proof could have been avoided and, of course, the final outcome.[82]

---

[77] *Crockett v. Crockett,* Extra Division, June 30, 1993, unreported.

[78] *Crockett, supra; Little v. Little,* 1990 S.L.T. 785 at p. 788E. "The matrimonial home is one of the clearest examples of a particular item of matrimonial property for which special arrangements may be justified" (*per* the Lord President in *Little, supra* at p. 788F).

[79] *Little, supra* at p. 790.

[80] *ibid.*

[81] *ibid.* See, *e.g. Scott v. Scott,* 1995 G.W.D. 36–1832 (no expenses found due to or by either party).

[82] *Adams v. Adams (No. 2),* 1997 S.L.T. 150. In *Adams* the Lord Ordinary awarded the husband defender the expenses of the proof and the procedure following thereon, and *quoad ultra* found no expenses due to or by either party, on the footing that the proof was necessitated because the wife insisted throughout on the two points of principle upon which she failed, whereas prior to the diet neither party could adopt a final position on financial matters, full and up-to-date information only being exchanged shortly before the proof. In *Macdonald v. Macdonald,* 1995 S.L.T. 72 (approved on appeal, 1994 G.W.D. 7–404) the Lord Ordinary awarded the wife pursuer the expenses of the action modified to 60 per cent, on the footing that her claims had, for the major part, been successful and that the defender had had no reasonable basis for contesting the issues which had generated much of the expense. In *Whittome v. Whittome (No. 2),* 1994 S.L.T. 130 the Lord Ordinary awarded the wife defender the expenses of the action modified to 75 per cent, having regard to the fact that she was partly successful, that her conduct throughout the litigation was generally reasonable and that it was reasonable that she should seek a decision from the court in respect of her claim

In applying Principle A, the court must not take account of the conduct of either party unless the conduct has adversely affected the financial resources which are relevant to the decision of the court on a claim for financial provision.[83]

Principle B. Fair account should be taken of any *economic advantage* derived by either party from *contributions* by the other, and of any *economic disadvantage* suffered by either party in the interests of the other party or of the family.[84]

Economic advantage means advantage gained whether before or during the marriage and includes gains in capital, in income and in earning capacity; and *economic disadvantage* is construed accordingly.[85]

Contributions are contributions made whether before or during the marriage, including indirect and non-financial contributions and, in particular, any such contribution made by looking after the family home or caring for the family.[85a]

In applying this principle, the court must have regard to the extent to which:

(a) the economic advantages or disadvantages sustained by either party have been balanced by the economic advantages or disadvantages sustained by the other party; and

---

for payment of a capital sum, given the dearth of authority regarding categorisation of assets such as the pursuer's as matrimonial property, and to the practical effect of an award of expenses on the respective assets of the parties, See also *De Winton v. De Winton (No. 2)*, 1997 G.W.D. 2–58. (*cf. Ferguson v. Maclennan Salmon Co. Ltd*, 1990 S.L.T. at p. 431, with regard to minutes of tender in divorce actions.)

[83] 1985 Act, s.11(7)(a). The dissipation of assets envisaged by s.11(7) requires the wanton using up or disposing of assets which were matrimonial property— *Russell v. Russell*, 1996 G.W.D. 15–895.

[84] Cases in which Principle B was explicitly considered are listed in App. VII.

[85] 1985 Act, s.9(2). As to what has been held to amount to "economic advantage" or "economic disadvantage", see cases listed in App. VII.

[85a] *ibid.* s.9(2). The Scottish Law Commission in its *Report on Family Law* (Scots. Law Com. No. 135, 1992) proposes the amendment of s.9(2) by substituting reference to the parties' children for "family" and defining the parties' children as including "children treated by both of the parties as children of their family".

(b) a resulting imbalance has been or will be corrected by a sharing of the value of the matrimonial property or otherwise.[86]

The court must not, on the other hand, take account of the conduct of either party unless the conduct has adversely affected the financial resources which are relevant to the decision of the court on a claim for financial provision.[87]

Principle C. Any economic burden of caring, after divorce, for a child of the marriage under the age of 16 years should be shared fairly between the parties.[88]

In applying this principle, the court must have regard to:

(a) any decree or arrangement for aliment for the child;
(b) any expenditure or loss of earning capacity caused by the need to care for the child[89];
(c) the need to provide suitable accommodation for the child;
(d) the age and health of the child;
(e) the educational, financial and other circumstances of the child;
(f) the availability and cost of suitable child-care facilities or services;
(g) the needs and resources of the parties; and
(h) all the other circumstances of the case (which *may* include, if the court thinks fit, taking account of any support, financial or otherwise, given by the party who is to make the financial provision to any person whom he maintains as a dependant in his household whether or not he owes an obligation of aliment to that person).[90]

---

[86] 1986 Act, s.11(2). In *De Winton v. DeWinton*, 1996 G.W.D. 29–1752, the Lord Ordinary noted that "where a balancing exercise requires to be carried out such as section 11(2)(a) provides for, the court must identify all the economic advantages derived by each party from the contributions of the other and all economic disadvantages suffered by either party in the interests of the other or of the family. Thereafter upon a consideration of that balancing exercise the court can determine whether an order should be made . . . it is plain from the interaction between section 9(1)(b) and section 11(2) that it is only where there is an imbalance that the court can then go on further to consider what order is called for."

[87] *ibid.* s.11(7)(a). See n.83 *supra.*

[88] Cases in which Principle C was explicitly considered are listed in App. VII.

[89] Expenditure on the child after his or her sixteenth birthday is not to be taken into account (*Monkman v. Monkman*, 1988 S.L.T. (Sh.Ct.) 37); nor should future expenditure on school fees (*Maclachlan v. Maclachlan*, 1997 G.W.D. 8–339).

[90] 1985 Act, s.11(3) and (6).

The court must not however take account of the conduct of either party unless the conduct has adversely affected the financial resources which are relevant to the decision of the court on a claim for financial provision.[91]

Principle D. A party who has been dependent to a substantial degree on the financial support of the other party should be awarded such financial provision as is reasonable to enable him to adjust, over a period of not more than three years from the date of the decree of divorce, to the loss of that support on divorce.[92]

In applying this principle, the court must have regard to:

  (a) the age, health and earning capacity of the party who is claiming the financial provision;
  (b) the duration and extent of the dependence of that party prior to divorce[93];
  (c) any intention of that party to undertake a course of education or training[94];
  (d) the needs and resources of the parties; and
  (e) all the other circumstances of the case (which *may* include, if the court thinks fit, taking account of any support, financial or otherwise, given by the party who is to make the financial provision to any person whom he maintains as a dependant in his household whether or not he owes an obligation of aliment to that person).[95]

The court must not, however, take account of the conduct of either party unless either (a) the conduct has adversely affected the financial resources which are relevant to the decision of the court on a claim for financial provision, or (b) it would be manifestly inequitable to leave the conduct out of account.[96]

---

[91] 1985 Act, s.11(7)(a). See n.83 *supra*.
[92] Cases in which Principle D was explicitly considered are listed in App. VII.
[93] Dependence prior to the marriage may be taken into account—*Petrie v. Petrie,* 1988 S.C.L.R. 390. The level of support afforded to the claimant between the date of separation and the date of divorce may be critical—*Millar v. Millar,* 1990 S.C.L.R. 666 at p. 671; failure to seek any financial support after separation may disentitle the claimant to an award under s.9(1)(d)—*Gray v. Gray,* 1991 S.C.L.R. 422. *cf.* n.98 *infra*.
[94] The absence of any such intention has been held not to be relevant (*Stott v. Stott,* 1987 G.W.D. 17–647).
[95] 1985 Act, s.11(4) and (6).
[96] *ibid.* s.11(7)(a) and (b). See n.83 *supra*.

Principle E. A party who at the time of the divorce seems likely to suffer serious financial hardship as a result of the divorce should be awarded such financial provision as is reasonable to relieve him of hardship over a reasonable period.[97]

In applying this principle, the court must have regard to:

(a) the age, health and earning capacity of the party who is claiming the financial provision;
(b) the duration of the marriage;
(c) the standard of living of the parties during the marriage;
(d) the needs and resources of the parties; and
(e) all the other circumstances of the case (which *may* include, if the court thinks fit, taking account of any support, financial or otherwise, given by the party who is to make the financial provision to any person whom he maintains as a dependant in his household whether or not he owes an obligation of aliment to that person).[98]

The court must not, though, take account of the conduct of either party unless either (a) the conduct has adversely affected the financial resources which are relevant to the decision of the court on a claim for financial provision, or (b) it would be manifestly inequitable to leave the conduct out of account.[99]

Where any parties have reached agreement in relation to any capital sum order, pension lump sum order or transfer of property order, a joint minute may be entered into expressing that agreement; and the sheriff may grant decree in respect of those parts of the joint minute in relation to which he could otherwise make an order, whether or not such a decree would include a matter for which there was no crave.[1] A joint minute is binding on the parties and cannot be set aside by the court unless: (1) the interests of third parties, such as the child of the marriage, are affected; (2) it

---

[97] Cases in which the application of Principle E was explicitly considered are listed in App. VII.
[98] 1985 Act, s.11(5) and (6). Failure to seek financial support after separation does not disentitle the claimant to an award under s.9(1)(e)—*Haughan v. Haughan*, 1996 S.C.L.R. 170. *cf.* n.93 *supra*.
[99] *ibid.* s.11(7)(a) and (b). See n.83 *supra*.
[1] r.33.26(c).

is void or voidable on some ground applicable to the general law of contract; or (3) there is specific statutory provision to that effect.[2]

In relation to (3), section 16(1)(b) and (2)(b) of the Family Law (Scotland) Act 1985 provides that where the parties to a marriage have entered into an agreement[3] as to the financial provision to be made on divorce, the court may on granting decree of divorce[4] (or within such time thereafter as the court may specify on granting decree of divorce) make an order setting aside or varying the agreement or any term of it where the agreement was not fair and reasonable at the time it was entered into.

In considering whether or not the agreement was fair and reasonable at the time it was entered into:

"the court has to look at all the circumstances prior to and at the time that the agreement was entered into and relevant to its negotiation and signing, to see whether there was some unfair or unconscionable advantage taken of some factor or of some relationship between the parties which enables the court to say that an agreement was not truly entered into by one party or the other as a free agent and that the agreement or any term of it was not in the circumstances fair and reasonable at the time it was entered into. In this determination, the extent of a party's professional qualifications and experience and the nature of any advice received from a professional source may well be important factors to bear in mind in the judgment of what is fair and reasonable. Nevertheless, they cannot in themselves be determinative of the issue where other circumstances suggesting unfair advantage or unreasonable conduct by one party to influence the other in the signing of an agreement which in its terms expressly

---

[2] *Anderson v. Anderson,* 1989 S.C.L.R. 475. See also cases cited therein, *Sochart v. Sochart,* 1988 S.L.T. 799, *Horton v. Horton,* 1992 S.L.T. (Sh.Ct.) 37 and *Jongejan v. Jongejan,* 1993 S.L.T. 595 (*cf. Davidson v. Davidson,* 1989 S.L.T. 466 and *Stewart v. Stewart,* 1990 S.C.L.R. 360).

[3] "Agreement" means an agreement entered into before or after the commencement of the 1985 Act—s.16(5). An agreement recorded in a joint minute falls within s.16(1)(b)—*Jongejan, supra.*

[4] While the court cannot make the order prior to granting decree of divorce, a preliminary proof on a crave for such an order is competent—*Gillon v. Gillon (No. 2),* 1994 S.L.T. 984; 1994 S.C. 162.

surrenders rights which that other party would have on divorce are averred."[5]

Any term of an agreement purporting to exclude the right to apply for an order under section 16(1)(b) is void.[6] Application for the order must be made by a crave in the initial writ or defences, as the case may be.[7]

Periodical allowance orders

An order for payment of a periodical allowance may be made on granting decree of divorce or within such period as the court on granting decree of divorce may specify.[8]

The order may be for a definite or indefinite period or until the happening of a specified event.[9] The order in any event ceases to have effect on the remarriage or death of the party receiving payment, except in relation to arrears due under it.[10] If the order is subsisting at the death of the party making the payment, it continues to operate against that party's estate.[11]

Application for a periodical allowance order may be made in similar fashion to an application for a capital sum or transfer of property order, except that the applicant's pleadings must contain an averment stating whether and, if so, when and by whom, a maintenance order has been granted in favour of or against that party or of any other person in respect of whom the order is sought.[12]

The court cannot make a periodical allowance order *unless* (i) the order is justified by Principle C, D or E (detailed *supra*) and (ii) the court is satisfied that an order for payment of a capital sum

---

[5] *McAfee v. McAfee,* 1990 S.C.L.R. 805 at p. 808, followed in *Gillon v. Gillon (No. 1),* 1994 S.L.T. 978 at p.982K. In *McAfee,* the order was refused after proof (1993 G.W.D. 28–1782); so also in *Gillon (No. 3)* (1995 S.L.T. 678). And see *Anderson v. Anderson,* 1991 S.L.T. (Sh.Ct.) 11, *Young v. Young (No. 2),* 1991 S.L.T. 869, *Worth v. Worth,* 1994 S.L.T. (Sh.Ct.) 54 and *Short v. Short,* 1994 G.W.D. 21–1300.

[6] 1985 Act, s.16(4).

[7] rr.33.48(1)(*a*) and (2)(*b*).

[8] 1985 Act, s.13(1)(a) and (b). As to s.13(1)(b), see *Mackin v. Mackin,* 1991 S.L.T. (Sh.Ct.) 22 (n.26 *supra*). The order may also be made after the granting of decree of divorce (as to which, see n.33 *infra* and accompanying text).

[9] *ibid.* s.13(3). A party is entitled to argue for a restriction in the duration of an order without having given advance notice of the intention so to contend (*Robertson v. Robertson,* 1989 S.C.L.R. 71).

[10] *ibid.* s.13(7)(*b*).

[11] *ibid.* s.13(7)(a), subject to the court's powers under s.13(4) (n.34, *infra*).

[12] Text accompanying n.38 *supra* and r.33.5.

or for transfer of property would be inappropriate or insufficient to satisfy the requirements of section 8(2) of the Act (namely that the order justified be by the principles in section 9 and reasonable having regard to the resources of the parties).[13] The claimant must aver and prove that these conditions are satisfied,[14] even in an undefended action.[15]

The rules of law and procedure concerning agreements anent capital payment or transfer of property[16] apply also to agreements anent periodical allowance, with the addition that the court has extra powers to vary the terms of an agreement relating to periodical allowance in certain specified circumstances.[17]

Incidental orders

"An incidental order" is defined by section 14(2) as one or more of the following orders:

---

[13] 1985 Act, s.13(2). Cases in which a periodical allowance has been awarded include *Stott v. Stott*, 1987 G.W.D. 17–645 (for three years with an award at a reduced rate for a further four years), *Monkman v. Monkman*, 1988 S.L.T. (Sh.Ct.) 37 (for 10 years), *Dever v. Dever*, 1988 S.C.L.R. 352 (for six months), *Petrie v. Petrie*, 1988 S.C.L.R. 390 (for one year), *Atkinson v. Atkinson*, 1988 S.C.L.R. 396 (for three years), *Bell v. Bell*, 1988 S.C.L.R. 457 (until death or remarriage of pursuer or sixtieth birthday of defender), *Park v. Park*, 1988 S.C.L.R. 584 (for one year with an award at a reduced rate for a further year), *Daley v. Daley*, 1988 G.W.D. 3–118 (for two years), *McDevitt v. McDevitt*, 1988 S.C.L.R. 206 (for three years), *Muir v. Muir*, 1989 S.L.T. (Sh.Ct.) 20 (for one year), *Tyrrell v. Tyrrell*, 1990 S.L.T. 406 (for one year), *Johnstone v. Johnstone*, 1990 S.L.T. (Sh.Ct.) 79 (until death or remarriage), *Sheret v. Sheret*, 1990 S.C.L.R. 799 (for 13 weeks), *Thomson v. Thomson*, 1991 S.L.T. 126 (for three years), *McKenzie v. McKenzie*, 1991 S.L.T. 461 (until death or remarriage), *Barclay v. Barclay*, 1991 S.C.L.R. 205 (for three years), *Toye v. Toye*, 1992 S.C.L.R. 95 (for three years), *Kelly v. Kelly*, 1992 G.W.D. 36–2130 (for three years), *Louden v. Louden*, 1994 S.L.T. 381 (for one year), *McConnell v. McConnell*, 1993 G.W.D. 34–2185 (for three years; reduced on appeal to six months (1995 G.W.D. 3–145)), *McCormick v. McCormick*, 1994 G.W.D. 35–2078 (for five years), *Gribb v. Gribb*, 1994 S.L.T. (Sh.Ct.) 43 (until death or remarriage; approved by the Inner House (1996 S.L.T. 719)), *Buckle v. Buckle*, 1995 S.C.L.R. 590 (for one year), and *Haughan v. Haughan*, 1996 S.C.L.R. 170 (until death or remarriage).

[14] *Mackin v. Mackin*, 1991 S.L.T. (Sh.Ct.) 22. See also *Savage v. Savage*, 1993 G.W.D. 28–1779.

[15] *Thirde v. Thirde*, 1987 S.C.L.R. 335 (*cf. Main v. Main*, 1988 G.W.D. 24–1036).

[16] See (second) nn.1–7 and accompanying text, *supra*.

[17] See 1985 Act, s.16(1)(a) and (2)(a) and (3). See also *Mills v. Mills*, 1990 S.C.L.R. 213 and *Ellerby v. Ellerby*, 1991 S.C.L.R. 608, and r.33.52.

(a) an order for the sale[18] of property[19];
(b) an order for the valuation[20] of property;
(c) an order determining any dispute between the parties to the marriage as to their respective property rights by means of a declarator thereof or otherwise;
(d) an order regulating the occupation of the matrimonial home or the use of furniture and plenishings therein or excluding either party to the marriage from such occupation[21];
(e) an order regulating liability, as between the parties, for outgoings in respect of the matrimonial home or furniture or plenishings therein[22];
(f) an order that security shall be given for any financial provision[23];
(g) an order that payments shall be made or property transferred to any curator bonis or trustee or other person for the benefit of the party to the marriage by whom or on whose behalf application has been made under section 8(1) of the Act;

---

[18] The order requires to be, at least principally, aimed at financial provision on divorce, so that it cannot be granted just to save the pursuer the trouble of raising a separate action for division and sale (*Reynolds v. Reynolds*, 1991 S.C.L.R. 175, approved in *MacClue v. MacClue*, 1994 S.C.L.R. 933 (motion for order for sale by party not craving financial provision refused as incompetent)). Orders for sale of the matrimonial home were made in *Reynolds, Lewis v. Lewis*, 1993 S.C.L.R. 32, *Jacques v. Jacques*, 1995 S.C. 327 and *Crosbie v. Crosbie*, 1996 S.L.T. (Sh.Ct.) 86.

[19] "Property" in s.14 can only refer to such property as is properly encompassed within the ambit of the Act, *i.e.* the property of one or other or both of the parties to the marriage—*Demarco v. Demarco*, 1990 S.L.T. 635 (order for valuation of property owned by company of which defender a shareholder refused).

[20] *cf. McKeown v. McKeown*, 1988 S.C.L.R. 355 and *Demarco, supra.*

[21] As long as such an incidental order remains in force, the former spouse is deemed to be, except to the extent that the order otherwise provides, a non-entitled spouse with occupancy rights in the property as regards (i) certain general powers of management in relation thereto and (ii) protection against certain arrangements intended to defeat those rights (see s.14(5)). An order under s.14(2)(d) was granted in *Little v. Little*, Lord Cameron of Lochbroom, May 24, 1990, unreported (on this point), whereby a period of "protected occupation" for one year from the date of decree of divorce was allowed; and in *Symon v. Symon*, 1991 S.C.L.R. 414.

[22] See *Little, supra* (order refused *in hoc statu*) and *McCormick v. McCormick*, 1994 G.W.D. 35–2078 (order granted for period until transfer of property order given effect to). In *Macdonald v. Macdonald*, 1995 S.L.T. 72, such order was held incompetent as regards mortgage payments already made.

[23] In *Macdonald, supra*, such order was held incompetent as regards alimentary payments; and an order for security for payment of a capital sum was held competent notwithstanding the absence of a specific conclusion seeking such security.

(h) an order setting aside or varying any term in an antenuptial or postnuptial marriage settlement[24];

(j) an order as to the date from which any interest on any amount awarded shall run[25];

---

[24] "Settlement" includes a settlement by way of a policy of assurance to which s.2 of the Married Women's Policies of Assurance (Scotland) Act 1880 relates.

[25] "[T]he purpose of s.14(2)(j) is to enable the court to award interest on the whole, or any part, of any amount awarded as a financial provision as from such date as it thinks appropriate, even although this may be a date earlier than the date of payment in terms of the decree . . . [If] an order for interest is to be made as an incidental order under s.14(2)(j) it must, as s.8(2) provides, be justified by the principles set out in s.9 of the Act and be reasonable having regard to the resources of the parties. It should therefore be seen as an integral part of the order for financial provision, and not as something which is to be added on afterwards once all the exercises to arrive at this provision are complete. The order must also be made having regard to the purpose for which interest is awarded by the court . . . What [the court] is required to do, when the capital sum is awarded with reference to the net value of the matrimonial property, is to share fairly the net value of all the matrimonial property as at the relevant date. In most cases this will be the date of the final separation: see s.10(3)(a). There may be circumstances where a party who has had the sole use or possession of an asset since the relevant date, the whole or part of the value of which is to be shared with the other party on divorce, should be required to pay interest as consideration for the use or possession which he has had between the relevant date and the date of decree. An order for interest may, for example, be appropriate where the use or possession has resulted in a benefit which has not been taken into account in some other way in making the order for financial provision. It may also be appropriate where . . . the amount of the principal sum is fixed by the decree but payment of it, in whole or in part, is postponed to a later date. Whether interest should be awarded on this basis, and if so on what part of the award, from what date and what the rate of interest should be is in the discretion of the court, bearing in mind that an incidental order for interest under s.14(2)(j) is an integral part of the order for financial provision under s.8(2) of the Act." (*per* the Lord President in *Geddes v. Geddes*, 1993 S.L.T. 494 at pp. 499I–J and 500L–501B). In *Savage v. Savage*, 1993 G.W.D. 28–779 and in *Bolton v. Bolton*, 1995 G.W.D. 14–799 the Lord Ordinary awarded a lump sum under the head of interest to date of decree. In *Welsh v. Welsh*, 1994 S.L.T. 828 the Lord Ordinary awarded interest from the relevant date upon the applicant's share of the equity in the matrimonial home as valued at that date, the non-applicant spouse having had exclusive occupation thereof since the relevant date. In *Gracie v. Gracie*, 1997 S.L.T. (Sh.Ct.) 15 payment of a proportion of the capital sum was deferred and the balance made payable by instalments, with interest on the whole outstanding balance from time to time at the rate of 3 per cent from the date of decree. In *MacLean v. MacLean*, 1996 G.W.D. 22–1278 the Lord Ordinary held that, having regard to the fact that the liable party had cared for the parties' children since separation, it was not appropriate to backdate any order for interest. See also *Tahir v. Tahir (No. 2)*, 1995 S.L.T. 451.

(k) any ancillary order which is expedient to give effect to the principles set out in section 9 of the Act or to any order made under section 8(2) of the Act.[26]

Orders (d) and (e) may only be made on or after the granting of decree of divorce; other incidental orders may be made before, on or after the granting or refusal of decree of divorce.[27]

Neither an incidental order, nor any rights conferred by such an order, prejudices any rights of any third party in so far as those rights existed immediately before the making of the order.[28]

Section 14 of the 1985 Act gives the court a discretionary power, to be exercised in the circumstances of a particular case.[29] The phrase "an incidental order" means what it says, namely something done by way of order incidental or ancillary to the making of an order under section 8(2) in relation to an order under section 8(1)(a), (aa), (b) or (ba).[30]

ORDERS MADE AFTER THE GRANTING OF DECREE

Ordinary cause rule 33.51 provides that certain applications after decree relative to orders for financial provision require to be made by minute lodged in the process of the action to which the application relates. The applications thus provided for include[31] applications:

---

[26] See *Little, supra* (order made regarding conveyancing expenses), *McConnell v. McConnell,* 1993 G.W.D. 34–2185 (order made requiring defender to arrange for discharge of debt secured over matrimonial home) and *Murley v. Murley,* 1995 S.C.L.R. 1138 (order made requiring pursuer to grant standard security over matrimonial home for balancing payment relative to transfer of property order in her favour).

[27] 1985 Act, s.14(1) and (3). As to the mode of application for an incidental order in a depending action, see n.13 *supra.* For an example of an incidental order made after decree of divorce had been granted, see *Walker v. Walker,* 1994 G.W.D. 8–496 (former wife ordained to sign and deliver indemnity and disclaimer forms on insurance policy).

[28] *ibid.* s.15(3).

[29] *McKeown v. McKeown,* 1988 S.C.L.R. 355, *Little v. Little,* Lord Cameron of Lochbroom, May 24, 1990, unreported.

[30] *Demarco v. Demarco,* 1990 S.L.T. 635.

[31] r.33.51(1)(a)(ii) bears to provide for applications for a capital sum or transfer of property order under s.12(1)(b) of the 1985 Act (which enables such orders to be made within such period as the court on granting decree of divorce may specify). It is submitted that s.12(1)(b) presupposes application prior to decree for any such order; and that therefore the rule is erroneous (see also n.26 *supra; cf.* s.13(1)(b) and (c)).

(a) after final decree for—
  (i) variation of the date or method of payment of a capital sum or the date of transfer of property[32];
  (ii) payment by one party to the marriage to the other of a periodical allowance[33];
  (iii) variation or recall of an order for a periodical allowance[34];
  (iv) conversion of such an order into an order for payment of a capital sum or for a transfer of property[35];
  (v) recall or variation of a pension lump sum order[36];
  (vi) variation of pension lump sum order to substitute trustees or managers[37]; or
(b) after the grant or refusal of an application for—
  (i) an incidental order[38];
  (ii) variation or recall of an incidental order.[39]

Where a minute is lodged, any party may apply by motion for any interim order which may be made pending the determination of the application.[40]

---

[32] 1985 Act, s.12(4), requiring that there has since the date of decree been a material change of circumstance (see n.34 *infra.*).

[33] *ibid.* s.13(1)(c), requiring that there has, since the date of decree, been a change of circumstances (see n.34 *infra*). In its *Report on Family Law* (Scot. Law Com. No. 135, 1992) the Scottish Law Commission proposes an amendment to the provision so as to require a *material* change of circumstances. As to an order setting aside or varying any term of an agreement relating to a periodical allowance in terms of s.16(1)(a) of the 1985 Act, see (second) n.17 *supra.*

[34] *ibid.* s.13(4)(a); requiring that since the date of the order there has been a material change of circumstances. Such change is not constituted merely by showing that the court at the time of the earlier award proceeded upon a particular hypothesis which has turned out to be incorrect—*Walker v. Walker,* 1995 S.L.T. 375. The application may be made by the executor of a party to the former marriage—(see *e.g. Sandison's Extrx. v. Sandison,* 1984 S.L.T. 111 and *Finlayson v. Finlayson's Extrx.,* 1986 S.L.T. 19). The court has power to backdate such variation or recall (s.13(4)(b)) and in that event to order repayment— s.13(6).

[35] *ibid.* s.13(4)(c).

[36] *ibid.* s.12A(5), applicable where the liability of the liable party under the capital sum order has been discharged in whole or in part, other than by a payment by the trustees or managers under the pension lump sum order. In that event, on an application by any person having an interest, the court may recall the order or vary the amount specified in the order, as appears to the court appropriate in the circumstance.

[37] *ibid.* s.12A(7).

[38] *ibid.* s.14(1).

[39] *ibid.* s.14(4), requiring that cause be shown for the variation or recall.

[40] r.33.51(2).

SPECIMEN CRAVES AND ASSOCIATED PLEAS-IN-LAW

1. MERITS

C— (i) To divorce the defender from the pursuer on the ground that the marriage has broken down irretrievably as established by the defender's adultery.

(ii) To divorce the defender from the pursuer on the ground that the marriage has broken down irretrievably as established by the defender's behaviour.

(iii) To divorce the defender from the pursuer on the ground that the marriage has broken down irretrievably as established by the defender's desertion of the pursuer for a continuous period of two years or more.

(iv) To divorce the defender from the pursuer on the ground that the marriage has broken down irretrievably as established by the parties' non-cohabitation for a continuous period of two years or more and the defender's consent to the granting of decree of divorce.

(v) To divorce the defender from the pursuer on the ground that the marriage has broken down irretrievably as established by the parties' non-cohabitation for a continuous period of five years or more.

P— The marriage of the parties having broken down irretrievably, the pursuer is entitled to decree of divorce as first craved.

2. MATRIMONIAL INTERDICT

C— To interdict the defender from molesting the pursuer by abusing her verbally, threatening her, putting her into a state of fear and alarm or distress or using violence towards her; and to attach a power of arrest to the said interdict.

P— The defender having molested the pursuer in the manner condescended on, and having shown an intention to persist therein, the pursuer is entitled to interdict as craved.

P—   There being no circumstances to indicate that a power of arrest is unnecessary, such a power should be attached to the aforesaid interdict.

C—   To ordain the defender to appear personally before the court on such day and at such hour as the court may appoint to answer to the charge against him of being guilty of contempt of court and breach of the interdict granted by the Sheriff of North Strathclyde at Oban on February 5, 1997, whereby the defender was interdicted from molesting the pursuer by *inter alia* using violence towards her; and failing his appearance before the court as aforesaid, to grant warrant to officers of the court to apprehend the defender and bring him before the court to answer as aforesaid; and, on the charge being admitted or proved, to find that the defender has been guilty of contempt of court and breach of interdict and in respect thereof to visit him with such punishment as to the court shall seem just; and to find the defender liable in expenses.

P—   The defender, being in breach of interdict as condescended on, should be found guilty and punished as craved.

3. EXCLUSION ORDER AND ANCILLARY REMEDIES

C— (1)   To grant an exclusion order suspending the defender's occupancy rights in the matrimonial home at 1 High Street, Seatown;

   (2)   To grant warrant for the summary ejection of the defender from the matrimonial home at 1 High Street, Seatown;

   (3)   To interdict the defender from entering the matrimonial home at 1 High Street, Seatown without the express permission of the pursuer; and to attach a power of arrest to the said interdict;

   (4)   To interdict the defender from entering or remaining in High Street, Seatown; and to attach a power of arrest to the said interdict; and

   (5)   To interdict the defender from removing, except with the written consent of the pursuer or by a further order of the court, any furniture or plenishings in the matrimonial home at 1 High Street, Seatown.

P—   An exclusion order being in the circumstances necessary for the protection of the pursuer from reasonably apprehended conduct of the defender which would be injurious to her health, and the pursuer being entitled to the ancillary orders craved, an exclusion order suspending the defender's occupancy rights and orders ancillary thereto should be granted as   craved.

4. PROPERTY ORDERS

C—   To find and declare that the pursuer is entitled to occupy the dwellinghouse at 110 High Street, Seatown.

P—   The said dwellinghouse being a matrimonial home, the pursuer is entitled to declarator as   craved.

C—   To grant leave to the pursuer to enter and occupy the matrimonial home at 110 High Street, Seatown.

P—   It being in the circumstances just and reasonable for the occupancy rights of the pursuer to be so enforced, leave to enter into and occupy the said matrimonial home should be granted as   craved.

C—   To interdict the defender from entering the upper storey of the dwellinghouse at 110 High Street, Seatown.

P—   It being in the circumstances just and reasonable for the occupancy rights of the defender to be so restricted, interdict should be granted as   craved.

C—   To grant to the pursuer the possession and use of the items of furniture and plenishings specified in the schedule hereto in the matrimonial home at 110 High Street, Seatown.

P—   It being in the circumstances just and reasonable for the pursuer to be granted the possession and use of the said items owned by the defender in the said matrimonial home, decree therefor should be granted as craved.

C—   To grant decree for the transfer of the tenancy of the matrimonial home at 22 High Street, Seatown from the defender to the pursuer.

P—   It being in the circumstances just and reasonable that the said tenancy should be transferred from the defender to the pursuer, decree therefor should be granted as   craved.

C—   To grant decree for the vesting of the joint tenancy of the dwellinghouse at 22 Low Street, Seatown in the pursuer solely.

P—   It being in the circumstances just and reasonable that the said joint tenancy should be vested in the pursuer solely, decree should be granted as   craved.

5. CHILDREN

C—   To make a residence order in respect of John Smith, child under the age of 16 years, whereby he is to live with the pursuer.

P—   It being in the best interests of the child that the residence order sought be made, decree should be granted as   craved.

C—   To make a contact order in respect of Alexander Robertson, child under the age of 16 years, whereby he is to be with the pursuer each Saturday from 10 a.m. until 6 p.m. and every fourth weekend from 6 p.m. on Friday until 6 p.m. on Sunday.

P—   It being in the best interests of the child that the contact order sought be made, decree should be granted as   craved.

C—   To make a specific issue order in respect of Thomas Thompson, child under the age of 16 years, whereby he is to attend Millerstone Academy for the academic year commencing August 16, 1998.

P—   It being in the best interests of the child that the specific issue order sought be made, decree should be granted as   craved.

C—   To vary the interlocutor of the Sheriff of Lothian and Borders at Edinburgh dated July 15, 1993 by making a residence order in respect of Elizabeth Ross, child under the age of 16 years, whereby she is to live with the pursuer.

P—   There having been a material change of circumstances and it now being in the best interests of the said child that the residence order sought be made, the said interlocutor should be varied as craved.

6. MONEY

C— (i) To grant decree against the defender for payment to the pursuer of a capital sum of ten thousand pounds (£10,000), payable on such date and by such method as the court thinks fit, with interest thereon at such rate and from such date as to the court seems appropriate until payment.

(ii) To grant decree for the transfer of the defender's right, title and interest in the heritable property at 4 Old Street, Avebury; to ordain the defender to make, execute and deliver to the pursuer a valid disposition of the said subjects and such other deeds as may be necessary to give the pursuer a valid title to the said subjects, and that within one month of the date of decree to follow hereon; and in the event of the defender failing to make, execute and deliver such disposition and other deeds, to authorise and ordain the sheriff clerk to subscribe on behalf of the defender a disposition of the said subjects and such other deeds as may be necessary to give the pursuer a valid title to the said subjects, all as adjusted at the sight of the sheriff clerk.

(iii) To grant decree requiring the Standard Assurance Company, trustees or managers of the Island Horse Ltd pension scheme, to pay the whole of any pension lump sum payable to the defender, when it becomes due, to the pursuer.

P— The order   craved being justified by the principle set forth in s.9(1)(a) of the Family Law (Scotland) Act 1985 and reasonable having regard to the resources of the parties, should be granted as craved.

C— (i) To grant an order for the sale of the parties' heritable property at 6 Abbey Street, Perth and for that purpose to grant warrant to such person as the court shall think proper to dispose of the said subjects, heritably and irredeemably, by public roup or private bargain, in such manner and under such conditions as the court shall direct; to ordain the pursuer and the defender to execute and deliver to the purchaser or purchasers of the said subjects such dispositions and other deeds as shall be necessary for constituting full right thereto in their persons, failing which to dispense with such execution and delivery and to direct the sheriff clerk to execute such dispositions and other deeds all as adjusted at his sight as shall be necessary aforesaid; and to make such order regarding the price of the said subjects when sold, after deduction of any debts or burdens affecting the same and all other expenses attending the sale, as to the court seems proper.

(ii)   To find and declare that the pursuer is the sole owner of the Ford Escort motorcar, registration number K123 ABC.

(iii) To grant an order entitling the pursuer to reside in the matrimonial home at 5 Low Street, Aberdeen and excluding the defender therefrom for such period following upon the granting of decree of divorce as to the court seems proper.

(iv)   To find the defender liable, as between the parties, for such period as to the court seems proper to make all payments due under the standard security granted by the parties in favour of the National Building Society on August 5, 1988 over the matrimonial home at 4 Princess Road, Carlops.

(v)   To ordain the defender to grant a standard security over his heritable property at 6 Royal Mews, Ayr in favour of the pursuer for all sums due and to become due to her in respect of the order for financial provision craved and failing his doing so within such time as the court may specify to authorise and direct the sheriff clerk to execute such standard security, as adjusted at his sight.

P—   The order craved being appropriate in the circumstances, should be granted.

C—   To grant decree against the defender for payment to the pursuer of a periodical allowance of thirty pounds (£30) per week for a period of three years, or such lesser period as the court thinks fit, from the date of decree of divorce or until the death or remarriage of the pursuer, if sooner.

P—   The order   craved being justified by the principle set forth in s.9(1)(d) of the Family Law (Scotland) Act 1985 and reasonable having regard to the resources of the parties and an order for payment of a capital sum or for transfer of property being insufficient *et separatim* inappropriate to satisfy the requirements of section 8(2) of the Family Law (Scotland) Act 1985, the order craved as aforesaid should be granted.

C—   To grant decree against the defender for payment to the pursuer of a periodical allowance of fifty-five pounds (£55) per week until the death or remarriage of the pursuer or for such other lesser period as the court thinks fit.

P—   The order   craved being justified by the principle detailed in s.9(1)(e) of the Family Law (Scotland) Act 1985 and reasonable having regard to the resources of the parties, and an order for payment of a capital sum or for transfer of property being insufficient *et separatim* inappropriate to satisfy the requirements of section 8(2) of the Family Law (Scotland) Act 1985, the order craved aforesaid should be granted.

C—   To interdict the defender from effecting any transfer of, or transaction involving, (1) his dwelling-house at 1 High Street, Seatown and (2) any redundancy payment received or to be received by him from Rosebank Ltd, 15 Gold Street, Seatown, which has the effect of defeating in whole or in part the pursuer's claim for financial provision as   craved; and to grant such other order as the court thinks fit.

P—   The defender being liable to effect a transfer of, or transaction involving, his said property which is likely to have the effect of defeating the pursuer's claim for financial provision in whole or in part, interdict should be granted as   craved.

C—   To grant an order setting aside the agreement between the parties entered into on March 13, 1995.

P—   The said agreement between the parties not being fair and reasonable at the time it was entered into, should be set aside as   craved.

C—   To vary the interlocutor dated August 7, 1996 insofar as providing for payment by the defender to the pursuer of a capital sum and that by substituting for the date of payment specified therein the date "August 7, 1998".

P—   There having been a material change of circumstances, the said interlocutor should be varied as craved.

C—   To recall the order for payment of a periodical allowance by the defender to the pursuer pronounced on July 15, 1995 with effect from such date as to the court seems appropriate and to ordain the repayment by the pursuer to the defender of such sum or sums as the court thinks fit.

P—   There having been a material change of circumstances the said order should be recalled as craved.

7. MISCELLANEOUS

C—   To grant warrant to arrest on the dependence of this action.

C—   To grant warrant to intimate this initial writ to Mrs Jane Jackson, residing at 2 Park Grove, Aytown, mother and one of the next of kin of the defender; and to Mamie Jackson, residing at 52 Maple Terrance, Beetown, daughter of the defender who has reached the age of 16 years.

C—   To grant warrant to intimate this initial writ to Miss Mary Black, residing at 2 Glebe Street, Seatown, as a person with whom the defender is alleged to have committed adultery.

C—   To grant warrant to intimate this initial writ to Mrs Indira Banda, 5 Calcutta Road, Bombay, as an additional spouse of the defender.

C—   To grant warrant to intimate this initial writ to Beetown Council, Central Avenue, Beetown, as a local authority having care of Mark White.

C—   To grant warrant to intimate this initial writ to Roger Allan, residing at 1 Main Street, Beetown, as a person liable to maintain Peter Jones.

C—   To grant warrant to intimate this initial writ to Henry Smith, residing at 4 Jeffrey Street, Deetown, as a person in fact exercising care or control in respect of Peter Smith.

C—   To grant warrant to intimate this initial writ to Deetown Council, The Square, Deetown, as the local authority within which area the pursuer resides.

C—   To grant warrant to intimate to Alan Smith, 101 High Road, Efftown, as a child to whom any section 11 order made as craved would relate.

C— To grant warrant to intimate to The Huddersfield Building Society, 123 High Street, Jaytown, as holders of a security in respect of the property at 1 Johnson Terrace, Leven.

C— To grant warrant to intimate this initial writ to Peter Evans, 1 Forth Road, Dunfermline, as a person in whose favour the transfer of the property referred to in the fourth crave was made.

C— To grant warrant to intimate this initial writ to Seatown Council, Main Square, Seatown, landlords of the matrimonial home at 1 High Street, Seatown.

C— To grant warrant to intimate this initial writ to Hugh White, residing at 4 George Place, Seatown, owner of the matrimonial home at 110 High Street, Seatown.

C— To dispense with intimation to George Banks in respect that his address is not known and cannot reasonably be ascertained.

C— To grant warrant to intimate to the Scottish Prudential Co. Ltd, managers of the White Rose Ltd pension scheme.

C— To find the defender liable in expenses.

SPECIMEN WRITS[1]

1. HUME v. HUME

A. Initial Writ

SHERIFFDOM OF NORTH STRATHCLYDE AT PAISLEY

INITIAL WRIT

in the cause

MRS KATHLEEN
ALICIA ANDREWS or
HUME (Assisted
Person), residing at 331
Main Street, Paisley
PURSUER

against

EDWARD HUME,
residing at 52 Great
Queen Street,
Edinburgh
DEFENDER

The pursuer craves the court:

1. To divorce the defender from the pursuer on the ground that the marriage has broken down irretrievably as established by the defender's adultery.
2. To grant warrant to intimate this initial writ to Miss Racquel Smith, residing at 52 Great Queen Street, Edinburgh, as a person with whom the defender is alleged to have committed adultery.
3. To find the defender liable in expenses.

---

[1] These are drawn from five fictitious sheriff court processes in late 1998.

CONDESCENDENCE

1. The parties were married in Glasgow on July 1, 1985. They have two children: Sheila Amy Alicia Hume, born July 5, 1986, and George Hume, born November 22, 1987. Relative marriage and birth certificates are produced.

2. The pursuer has been habitually resident in Scotland throughout the period of one year immediately preceding the raising of this action. She has been resident within the Sheriffdom of North Strathclyde for a period exceeding 40 days immediately preceding the raising of this action. She is unaware of any proceedings continuing in Scotland or elsewhere which are in respect of the marriage or capable of affecting its validity or subsistence.

3. After their marriage the parties lived together until about May 4, 1996. Since then they have not lived together nor had marital relations. The defender has formed an adulterous association with Miss Racquel Smith, designed in the third crave. Since the said date they have resided together at 52 Great Queen Street, Edinburgh and have there committed adultery. On or about December 7, 1996, at said address, the defender admitted adultery to agents instructed by the pursuer. The marriage has broken down irretrievably. There is no prospect of a reconciliation. The pursuer now seeks decree of divorce.

4. The said children reside with the pursuer. They are happy and well cared for. The pursuer is willing and able to devote her whole time and attention to them and provide them with a good home.

PLEA-IN-LAW

The marriage of the parties having broken down irretrievably, the pursuer is entitled to decree of divorce as first craved.

IN RESPECT
WHEREOF

Enrolled Solicitor
503 Bank Street, Paisley
Solicitor for Pursuer

2. SMART v. SMART

A. Initial Writ, including Minute for Decree

SHERIFFDOM OF GLASGOW AND STRATHKELVIN AT
GLASGOW

INITIAL WRIT

in the cause

JOANNA WYSE or
SMART (Assisted
Person), residing at 4
Gardeners Crescent,
Springboig, Glasgow
PURSUER

against

HENRY JOSEPH
SMART, residing at 14
Grove Place,
Dennistoun, Glasgow
DEFENDER

The pursuer craves the court:

1. To divorce the defender from the pursuer on the ground that the marriage has broken down irretrievably as established by the defender's behaviour.
2. To interdict the defender from molesting the pursuer by abusing her verbally, threatening her, putting her into a state of fear and alarm or distress or using violence towards her; and to attach a power of arrest to the said interdict.
3. To find the defender liable in expenses.

CONDESCENDENCE

1. The parties were married at Glasgow on November 20, 1994. They have no children. Relative marriage certificate is produced.
2. The pursuer was born in Scotland and has lived in Scotland all her life. She intends to remain permanently resident in

Scotland. She is domiciled in Scotland. She has been resident in the Sheriffdom of Glasgow and Strathkelvin for a period exceeding 40 days immediately preceding the raising of this action. She knows of no proceedings continuing in Scotland or elsewhere which are in respect of the marriage or capable of affecting its validity or subsistence.

3. The marriage has broken down irretrievably as established by the defender's behaviour. He developed an alcohol problem. Latterly he drank every day. He would regularly return home drunk late at night. He would become heavily intoxicated at social events to the embarrassment and humiliation of the pursuer. He spent little time at home. He did little to assist in the management of the household. The defender's said behaviour adversely affected the pursuer's health. On or about June 6, 1997, the parties separated. Since then they have not lived together nor had marital relations. The pursuer cannot reasonably be expected to cohabit with the defender. There is no prospect of a reconciliation. The pursuer now seeks decree of divorce.

4. Following the parties' separation aforesaid the defender has persistently molested the pursuer. He has frequently abused her by telephone. He has threatened to assault her if she does not resume cohabitation with him. He has followed her in the street demanding a reconciliation. In particular, on or about August 5, 1997, the defender shouted abuse and threats at the pursuer from the street outside her house. The pursuer is apprehensive that he will continue so to act. She is fearful lest he carry out the said threats. She accordingly seeks the protection of the interdict and power of arrest second craved.

PLEAS-IN-LAW

1. The marriage of the parties having broken down irretrievably, the pursuer is entitled to decree of divorce as first craved.
2. The defender having molested the pursuer in the manner condescended on, and having shown an intention to persist therein, the pursuer is entitled to interdict as second craved.
3. There being no circumstances to indicate that a power of arrest is unnecessary, such a power should be attached to the aforesaid interdict.

IN RESPECT
WHEREOF

Enrolled Solicitor
692 West George Street,
Glasgow
Solicitor for Pursuer

WADDELL having considered the evidence contained in the affidavits and the other documents all as specified in the schedule hereto and being satisfied that upon the evidence a motion for decree in terms of the first and third craves of the initial writ may properly be made, moves the court accordingly.

IN RESPECT
WHEREOF

Solicitor for Pursuer

SCHEDULE

1.   Affidavit of pursuer.
2.   Affidavit of Glenda Parkes or Wilson.
3.   Marriage certificate no. 2/1 of process.

B. Affidavit of Pursuer

SHERIFFDOM OF GLASGOW AND STRATHKELVIN AT
GLASGOW

AFFIDAVIT

of the pursuer

in the cause

JOANNA WYSE or
SMART (Assisted
Person), residing at
4 Gardeners Crescent,
Springboig, Glasgow
PURSUER

against

HENRY JOSEPH
SMART, residing at 14
Grove Place,
Dennistoun, Glasgow
DEFENDER

At Glasgow, the Fifteenth day of December Nineteen Hundred
and Ninety Seven, in the presence of ALLAN WADDELL,
Solicitor and Notary Public, 692 West George Street, Glasgow,
Compeared: JOANNA WYSE or SMART, residing at 4 Gar-
deners Crescent, Springboig, Glasgow, who being solemnly sworn,
Depones as follows:

1. My full name is Joanne Wyse or Smart. I am 25 years of age,
    a part-time teller in Citibank, and I reside at 4 Gardeners
    Crescent, Springboig, Glasgow.
2. I married my husband, Henry Joseph Smart, at present
    residing at 14 Grove Place, Dennistoun, Glasgow, at Glasgow
    on November 20, 1994. We have no children. I produce an
    extract of the entry in the Register of Marriages, no. 2/1 of
    process, which I have signed as relative hereto.
3. I was born in Scotland and have lived here all my life and
    intend to continue doing so. I was resident in the Sheriffdom
    of Glasgow and Strathkelvin for at least forty days prior to
    raising this action of divorce. I do not know of any proceed-
    ings continuing in Scotland or elsewhere concerning my
    marriage or capable of affecting its validity or subsistence.
4. My marriage has broken down irretrievably. I believe that my
    husband had a drinking problem when we got married but it
    became progressively worse. Eventually he would never come
    home without calling in at the pub on the way. When he
    returned home, he would stay for a short time only before
    going back out to the pub, where he would stay drinking until
    closing time. He would then come home drunk. He worked
    as a TV engineer with Johnsons of Edinburgh Road, Glasgow
    until he was sacked on account of his drinking.
      My husband's drinking caused me humiliation and embar-
    rassment at the few social events that we attended. My
    husband behaved so badly at these, because he was hopelessly
    drunk, that I had to spend almost the entire evening apologis-
    ing. On one particular occasion, at a disco for a charity held
    after the death of a friend of mine, I felt particularly bad
    because my husband had been rude and unpleasant to
    everybody and had embarrassed and humiliated me in front
    of a good number of my friends.

My husband also did virtually nothing to assist with running the house, although I cannot say that he kept me short of money. It was only grudgingly that he ever helped in the decoration of our home, and apart from that he never did anything at all, not even drying the dishes.

Although my husband never assaulted me, his behaviour certainly affected my health and nerves. I would often get asthmatic attacks because of the stress I felt. Eventually, I felt that I could no longer tolerate his behaviour. On June 6, 1997, I left him and we have neither lived together nor had marital relations since. I confirm that there is no prospect of a reconciliation between us.

5. Following our separation my husband pestered me by telephone and in the streets, making various threats to hurt me if I did not go back to him. Since I obtained an interim interdict against him to stop him molesting me, I have heard nothing more from him.

All of which is truth as the deponent shall answer to God.

. . . . .Deponent

. . . . .Notary Public

C. Affidavit of Glenda Parkes or Wilson

SHERIFFDOM OF GLASGOW AND STRATHKELVIN AT GLASGOW

AFFIDAVIT

of Mrs Glenda Parkes or Wilson

in the cause

JOANNA WYSE or SMART (Assisted Person), residing at 4 Gardeners Crescent, Springboig, Glasgow
PURSUER

against

HENRY JOSEPH
SMART, residing at
14 Grove Place,
Dennistoun, Glasgow
DEFENDER

At Glasgow, the Fifteenth day of December Nineteen Hundred
and Ninety Seven, in the presence of ALLAN WADDELL,
Solicitor and Notary Public, 692 West George Street, Glasgow,
Compeared GLENDA PARKES or WILSON, residing at
43 Queen's Road, Springboig, Glasgow, who being solemnly sworn,
Depones as follows:

1. My full name is Glenda Parkes or Wilson. I am 27 years of
    age, a part-time sales assistant and reside at 43 Queen's
    Road, Springboig, Glasgow.
2. I have been a friend of Joanna Smart, the pursuer in this
    action, for several years. I came to know her husband pretty
    well and am able to speak to events during their marriage
    from my own personal knowledge. I am aware that Mrs
    Smart and her husband have been separated since about June
    of this year. I also know why their relationship broke down: it
    was solely as a result of the defender's increasing addiction to
    drink. He seemed to drink virtually every day. He often came
    round to my house to try to persuade my husband to go
    drinking with him. Usually he had already had a few and was
    quite drunk.
        I would say that there was a definite effect on Mrs Smart's
    health. She has asthma and his behaviour affected her
    asthmatic condition. Before the separation she had to use her
    inhaler far more than ever before. There were days also when
    I went to her house and found her sitting in the kitchen in
    floods of tears. The whole marital relationship slid to rock-
    bottom as a result of his drinking and its effect on her. I have
    been at a number of social occasions which they attended
    before they separated at which he was drunk and I know that
    she was embarrassed by his behaviour at them. I do not see
    them ever getting back together again.

All of which is truth as the deponent shall answer to God.

. . . . .Deponent

. . . . .Notary Public

3. SCOTT v. SCOTT

A. Initial Writ

SHERIFFDOM OF LOTHIAN AND BORDERS AT EDINBURGH

INITIAL WRIT

in the cause

MRS ANN GEORGE
or SCOTT (Assisted
Person), residing at
5 Merton Grove,
Edinburgh
PURSUER

against

PHILIP SCOTT,
residing at 14 Elm
Grove, Dalkeith
DEFENDER

The pursuer craves the court:

1. To divorce the defender from the pursuer on the ground that the marriage has broken down irretrievably as established by the defender's desertion of the pursuer for a continuous period of two years or more.
2. To make a residence order in respect of Daphne Scott, child under the age of 16 years, whereby she is to live with the pursuer.
3. Failing an order in terms of the second crave, to make a contact order in respect of Daphne Scott, child under the age of 16 years, whereby she is to be with the pursuer each Saturday from 10 a.m. until 6 p.m. and every fourth weekend from 6 p.m. on Friday until 6 p.m. on Sunday.
4. To grant warrant to intimate this initial writ to Mrs Elspeth Scott, residing at 22 George Place, Dalkeith as a person in fact exercising care or control in respect of Daphne Scott.
5. To grant warrant to intimate to Daphne Scott, 22 George Place, Dalkeith, as a child to whom any section 11 order made as craved would relate.
6. To find the defender liable in expenses.

CONDESCENDENCE

1. The parties were married at Edinburgh on March 1, 1986. They have one child, Daphne Scott born June 25, 1987. Relative marriage and birth certificates are produced.

2. The pursuer was born in Scotland of Scottish parents and has lived most of her life in Scotland. She intends to reside permanently in Scotland. She is domiciled in Scotland. She has been resident within the Sheriffdom of Lothian and Borders for a period exceeding 40 days immediately preceding the raising of this action. She is unaware of any proceedings continuing in Scotland or elsewhere which are in respect of the marriage or capable of affecting its validity or subsistence. She is unaware of any proceedings continuing or concluded in Scotland or elsewhere which relate to the said child.

3. After the marriage the parties lived together until about June 1994, when the defender deserted the pursuer. The pursuer was then willing to adhere. The defender had no reasonable cause so to act. Since then the parties have not lived together nor had marital relations. The pursuer has not refused a genuine and reasonable offer by the defender to adhere. The marriage has broken down irretrievably. There is no prospect of a reconciliation. The pursuer now seeks decree of divorce.

4. After the parties' separation the child resided with the pursuer. On or about March 4, 1997 at or about 7 p.m. the defender came to the pursuer's house. He demanded to see the said child forthwith. The pursuer declined to accede. The defender thereupon assaulted her. He forcibly entered the said house and seized the child. He removed the child to the house of his mother, Mrs Elspeth Scott, designed in the third crave. The child remains in the care or control of Mrs Scott. It is not in the best interests of the child to live with the said Mrs Scott or with the defender. The child was well settled and happy with the pursuer. She attended the local school where she performed well. The child wishes to live with the pursuer. It is in her best interests so to do. It is better for her that the residence order which failing the contact order be made than that no order be made at all.

PLEAS-IN-LAW

1. The marriage of the parties having broken down irretrievably, the pursuer is entitled to decree of divorce as first craved.

2. It being in the best interests of the child that the residence order which failing the contact order sought be made, decree should be granted as second or third craved.

IN RESPECT
WHEREOF

Enrolled Solicitor
42 St. Charlotte Street,
Edinburgh
Solicitor for Pursuer

B. Defences

SHERIFFDOM OF LOTHIAN AND BORDER AT
EDINBURGH

DEFENCES

in the cause

MRS ANN GEORGE
or SCOTT (Assisted
Person), residing at
5 Merton Grove,
Edinburgh
PURSUER

against

PHILIP SCOTT,
residing at 14 Elm
Grove, Dalkeith
DEFENDER

The defender craves the court:

1. To make a residence order in respect of Daphne Scott, child under the age of 16 years, whereby she is to live with the defender.
2. To grant warrant to intimate to Daphne Scott, 22 George Place, Dalkeith, as a child to whom any section 11 order made as craved would relate.

ANSWERS TO CONDESCENDENCE

1. Admitted under explanation that the defender now resides at 22 George Place, Dalkeith.
2. Believed to be true. The defender knows of no such proceedings.
3. No admission is made.
4. Admitted that after the parties' separation the child resided with the pursuer. Admitted that on March 4, 1997 at about 7 p.m. the defender came to the pursuer's house. Admitted that he requested access to the child. Admitted that he removed the said child to the house of his mother, Mrs Elspeth Scott. Admitted that the child attended the local school. Not known and not admitted how she performed there. *Quoad ultra* denied. Explained and averred that on March 4, 1997 at about 7 p.m. the defender called at the pursuer's house. He requested access to the child. The pursuer thrust the child into the defender's arms. She told him to keep her for good. The pursuer was drunk at the time. The defender believes and avers that the pursuer is frequently under the influence of alcohol. Her house is dirty. The child was not being properly looked after. Her clothing was torn and filthy. She required to be thoroughly scrubbed at the defender's mother's house where she now lives. There is ample accommodation for her. She is well looked after by both the defender and his mother. She is happy living with them. She is settling well at her new school. It is in her best interests to live with the defender. It is better for her that the residence order be made than that no order be made at all. The defender believes and avers that it is further in the best interests of the child not to stay overnight with the pursuer.

PLEAS-IN-LAW

1. It being in the best interests of the child that the residence order sought by the defender be made, decree therefor should be pronounced as first craved.
2. It not being in the best interests of the child that the residence order sought by the pursuer be made, decree therefor should not be pronounced as second craved by the pursuer.
3. It not being in the best interests of the child that the contact order sought by the pursuer be made, decree therefor should not be pronounced as third craved by the pursuer.

IN RESPECT
WHEREOF

Enrolled Solicitor
4 Market Street,
Dalkeith
Solicitor for Defender

4. JAMIESON v. JAMIESON

A. Initial writ, including Minute for Decree

SHERIFFDOM OF GRAMPIAN, HIGHLAND AND ISLANDS AT STONEHAVEN

INITIAL WRIT

in the cause

ROBERT JAMIESON,
residing at 4 Dundas
Street, Stonehaven
PURSUER

against

MRS OLIVE HANSON
or ROBERTSON or
JAMIESON, residing at
4 Nursery Street,
Stonehaven
DEFENDER

The pursuer craves the court:

1. To divorce the defender from the pursuer on the ground that the marriage has broken down irretrievably as established by the parties' non-cohabitation for a continous period of two years or more and the defender's consent to the granting of decree of divorce.
2. To grant warrant to intimate this initial writ to Hamish Wilson Robertson, residing at 1 Forge Park, Brechin, Angus as a person who is liable to maintain Peter Robertson.

CONDESCENDENCE

1. The parties were married at Edinburgh on December 5, 1993. They have no children. The defender has a child treated as one of the family by the pursuer: Peter Robertson, born July 5, 1991. Relative marriage and birth certificates are produced. The natural father of the said Peter Robertson is Hamish Wilson Robertson, designed in the second crave.
2. The pursuer has been habitually resident in Scotland throughout the period of one year immediately preceding the raising of this action. He has been resident within the Sheriffdom of Grampian, Highland and Islands for a period exceeding 40 days immediately preceding the raising of this action. He is unaware of any proceedings continuing in Scotland or elsewhere which are in respect of the marriage or capable of affecting its validity or subsistence.
3. After their marriage the parties lived together until about January 1995. Since then they have not lived together nor had marital relations. The defender is prepared to consent to the granting of decree of divorce. The marriage has broken down irretrievably. There is no prospect of a reconcilation. The pursuer seeks decree of divorce.
4. The said child resides with the defender and is well looked after. The present arrangements for his care and upbringing are satisfactory.

PLEA-IN-LAW

The marriage of the parties having broken down irretrievably, the pursuer is entitled to decree of divorce as first craved.

IN RESPECT
WHEREOF

Enrolled Solicitor
10 Main Square,
Stonehaven
Solicitor for Pursuer

THOMSON having considered the evidence contained in the affidavits and the other documents all as specified in the schedule hereto and being satisfied that upon the evidence a motion for decree in terms of the first crave of the initial writ may properly be made, moves the court accordingly.

IN RESPECT
WHEREOF

Solicitor for Pursuer

SCHEDULE

1. Affidavit of pursuer.
2. Affidavit of defender.
3. Affidavit of Mrs Jeannie Hogg or Hanson.
4. Marriage certificate, No. 2/1 of process.
5. Birth certificate, No. 2/2 of process.
6. Notice of Consent, No. 2/3 of process.

B. Affidavit of Pursuer

SHERIFFDOM OF GRAMPIAN, HIGHLAND AND ISLANDS
AT STONEHAVEN

AFFIDAVIT

of the pursuer

in the cause

ROBERT JAMIESON,
residing at 4 Dundas
Street, Stonehaven
PURSUER

against

MRS OLIVE HANSON
or ROBERTSON or
JAMIESON, residing at
4 Nursery Street,
Stonehaven
DEFENDER

At Stonehaven, the Seventh day of September Nineteen Hundred and Ninety Seven, in the presence of JOHN UNMAN, Notary Public, 10 Main Square, Stonehaven, Compeared: ROBERT JAMIESON, residing at 4 Dundas Street, Stonehaven, who being solemnly sworn, Depones as follows:

1. My full name is Robert Jamieson. I am aged 42 years and I reside at 4 Dundas Street, Stonehaven. I am unemployed.

2. I was married to Olive Hanson or Robertson or Jamieson, presently residing at 4 Nursery Street, Stonehaven at Edinburgh on December 5, 1993. We have no children. My wife has a child from a previous marriage: Peter Robertson, born July 5, 1991 whose natural father is Hamish Wilson Robertson, residing at 1 Forge Park, Brechin, Angus. I treated Peter Robertson as one of the family. I produce extracts of the relevant entries in the Registers of Marriages and Births, numbers 2/1 and 2/2 of process, which I have docqueted as relative hereto.

3. I have been habitually resident in Scotland throughout the period of one year immediately preceding the raising of this action. I have been resident within the Sheriffdom of Grampian, Highland and Islands for a period exceeding 40 days immediately preceding the raising of this action. I am not aware of any proceedings continuing in Scotland or elsewhere which are in respect of the marriage or capable of affecting its validity or subsistence.

4. After the marriage my wife and I lived together until about January 1995. Since then we have not lived together nor had marital relations. There is no prospect of a reconciliation. My wife consents to the granting of decree of divorce. I identify her signature on the Form of Consent, No. 2/3 of process, which I have docqueted as relative hereto.

5. Since the separation I have seen very little of the child, Peter. I am not in a position to speak to the present arrangements for his care and upbringing.

All of which is truth as the Deponent shall answer to God.

. . . . Deponent

. . . . Notary Public

C. Affidavit of Oliver Jamieson

SHERIFFDOM OF GRAMPIAN, HIGHLAND AND ISLANDS
AT STONEHAVEN

AFFIDAVIT

of Oliver Jamieson

in the cause

ROBERT JAMIESON,
residing at 4 Dundas
Street, Stonehaven
PURSUER

against

MRS OLIVE HANSON
or ROBERTSON or
JAMIESON, residing at
4 Nursery Street,
Stonehaven
DEFENDER

At Stonehaven, the Seventh day of September Nineteen Hundred and Ninety Seven, in the presence of JOHN UNMAN, Notary Public, 10 Main Square, Stonehaven, Compeared: Oliver Jamieson, residing at 4 Dundas Street, Stonehaven, who being solemnly sworn, Depones as follows:

1. My full name is Oliver Jamieson. I am aged 67 years. I reside at 4 Dundas Street, Stonehaven. I am retired. I am the father of Robert Jamieson, the pursuer in this action.
2. My son lives with me. I am aware that he separated from his wife in January 1995. He did in fact come to stay with me at that time and has lived with me ever since. I therefore know that he has not lived as man and wife with her since then.

All of which is truth as the Deponent shall answer to God.

. . . . Deponent

. . . . Notary Public

D. Affidavit of Defender

SHERIFFDOM OF GRAMPIAN, HIGHLAND AND ISLANDS
AT STONEHAVEN

AFFIDAVIT

of the defender

in the cause

ROBERT JAMIESON,
residing at 4 Dundas
Street, Stonehaven
PURSUER

against

MRS OLIVE HANSON
or ROBERTSON or
JAMIESON, residing at
4 Nursery Street,
Stonehaven
DEFENDER

At Stonehaven, the Twenty First day of September Nineteen Hundred and Ninety Seven, in the presence of ALAN MARSH, Notary Public, 11 New Street, Stonehaven, Compeared: MRS OLIVE HANSON or ROBERTSON or JAMIESON, residing at 4 Nursey Street, Stonehaven, who being solemnly sworn, Depones as follows:

1. My full name is Olive Hanson or Robertson or Jamieson. I am aged 32 years and reside at 4 Nursery Street, Stonehaven. I am a housewife.
2. My son Peter Robertson has lived with me since my separation from my husband. Although Peter was a bit upset at the break-up of our marriage, he has come on well since. He stays with me in the former matrimonial home at 4 Nursery Street, Stonehaven. The house is a Scottish Homes house and is well furnished. It comprises a livingroom, two bedrooms, livingroom/kitchenette and bathroom. Peter has one bedroom and I have the other. Peter attends St. Mark's Primary School near my house and is getting on well there. He has lots of friends with whom he plays regularly. I do not work and devote my whole time and attention to Peter's care and wellbeing. He is a happy and healthy boy. Peter has little contact with my husband and does not seem to miss him now.

All of which is truth as the Deponent shall answer to God.

. . . . Deponent

. . . . Notary Public

E. Affidavit of Mrs Jeannie Hogg or Hanson

SHERIFFDOM OF GRAMPIAN, HIGHLAND AND ISLANDS
AT STONEHAVEN

AFFIDAVIT

of Mrs Jeannie Hogg or
Hanson

in the cause

ROBERT JAMIESON,
residing at 4 Dundas
Street, Stonehaven
                    PURSUER

against

MRS OLIVE HANSON
or ROBERTSON or
JAMIESON, residing at
4 Nursery Street,
Stonehaven
                    DEFENDER

At Stonehaven, the Twenty-First day of September Nineteen
Hundred and Ninety Seven in the presence of ALAN MARSH,
Notary Public. 11 New Street, Stonehaven, Compeared: MRS
JEANNIE HOGG or HANSON, residing at 66 Nursery Street,
Stonehaven, who being solemnly sworn, Depones as follows:

1.   My full name is Jeannie Hogg or Hanson. I am 55 years of
     age and reside at 66 Nursery Street, Stonehaven. I am a
     housewife. I am the mother of the defender, Mrs Olive
     Hanson or Robertson or Jamieson.
2.   I remember my daugher and her husband separating in about
     January 1995. Since then my grandson Peter has lived with
     my daugher in the former matrimonial home at 4 Nursery
     Street, Stonehaven. My daughter does not work and devotes
     all her time to looking after Peter. He is always healthy and
     happy. Although he was upset when my son-in-law left the
     family home, he seems to be over it now and rarely sees my
     son-in-law now. My daughter and Peter live in a Scottish
     Homes house which has a livingroom, livingroom/kitchenette,
     two bedrooms and bathroom. Peter has his own bedroom, my
     daughter has the other. Peter now attends St. Mark's Primary
     School, Stonehaven and I know he enjoys it. He is forever off
     to play with some new friend or other. He really loves his
     mother.

All of which is truth as the Deponent shall answer to God.

. . . . Deponent

. . . . Notary Public

5. BANKS v. BANKS

A. Initial Writ

SHERIFFDOM OF SOUTH STRATHCLYDE, DUMFRIES AND GALLOWAY AT STRANRAER

INITIAL WRIT

in the cause

JOHN BANKS, residing
at 4 Almond Place,
Stranraer
PURSUER

against

MRS ANNIE
ALLISON or BANKS,
his wife, residing at 1
Park Street, Glasgow
DEFENDER

The pursuer craves the court:

1. To divorce the defender from the pursuer on the ground that the marriage has broken down irretrievably as established by the parties' non-cohabitation for a continous period of five years or more.
2. To grant warrant to intimate this initial writ to City of Glasgow Council, City Chambers, George Square, Glasgow, as a local authority having care of Peter Banks.

CONDESCENDENCE

1. The parties were married at Hamilton on June 5, 1970. There is one child of the marriage under the age of 16 years: Peter Banks, born June 5, 1982. Relative marriage and birth certificates are produced.
2. The defender has been habitually resident in Scotland throughout the period of one year immediately preceding the raising of this action. The pursuer has been resident within the Sheriffdom of South Strathclyde, Dumfries and Galloway for a period exceeding 40 days immediately preceding the

raising of this action. He is unaware of any proceedings continuing in Scotland or elsewhere which are in respect of the marriage or capable of affecting its validity or subsistence.

3.   After their marriage the parties lived together until about January 1992. Since then they have not lived together nor had marital relations. The marriage has broken down irretrievably. There is no prospect of a reconciliation. The pursuer seeks decree of divorce.

4.   The said child is at present in the care of City of Glasgow Council, designed in the second crave.

5.   The pursuer is employed as a labourer and earns about £250 per week. He has savings of about £2,000. He has no other capital. He aliments the defender at the rate of £50 per week in terms of an order by the Sheriff at Peebles dated March 4, 1995. He is otherwise unaware of the defender's present financial circumstances.

PLEA-IN-LAW

The marriage of the parties having broken down irretrievably, the pursuer is entitled to decree of divorce as first craved.

IN RESPECT
WHEREOF

Enrolled Solicitor,
1 Fleet Street, Stranraer
Solicitor for Pursuer

SHERIFFDOM OF SOUTH STRATHCLYDE, DUMFRIES
AND GALLOWAY AT STRANRAER

DEFENCES

in the cause

JOHN BANKS, residing
at 4 Almond Place,
Stranraer
PURSUER

against

MRS ANNIE
ALLISON or BANKS,
residing at 1 Park Street,
Glasgow

DEFENDER

The defender craves the court:

1. To grant decree against the pursuer for payment to the defender of a capital sum of one thousand pounds (£1,000), payable at such date and by such method as the court thinks fit, with interest on such proportion thereof at such rate and from such date as the court thinks fit until payment.
2. To grant decree against the pursuer for payment to the defender of a periodical allowance of sixty five pounds (£65) per week for a period of three years, or such lesser period as the court thinks fit, from the date of decree of divorce or until the death or remarriage of the defender, if sooner.

ANSWERS TO CONDESCENDENCE

1. Admitted.
2. Admitted. The defender knows of no such proceedings.
3. Admitted.
4. Admitted.
5. The averment anent the maintenance order is admitted. *Quoad ultra* not known and not admitted. Explained and averred that the defender is aged 52 years. She keeps reasonable health. She has no qualifications. She is in employment as a clerkess and earns about £150 per week. She has been dependent on the pursuer for financial support throughout the marriage. She has enjoyed a reasonably comfortable standard of living. She has no capital. She made a substantial contribution to the marriage. She looked after the family home and cared for the pursuer and the parties' five children. In all the circumstances, the pursuer is entitled to a fair sharing of the matrimonial property and an order enabling her to adjust to the loss of financial support. Decree should in these circumstances be granted as first and second craved.

PLEAS-IN-LAW

1. The order first craved being justified by the principle set forth in s.9(1)(a) of the Family Law (Scotland) Act 1985 and

    reasonable having regard to the parties' resources should be granted.

2.   The order second craved being justified by the principle set forth in s.9(1)(d) of the Family Law (Scotland) Act 1985 and reasonable having regard to the parties' resources and an order for payment of a capital sum being insufficient to satisfy the requirements of section 8(2) of the Act, the order second craved should be granted.

IN RESPECT
WHEREOF

Enrolled Solicitor,
42 Ainslie Street,
Glasgow
Solicitor for Defender

C. Joint Minute for Parties

SHERIFFDOM OF SOUTH STRATHCLYDE, DUMFRIES
AND GALLOWAY AT STRANRAER

JOINT MINUTE

for the parties

in the cause

JOHN BANKS, residing
at 4 Almond Place,
Stranraer
PURSUER

against

MRS ANNIE
ALLISON or BANKS,
residing at 1 Park Street,
Glasgow
DEFENDER

JONES for the pursuer and
ADAMS for the defender concurred and hereby concur in stating to the court that in the event of decree of divorce being granted and subject to the approval of the court the parties have agreed and hereby agree as follows:

1. The pursuer shall pay to the defender a capital sum of nine hundred pounds (£900), payable upon the granting of decree of divorce, with interest thereon at the rate of eight per cent a year from the date of decree to follow hereon until payment; and
2. The pursuer shall pay to the defender a periodical allowance of sixty pounds (£60) per week for a period of two years from the date of decree of divorce or until the death or remarriage of the defender, if sooner.

The parties therefore craved and hereby crave the court to interpone authority hereto and grant decree in terms hereof.

IN RESPECT
WHEREOF

Enrolled Solicitor,
1 Fleet Street, Stranraer
Solicitor for Pursuer

Enrolled Solicitor,
42 Ainslie Street,
Glasgow
Solicitor for Defender

APPENDIX III

COURT PRACTICE RE DIVORCE AFFIDAVITS[1]

1. An affidavit is no substitute for a reliable and adequate precognition, though a precognition may eventually be the basis for an affidavit.

2. The affidavit should be typed on substantial paper, should be backed up longways, and should be stitched or stapled. It must commence with the words "At   , the   day of   19 , in the presence of   Compeared   who being solemnly sworn, Depones as follows   ,". The full name, age, address and occupation must be given, and it must thereafter proceed in the first person and should take the form of numbered paragraphs. The witness should be made to appreciate the importance of the affidavit. The witness must be placed on oath, or must affirm, and each page will require to be signed by both the witness and the notary. It is not essential that it should be sealed by the notary. The document should be of a shape and size convenient to be lodged as part of the process. The affidavit should end with the words, "All of which is truth as the deponent shall answer to God," or "All of which is affirmed to be true," as appropriate.

3. Affidavits of parties and witnesses should follow step-by-step the averments in the initial writ. The drafter of an affidavit should provide himself, before drawing it, with a copy of the initial writ, a copy of the appropriate precognition, and the relative productions. The affidavit to be taken from a witness should follow the averments in the initial writ to the extent that these are within the knowledge of that particular witness. It is not a requirement that the wording of an affidavit should follow exactly the wording of the initial writ.

4. [*No hearsay.*] The drafter must take care that an affidavit [contains only matters of fact to which the party or the witness in

---

[1] Appendix III comprises the terms of the Acts of Court or Practice Notes of all the sheriffdoms relative to affidavits in undefended actions of divorce, with local variations as indicated.

130

question can testify, and that it] is correct at the date at which it is sworn.[2]

5. On the matter of the qualifications of the person before whom the affidavit is taken, the Rules provide that the affidavit is admissible if it is duly emitted before a notary public or other competent authority. This means a notary public, justice of the peace, commissioner of oaths or other statutory authority within the meaning of the Statutory Declarations Act 1835. In the examples given hereafter, it is assumed that the affidavit is in fact taken before a solicitor who is a notary public, and therefore the references to the party before whom the affidavit is sworn are to "the notary". The solicitor acting in the action may well be called on also to act in a notarial capacity when the affidavit is subsequently sworn. This is permissible. In acting in a notarial capacity he must, however, as a competent authority, observe all the normal rules in this connection, and must satisfy himself as to the capacity of the witness to make the statement, and ensure that the witness understands that it constitutes his or her evidence in the case.

6. On the matter of productions, those required, when an affidavit is being taken, may already have been lodged in process, but there may be some productions (such as photographs) which are produced by the witness to the notary when the affidavit is sworn, and which may not by that time have been lodged in process.

7. Productions already lodged in process must be borrowed up, and put to the party or the witness who makes them part of his evidence in the appropriate part of the affidavit. Each production will require to be referred to in the affidavit by its number of process and must be docqueted and signed by the party or witness and the notary. If a production has not yet been lodged when the affidavit is being taken, it will require to be identified by the witness in his evidence in the affidavit, and will then be docqueted with regard to the affidavit and signed by the party or witness and the notary. It will then be lodged as a production. Obviously, certain productions will be docqueted with regard to more than one affidavit.

8. In adultery cases, photographs of both the pursuer and the defender will require to be produced, put to the appropriate party or witnesses in the affidavit, and signed and docqueted with

[2] Words in square brackets deleted by Practice Note, June 1991, by the Sheriff Principal of Glasgow and Strathkelvin; and the whole paragraph omitted from the Sheriffdom of Lothian and Borders Act of Court (Consolidation, etc.) 1990 No. 1.

reference thereto in the manner already described. [In certain circumstances, a photograph may have to be identified and docqueted by more than one person, as in the case of the photograph of a party requiring to be spoken to by the pursuer and two inquiry agents.][3]

9. All affidavits lodged must be of as recent a date as is possible in the circumstances. This factor is particularly important in (1) cases involving children, (2) those in which financial craves are involved, or (3) in any other circumstances where the evidence of a party or witness is liable to change through the passage of time. The notary will require to ensure, therefore, that an affidavit represents the deponent's evidence on such matters at the time the affidavit is sworn.

10. In cases involving custody of or access to children, an affidavit or affidavits providing corroborating evidence about the welfare of the children should be provided. The evidence of that witness must present the court with a full picture of the position regarding the child or children. It is, however, clear that such independent evidence in no way relieves the pursuer from testifying fully the position regarding the children in his or her own affidavit, so far as within his or her knowledge. Whatever else the affidavits of the pursuer and the independent witness contain, the evidence should certainly include the following:

> (a) the qualifications of the witness, if not a parent, to speak about the child; how often, for example, and in what circumstances, does the witness normally see the child;
>
> (b) a description of the home conditions in which the child lives;
>
> (c) observations upon the child's general appearance, interests, state of health and well-being;
>
> (d) information, where relevant, about the school the child attends; whether and to what extent he has contact with other children and relatives;
>
> (e) observations on the relationship between the child and the person in whose care he or she lives, on the child's attitude towards each of the parents and on the extent of contact with the parent or parents with whom the child is not living;

---

[3] Words in square brackets deleted by Practice Note, June 1991, by the Sheriff Principal of Glasgow and Strathkelvin and omitted from the Sheriffdom of North Strathclyde Act of Court (Consolidation, etc.) 1992.

(f) details of child care arrangements at all times including arrangements during working hours (outwith school hours);

(g) the means and status of the person craving custody with a view to enabling him or her to maintain and bring up the child in a suitable manner.

11. The attention of solicitors is drawn to the provisions of the Matrimonial Proceedings (Children) Act 1958. The court will not (unless the provisions of section 8(2) are shown to apply) grant decree of divorce until the court is satisfied, as respects every child for whose custody, maintenance and education the court has jurisdiction to make provision in that action, (a) that arrangements have been made for the care and upbringing of the child and that those arrangements are satisfactory or are the best which can be devised in the circumstances; or (b) that it is impracticable for the party or parties appearing before the court to make any such arrangements.

12. Where financial conclusions are involved, it is even more important that the evidence is full, accurate and up-to-date. In parole proofs the evidence of the pursuer and the witnesses on these matters can be supplemented at the proof by questions from the bench or from the solicitor for the pursuer. This will not be possible where evidence is taken by affidavit, and the affidavits must be so framed as to exclude the necessity for supplementary questions. Failure to do so may result in the sheriff requiring the attendance of the solicitor in court. If, after an affidavit has been taken, and the solicitor concerned has parted with it, a material change of circumstances occurs, it is essential that the court be immediately informed, and where necessary, that a further affidavit be sworn.

13. Where the pursuer in an action is speaking in the affidavit of the financial position of the defender, it is essential that the affidavit should state the date, as precisely as possible, at which that information was valid. Otherwise it may be assumed by the court that the pursuer is speaking to the defender's position at the date of the affidavit. The court must be provided with as up-to-date information as possible about the defender's ability to pay the sums the pursuer is seeking, and these sums should be such as that evidence justifies. The pursuer must, of course, speak also to his or her own financial position, at the date of the affidavit. Where the pursuer cannot obtain recent information as to the defender's means, it is suggested that, if the pursuer's advisers approve, assessment should be left to the sheriff, and in such cases it may be that the solicitors representing the pursuer would be willing to incorporate in the terms of the minute for decree, after the words "in terms of the crave of the initial writ," the words "or such other sum (or sums) as the Court may think proper."

14. The minute for decree must be signed by a solicitor who has examined the affidavits and other documents and takes responsibility therefor, whether or not he is the person who drew the initial writ or affidavits.

15. In consent cases, the defender's written consent form will also have to be borrowed up, put to the pursuer in his or her affidavit, and docqueted and identified in the same way as other productions.

16. Affidavit procedure will not prevent the parties to the action agreeing the financial or other ancillary craves by joint minute. For so long as these ancillary craves are opposed, the affidavit procedure cannot be used for them, but it can be used for the merits of the action. If a joint minute is signed before an affidavit or supplementary affidavit is emitted by the pursuer, that affidavit must refer to the arrangements in the joint minute. Decree of divorce will not be granted before any issues relating to financial provisions consequent upon the divorce which require to be decided by the court, have been so decided.

17. Where the pursuer has craved a capital allowance, a periodical allowance, aliment for the child or children, or expenses, and in the minute for decree does not seek decree for one or any of these, it is essential that the reasons for this are fully narrated in the affidavit. Where these reasons are capable of corroboration by witnesses, they should be dealt with in the witnesses' affidavits.

[18. Solicitors are reminded that the normal rules of evidence about corroboration still apply except where:

    (a) the action is brought in reliance on the facts set out in section 1(2)(d) (2 years non-cohabitation and the defender's consent to decree) or in section 1(2)(e) (5 years non-cohabitation) of the Divorce (Scotland) Act 1976;

    (b) no other proceedings are pending in any court which could have the effect of bringing the marriage to an end;

    (c) there are no children of the marriage under the age of 16 years;

    (d) neither party applies for an order for financial provision on divorce; and

    (e) neither party suffers from mental disorder within the meaning of Section 6 of the Mental Health (Scotland) Act 1960.][4]

---

[4] Words in square brackets omitted from Sheriffdom of Lothian and Borders Act of Court (Consolidation, etc.) 1990 No. 1 wherein there is substituted the following: "While it is no longer necessary to corroborate any fact, proof of which is required to establish a ground of divorce or any other matter, solicitors are nonetheless reminded that any affidavit or affidavits must satisfy the requirements of section 8 of the Civil Evidence (Scotland) Act 1988."

ORDINARY CAUSE FORMS RELATIVE TO DIVORCE ACTIONS

FORM F1   **Rule 33.7(1)(a)**

FORM OF INTIMATION TO CHILDREN AND NEXT-OF-KIN IN AN ACTION OF DIVORCE OR SEPARATION WHERE THE DEFENDER'S ADDRESS IS NOT KNOWN

To (*insert name and address as in warrant*)   Court ref. no.

You are given NOTICE that an action of divorce [*or* separation] has been raised against (*insert name*) your (*insert relationship, e.g. father, mother, brother or other relative as the case may be*). If you know of his [*or* her] present address, you are requested to inform the sheriff clerk (*insert address of sheriff clerk*) in writing immediately. If you wish to appear as a party you must lodge a minute with the sheriff clerk for leave to do so. Your minute must be lodged within 21 days of (*insert date on which intimation was given. N.B. Rule 5.3(2) relating to postal service or intimation*).

Date (*insert date*)   (*Signed*) A.B.
                            [Solicitor for the pursuer (*add designation and business address*)]

NOTE
If you decide to lodge a minute it may be in your best interest to consult a solicitor. The minute should be lodged with the sheriff clerk with the appropriate fee of (*insert amount*) and a copy of this intimation.

IF YOU ARE UNCERTAIN WHAT ACTION TO TAKE you should consult a solicitor. You may be entitled to legal aid depending on your financial circumstances, and you can get information about legal aid from a solicitor. You may also obtain advice from any Citizens Advice Bureau or other advice agency.

FORM F2   **Rule 33.7(1)(b)**

FORM OF INTIMATION TO ALLEGED ADULTERER IN ACTION OF DIVORCE OR SEPARATION

To (*insert name and address as in warrant*)   Court ref. no.

You are given NOTICE that in this action, you are alleged to have committed adultery. A copy of the initial writ is attached. If you wish to dispute the truth of the allegation made against you, you must lodge a minute with the sheriff clerk (*insert address of sheriff clerk*) for leave to appear as a party. Your minute must be lodged within 21 days of (*insert date on which intimation given N.B. Rule 5.3(2) relating to postal service or intimation*).

Date (*insert date*)   (*Signed*) A.B.
                              [Solicitor for the pursuer]

NOTE
If you decide to lodge a minute it may be in your best interest to consult a solicitor. The minute should be lodged with the sheriff clerk with the appropriate fee of (*insert amount*) and a copy of this intimation.

IF YOU ARE UNCERTAIN WHAT ACTION TO TAKE you should consult a solicitor. You may be entitled to legal aid depending on your financial circumstances, and you can get information about legal aid from a solicitor. You may also obtain advice from any Citizens Advice Bureau or other advice agency.

FORM F3   **Rule 33.7(1)(c)**

FORM OF INTIMATION TO CHILDREN, NEXT OF KIN AND *CURATOR BONIS* IN AN ACTION OF DIVORCE OR SEPARATION WHERE THE DEFENDER SUFFERS FROM A MENTAL DISORDER

To (*insert name and address as in warrant*)   Court ref. no.

You are given NOTICE that an action of divorce [*or* separation] has been raised against (*insert name, and designation*) your (*insert relationship, e.g. father, mother, brother or other relative, or ward, as the case may be*). A copy of the initial writ is enclosed. If you wish to appear as a party, you must lodge a minute with the sheriff clerk (*insert address of sheriff clerk*), for leave to do so. Your minute must be lodged within 21 days of (*insert date on which intimation was given. N.B. Rule 5.3(2) relating to postal service or intimation*).

Date (*insert date*)   (*Signed*) A.B.
                            [Solicitor for the pursuer (*insert designation and business address*)]

NOTE
If you decide to lodge a minute it may be in your best interest to consult a solicitor. The minute should be lodged with the sheriff clerk with the appropriate fee of (*insert amount*) and a copy of this intimation.

IF YOU ARE UNCERTAIN WHAT ACTION TO TAKE you should consult a solicitor. You may be entitled to legal aid depending on your financial circumstances, and you can get information about legal aid from a solicitor. You may also obtain advice from any Citizens Advice Bureau or other advice agency.

FORM F4   **Rule 33.7(1)(d)**

FORM OF INTIMATION TO ADDITIONAL SPOUSE OF EITHER PARTY IN PROCEEDINGS RELATING TO A POLYGAMOUS MARRIAGE

To (*name and address as in warrant*)   Court ref. no.

You are given NOTICE that this action for divorce [*or* separation] involves (*insert name and designation*) your spouse. A copy of the initial writ is attached. If you wish to appear as a party, you must lodge a minute with the sheriff clerk (*insert address of sheriff clerk*) for leave to do so. Your minute must be lodged within 21 days of (*insert date on which intimation was given. N.B. Rule 5.3(2) relating to postal service or intimation*).

Date (*insert date*)   (*Signed*) A.B.
                              [Solicitor for the pursuer]

NOTE
If you decide to lodge a minute it may be in your best interest to consult a solicitor. The minute should be lodged with the sheriff clerk with the appropriate fee of (*insert amount*) and a copy of this intimation.

IF YOU ARE UNCERTAIN WHAT ACTION TO TAKE you should consult a solicitor. You may be entitled to legal aid depending on your financial circumstances, and you can get information about legal aid from a solicitor. You may also obtain advice from any Citizens Advice Bureau or other advice agency.

FORM F5   **Rule 33.7(1)(e)(i) and (ii)**

FORM OF INTIMATION TO A LOCAL AUTHORITY OR THIRD PARTY WHO MAY BE LIABLE TO MAINTAIN A CHILD

To (*insert name and address as in warrant*)   Court ref. no.

You are given NOTICE that in this action, the court may make an order under section 11 of the Children (Scotland) Act 1995 in respect of (*insert name and address*), a child in your care [*or* liable to be maintained by you]. A copy of the initial writ is attached. If you wish to appear as a party, you must lodge a minute with the sheriff clerk (*insert address of sheriff clerk*) for leave to do so. Your minute must be lodged within 21 days of (*insert date on which intimation was given. N.B. Rule 5.3(2) relating to postal service or intimation*).

Date (*insert date*)   (*Signed*)
                             [Solicitor for the pursuer]

NOTE
If you decide to lodge a minute it may be in your best interest to consult a solicitor. The minute should be lodged with the sheriff clerk with the appropriate fee of (*insert amount*) and a copy of this intimation.

IF YOU ARE UNCERTAIN WHAT ACTION TO TAKE you should consult a solicitor. You may be entitled to legal aid depending on your financial circumstances, and you can get information about legal aid from a solicitor. You may also obtain advice from any Citizens Advice Bureau or other advice agency.

FORM F6   **Rule 33.7(1)(e)(iii)**

FORM OF INTIMATION TO PERSON WHO IN FACT EXERCISES CARE OR CONTROL OF A CHILD

To (*insert name and address as in warrant*)   Court ref. no.

You are given NOTICE that in this action, the court may make an order under section 11 of the Children (Scotland) Act 1995 in respect of (*insert name and address*) a child at present in your care or control. A copy of the initial writ is attached. If you wish to appear as a party, you must lodge a minute with the sheriff clerk (*insert address of sheriff clerk*) for leave to do so. Your minute must be lodged within 21 days of (*insert date on which intimation was given. N.B. Rule 5.3(2) relating to postal service or intimation*).

Date (*insert date*)   (*Signed*)
                            [Solicitor for the pursuer]

NOTE
If you decide to lodge a minute it may be in your best interest to consult a solicitor. The minute should be lodged with the sheriff clerk with the appropriate fee of (*insert amount*) and a copy of this intimation.

IF YOU ARE UNCERTAIN WHAT ACTION TO TAKE you should consult a solicitor. You may be entitled to legal aid depending on your financial circumstances, and you can get information about legal aid from a solicitor. You may also obtain advice from any Citizens Advice Bureau or other advice agency.

FORM F7   **Rule 33.7(1)(f)**

FORM OF NOTICE TO PARENT OR GUARDIAN IN ACTION FOR A SECTION 11 ORDER IN RESPECT OF A CHILD

1. You are given NOTICE that in this action, the pursuer is applying for an order under section 11 of the Children (Scotland) Act 1995 in respect of the child (*insert name of child*). A copy of the initial writ is served on you and is attached to this notice.

2. If you wish to oppose this action, or oppose the granting of any order applied for by the pursuer in respect of the child, you must lodge a notice of invention to defend (Form F26). see Form F26 attached for further details.

Date (*insert date*)   (*Signed*)
                              Pursuer
                              or Solicitor for the pursuer (*add designation and business address*)

NOTE

IF YOU ARE UNCERTAIN WHAT ACTION TO TAKE you should consult a solicitor. You may be entitled to legal aid depending on your financial circumstances, and you can get information about legal aid from a solicitor. You may also obtain advice from any Citizens Advice Bureau or other advice agency.

FORM F8   **Rule 33.7(1)(g), 33.7(4)
and 33.12(2) and (3)**

FORM OF NOTICE TO LOCAL AUTHORITY
REQUESTING A REPORT IN RESPECT OF A CHILD

To (*insert name and address*)   Court ref. no.

1. You are given NOTICE that in an action in the Sheriff Court at (*insert address*) the pursuer has applied for a residence order in respect of the child (*insert name of child*). A copy of the initial writ is enclosed.
2. You are required to submit to the court a report on all the circumstances of the child and on the proposed arrangements for the care and upbringing of the child.

Date (*insert date*)   (*Signed*)
                              [Solicitor for the pursuer (*add designa-
                              tion and business address*)]

FORM F9   **Rule 33.7(1)(h)**

FORM OF INTIMATION IN AN ACTION WHICH INCLUDES A CRAVE FOR A SECTION 11 ORDER

PART A   Court ref. no.

This part must be completed by the Pursuer's solicitor in language a child is capable of understanding.

To **(1)**
The Sheriff (the person who has to decide about your future) has been asked by **(2)**   to decide—

(a) **(3)** and **(4)**

(b) **(5)**

(c) **(6)**

If you want to tell the Sheriff what you think about the things your **(2)**   has asked the Sheriff to decide about your future you should complete Part B of this form and send it to the Sheriff Clerk at **(7)** by **(8)**   . An envelope which does not need a postage stamp is enclosed for you to use to return the form.

If you do not understand this form or if you want help to complete it you may get help from a solicitor or contact the Scottish Child Law Centre on the Free Advice Telephone Line on 0800 317 500.

If you return the form it will be given to the Sheriff. The Sheriff may wish to speak with you and may ask you to come and see him or her.

PART B

IF YOU WISH THE SHERIFF TO KNOW YOUR VIEWS ABOUT YOUR FUTURE YOU SHOULD COMPLETE THIS PART OF THE FORM.

To the Sheriff Clerk, **(7)**
Court Ref. No. **(9)**
(10) ....

QUESTION **(1)**: DO YOU WISH THE SHERIFF TO KNOW WHAT YOUR VIEWS ARE ABOUT YOUR FUTURE?

(PLEASE TICK BOX)

Yes	
No	

If you have ticked YES please also answer Question (2) *or* (3)

QUESTION (2): WOULD YOU LIKE A FRIEND, RELATIVE OR OTHER PERSON TO TELL THE SHERIFF YOUR VIEWS ABOUT YOUR FUTURE?

(PLEASE TICK BOX)

Yes	
No	

If you have ticked YES please write the name and address of the person you wish to tell the Sheriff your views in Box (A) below. You should also tell that person what your views about your future.

BOX A: (NAME) ....
(ADDRESS).....................................
....
Is this person: A friend?   ☐   A relative   ☐
                  A teacher? ☐   Other   ☐

OR

QUESTION (3) WOULD YOU LIKE TO WRITE TO THE SHERIFF AND TELL HIM WHAT YOUR VIEWS ARE ABOUT YOUR FUTURE?

(PLEASE TICK BOX)

Yes	
No	

If you decide that you wish to write to the Sheriff you can write what your views are about your future in Box (B) below or on a separate piece of paper. If you decide to write your views on a separate piece of paper you should send it along with this form to the Sheriff Clerk in the envelope provided.

```
┌─────────────────────────────────────────────────────────────┐
│ BOX B:  WHAT I HAVE TO SAY ABOUT MY FUTURE:                   │
│                                                               │
│                                                               │
│                                                               │
│                                                               │
│                                                               │
└─────────────────────────────────────────────────────────────┘
```

NAME:..

ADDRESS: ....

DATE: ....

NOTES FOR COMPLETION

(1) Insert name and address of child.	(2) Insert relationship to the child of party making the application to court.
(3) Insert appropriate wording for residence order sought.	(4) Insert address.
(5) Insert appropriate wording for contact order sought.	(6) Insert appropriate wording for any other order sought.
(7) Insert address of sheriff clerk.	(8) Insert the date occurring 21 days after the date on which intimation is given. N.B. Rule 5.3(2) relating to intimation and service.
(9) Insert court reference number.	(10) Insert name and address of parties to the action.

FORM F10   **Rule 33.7(1)(i)**

FORM OF INTIMATION TO CREDITOR IN APPLICATION FOR ORDER FOR THE TRANSFER OF PROPERTY UNDER SECTION 8 OF THE FAMILY LAW (SCOTLAND) ACT 1985

To (*insert name and address as in warrant*)   Court ref. no.

You are given NOTICE that in this action an order is sought for the transfer of property (*specify the order*), over which you hold a security. A copy of the initial writ is attached. If you wish to appear as a party you must lodge a minute with the sheriff clerk (*insert address of sheriff clerk*) for leave to do so. Your minute must be lodged within 21 days of (*insert date on which intimation was given. N.B. Rule 5.3(2) relating to postal service or intimation*).

Date (*insert date*)   (*Signed*) A.B.
                              [Solicitor for the pursuer]

NOTE
If you decide to lodge a minute it may be in your best interest to consult a solicitor. The minute should be lodged with the sheriff clerk with the appropriate fee of (*insert amount*) and a copy of this intimation.

IF YOU ARE UNCERTAIN WHAT ACTION TO TAKE you should consult a solicitor. You may be entitled to legal aid depending on your financial circumstances, and you can get information about legal aid from a solicitor. You may also obtain advice from any Citizens Advice Bureau or other advice agency.

FORM F11   **Rule 33.7(1)(j)**

FORM OF INTIMATION IN AN ACTION WHERE THE PURSUER MAKES AN APPLICATION FOR AN ORDER UNDER SECTION 18 OF THE FAMILY LAW (SCOTLAND) ACT 1985

To (*insert name and address as in warrant*)   Court ref. no.

You are given NOTICE that in this action, the pursuer craves the court to make an order under section 18 of the Family Law (Scotland) Act 1985. A copy of the initial writ is attached. If you wish to appear as a party, you must lodge a minute with the sheriff clerk (*insert address of sheriff clerk*) for leave to do so. Your minute must be lodged within 21 days of (*insert date on which intimation was given. N.B. Rule 5.3(2) relating to postal service or intimation*).

Date (*insert date*)   (*Signed*) A.B.
                              [Solicitor for the pursuer]

NOTE
If you decide to lodge a minute it may be in your best interest to consult a solicitor. The minute should be lodged with the sheriff clerk with the appropriate fee of (*insert amount*) and a copy of this intimation.

IF YOU ARE UNCERTAIN WHAT ACTION TO TAKE you should consult a solicitor. You may be entitled to legal aid depending on your financial circumstances, and you can get information about legal aid from a solicitor. You may also obtain advice from any Citizens Advice Bureau or other advice agency.

FORM F12   **Rule 33.7(1)(k)**

FORM OF INTIMATION IN AN ACTION WHERE A NON-ENTITLED PURSUER MAKES AN APPLICATION FOR AN ORDER UNDER THE MATRIMONIAL HOMES (FAMILY PROTECTION) (SCOTLAND) ACT 1981

To (*insert name and address as in warrant*)   Court ref. no.

You are given NOTICE that in this action, the pursuer craves the court to make an order under section (*insert the section under which the order(s) sought*) of the Matrimonial Homes (Family Protection) (Scotland) Act 1981. A copy of the initial writ is attached. If you wish to appear as a party you must lodge a minute with the sheriff clerk (*insert address of sheriff clerk*) for leave to do so. Your minute must be lodged within 21 days of (*insert date on which intimation was given. N.B. Rule 5.3(2) relating to postal service or intimation*).

Date (*insert date*)   (*Signed*) A.B.
                              [Solicitor for the pursuer]

NOTE
If you decide to lodge a minute it may be in your best interest to consult a solicitor. The minute should be lodged with the sheriff clerk with the appropriate fee of (*insert amount*) and a copy of this intimation.

IF YOU ARE UNCERTAIN WHAT ACTION TO TAKE you should consult a solicitor. You may be entitled to legal aid depending on your financial circumstances, and you can get information about legal aid from a solicitor. You may also obtain advice from any Citizens Advice Bureau or other advice agency.

FORM F12A   **Rule 33.7(1)(l)**

FORM OF INTIMATION TO TRUSTEES OR MANAGERS OF PENSION SCHEME IN RELATION TO ORDER FOR PAYMENT IN RESPECT OF PENSION LUMP SUM UNDER SECTION 12A OF THE FAMILY LAW (SCOTLAND) ACT 1985

To (*insert name and address as in warrant*)   Court ref. no.

You are given NOTICE that in this action the pursuer has applied for an order under section 8 of the Family Law (Scotland) Act 1985 for a capital sum in circumstances where the matrimonial property includes rights in a pension scheme under which a lump sum is payable. The relevant pension scheme is (*give brief details, including number, if known*). If you wish to apply to appear as a party you must lodge a minute with the sheriff clerk (*insert address of sheriff clerk*) for leave to do so. Your minute must be lodged within 21 days of (*insert date on which intimation was given. N.B. Rule 5.3(2) relating to postal service or intimation*).

Date (*insert date*)   Signed
                        Solicitor for the pursuer (*add designation and business address*)

NOTE
If you decide to lodge a minute it may be in your best interest to consult a solicitor. The minute should be lodged with the sheriff clerk with the appropriate fee of (*insert amount*) and a copy of this intimation.

IF YOU ARE UNCERTAIN WHAT ACTION TO TAKE you should consult a solicitor. You may be entitled to legal aid depending on your financial circumstances, and you can get information about legal aid from a solicitor. You may also obtain advice from any Citizens Advice Bureau or other advice agency.

FORM F13   **Rule 33.8(3)**

FORM OF INTIMATION TO PERSON WITH WHOM AN IMPROPER ASSOCIATION IS ALLEGED TO HAVE OCCURRED

To (*insert name and address as in warrant*)   Court ref. no.

You are given NOTICE that in this action, the defender is alleged to have had an improper association with you. A copy of the initial writ is attached. If you wish to dispute the truth of the allegation made against you, you must lodge a minute with the sheriff clerk (*insert address of sheriff clerk*) for leave to appear as a party. Your minute must be lodged within 21 days of (*insert date on which intimation was given. N.B. Rule 5.3(2) relating to postal service or intimation*).

Date (*insert date*)   (*Signed*) A.B.
                              [Solicitor for the pursuer]

NOTE
If you decide to lodge a minute it may be in your best interest to consult a solicitor. The minute should be lodged with the sheriff clerk with the appropriate fee of (*insert amount*) and a copy of this intimation.

IF YOU ARE UNCERTAIN WHAT ACTION TO TAKE you should consult a solicitor. You may be entitled to legal aid depending on your financial circumstances, and you can get information about legal aid from a solicitor. You may also obtain advice from any Citizens Advice Bureau or other advice agency.

FORM F14   **Rule 33.10**

FORM OF WARRANT OF CITATION IN FAMILY ACTION

(*Insert place and date*)

Grants warrant to cite the defender (*insert name and address of defender*) by serving upon him [*or* her] a copy of the writ and warrant upon a period of notice of (*insert period of notice*) days, and ordains the defender to lodge a notice of intention to defend with the sheriff clerk at (*insert address of sheriff clerk*) if he [*or* she] wishes to:

(a) challenge the jurisdiction of the court;
(b) oppose any claim made or order sought;
(c) make any claim or seek any order.

[Meantime grants interim interdict, *or* warrant to arrest on the dependence].

FORM F15   **Rule 33.11(1) and
                              33.13(1)(a)**

FORM OF CITATION IN FAMILY ACTION

CITATION

SHERIFFDOM OF (*insert name of sheriffdom*)
AT (*insert place of sheriff court*)

[A.B.], (*insert designation and address*) Pursuer, against [C.D.], (*insert designation and address*), Defender.
          Court ref. no.

(*Insert place and date*) You [C.D.] are hereby served with this copy writ and warrant, with Form F26 (notice of intention to defend) [and (*insert details of any other form of notice served, e.g. any of the forms served in accordance with rule 33.14*].

FORM F26 is served on you for use should you wish to intimate an intention to defend the action.

IF YOU WISH TO—

    (a) challenge the jurisdiction of the court;
    (b) oppose any claim made or order sought;
    (c) make any claim or seek any order; or
    (d) seek any order;

you should consult a solicitor with a view to lodging a notice of intention to defend (Form F26). The notice of intention to defend, together with the court fee of £(*insert amount*) must be lodged with the sheriff clerk at the above address within 21 days (*or insert appropriate period of notice*) of (*insert the date on which service was executed. N.B. Rule 5.3(2) relating to postal service or intimation*).

IF YOU ARE UNCERTAIN WHAT ACTION TO TAKE you should consult a solicitor. You may be entitled to legal aid depending on your financial circumstances, and you can get information about legal aid from a solicitor. You may also obtain advice from any Citizens Advice Bureau or other advice agency.

PLEASE NOTE THAT IF YOU DO NOTHING IN ANSWER TO THIS DOCUMENT the court may regard you as admitting the claim made against you and the pursuer may obtain decree against you in your absence.

> (*Signed*)
> [P.Q.], Sheriff officer
> *or*
> [X.Y.] (*add designation and business address*)
> [Solicitor for the pursuer]

FORM F16   **Rule 33.11(2)**

FORM OF CERTIFICATE OF CITATION IN FAMILY ACTION

CERTIFICATE OF CITATION

(*Insert place and date*) I,   hereby certify that upon the   day of   I duly cited [C.D.], Defender, to answer to the foregoing writ. This I did by (*state method of service; if by officer and not by post, add:* in presence of (L.M.), (*insert designation*)), witness hereto with me subscribing and (*insert details of any forms of intimation or notice sent including details of the person to whom intimation sent and the method of service*).

> (*Signed*)
> [P.Q.], Sheriff officer
> [L.M.], witness
> *or*
> [X.Y.] (*add designation and business address*)
> Solicitor for the pursuer

FORM F17   **Rule 33.13(1)(c)**

FORM OF REQUEST TO MEDICAL OFFICER OF HOSPITAL OR SIMILAR INSTITUTION

To (*insert name and address of medical officer*)

In terms of rule 33.13(1)(*c*) of the Ordinary Cause Rules of the Sheriff Court a copy of the initial writ at the instance of (*insert name and address of pursuer*), Pursuer, against (*insert name and address of defender*), Defender, is enclosed and you are requested to:

(a) deliver it personally to (*insert name of defender*), and
(b) explain the contents to him or her,

unless you are satisfied that such delivery of explanation would be dangerous to his or her health or mental condition. You are further requested to complete and return to me in the enclosed stamped addressed envelope the certificate appended hereto, making necessary deletions.

Date (*insert date*)   (*Signed*) A.B.
                        [Solicitor for the pursuer (*add designation and business address*)]

FORM F18   **Rule 33.13(1)(d) and
33.13(2)**

FORM OF CERTIFICATE BY MEDICAL OFFICER OF HOSPITAL OR SIMILAR INSTITUTION

Court ref. no.

I (*insert name and designation*) certify that I have received a copy initial writ in an action of (*type of family action to be inserted by the party requesting service*) at the instance of (*insert name and designation*), Pursuer against (*insert name and designation*), Defender, and that
*I have on the   day of   personally delivered a copy thereof to the said defender who is under my care at (*insert address*) and I have explained the contents or purport thereof to him or her, *or*
*I have not delivered a copy thereof to the said defender who is under my care at (*insert address*) and I have not explained the contents or purport thereof to him or her because (*state reasons*).

Date (*insert date*)   (*Signed*) A.B.
[Medical officer (*add designation and business address*)]

    *Delete as appropriate.

FORM F19   **Rule 33.14(1)(a)(i)**

FORM OF NOTICE TO DEFENDER WHERE IT IS STATED THAT DEFENDER CONSENTS TO THE GRANTING OF DECREE OF DIVORCE

You are given NOTICE that the copy initial writ served on you with this notice states that you consent to the grant of decree of divorce.
1. If you do so consent the consequences for you are that:—

  (a) provided the pursuer establishes the fact that he [*or* she] has not cohabited with you at any time during a continuous period of two years after the date of your marriage and immediately preceding the bringing of this action and that you consent, a decree of divorce will be granted;
  (b) on the grant of a decree of divorce you may lose your rights of succession to the pursuer's estate; and
  (c) decree of divorce will end the marriage thereby affecting any right to such pension as may depend on the marriage continuing, or, on your being left a widow the state widow's pension will not be payable to you when the pursuer dies.

Apart from these, there may be other consequences for you depending upon your particular circumstances.
2. You are entitled, whether or not you consent to the grant of decree of divorce in this action, to apply to the sheriff in this action—

  (a) to make financial or other provision for you under the Family Law (Scotland) Act 1985;
  (b) for an order under section 11 of the Children (Scotland) Act 1995 in respect of any child of the marriage, or any child accepted as such, who is under 16 years of age; or
  (c) for any other competent order.

3. IF YOU WISH TO APPLY FOR ANY OF THE ABOVE ORDERS you should consult a solicitor with a view to lodging a notice of intention to defend (Form F26).
4. If, after consideration, you wish to consent to the grant of decree of divorce in this action, you should complete and sign the attached notice of consent (Form F20) and send it to the sheriff clerk at the sheriff court referred to in the initial writ within 21 days of (*insert the date on which service was executed. N.B. Rule 5.3(2) relating to postal service*).

5. If, at a later stage, you wish to withdraw your consent to decree being granted against you in this action, you must inform the sheriff clerk immediately in writing.

Date (*insert date*)   (*Signed*)
                              Solicitor for the pursuer (*add designation and business address*)

FORM F20   **Rule 33.14(1)(a)(i)
                                    and 33.18(1)**

FORM OF NOTICE OF CONSENT IN ACTIONS OF DIVORCE UNDER SECTION 1(2)(D) OF THE DIVORCE (SCOTLAND) ACT 1976

[A.B.], (*insert designation and address*), Pursuer, against [C.D.], (*insert designation and address*), Defender

I (*full name and address of the defender to be inserted by pursuer or pursuer's solicitor before sending notice*) have received a copy of the initial writ in the action against me at the instance of (*full name and address of pursuer to be inserted by pursuer or pursuer's solicitor before sending notice*). I understand that it states that I consent to the grant of decree of divorce in this action. I have considered the consequences for me mentioned in the notice (Form F19) sent to me with this notice. I consent to the grant of decree of divorce in this action.

Date (*insert date*)   (*Signed*) A.B.
                                   |Defender|

FORM F21   **Rule 33.14(1)(a)(ii)**

FORM OF NOTICE TO DEFENDER WHERE IT IS STATED THAT DEFENDER CONSENTS TO THE GRANTING OF DECREE OF SEPARATION

You are given NOTICE that the copy initial writ served on you with this notice states that you consent to the grant of decree of separation.

1. If you do so consent the consequences for you are that—

   (a) provided the pursuer establishes the fact that he [*or* she] has not cohabited with you at any time during a continuous period of two years after the date of your marriage and immediately preceding the bringing of this action and that you consent, a decree of divorce will be granted;
   (b) on the grant of a decree of separation you will be obliged to live apart from the pursuer but the marriage will continue to subsist; you will continue to have a legal obligation to support your wife [*or* husband] and children.

Apart from these, there may be other consequences for you depending upon your particular circumstances.

2. You are entitled, whether or not you consent to the grant of decree of separation in this action, to apply to the sheriff in this action—

   (a) to make financial or other provision for you under the Family Law (Scotland) Act 1985;
   (b) for an order under section 11 of the Children (Scotland) Act 1995 in respect of any child of the marriage, or any child accepted as such, who is under 16 years of age; or
   (c) for any other competent order.

3. IF YOU WISH TO APPLY FOR ANY OF THE ABOVE ORDERS you should consult a solicitor with a view to lodging a notice of intention to defend (Form F26).

4. If, after consideration, you wish to consent to the grant of decree of separation in this action, you should complete and sign the attached notice of consent (Form F22) and send it to the sheriff clerk at the sheriff court referred to in the initial writ and other paper within 21 days of (*insert the date on which service was executed. N.B. Rule 5.3(2) relating to postal service or intimation*).

5. If, at a later stage, you wish to withdraw your consent to decree being granted against you in this action, you must inform the sheriff clerk immediately in writing.

Date (*insert date*)   *Signed*
                                   Solicitor for the pursuer (*add designation and business address*)

FORM F22   **Rule 33.14(1)(a)(ii)
                        and 33.18(1)**

FORM OF NOTICE OF CONSENT IN ACTIONS OF SEPARATION UNDER SECTION 1(2)(D) OF THE DIVORCE (SCOTLAND) ACT 1976

[A.B.], (*insert designation and address*), Pursuer against [C.D.], (*insert designation and address*), Defender

I (*full name and address of the defender to be inserted by pursuer or pursuer's solicitor before sending notice*) confirm that I have received a copy of the initial writ in the action against me at the instance of (*full name and address of pursuer to be inserted by pursuer or pursuer's solicitor before sending notice*). I understand that it states that I consent to the grant of decree of separation in this action. I have considered the consequences for me mentioned in the notice (Form F21) sent together with this notice. I consent to the grant of decree of separation in this action.

Date (*insert date*)   (*Signed*) A.B.
                                [Defender]

FORM F23   **Rule 33.14(1)(b)(i)**

FORM OF NOTICE TO DEFENDER IN AN ACTION OF DIVORCE WHERE IT IS STATED THAT THERE HAS BEEN FIVE YEARS' NON-COHABITATION

You are given NOTICE that—

1. The copy initial writ served on you with this notice states that there has been no cohabitation between you and the pursuer at any time during a continuous period of five years after the date of the marriage and immediately preceding the commencement of this action. If the pursuer establishes this as a fact and the sheriff is satisfied that the marriage has broken down irretrievably, a decree will be granted, unless the sheriff is of the opinion that to grant decree would result in grave financial hardship to you.

2. Decree of divorce will end the marriage thereby affecting any right to such pension as may depend on the marriage continuing, or, on your being left a widow the state widow's pension will not be payable to you when the pursuer dies. You may also lose your rights of succession to the pursuer's estate.

3. You are entitled, whether or not you dispute that there has been no such cohabitation during that five year period, to apply to the sheriff in this action—

   (a) to make financial or other provision for you under the Family Law (Scotland) Act 1985;
   (b) for an order under section 11 of the Children (Scotland) Act 1995 in respect of any child of the marriage, or any child accepted as such, who is under 16 years of age; or
   (c) for any other competent order.

4. IF YOU WISH TO APPLY FOR ANY OF THE ABOVE ORDERS you should consult a solicitor with a view to lodging a notice of intention to defend (Form F26).

Date (*insert date*)   Signed
Solicitor for the pursuer (*add designation and business address*)

FORM F24   **Rule 33.14(1)(b)(ii)**

FORM OF NOTICE TO DEFENDER IN AN ACTION OF SEPARATION WHERE IT IS STATED THAT THERE HAS BEEN FIVE YEARS' NON-COHABITATION

You are given NOTICE that—

1. The copy initial writ served on you together with this notice states that there has been no cohabitation between you and the pursuer at any time during a continuous period of five years after the date of the marriage and immediately preceding the commencement of this action and that if the pursuer establishes this as a fact, and the sheriff is satisfied that there are grounds justifying decree of separation, a decree will be granted, unless the sheriff is of the opinion that to grant decree would result in grave financial hardship to you.

2. On the granting of decree of separation you will be obliged to live apart from the pursuer but the marriage will continue to subsist. You will continue to have a legal obligation to support your wife [*or* husband] and children.

3. You are entitled, whether or not you dispute that there has been no such cohabitation during that five year period, to apply to the sheriff in this action—

   (a) to make provision under the Family Law (Scotland) Act 1985;
   (b) for an order under section 11 of the Children (Scotland) Act 1995 in respect of any child of the marriage, or any child accepted as such, who is under 16 years of age; or
   (c) for any other competent order.

4. IF YOU WISH TO APPLY FOR ANY OF THE ABOVE ORDERS you should consult a solicitor with a view to lodging a notice of intention to defend (Form F26).

Date (*insert date*)   Signed
Solicitor for the pursuer (*add designation and business address*)

FORM F25   **Rule 33.19(1)(a)(ii)**
and 33.19(2)(i)

FORM OF CONSENT OF PARENT OR GUARDIAN IN
PROCEEDINGS FOR CUSTODY OF CHILDREN UNDER
SECTION 47 OF THE CHILDREN ACT 1975

Court ref. no.

[A.B.], (*insert designation and address*), Pursuer, against [C.D.], (*insert designation and address*), Defender

I (*insert name and address*) confirm that I am the mother [*or* father *or* guardian] of the child (*insert full name of the child as given on birth certificate, and the child's present address*). I understand that if I consent to the granting of custody to the pursuer, the care, possession and control of the child may be granted to the pursuer by the court. I hereby consent to the making of a custody order in relation to the child (*insert name of child*) in favour of (*insert name and address or pursuer*).

Dated at (*insert place*) on the   day of   19 .

Signature of person consenting . . . .

Signature of Witness . . . .   Signature of Witness . . . .

*Full Name . . . .   *Full Name . . . .

*Designation . . . .   *Designation . . . .

*Address . . . .   *Address . . . .

. . . .

*Please complete in block capitals.

FORM F26   **Rule 33.11(1)
                                  and 33.34(2)(a)**

FORM OF NOTICE OF INTENTION TO DEFEND IN A FAMILY ACTION

NOTICE OF INTENTION TO DEFEND

PART A
(This section to be completed by the pursuer's solicitor before service.)

Court ref. no.
In an action brought in
Sheriff Court ....

(*Insert name and business address of solicitor for the pursuer*)

....
....

Pursuer

....
....

Defender

Date of service   Date of expiry of period of notice:

PART B
(This section to be completed by the defender or defender's solicitor, and both parts of the form to be returned to the sheriff clerk at the above sheriff court on or before the date of expiry of the period of notice referred to in Part A above.)
(*Insert place and date*)
[C.D.] (*insert designation and address*), Defender, intends to

    (a) challenge the jurisdiction of the court;
    (b) oppose a crave in the initial writ;
    (c) make a claim;
    (d) seek an order;

in the action against him [*or* her] raised by [A.B.], (*insert designation and address*), Pursuer.

PART C
(This section to be completed by the defender or the defender's solicitor where an order under section 11 of the Children (Scotland) Act 1995 in respect of a child is sought by the pursuer or is to be sought by the defender.)

DO YOU WISH TO OPPOSE THE MAKING OF ANY ORDER CRAVED BY THE PURSUER IN RESPECT OF A CHILD?

YES/NO*
*delete as appropriate

If you have answered YES to the above question, please state here the order(s) which you wish to oppose and the reasons why the court should not make such order(s).

DO YOU WISH THE COURT TO MAKE ANY ORDER UNDER SECTION 11 OF THE CHILDREN (SCOTLAND) ACT 1995 IN RESPECT OF A CHILD?

YES/NO*
*delete as appropriate

If you have answered YES to the above question, please state here the order(s) which you wish the court to make and the reasons why the court should not make such order(s).

PART D
IF YOU HAVE COMPLETED PART C OF THIS FORM YOU MUST INCLUDE EITHER CRAVE (1) OR (2) BELOW (*delete as appropriate)

    (1)   ***Warrant for intimation of notice in terms of Form F9 on the child(ren)** (*insert name(s)*) **is sought.**
    (2)   ***I seek to dispense with intimation on the child(ren)** (*insert names*) **for the following reasons—**

                Signed
                [C.D.] Defender
                or [X,Y] (*add designation and business address*)
                Solicitor for Defender

FORM F27   **Rule 33.29(1)(b)**

FORM OF MINUTE FOR DECREE IN FAMILY ACTION TO WHICH RULE 33.28 APPLIES

(*Insert name of solicitor for the pursuer*) having considered the evidence contained in the affidavits and the other documents all as specified in the schedule hereto, and being satisfied that upon the evidence a motion for decree (in terms of the crave of the initial writ) [*or in such restricted terms as may be appropriate*] may properly be made, moves the court accordingly.

In respect whereof

> (*Signed*) A.B.
> [Solicitor for the pursuer (*add designation and business address*)]

SCHEDULE

(*Number and specify documents considered*)

5. If, at a later stage, you wish to withdraw your consent to decree being granted against you in this action, you must inform the sheriff clerk immediately in writing.

Date (*insert date*)   *Signed*
                                  Solicitor for the pursuer (*add designation and business address*)

FORM F22   **Rule 33.14(1)(a)(ii)
                            and 33.18(1)**

FORM OF NOTICE OF CONSENT IN ACTIONS OF SEPARATION UNDER SECTION 1(2)(D) OF THE DIVORCE (SCOTLAND) ACT 1976

[A.B.], *(insert designation and address)*, Pursuer against [C.D.], *(insert designation and address)*, Defender

I *(full name and address of the defender to be inserted by pursuer or pursuer's solicitor before sending notice)* confirm that I have received a copy of the initial writ in the action against me at the instance of *(full name and address of pursuer to be inserted by pursuer or pursuer's solicitor before sending notice)*. I understand that it states that I consent to the grant of decree of separation in this action. I have considered the consequences for me mentioned in the notice (Form F21) sent together with this notice. I consent to the grant of decree of separation in this action.

Date *(insert date)*   *(Signed)* A.B.
                              [Defender]

FORM F23   **Rule 33.14(1)(b)(i)**

FORM OF NOTICE TO DEFENDER IN AN ACTION OF DIVORCE WHERE IT IS STATED THAT THERE HAS BEEN FIVE YEARS' NON-COHABITATION

You are given NOTICE that—

1. The copy initial writ served on you with this notice states that there has been no cohabitation between you and the pursuer at any time during a continuous period of five years after the date of the marriage and immediately preceding the commencement of this action. If the pursuer establishes this as a fact and the sheriff is satisfied that the marriage has broken down irretrievably, a decree will be granted, unless the sheriff is of the opinion that to grant decree would result in grave financial hardship to you.

2. Decree of divorce will end the marriage thereby affecting any right to such pension as may depend on the marriage continuing, or, on your being left a widow the state widow's pension will not be payable to you when the pursuer dies. You may also lose your rights of succession to the pursuer's estate.

3. You are entitled, whether or not you dispute that there has been no such cohabitation during that five year period, to apply to the sheriff in this action—

(a) to make financial or other provision for you under the Family Law (Scotland) Act 1985;

(b) for an order under section 11 of the Children (Scotland) Act 1995 in respect of any child of the marriage, or any child accepted as such, who is under 16 years of age; or

(c) for any other competent order.

4. IF YOU WISH TO APPLY FOR ANY OF THE ABOVE ORDERS you should consult a solicitor with a view to lodging a notice of intention to defend (Form F26).

Date (*insert date*)   Signed
                              Solicitor for the pursuer (*add designation and business address*)

FORM F24   **Rule 33.14(1)(b)(ii)**

FORM OF NOTICE TO DEFENDER IN AN ACTION OF SEPARATION WHERE IT IS STATED THAT THERE HAS BEEN FIVE YEARS' NON-COHABITATION

You are given NOTICE that—
1. The copy initial writ served on you together with this notice states that there has been no cohabitation between you and the pursuer at any time during a continuous period of five years after the date of the marriage and immediately preceding the commencement of this action and that if the pursuer establishes this as a fact, and the sheriff is satisfied that there are grounds justifying decree of separation, a decree will be granted, unless the sheriff is of the opinion that to grant decree would result in grave financial hardship to you.
2. On the granting of decree of separation you will be obliged to live apart from the pursuer but the marriage will continue to subsist. You will continue to have a legal obligation to support your wife [*or* husband] and children.
3. You are entitled, whether or not you dispute that there has been no such cohabitation during that five year period, to apply to the sheriff in this action—

  (a) to make provision under the Family Law (Scotland) Act 1985;
  (b) for an order under section 11 of the Children (Scotland) Act 1995 in respect of any child of the marriage, or any child accepted as such, who is under 16 years of age; or
  (c) for any other competent order.

4. IF YOU WISH TO APPLY FOR ANY OF THE ABOVE ORDERS you should consult a solicitor with a view to lodging a notice of intention to defend (Form F26).

Date (*insert date*)   Signed
                          Solicitor for the pursuer (*add designation and business address*)

FORM F25   **Rule 33.19(1)(a)(ii)
and 33.19(2)(i)**

FORM OF CONSENT OF PARENT OR GUARDIAN IN PROCEEDINGS FOR CUSTODY OF CHILDREN UNDER SECTION 47 OF THE CHILDREN ACT 1975

Court ref. no.

[A.B.], (*insert designation and address*), Pursuer, against [C.D.], (*insert designation and address*), Defender

I (*insert name and address*) confirm that I am the mother [*or* father *or* guardian] of the child (*insert full name of the child as given on birth certificate, and the child's present address*). I understand that if I consent to the granting of custody to the pursuer, the care, possession and control of the child may be granted to the pursuer by the court. I hereby consent to the making of a custody order in relation to the child (*insert name of child*) in favour of (*insert name and address or pursuer*).

Dated at (*insert place*) on the   day of   19 .

Signature of person consenting . . . .

Signature of Witness . . . .   Signature of Witness . . . .

*Full Name . . . .   *Full Name . . . .

*Designation . . . .   *Designation . . . .

*Address . . . .   *Address . . . .

. . . .

*Please complete in block capitals.

FORM F26   **Rule 33.11(1)
                                  and 33.34(2)(a)**

FORM OF NOTICE OF INTENTION TO DEFEND IN A FAMILY ACTION

NOTICE OF INTENTION TO DEFEND

PART A
**(This section to be completed
by the pursuer's solicitor
before service.)**   Court ref. no.
                                      In an action brought in
| *(Insert name and business address of solicitor for the pursuer)* | Sheriff Court .... |

....
....
                                      Pursuer
....
....
                                      Defender

Date of service   Date of expiry of period of notice:

_____

PART B
**(This section to be completed by the defender or defender's
solicitor, and both parts of the form to be returned to the sheriff
clerk at the above sheriff court on or before the date of expiry of
the period of notice referred to in Part A above.)**
(Insert place and date)
[C.D.] *(insert designation and address)*, Defender, intends to

   (a) challenge the jurisdiction of the court;
   (b) oppose a crave in the initial writ;
   (c) make a claim;
   (d) seek an order;

in the action against him [*or* her] raised by [A.B.], *(insert designation and address)*, Pursuer.

PART C
**(This section to be completed by the defender or the defender's
solicitor where an order under section 11 of the Children
(Scotland) Act 1995 in respect of a child is sought by the pursuer
or is to be sought by the defender.)**

DO YOU WISH TO OPPOSE THE MAKING OF ANY ORDER CRAVED BY THE PURSUER IN RESPECT OF A CHILD?

YES/NO*

*delete as appropriate

> If you have answered YES to the above question, please state here the order(s) which you wish to oppose and the reasons why the court should not make such order(s).

DO YOU WISH THE COURT TO MAKE ANY ORDER UNDER SECTION 11 OF THE CHILDREN (SCOTLAND) ACT 1995 IN RESPECT OF A CHILD?

YES/NO*

*delete as appropriate

> If you have answered YES to the above question, please state here the order(s) which you wish the court to make and the reasons why the court should not make such order(s).

PART D

IF YOU HAVE COMPLETED PART C OF THIS FORM YOU MUST INCLUDE EITHER CRAVE (1) OR (2) BELOW (*delete as appropriate)

(1) *Warrant for Intimation of notice in terms of Form F9 on the child(ren) (*insert name(s)*) is sought.

(2) *I seek to dispense with intimation on the child(ren) (*insert names*) for the following reasons—

Signed
[C.D.] Defender
or [X,Y] (*add designation and business address*)
Solicitor for Defender

FORM F27 **Rule 33.29(1)(b)**

FORM OF MINUTE FOR DECREE IN FAMILY ACTION TO WHICH RULE 33.28 APPLIES

(*Insert name of solicitor for the pursuer*) having considered the evidence contained in the affidavits and the other documents all as specified in the schedule hereto, and being satisfied that upon the evidence a motion for decree (in terms of the crave of the initial writ) [*or in such restricted terms as may be appropriate*] may properly be made, moves the court accordingly.

In respect whereof

(*Signed*) A.B.
[Solicitor for the pursuer (*add designation and business address*)]

SCHEDULE

(*Number and specify documents considered*)

FORM F28   **Rule 33.40(c) and
33.64(1)(c)**

FORM OF NOTICE OF INTIMATION TO LOCAL AUTHORITY OR THIRD PARTY TO WHOM CARE OF A CHILD IS TO BE GIVEN

To (*name and address as in warrant*)   Court ref. no.

You are given NOTICE that in this action, the sheriff proposes to commit to your care the child (*insert name and address*). A copy of the initial writ is attached. If you wish to appear as a party, you must lodge a minute with the sheriff clerk (*insert address of sheriff clerk*) for leave to do so. Your minute must be lodged within 21 days of (*insert date on which intimation was given. N.B. Rule 5.3(2) relating to postal service or intimation*).

Date (*insert date*)   (*Signed*) A.B.
                        [Solicitor for the pursuer]

NOTE
If you decide to lodge a minute it may be in your best interest to consult a solicitor. The minute should be lodged with the sheriff clerk with the appropriate fee of (*insert amount*) and a copy of this intimation.

IF YOU ARE UNCERTAIN WHAT ACTION TO TAKE you should consult a solicitor. You may be entitled to legal aid depending on your financial circumstances, and you can get information about legal aid from a solicitor. You may also obtain advice from any Citizens Advice Bureau or other advice agency.

FORM F29   **Rule 33.41 and**
                                33.64(2)

FORM OF NOTICE OF INTIMATION TO LOCAL AUTHORITY OF SUPERVISION ORDER

[A.B.], (*insert designation and address*), Pursuer, against [C.D.], (*insert designation and address*), Defender

To (*insert name and address of local authority*)   Court ref. no.

You are given NOTICE that on (*insert date*) in the Sheriff Court at (*insert place*) the sheriff made a supervision order under section 12 of the Matrimonial Proceedings (Children) Act 1958 [*or* section 11(1)(b) of the Guardianship Act 1973] placing the child (*insert name and address of child*) under your supervision. A certified copy of the sheriff's interlocutor is attached.

Date (*insert date*)   (*Signed*)
                                [Sheriff clerk (depute)]

FORM F30   **Rule 33.72(1) and
                                 33.72(2)**

FORM OF CERTIFICATE OF DELIVERY OF DOCUMENTS TO CHIEF CONSTABLE

(*Insert place and date*) I,   hereby certify that upon the
         day of   I duly delivered to (*insert name and
address*) chief constable of (*insert name of constabulary*) (*insert
details of the documents delivered*). This I did by (*state method of
service*).

Date (*insert date*)   (*Signed*) A.B.
                                        [Solicitor for the pur-
                                        suer (*add designation
                                        and business address*)]

THE DIVORCE ETC (PENSIONS) (SCOTLAND) REGULATIONS 1996[1]

The Secretary of State, in exercise of the powers conferred upon him by sections 10(8) and (10) and 12A(8) and of the Family Law (Scotland) Act 1985 and of all other powers enabling him in that behalf, hereby makes the following Regulations.

Citation, commencement and application

1.—(1) These Regulations may be cited as the Divorce etc (Pensions) (Scotland) Regulations 1996 and shall come into force on 19th August 1996.

(2) These Regulations shall not affect any action for divorce commenced before 19th August 1996 or any action for declarator of nullity of marriage commenced before that date.

Interpretation

2.—(1) Unless the contrary intention appears, in these Regulations—

"the Act" means the Family Law (Scotland) Act 1985;

"the 1993 Act" means the Pensions Schemes Act 1993;

"the 1995 Act" means the Pensions Act 1995;

"active member" has the same meaning as in section 124 of the 1995 Act;

"benefits under a pension scheme" has the same meaning as in section 10(10), subject to section 12A(10) and any reference to the rights or interests which a party has or may have in benefits under a pension scheme includes a reference to the rights or interests which a party has or may have in such benefits which are payable in respect of the death of either party;

"deferred member" has the same meaning as in section 124 of the 1995 Act;

"a party" means a party to a marriage;

---

[1] See Chap. 7, nn.30 and 61 and accompanying text.

"occupational pension scheme" has the same meaning as in
   section 1 of the 1993 Act;
"pension scheme" has the same meaning as in section 10(10);
"personal pension scheme" has the same meaning as in
   section 1 of the 1993 Act but, as if the reference to
   employed earners in that definition were to any earner;
"matrimonial property" has the same meaning as in section
   10(4) and (5);
"relevant date" has the same meaning as in section 10(3);
"trustee or manager of a pension scheme" shall be construed
   as in section 10(11),

and any expression used in regulations 5 to 10 to which a meaning
is assigned in section 12A shall have the same meaning in these
Regulations as in that section.

(2) Unless the contrary appears, any reference in these Regulations to—

(*a*) a numbered section is to a section bearing that number in
     the Act;
(*b*) a numbered regulation is to a regulation bearing that
     number in these Regulations.

Valuation

3.—(1) The value of any benefits under a pension scheme shall
be calculated and verified, for the purposes of the Act, in accordance with this regulation.

(2) The value, as at the relevant date, of the rights or interests
which a party has or may have in any benefits under a pension
scheme as at that date shall be calculated as follows and in
accordance with paragraphs (4) and (5) below—

(*a*) where, on the relevant date, the party is an active member
     of an occupational pension scheme, the value of the
     benefits which he has under that scheme shall be taken to
     be the cash equivalent to which he would have acquired a
     right under section 94(1)(a) of the 1993 Act if his pensionable service had terminated at that date;
(*b*) where, on the relevant date, the party is a deferred
     member of an occupational pension scheme, the value of
     the benefits which he has under that scheme shall be taken
     to be the cash equivalent to which he acquired a right
     under section 94(1)(a) of that Act on the termination of
     his pensionable service valued as at the relevant date;
(*c*) where, on the relevant date, the party is a member of a
     personal pension scheme, the value of the benefits which
     he has under that scheme shall be taken to be the cash

equivalent to which he would have acquired a right under section 94(1)(b) if he had made an application under section 95(1) of that Act on that date; and

(*d*) where any benefits which a party has or may have under a pension scheme as at the relevant date are not valued in accordance with sub-paragraphs (a), (b) or (c) above, their value, as at that date, shall be such as may be calculated by the court by such method as it shall see fit.

(3) The value of the proportion of any rights or interests which a party has or may have in any benefits under a pension scheme as at the relevant date and which forms part of the matrimonial property by virtue of section 10(5) shall be calculated in accordance with the following formula—

$$A \times \frac{B}{C}$$

where—

A is the value of these rights or interests in any benefits under the pension scheme which is calculated, as at the relevant date, in accordance with paragraph (2) above; and

B is the period of C which falls within the period of the marriage of the parties before the relevant date and, if there is no such period, the amount shall be zero; and

C is the period of the membership of that party in the pension scheme before the relevant date.

(4) For the purposes of paragraph 2(a), (b) and (c) of this regulation, the value of any benefits which a party has under a pension scheme shall be calculated and verified in accordance with any guidance for the time being in force which has been prepared or from time to time revised by the Institute of Actuaries and Faculty of Actuaries and approved for the purposes of these Regulations by the Secretary of State.

(5) In making any calculation for the purposes of this regulation, regard may be had to any information furnished by the trustees or managers of the pension scheme pursuant to

(i) regulation 6 of, and Schedule 2 to, the Occupational Pension Schemes (Disclosure of Information) Regulations 1986;

(ii) paragraph 2(a) or, where applicable, paragraph 2(b), of Schedule 2 to the Personal Pensions Schemes (Disclosure of Information) Regulations 1987; or

(iii) regulation 4,

but this is without prejudice to any other information or evidence to which regard may also be had.

Information

4.—(1) The trustees or managers of a pension scheme shall furnish, within 3 months of being requested to do so, the information described in paragraph (2) below where—

(a) the member of the pension scheme is the pursuer or defender in an action for divorce or an action for declarator of nullity of marriage; and either

(b) that member has requested the information and has not previously received information under this regulation for the purpose of those proceedings; or

(c) the member has been required by the court to request the information.

(2) In the circumstances described in paragraph (1) above—

(a) the trustees or managers of any occupational pension scheme shall furnish in writing the information mentioned in regulation 6(7) of, and paragraphs 8 and 9 of Schedule 2 to the Occupational Pension Schemes (Disclosure of Information) Regulations 1986 to the member of the scheme requesting the information;

(b) the trustees or managers of any personal pension scheme shall furnish in writing the information mentioned in paragraph 2(a) or, where applicable, paragraph 2(b), of Schedule 2 to the Personal Pensions Schemes (Disclosure of Information) Regulations 1987 to the member of the scheme requesting such information.

(3) For the purposes of any information to be furnished under paragraph (1) or (2) above, the value of any rights or interests in any benefits under a pension scheme shall be calculated as mentioned in regulation 3.

(4) The trustees or managers of a pension scheme shall be entitled to recover from the member any reasonable administrative expenses incurred by them in furnishing the information under paragraph (1) or (2) above.

Notices

5.—(1) This regulation applies in the circumstances set out in section 12A(6)(a).

(2) Where this regulation applies, the trustees or managers of the first scheme shall, within 14 days after the date of the transfer,

give notice in accordance with the following paragraphs of this regulation to—

(*a*) the trustees or managers of the new scheme, and
(*b*) the other party.

(3) The notice to the trustees or managers of the new scheme shall consist of a copy of every order made under section 12A(2) or (3) imposing any requirement upon the trustees or managers of the first scheme and of any order under section 12A(7) varying such an order.

(4) The notice to the other party shall contain the following particulars—

(*a*) the fact that all the accrued rights of the liable party under the first scheme have been transferred to the new scheme;
(*b*) the date on which the transfer takes effect;
(*c*) the name and address of the trustees or managers of the new scheme;
(*d*) the fact that the order made under section 12A(2) or (3) is to have effect as if it had been made instead in respect of the trustees or managers of the new scheme.

6.—(1) This regulation applies where—

(*a*) section 12A(6) has already applied, and
(*b*) the liable party has transferred all his accrued rights for the second or any subsequent time to another new scheme.

(2) Where this regulation applies, the trustees or managers of the pension scheme from which the transfer is made to the other new scheme shall, within 14 days after the date of the transfer, give notice to the other party of—

(*a*) the fact that all the accrued rights of the liable party have been transferred to the other new scheme;
(*b*) the date on which the transfer takes effect;
(*c*) the name and address of the trustees or managers of the other new scheme; and
(*d*) the fact that the court may, on an application by any person having interest, vary any order under section 12A(2) or (3).

7.—(1) This regulation applies where—

(*a*) an order under section 12A(2) or (3) has been made imposing any requirement on the trustees or managers of a pension scheme; and
(*b*) some but not all of the accrued rights of the liable party have been transferred from the pension scheme.

(2) Where this regulation applies, the trustees or managers of the pension scheme from which the transfer is made shall, within 14 days after the date of the transfer, give notice to the other party of—

(*a*) the likely extent of the reduction in the benefits payable under the scheme as a result of the transfer;

(*b*) the name and address of the trustees or managers of any pension scheme under which the liable party has acquired transfer of credits as a result of the transfer;

(*c*) the date on which the transfer takes effect; and

(*d*) the fact that the court may, on an application by any person having an interest, vary an order under section 12A(2) or (3).

8.—(1) This regulation applies where—

(*a*) an order under section 12A(2) or (3) has been made imposing any requirement on the trustees or managers of a pension scheme; and

(*b*) there has been a change in the name or address of the other party.

(2) Where this regulation applies, the other party shall, within 14 days of the occurrence of the change mentioned in paragraph 1(b), give notice of that change to the trustees or managers of the pension scheme.

9. A notice under regulation 5, 6, 7 or 8 may be sent by ordinary first class post to the last known address of the intended recipient and shall be deemed to have been received on the seventh day following the date of posting.

Expenses

10.—(1) Where an order has been made under section 12A(2) or (3) imposing any requirement on the trustees or managers of the first scheme, the trustees or managers of that scheme shall be entitled to recover from the liable party such sum as represents the reasonable administrative expenses which they have incurred by complying with that order and, in the event of a dispute as to what constitutes this sum, it shall be determined by the court.

(2) Paragraph (1) shall also apply—

(*a*) where the order under section 12A(2) or (3) has effect, by
virtue of section 12A(6), as if it had been made in respect
of the trustees or managers of a new scheme, to the
trustees and managers of the new scheme, and

(*b*) where the order under section 12A(2) or (3) has been
varied under section 12A(7), to the trustees or managers
of the pension scheme who were substituted for the
trustees or managers specified in the order,

as it applies to the trustees or managers of the first scheme.

TABLE OF MATRIMONIAL PROPERTY AND RESOURCES[1]

PURSUER	£	DEFENDER	£
At relevant date:		*At relevant date:*	
(i) one-half interest in matrimonial home	96,937	(i) one-half interest in matrimonial home	96,937
(ii) one-half interest in Scottish Widows Insurance Policy ...	3,684	(ii) one-half interest in Scottish Widows Insurance Policy ...	3,684
(iii) 38.03% interest in C.C. Hornig & Son Ltd Executive Pension Fund	43,318	(iii) 61.97% interest in C.C. Hornig & Son Ltd Executive Pension Fund	70,588
		(iv) interest in Legal & General Pension Plan Policy	4,000
		(v) interest in Liverpool and Victoria Insurance Policy ...	2,200
		(vi) cash in Bank of Scotland	3,567.32
		(vii) shares in C.C. Hornig & Son Ltd	69,000
SUBTOTAL	**143,939**	**SUBTOTAL**	**249,976.32**
Less		*Less*	
(a) one-half liability to Bank of Scotland ..	1,763.71	(a) one-half liability to Bank of Scotland ..	1,763.71
TOTAL	**142,175.29**	**TOTAL**	**248,212.61**

---

[1] This is the table (revised) presented to the court on behalf of the defender in *Crockett v. Crockett*, 1992 S.C.L.R. 591.

180   *Divorce in the Sheriff Court*

At present date:	£	At present date:	£
(i) 14 Glenorchy Terrace, Edinburgh	100,000	(i) 10 Ventnor Terrace, Edinburgh	90,000
(ii) one-half interest in Scottish Widows Insurance Policy ...	6,449	(ii) one-half interest in Scottish Widows Insurance Policy	6,449
[(iii) 38.03% interest in C.C. Hornig & Son Ltd Executive Pension Fund	54,390]	[(iii) 61.97% interest in C.C. Hornig & Son Ltd Executive Pension Fund	88,628]
[(iv) personal jewellery	8,000]	[(iv) interest in Legal & General Pension Plan Policy	7,444]
		(v) interest in Liverpool and Victoria Insurance Policy ...	10,343
		(vi) shares in Abbey National	2,000
		(vii) cash in Bank of Scotland	3,567.22
		(viii) cash in Bank of Scotland	41,136.52
		(ix) shares in C.C. Hornig & Son Ltd	nil
		[(x) personal jewellery	8,000)]
SUBTOTAL	106,449*	**SUBTOTAL**	153,495.74*
Less		*Less*	
(a) mortgage	16,000	(a) mortgage	30,312
(b) one-half liability to Bank of Scotland ..	273.39	(b) one-half liability to Bank of Scotland ..	273.39
(c) cheque account overdraft with Bank of Scotland	2,000	(c) current account overdraft with Bank of Scotland	8,620
(d) legal fees	10,000	(d) legal fees	10,000
	28,273.39		49,205.39
TOTAL	**78,175.61**	**TOTAL**	**104,290.35**

*excludes (illiquid) pension(s) and personal jewellery

REPORTED CASES INVOLVING PRINCIPLES B to E[1]

PRINCIPLE B

Cases in which Principle B was explicitly considered include the following:

(1) *Petrie v. Petrie*, 1988 S.C.L.R. 390 (husband held not to have derived economic advantage from presence of wife in the home).

(2) *Kerrigan v. Kerrigan*, 1988 S.C.L.R. 603 (wife held to have derived economic advantage from husband's mortgage payments by increase in value of jointly owned matrimonial home).

(3) *Muir v. Muir*, 1989 S.L.T. (Sh.Ct.) 20 (husband held not to have derived economic advantage from wife's occupation of his house since separation).

(4) *Little v. Little*, 1989 S.C.L.R. 613 (wife held to have suffered economic disadvantage in the family interest by the interruption of her professional career in order to look after house and family for a period).

(5) *Tyrrell v. Tyrrell*, 1990 S.L.T. 406 (husband held not to have derived any economic advantage from any contribution by wife by increase in value of his pension since separation).

(6) *Skarpaas v. Skarpaas*, 1991 S.L.T. (Sh.Ct.) 15 (wife held to have suffered economic disadvantage in relation to her business because of need to look after injured husband).

(7) *Jesner v. Jesner*, 1992 S.L.T. 999 (husband held to have derived economic advantage from wife's contribution in looking after family home and caring for family).

(8) *Shipton v. Shipton*, 1992 S.C.L.R. 23 (wife held to have suffered economic disadvantage through her inability to work during the marriage).

(9) *Toye v. Toye*, 1992 S.C.L.R. 95 (wife held to have suffered economic disadvantage by giving up work which she could not readily resume).

[1] See Chap. 7, text accompanny nn.84–87.

(10) *Luckwell v. Luckwell,* 1992 G.W.D. 34–2005 (wife held to have suffered economic disadvantage where parties living in relatively remote area and wife not resuming work after children had left home).

(11) *Kelly v. Kelly,* 1992 G.W.D. 36–2130 (wife held to have suffered economic disadvantage: (i) as a result of giving up work to carry out home duties; and (ii) as a result of not exercising, at husband's urging, her entitlement to buy back pension rights foregone by her upon marriage).

(12) *Macdonald v. Macdonald,* 1993 S.C.L.R. 132 (wife held to have suffered economic disadvantage through having assumed greater economic burden of caring for children than husband hitherto).

(13) *Davidson v. Davidson,* 1993 G.W.D. 31–2000 (husband held to have derived economic advantage from gifts of money from wife).

(14) *Ranaldi v. Ranaldi,* 1994 S.L.T. (Sh.Ct.) 25 (husband held to have derived economic advantage through wife having taken in lodgers throughout marriage).

(15) *Louden v. Louden,* 1994 S.L.T. 381 (wife held to have suffered economic disadvantage by giving up work and losing earning potential).

(16) *Welsh v. Welsh,* 1994 S.L.T. 828 (wife's economic disadvantage in giving up well-paid employment to look after husband and children held to have been balanced by economic advantage from being maintained by husband and from enjoying the results of mortgage payments made exclusively by him in respect of jointly owned matrimonial home and by economic disadvantage suffered by him accordingly; but economic advantage held to have been enjoyed by husband in having exclusive use of house after separation with corresponding economic disadvantage to wife).

(17) *McCormick v. McCormick,* 1994 G.W.D. 35–2078 (wife held to have suffered economic disadvantage through having given up career as nurse and midwife to become a full-time wife and mother and to have continuing disadvantage in respect of securing regular employment).

(18) *Miller v. Miller,* 1995 G.W.D. 23–1248 (wife held to have suffered economic disadvantage by the loss of employment and career prospects on the birth of the parties' children).

(19) *Tahir v. Tahir (No. 2),* 1995 S.L.T. 451 (husband held to have gained economic advantage, and the wife a corresponding economic disadvantage, by his forcibly dispossessing her of her jewellery).

(20) *De Winton v. De Winton*, 1996 G.W.D. 29–1752 (husband held to have gained economic advantage from wife's financial investment in farming partnership which had allowed the firm overdraft to be lowered and certain improvements to be carried out at the expense of disabling her from dealing with her own money to her own profit — an advantage not cancelled out by her receiving her share of the partnership assets — and from her management of holiday cottages which had enhanced their revenue earning capacity to his financial benefit; but wife's contribution to the children's school fees not an economic disadvantage to wife nor, in any event, a corresponding economic advantage to husband).

(21) *Adams v. Adams (No. 1)*, 1997 S.L.T. 144 (wife's economic disadvantage in prejudicing her career by bringing up the parties' children held to have been counter-balanced by husband's greater contribution to household finances).

(22) *McVinnie v. McVinnie (No. 2)*, 1997 S.L.T. (Sh.Ct.) 12 (husband held to have derived economic advantage through childcaring contribution by wife and from portion of wife's receipts from sale of her interest in two houses).

PRINCIPLE C[2]

Cases in which Principle C was explicitly considered include the following:

(1) *Monkman v. Monkman*, 1988 S.L.T. (Sh.Ct.) 37 (economic burden held to be shared fairly by periodical allowance under s.9(1)(c) for wife until child about 20 years old).

(2) *Morrison v. Morrison*, 1989 S.C.L.R. 574 (economic burden held to be shared fairly by award to wife under s.9(1)(c) of two-thirds of value of matrimonial home and contents).

(3) *White v. White*, 1990 G.W.D. 12–616 (economic burden held to be shared fairly by relatively token compensation under s.9(1)(c) in the form of capital).

(4) *Millar v. Millar*, 1990 S.C.L.R. 666 (economic burden held to be shared fairly under reference to alimentary award in child's favour).

(5) *Shipton v. Shipton*, 1992 S.C.L.R. 23 (economic burden held to be shared fairly by award of greater share of matrimonial property).

---

[2] See Chap. 7, nn.88–91 and accompanying text.

(6) *Toye v. Toye*, 1992 S.C.L.R. 95 (economic burden held to be shared fairly by award of periodical allowance for three years).

(7) *Macdonald v. Macdonald*, 1993 S.C.L.R. 132 (economic burden held to be shared fairly by award of capital sum to enable need to provide accommodation for children to be met).

(8) *Proctor v. Proctor*, 1994 G.W.D. 30–1814 (economic burden held to be shared fairly by award of a modest capital sum and a periodical allowance for three years).

(9) *McCormick v. McCormick*, 1994 G.W.D. 35–2078 (economic burden held to be shared fairly by award of a periodical allowance for five years).

(10) *Adams v. Adams (No. 1)*, 1997 S.L.T. 144 (economic burden held to be shared fairly by resumption of alimentary payments by husband).

(11) *Maclachlan v. Maclachlan*, 1997 G.W.D. 8–339 (economic burden held to be shared fairly by substantial adjustment of capital in wife's favour — cancelled out by husband's entitlement under s.9(1)(a)).

PRINCIPLE D[3]

Cases in which Principle D was explicitly considered include the following:

(1) *Stott v. Stott*, 1987 G.W.D. 17–645 (wife aged 42 years and married for 24 years, no dependent children, in low-paid, part-time employment and not well educated, awarded periodical allowance under s.9(1)(d) for maximum period of three years from date of decree and at reduced rate for a further four years under s.9(1)(e)).

(2) *Dever v. Dever*, 1988 S.C.L.R. 352 (wife aged 27 years and married living with husband for six years, no children, in receipt of state benefits, claimed no maintenance since separation 18 months prior to diet of proof, awarded periodical allowance under s.9(1)(d) for six months from date of decree).

(3) *Petrie v. Petrie*, 1988 S.C.L.R. 390 (wife aged 42 years and married and living with husband for two years, one child, cohabited with husband for several years before marriage,

---

[3] See Chap. 7, nn.92–96 and accompanying text.

in receipt of state benefits, no skills or qualifications but fit for work, claimed no maintenance since separation in belief that her adultery disentitled her, awarded periodical allowance under s.9(1)(d) for one year from date of decree).

(4) *Atkinson v. Atkinson,* 1988 S.C.L.R. 396 (wife earning salary insufficient for her upkeep in the standard of life she enjoyed during marriage, awarded a periodical allowance under s.9(1)(d) for three years from date of decree).

(5) *Park v. Park,* 1988 S.C.L.R. 584 (wife married and living with husband for five years, no children, earning one-fifth of the total amount earned by the parties, awarded a periodical allowance under s.9(1)(d) to increase her "share" to one-third and allow her to adjust back to one-fifth, award being made for one year and at reduced rate for further year).

(6) *Muir v. Muir,* 1989 S.L.T. (Sh.Ct.) 20 (wife aged 47 years, no dependent children, in receipt of invalidity benefit, hoping to resume work as shop assistant, separated for four years and in receipt of maintenance during last of those years, awarded a periodical allowance under s.9(1)(d) for one year from date of decree).

(7) *Tyrrell v. Tyrrell,* 1990 S.L.T. 406 (wife married and living with husband for 18 years, in part-time employment and in receipt of maintenance for seven years after separation until date of proof, awarded a periodical allowance under s.9(1)(d) for one year from date of decree).

(8) *Sheret v. Sheret,* 1990 S.C.L.R. 799 (wife married and living with husband for two years, aged 42 years, with no immediate prospects of employment, supported only periodically by husband, awarded a periodical allowance under s.9(1)(d) for 13 weeks from date of decree).

(9) *Millar v. Millar,* 1990 S.C.L.R. 666 (wife married and living with husband for 10 years, one child in joint custody, wife in part-time employment and in receipt of interim aliment for herself and child, awarded aliment in larger amount for child leaving small shortfall, held not entitled to a periodical allowance under s.9(1)(d)).

(10) *Thomson v. Thomson,* 1991 S.L.T. 126 (wife dependent wholly for her financial support on husband for five years before separation, awarded interim aliment three years later against husband held to have taken every opportunity to avoid his financial responsibilities since separation, awarded a periodical allowance under s.9(1)(d) for three years).

(11) *Barclay v. Barclay*, 1991 S.C.L.R. 205 (wife aged 29 years, married and living with husband for some three years, no children, permanently disabled by multiple sclerosis and resident in a nursing home, not envisaged that she would ever be able to resume life in the community, awarded a periodical allowance under s.9(1)(d) for three years).

(12) *Gray v. Gray*, 1991 S.C.L.R. 422 (wife dependent to substantial degree on husband's financial support prior to separation, since then not provided with, nor had she sought, financial support from husband, held to have adjusted to withdrawal of support and no award made).

(13) *Kelly v. Kelly*, 1992 G.W.D. 36–2130 (wife with secure job and reasonable salary held to have suffered loss of support, account taken of fact that equal sharing of matrimonial property not possible and of wife's need to build up pension fund, wife awarded a periodical allowance under s.9(1)(d) for three years).

(14) *Murray v. Murray*, 1993 G.W.D. 16–1058 (wife aged 56 years, married and living with husband for 26 years, in part-time employment but held not to have sought to decrease her dependence on husband through choice, due to retire at the age of 60, held entitled to a further short period to adjust to loss of husband's support, awarded a periodical allowance under s.9(1)(d) for two years).

(15) *Louden v. Louden*, 1994 S.L.T. 381 (wife aged 45 years, married and living with husband for 17 years, one child (aged 17), wife unemployed and requiring to retrain to "get back on employment ladder", awarded a periodical allowance under s.9(1)(d) for one year).

(16) *McConnell v. McConnell*, 1993 G.W.D. 34–2185 (wife married and living with husband for 16 years, three children, wife almost exclusively dependent upon income from husband, held reasonable for her to have period of time to adjust to new circumstances created by determination of the litigation, awarded a periodical allowance under s.9(1)(d) for three years, reduced on appeal to six months (1995 G.W.D. 3–145)).

(17) *Wilson v. Wilson*, 1993 G.W.D. 38–2521 (wife a qualified vet but unable to work by reason of commitments to parties' children, had applied for teacher training course, awarded a periodical allowance under s.9(1)(d) for one year).

(18) *Buckle v. Buckle*, 1995 S.C.L.R. 590 (wife financially dependent on husband after 30 years marriage but undergoing one-year college course in office technology, held

entitled to a capital sum payable by instalments over five years, awarded a periodical allowance for one year under s.9(1)(d)).

PRINCIPLE E[4]

Cases in which the application of Principle E was explicitly considered include the following:

(1) *Stott v. Stott,* 1987 G.W.D. 17–645 (wife aged 42 years and married for 24 years, no dependent children, in low-paid, part-time employment and not well educated, awarded periodical allowance under s.9(1)(d) for maximum period of three years from date of decree and at reduced rate for a further four years under s.9(1)(e)).

(2) *Atkinson v. Atkinson,* 1988 S.C.L.R. 396 (wife with salary insufficient for her upkeep in the standard of life she enjoyed during marriage, but her income and substantial capital made it "quite out of the question" to make award under s.9(1)(e)).

(3) *Bell v. Bell,* 1988 S.C.L.R. 457 (wife aged 51 years, married and living with husband for 26 years, no dependent children, a qualified teacher but a full-time housewife and mother dependent on husband's support throughout the marriage, unlikely to find work affording reasonable remuneration, with sufficient capital to retain a nice house but with no income after divorce, awarded a periodical allowance under s.9(1)(e) until husband's sixtieth birthday or her own death or remarriage).

(4) *Muir v. Muir,* 1989 S.L.T. (Sh.Ct.) 20 (wife aged 47 years, no dependent children, in receipt of invalidity benefit, hoping to resume work as shop assistant, separated for four years and in receipt of maintenance during last of those years, awarded a periodical allowance under s.9(1)(d) for one year from date of decree, but s.9(1)(e) held inapplicable).

(5) *Tyrrell v. Tyrrell,* 1990 S.L.T. 406 (wife married and living with husband for 18 years, in part-time employment and in receipt of maintenance for seven years after separation until date of proof, had received substantial capital at time of separation, with further capital sum upon decree, held

---

[4] See Chap. 7, nn.97–99 and accompanying text.

entitled to award of a periodical allowance under s.9(1)(d),
but to no award under s.9(1)(e)).

(6) *Johnstone v. Johnstone*, 1990 S.L.T. (Sh.Ct.) 79 (wife aged
35 years, married and living with husband for 13 years, one
child, unfit for work because of epilepsy, awarded a
periodical allowance until her death or remarriage under
s.9(1)(e)).

(7) *McKenzie v. McKenzie*, 1991 S.L.T. 461 (wife aged nearly
60 years, married and living with husband for 16 years, no
dependent children, ran small business with low income
with possibility of income from lodger, entitled to small
pension at 60, held liable to be "seriously short of money"
notwithstanding award of capital sum if no maintenance
awarded, awarded a periodical allowance until death or
remarriage).

(8) *Barclay v. Barclay*, 1991 S.C.L.R. 205 (wife aged 29 years,
married and living with husband for some three years, no
children, permanently disabled by multiple sclerosis and
resident in a nursing home, not envisaged that she would
ever be able to resume life in the community, awarded a
periodical allowance under s.9(1)(d) for three years from
date of decree but, requiring substantial support anyway
from public funds, given award under s.9(1)(e)).

(9) *Kelly v. Kelly*, 1992 G.W.D. 36–2130 (wife with secure job
and reasonable salary held entitled to award of a periodical allowance under s.9(1)(d), but could not be said to be
likely to suffer serious financial hardship within s.9(1)(e)).

(10) *Murray v. Murray*, 1993 G.W.D. 16–1058 (wife aged
56 years, married and living with husband for 26 years, in
part-time employment with the prospect of retirement on
very small income at the age of 60, held entitled to award
of a periodical allowance under s.9(1)(d), accepted as
being liable to suffer financial hardship thereafter, but
such held not likely to be "serious" and award under
s.9(1)(e) refused).

(11) *Savage v. Savage*, 1993 G.W.D. 28–1779 (wife unfit for
work and unlikely to find employment, but awarded a "not
insubstantial" capital sum, husband's business drawings at
very modest level, no award under s.9(1)(e)).

(12) *Davidson v. Davidson*, 1993 G.W.D. 31–2000 (husband
aged 46 years with very restricted earning capacity and
without sound mental health, wife a very wealthy woman,
marriage of five years' duration, husband awarded capital
sum under s.9(1)(e) in respect of loss of home and
"considerable financial comfort" of wife's money).

(13) *Gribb v. Gribb*, 1994 S.L.T. (Sh.Ct.) 43 (approved by Inner House, 1996 S.L.T. 719) (wife aged 62 years, married and living with her husband for 38 years, in part-time employment and in receipt of modest pension payments, awarded transfer of property order in respect of husband's interest in the matrimonial home and held entitled to award of a periodical allowance until her death or remarriage under s.9(1)(e)).

(14) *Buckle v. Buckle*, 1995 S.C.L.R. 590 (wife financially dependent on husband after 30 years marriage but undergoing one-year college course in office technology, awarded a capital sum payable by instalments over five years, held entitled to a periodical allowance for one year under s.9(1)(d) but any financial hardship occasioned by the divorce held to be mitigated by capital award and so no award under s.9(1)(e)).

(15) *Bolton v. Bolton*, 1995 G.W.D. 14–799 (wife aged 60 years, married and living with husband for 33½ years enjoying a comfortable lifestyle, unemployed and with a nil earning capacity, awarded a substantial capital sum and interest to supplement certain resources of her own, held not entitled to award of a periodical allowance under s.9(1)(c), except for the period until payment of the capital sum, in respect that she would have sufficient resources to live comfortably).

(16) *Haughan v. Haughan*, 1996 S.C.L.R. 170 (wife aged 51 years, married and living with husband for 26 years, suffering impaired hearing, chronic high blood pressure and fibrositis and moderate to severe depression, in penurious circumstances with very restricted earning capacity, held entitled to award of a periodical allowance until her death or remarriage under s.9(1)(e)).

INDEX

address, accommodation, pursuers
36
admissibility of evidence, from
marriage parties 25
adultery
affidavits 27n14
photographs 131–132
evidence 26, 27, 28–29
intimations 3, 29
form 136
advertisements, citations 2
affidavits 8–9
adultery 27n14
court practice 130–134
curators ad litem 8
dates 132, 133
medical practitioners 8n31
parental rights 132–133
quality of evidence 133
styles
defenders 122–124
pursuers 110–113, 120–122
agricultural holdings, exclusion from
matrimonial homes 43
alcohol abuse 30
children 70
aliment
affidavits 134
children over 18 60n33
claims, defended actions 10
interim orders 71–72
appeals, simplified procedure 13
arrest *see* **powers of arrest**
arrestments on the dependence
47–48
specimen crave 104
avoidance transactions
intimations 6, 47
orders 46–47

bestiality 30
burden of proof, irretrievable
breakdown 27
businesses, matrimonial property 81

capital sums 74
affidavits 134
instalments 75
joint minutes 88
variation of orders 95

children *see also* **parental
responsibilities; parental rights**
alcohol abuse 70
contact orders 68
courts' duties 56–60
courts' powers 60–70
custody, form of consent 165
definition 62n36
domicile 16–17
drug abuse 70
expression of views 58–59
fair share of economic burden
86–87
reported cases 183–184
financial support 60
interdicts, removal from the UK 46
intimations 3, 4
forms 135, 137, 143
jurisdiction 55–56, 68–69
local authority reports 67
minimum intervention principle 58
orders, specimen craves 100
references to Principal Reporter
69–70
restrictions on decrees affecting
children 56–57, 133
sexual offences 70
third-party rights 60
welfare hearings 65–66
welfare principle 57–58
Children's Reporter, references
69–70
citations
advertisements 2
certificates 1
form 154
defenders' address unknown 1
display on walls of court 2
form 152
mental disorder 23
notices 2
simplified procedure 12
warrants 1–2
form 151
cohabitation, meaning 33
concurrent proceedings
discretionary sists 21–22
information 18–20, 65
jurisdiction 18–22
mandatory sists 20–21

191

consent
  custody of children, form 165
  dealing with matrimonial homes 52
  defenders to divorce decrees, forms
    157–159
  defenders to separation decrees,
    forms 160–162
  two-year actions 34
contact orders, breaches 68
contempt of court, breaches of
    matrimonial interdicts 38
corroboration, affidavits 134
craves
  specimen craves 97–105
  warrants for intimation 3
creditors
  intimations 6
  form 146
curators ad litem
  affidavits 8
  appointment 23
  discharge 24
curators bonis
  intimations 4
  form 137

damages, matrimonial property 79,
    81
decrees, minutes, form 168
defences, styles 116–118
defended actions 9–11
  attendance of parties 10
  claims for aliment 10
  financial provision orders 10
  matrimonial homes 10
  notices of intention to defend 10
  form 166
defenders
  affidavits, styles 122–124
  consent to divorce decree, forms
    157–159
  consent to separation decrees,
    forms 160–162
  five-year non-cohabitation, forms
    of notice 163, 164
  grave financial hardship 35
  mental disorder 22–24
  forms of intimation 137
delivery of documents, form of
    certificate 171
desertion, evidence 31–32
documents, delivery, form of
    certificate 171

domicile
  definition 16–17
  of choice 17
drug abuse 30
  children 70

evidence *see also* **affidavits**
  admissibility, from marriage parties
    25
  adultery 26, 27, 28–29
  corroboration, affidavits 134
  desertion 31–32
  exclusion orders 44
  hearsay, affidavits 130
  marital intercourse 28
  parole evidence, simplified
    procedure 13
  proof 7–9
  proof of marriage 14
  separation 32–35
  sufficiency 25–26
  undefended actions 25
  unreasonable behaviour 29–30
exclusion orders 41–46
  evidence 44
  intimations 46
  powers of arrest 39
  specimen craves 98–99
expenses, division of matrimonial
    property 84

family mediation 66
financial provision *see also* **capital
    sums; matrimonial property;
    pensions; periodical allowances;
    transfers of property**
  affidavits 133
  agreements 89
  avoidance transactions 46–47
  defended actions 10
  economic dependence of spouses
    87
    reported cases 184–187
  fair share of economic burden of
    children 86–87
    reported cases 183–184
  incidental orders 72–73, 74, 91–94
  judicial discretion 74
  principles 77–88
  procedure 74–78
  serious financial hardship 88
    reported cases 187–189
  specimen craves 101–104

guardians, intimations, form 141

habitual residence 18
hearsay, divorce affidavits 130
homosexual relations, intimations
 3n11, 30n33

improper associations
 intimations 3n11, 30n33
 form 150
incest, intimations 3n11, 4, 30n33
incidental orders, financial provision
 72–73, 74, 91–94
information, on concurrent
 proceedings 18–20, 65
inhibitions on the dependence 47–48
initial writs
 amendment when address becomes
 known 2
 specimen writs 106–129
interdicts *see also* **exclusion orders**
 breaches 38–39
 law reform 37n5
 meaning of matrimonial interdicts
 36–38
 removal of children from UK 46
 specimen craves 97–98
interest, incidental orders 93
interim interdicts, breaches 38–39
intimations 2–7
 address unknown 3, 7
 form 135
 adultery actions 3, 29
 form 136
 avoidance transactions 6, 47
 children 3, 4
 form 135
 creditors 6
 form 146
 curators bonis 4
 dispensation 2
 exclusion orders 46
 homosexual relations 3n11, 30n33
 improper associations 3n11, 30n33
 form 150
 incest 3n11, 30n33
 local authorities 3n6, 4
 form 139, 169, 170
 matrimonial homes 6
 form 148
 mental disorder 4
 form 137
 next-of-kins 3

 form 135
 pension trustees 6
 form 149
 persons with parental
 responsibilities, form 140
 polygamy 4
 form 138
 postponement 2
 rape 4
 residence orders 5
 s.11 orders, forms 141, 143
 simplified procedure 12
 sodomy 3n11, 30n33
 specimen craves 104–105
 transfers of property 6
irretrievable breakdown *see also*
 adultery; separation;
 unreasonable behaviour
 burden of proof 27
 desertion, evidence 31–32
 standard of proof 27

joint minutes
 affidavits 134
 styles 128–129
jurisdiction
 challenge, simplified procedure 12
 children 55–56, 68–69
 concurrent proceedings 18–22
 sheriff court 15–18

law reform, matrimonial interdicts
 37n5
lenocinium 29
life policies, matrimonial property
 79, 80
local authorities
 intimations 3n6, 4
 form 139, 169, 170
 reports on children 67
 form of request 142

maintenance orders 60n33
marital intercourse, evidence 28
marriage
 certificates 15
 proof 14
marriage counselling 14
marriage settlements, variation
 orders 93

matrimonial homes *see also* **exclusion orders**
  intimations 6
    form 148
  meaning 42n38
  orders
  dispensing with consent to dealing 51–53
    occupancy rights 49–51, 92
    sale 92
    transfer of tenancies 53–54
matrimonial interdicts *see* **interdicts**
matrimonial property *see also*
    transfers of property
  economic advantages of parties 85–86
  fair division 77, 78–85
    reported cases 181–183
    special circumstances 82–83
  meaning 78–80
  net value 80
  tables, specimen 179–180
medical practitioners, affidavits 8n31
mental disorder 22–24
  certificates by medical officers, Form F18 156
  citations 23
  defenders 22–24
    form 137
  evidence 26
  intimations 4
    form 137
  pursuers 22
  requests to medical officers, form F17 155

next-of-kin
  intimations 3
  forms 135, 137
occupancy rights *see also* **exclusion orders**
  orders 49–51, 92
orders *see also* **exclusion orders;**
    financial provision
  after grants of decree 94–95
  avoidance transactions 46–47
  before grants of decrees 71–73
  dispensing with consent to dealing with matrimonial homes 51–53
  incidental orders 72–73, 74, 91–94
  interim aliment orders 71–72
  occupancy rights 49–51
  parental responsibilities 61–69

orders—*cont.*
  parental rights 61–69
  property orders, specimen craves 99
  provision of details of resources 73
  s.11 orders 61–69
    form of intimation 141, 143
  supervision orders, form of intimation to local authorities 170
  transfer of tenancies 53–54
  with grants of decrees 74–78
ordinary causes, forms 135–171

parental responsibilities
  intimations, form 140
  s.11 orders 61–69
    form of intimation 141
parental rights
  affidavits 132–133
  s.11 orders 61–69
  form of intimation 141
parents, intimations, form 141
parole evidence, simplified procedure 13
pensions
  divorce, 1996 regulations 172–178
  joint minutes 88
  lump sums 74
    form of intimation 149
    payment orders 75
    variation orders 95
  matrimonial property 79
  trustees, intimations 6
  valuation 81
periodical allowances 74
  affidavits 134
  orders 90–91
  orders after decrees 95
  variation orders 95
photographs, affidavits 131–132
polygamy
  intimations 4
  Form 138
powers of arrest
  breaches of matrimonial interdicts 39–41
  expiry period 41n32
  recall 41
privilege
  accommodation address 36
  communications between spouses 27
productions, affidavits 131

proof 7–9
  of marriage 14
  requirement 7
property *see also* **matrimonial
    property; transfers of property**
  orders, specimen craves 99
pursuers
  affidavits 110–113
  mental disorder 22
  minutes for decree, form 168

rape, intimations 4
reconciliation 14
residence, habitual residence 18
residence orders, intimations 5
right to purchase, compensation
    53n30

securities
  intimation to creditors 6
  standard securities, consent of
      holders to transfers of
      property 76
separation
  consent to decrees, forms 160–162
  evidence 26, 32–35
  five-year actions 34–35
    form of notice 163, 164
  two-year actions 33–34
sexual offences, children 70
shares, matrimonial property 79
sheriff court, jurisdiction 15–18
simplified procedure
  appeals 13
  challenge of jurisdiction 12
  citations 12
  conditions 11–12
  intimations 12
  parole evidence 13
sists
  discretionary, concurrent
      proceedings 21–22
  mandatory, concurrent proceedings
      20–21
  proceedings relating to children 56
sodomy, intimations 3n11, 30n33
standard of proof
  breaches of matrimonial interdicts
      39
  irretrievable breakdown 27

standard securities, consent of
    security holders to transfers of
    property 76
supervision orders, intimations to
    local authorities, form 170

tenancies, transfer orders 53–54
transfers of property *see also*
    matrimonial property 74
  consent of third parties 76
  description of property 77n37
  intimations, form 146
  joint minutes 88
  variation of orders 95

undefended actions, evidence 25
unreasonable behaviour, evidence
    29–30

valuation
  incidental orders 92
  matrimonial property 80–81
violence 30

warrants
  citations 1–2
    form 151
welfare principle, children 57–58
witnesses
  compellability 27–28
  competency 27–28
words and phrases
  agreements 89n3
  child 62n36
  child of the family 43n42
  cohabitation 33
  domicile 16–17
  furniture and plenishings 45n54
  gift 78n42
  habitual residence 18
  hardship 35
  incidental order 91–92
  matrimonial home 42n38
  mental disorder 22
  non-entitled spouse 41n37
  pension scheme 79
  relevant date 78n41
  resources 73n15
  welfare 57

Les tribulations
d'une cuisinière anglaise

Margaret Powell

Les tribulations
d'une cuisinière anglaise

Traduit de l'anglais par Hélène Hinfray
Présentation de Mario Pasa

PAYOT

Titre original :
BELOW STAIRS

PRÉSENTATION

« Ne t'en fais pas, va ! Dis-toi qu'ils font leurs besoins exactement comme nous. »

C'est en ces termes qu'au début des années 1920 Mrs McIlroy, cuisinière chez le révérend Clydesdale, console Margaret (née Langley), alors âgée de quinze ans, lorsque Mrs Clydesdale lui reproche de ne pas avoir suffisamment astiqué les cuivres de la porte d'entrée. Car si elle vient d'« entrer en condition » comme fille de cuisine dans sa ville natale de Hove (Sussex), si elle doit par exemple disposer sur la table de l'office, comme avant une opération chirurgicale, tous les instruments nécessaires à la confection des plats, elle doit en outre accomplir dès l'aube nombre de tâches ménagères ingrates et épuisantes qui n'ont rien à voir avec l'art culinaire, notamment le nettoyage de cette maudite porte d'entrée et des marches du perron, ou encore le repassage des lacets. Et le comble, c'est qu'elle doit servir les autres domestiques !

À l'époque, il faut le plus souvent en passer par là si l'on veut devenir une vraie cuisinière, personnage aussi important qu'un majordome, si important, même, qu'en général seule une maîtresse de maison peut pénétrer dans son royaume sans lui en demander la permission – et encore, une fois par jour, le matin, pour l'élaboration des menus.

Dès l'âge de dix-huit ans Margaret va accéder à une telle fonction, mais pas chez les Clydesdale, pas en province : à Londres, où deux ans plus tôt elle a décidé de tenter sa chance. Elle cuisine pour une certaine Lady Gibbons, et peu importe que celle-ci soit un « vieux chameau » : la jeune fille n'a pas l'intention de passer sa vie à son service ; elle n'est pas de ces gens de maison trop zélés qui, plus snobs que leurs patrons, finissent par se croire de la famille. Elle, au contraire, ne tarit pas de griefs contre ceux qu'avec ses « collègues » elle nomme « Eux » : « C'étaient "Eux" qui nous donnaient trop de travail, "Eux" qui ne nous payaient pas assez, et pour "Eux" les domestiques étaient une race à part, un mal nécessaire. On était d'ailleurs leur principal sujet de conversation. »

Dans son journal, Virginia Woolf elle-même exprime son exaspération devant des servantes qu'elle juge « à l'état de nature, sans formation, sans éducation ». Les petits-enfants des Cutler, premiers employeurs londoniens de Margaret, ne pensent pas autrement quand à Noël les serviteurs reçoivent du couple des cadeaux moches et utiles : « [Ils] nous regardaient comme si on venait d'un autre monde. Et pour eux c'est sûrement ça qu'on était : une sous-espèce vivant sous terre. »

Sous terre, ou plutôt « en bas », car toujours la cuisine et l'ensemble de l'office sont en demi-sous-sol ou en sous-sol, y compris la pièce réservée au repos et aux repas du personnel, et cette configuration concerne aussi bien les maisons de ville que les châteaux. « En haut », il y a sur plusieurs étages le saint des saints : le territoire des maîtres, où les domestiques doivent œuvrer en sachant se rendre invisibles. Cette règle n'a pas totalement disparu en ces années 1920 ; voilà pourquoi le dixième duc de Marlborough, en visite chez sa fille sans avoir pu emmener de valets, ne comprend pas que sa brosse à dents ne sécrète plus de dentifrice automatiquement chaque fois qu'il veut s'en servir.

Margaret ne travaille pas chez d'aussi grands aristocrates, mais à ses débuts, un matin où elle a spontanément tendu le journal à Mrs Clydesdale, celle-ci lui déclare : « Langley, vous ne devez jamais, jamais, vous m'entendez, sous aucun prétexte, me tendre quoi que ce soit avec vos mains ; toujours sur un plateau d'argent. »

Ainsi « en haut » et « en bas » sont-ils deux univers tout à la fois séparés et interdépendants, comme dans les histoires de mondes parallèles. Entre les deux, le poste pivot de cuisinière offre une certaine liberté, d'autant que Margaret change souvent de cuisine et finit par préférer les remplacements, toujours en milieu urbain. On la voit dans des habitations plus ou moins grandes où vivent des gens plus ou moins riches, plus ou moins méchants (parfois même gentils) et plus ou moins nobles (souvent pas du tout).

En attendant le mari qui la fera remonter définitivement du sous-sol, sa bougeotte lui permet de perfectionner son art, d'obtenir de meilleurs gages, et nous vaut une galerie de portraits, une succession de décors, un enchaînement de mésaventures burlesques ou émouvantes qui confèrent à son récit toutes les saveurs d'un bon roman, le tout assaisonné de conseils divers pour faire briller l'argenterie ou accommoder (raccommoder, plutôt) du hareng fumé qu'on a jeté à la poubelle par erreur.

Au-delà du plaisir procuré par la lecture d'un témoignage au style « parlé » qui ne mâche pas ses mots, on mesure les changements qui s'opèrent en ce temps-là sur le marché du travail pour la domesticité anglaise. Dès avant 1914, l'appauvrissement d'une partie de la haute noblesse terrienne, l'allègement des corvées grâce au progrès technique (électricité, eau chaude courante, etc.) ou encore l'instauration de charges sociales pour les emplois manuels ont contrarié la demande de la part des classes aisées, et rares sont ceux qui, tel le duc de Westminster, peuvent s'offrir une ménagerie humaine de plusieurs centaines de serviteurs. Mais il reste indispensable d'en avoir pour asseoir un statut social ou l'améliorer. À l'inverse, ces métiers apparaissent déjà peu attirants au début du XXe siècle, notamment à cause de la privation de liberté qu'ils impliquent.

À la fin des années 1920, près des trois quarts des foyers qui peuvent s'offrir des gens de maison n'ont qu'une personne à leur service, or ce chiffre cache une autre réalité : les femmes, dont beaucoup ont participé à l'industrie de guerre, préfèrent se faire embaucher dans les usines, les bureaux et les commerces, mais elles sont frappées par le chômage plus que les hommes, et beaucoup se résolvent à devenir ou à rester domestiques. Elles sont 1,1 million en 1921, 1,3 million en 1931 et plus d'1,4 million en 1939 [1]. Cette population tend à vieillir et à devenir plus autonome :

---

1. Devenus très minoritaires dans la domesticité britannique, les hommes sont passés dans les années 1920 de 60 000 à près de 80 000, la moitié ne travaillant pas chez des particuliers mais dans des établissements comme les

en 1931, 1 sur 3 a plus de trente-cinq ans et 4 sur 10 ne logent pas chez leur employeur. Les plus jeunes aspirent à plus de mobilité et n'hésitent pas, comme Margaret, à quitter Mrs X. dès qu'elles savent pouvoir être mieux payées chez Mrs Y. Les autres sont plus stables mais ont appris à monnayer leur expérience et supportent de plus en plus mal toute ingérence dans leur vie privée.

C'est dans ce contexte que notre héroïne et narratrice, qui aurait préféré devenir institutrice, passe rapidement du statut de fille de cuisine à celui de cuisinière puis de cuisinière confirmée, grâce à une émulsion de volonté et de chance, à un concentré d'astuce et d'instinct. De toute façon, on ne peut rester fille de cuisine lorsqu'on s'appelle Margaret Langley. En débarquant à Londres à l'âge de seize ans, elle a bien senti que sa nouvelle patronne, Mrs Cutler, trouvait son nom « tout à fait déplacé pour une fille de cuisine. C'était un genre de nom pour faire de la scène, pas pour travailler au sous-sol ».

Mrs Cutler n'avait pas tort : près de cinquante ans plus tard, Margaret va faire de la scène à sa manière et devenir célèbre, mais sous son nom d'épouse, Powell. Il faut savoir que pendant ses années en condition elle s'est adonnée à la lecture, d'où les références littéraires qui émaillent son récit. Une fois ses enfants élevés, elle s'autorise à entreprendre les études que ses parents n'ont pu financer. Elle découvre l'histoire et la philosophie puis décide, à l'approche de la soixantaine, de préparer l'équivalent anglais du baccalauréat, qu'elle obtiendra.

hôtels et les clubs. (Les données de ce paragraphe sont empruntées au livre de Pamela HORN, *Life Below Stairs : The Real Life of Servants, the Edwardian Era to 1939*, Amberley Publishing, 2010.)

Interviewée par la BBC durant l'un de ces cours du soir qu'elle affectionne, elle se met à évoquer le vieux temps « en bas », pas toujours si bon. Un éditeur la repère sur les ondes, et en 1968 paraît le présent ouvrage sous le titre *Below Stairs*[2].

Non seulement c'est un best-seller, mais Margaret Powell, qui jusqu'à sa mort en 1984 signera d'autres titres dans la même veine, se fait très présente sur les plateaux de télévision. Avec son collier de perles et sa permanente immaculée, elle ressemblerait presque à « Eux », s'il n'y avait ses grosses lunettes pour lui donner un air de gentille institutrice et son grand sourire pour la distinguer des hautaines Mrs Clydesdale, Cutler et autres Lady Gibbons. Lorsque en 1971 elle encourage la consommation de poulet britannique dans un spot publicitaire[3], il faut bien convenir qu'elle est aussi chic qu'une duchesse !

Son livre vient d'ailleurs rejoindre aux éditions Payot ceux d'une authentique duchesse anglaise, Deborah Devonshire[4]. Après avoir donné la parole à quelqu'un d'« en haut », laisser s'exprimer quelqu'un d'« en bas » n'était que justice, surtout que l'humour dont l'une et l'autre font preuve réconcilie parfois leurs deux mondes dans des morceaux d'anthologie.

Autre point commun entre elles : le cinéma. Deborah Devonshire a souvent prêté pour des tournages son somptueux palais de Chatsworth, dans le Derbyshire. Les Mémoires

---

2. Littéralement : *Tout en bas de l'escalier.*
3. À déguster en boucle sur Youtube !
4. La dernière des sœurs Mitford, dont on pourra lire dans la « Petite Bibliothèque Payot » : *Les Humeurs d'une châtelaine anglaise, La châtelaine déménage* et *Duchesse à l'anglaise.*

de Margaret Powell ont inspiré en Angleterre trois séries télévisées : *Maîtres et valets (Upstairs Downstairs)*[5] ainsi que *Beryl's Lot*[6] dans les années 1970, puis *Downton Abbey* à partir de 2010, qui a repris avec succès le thème d'une triple saga – entre maîtres, entre serviteurs, entre maîtres et serviteurs.

Son créateur, Julian Fellowes, qui est aussi le scénariste de *Gosford Park*[7], a souvent déclaré devoir beaucoup à notre cuisinière : au travers de ses Mémoires elle a été la première personne à initier ce fils de diplomate au quotidien des domestiques et de leurs employeurs, « qui, dit-il, vivaient des vies si différentes sous un même toit ». Il a transposé cette matière aussi réaliste que romanesque des étroites et hautes maisons urbaines aux demeures aristocratiques de la campagne anglaise. En cela il est resté dans le sillage du double chef-d'œuvre que sont dans la littérature et au cinéma *Les Vestiges du jour*[8], avec son inoubliable majordome, Mr Stevens, incarné par Anthony Hopkins. Margaret aurait bien fini par dérider cet homme plus pudique qu'austère si elle avait fait irruption dans l'histoire, tout en pensant de lui ce qu'elle écrit d'un autre majordome de sa connaissance : « On aurait dit que le prestige de la classe pour laquelle il bossait déteignait sur lui. »

---

5. Diffusée en France à partir de 1975, et dont les deux saisons du remake (2010-2012) ont été boudées par le public anglais.

6. Chronique d'une femme de quarante ans qui suit des cours du soir en philosophie (1973-1977).

7. Réalisé par Robert Altman (2001) : autre intrigue mêlant maîtres et valets anglais, avec un meurtre en prime.

8. Le roman de Kazuo Ishiguro (1989) a été porté à l'écran par James Ivory (1993).

Par rapport à la plupart de ses ex-patrons, elle aurait sans doute trouvé que dans *Downton Abbey* Julian Fellowes avait un peu forcé le trait de la bienveillance chez Lord et Lady Bantham, qui habitent un château aux allures de parlement de Londres, mais elle n'en doit pas moins à la popularité de la série la résurrection de son récit.

Quand enfin elle a pu fonder une famille, elle s'est rendu compte qu'il ne lui servait à rien de savoir préparer un dîner de sept plats, et pourtant elle aurait certainement été fière d'apprendre que ce que préfèrent désormais les touristes dans les belles demeures anglaises, ce sont les cuisines. En revanche, elle aurait trouvé ses compatriotes un peu fous en découvrant que, pour une émission de télé-réalité reconstituant la vie dans un manoir anglais au début du XXe siècle [9], il y avait eu moins de candidats aux rôles de maîtres qu'à ceux de domestiques.

Et vous, qui auriez-vous choisi d'être ? Avant de répondre, goûtez ces *Tribulations d'une cuisinière anglaise.*

C'est en bas que ça se passe.

Mario PASA.

---

9. *The Edwardian Country House*, Channel 4, 2002.

Les tribulations
d'une cuisinière anglaise

I

Je suis née en 1907 à Hove, près de Brighton, et j'étais la deuxième d'une famille de sept enfants. Mon souvenir le plus ancien, c'est que les autres gosses avaient l'air plus riches que nous. Mais nos parents nous aimaient tellement ! Par exemple, une chose qui m'est restée c'est que tous les dimanches matin mon père nous apportait un illustré et un paquet de bonbons. À l'époque, un illustré en noir et blanc c'était un demi-penny, et un en couleurs, un penny. Parfois, quand j'y repense maintenant, je me demande comment il se débrouillait lorsqu'il était au chômage et qu'il ne gagnait rien du tout.

Il était artisan peintre, mon père. En fait il savait pratiquement tout faire, réparer les toits, poser du plâtre, mais son domaine c'était surtout la peinture et le papier peint. Par contre, dans le quartier où on habitait il n'y avait presque pas de travail en hiver. Les gens ne faisaient pas rénover leur maison à cette période de l'année. Alors pour nous c'était la saison la plus dure.

Ma mère faisait des ménages d'environ huit heures du matin à six heures du soir pour deux shillings par jour. Parfois elle rapportait des trésors à la maison : un peu de graisse de rôti, la moitié d'une miche de pain, un petit morceau de beurre ou un bol de soupe. Elle avait horreur qu'on lui donne quoi que ce soit. Elle avait horreur de la charité. Mais nous on était tellement contents, quand on la voyait revenir avec quelque chose, qu'on se précipitait pour voir ce que c'était.

Ça paraît sûrement bizarre, aujourd'hui, cette horreur de la charité, mais quand on était mômes il n'y avait pas d'allocations de chômage. Alors si on recevait quelque chose c'était forcément qu'on nous faisait l'aumône.

Je me rappelle que ma mère, à un moment où on n'avait qu'une paire de chaussures chacun et qu'elles avaient toutes besoin d'être réparées, elle est allée à la mairie pour essayer de nous en avoir d'autres. On lui a posé tout un tas de questions, et on lui a bien fait sentir qu'elle était coupable de ne pas avoir de quoi vivre.

Pour trouver à se loger, ce n'était pas du tout comme maintenant. Il suffisait de se promener dans la rue pour voir où il y avait des panneaux « À louer ».

Quand on était vraiment ric-rac, on vivait dans une ou deux pièces chez quelqu'un. Mais quand papa avait du boulot on louait la moitié d'une maison. On n'a jamais eu toute une maison à nous. C'était rare, les gens qui pouvaient avoir toute une maison à eux. Et en acheter une, alors là, on n'en rêvait même pas !

Je me demandais pourquoi maman continuait à avoir des enfants alors que la vie était si dure, et je me rappelle qu'elle se mettait drôlement en colère quand deux vieilles filles chez qui elle travaillait lui serinaient qu'elle ne devait plus en avoir, qu'elle n'avait pas les moyens de les élever. Un jour, je me souviens que je lui ai demandé :

« Dis, maman, pourquoi tu as autant d'enfants ? C'est difficile d'avoir des enfants ? »

Elle m'a répondu :

« Oh non ! C'est facile comme bonjour. »

Vous comprenez, c'était le seul plaisir que les pauvres pouvaient s'offrir. Ça ne coûtait rien, du moins au moment où on les faisait. Du coup certaines femmes avaient des enfants sans arrêt. Personne ne pouvait se permettre de faire venir le médecin, mais il y avait une sage-femme qui se déplaçait pour presque rien. Naturellement, ça coûterait des sous plus tard, mais les ouvriers ne pensaient pas à l'avenir. Ils n'osaient pas. C'était déjà bien assez dur de vivre au présent.

De toute façon, à l'époque on ne cherchait pas à limiter les naissances. L'idée, c'était justement d'avoir des enfants – un souvenir de l'époque victorienne, peut-être… Plus on en avait, plus on était vu comme un bon citoyen ; on faisait pour ainsi dire son devoir de chrétien.

Enfin, on ne peut pas dire non plus que l'Église jouait un grand rôle dans la vie de mes parents. Je crois qu'ils n'avaient pas vraiment de temps à consacrer à ça ; ou plus exactement ils n'en avaient pas envie. D'ailleurs on était plusieurs dans la famille à ne pas être baptisés. Moi je ne l'étais pas, et je ne l'ai jamais été. N'empêche qu'on devait tous aller au catéchisme le dimanche. Pas parce que nos parents étaient croyants, mais parce que pendant ce temps-là on n'était pas dans leurs jambes.

Le dimanche après-midi, c'était le moment où ils faisaient l'amour. Il faut dire que, chez les ouvriers, il n'y avait pas beaucoup d'intimité. Quand toute une famille vivait dans deux ou trois pièces, les parents devaient prendre quelques-uns de leurs enfants avec eux dans leur chambre, et s'ils avaient un peu de pudeur ils attendaient que les gosses soient endormis, ou carrément ailleurs. Mes parents étaient pudiques, ça c'est sûr : pendant toute mon enfance je ne me suis jamais doutée qu'ils faisaient l'amour. Je ne les ai même jamais vus s'embrasser, et d'ailleurs mon père était plutôt froid extérieurement. Du coup j'ai été stupéfaite quand ma mère m'a confié plus tard qu'en fait il était tout feu tout flamme avec elle. Bref, c'est seulement quand la marmaille n'était pas là qu'ils pouvaient se laisser aller.

Le dimanche après-midi, donc, après un déjeuner bien copieux (tout le monde essayait de faire un déjeuner bien copieux le dimanche), ils se mettaient au lit pour faire des câlins et un bon petit somme. Comme m'a dit ma mère, si on fait l'amour, autant le faire confortablement. Quand on prend de l'âge, ce n'est pas très marrant de faire ça dans les coins. Voilà pourquoi le catéchisme avait autant de succès ! Je ne sais pas si c'est toujours pareil…

Mon frère et moi on a commencé à aller à l'école la même année. En ce temps-là ils prenaient les gosses à partir de quatre ans. Ma mère m'y a envoyée en même temps que mon frère parce qu'elle attendait un autre enfant, et elle s'est dit que ça en ferait toujours deux de moins dans ses jambes.

Le midi on devait rentrer chez nous pour manger. Il n'y avait pas de cantine ni de distribution de lait. On emportait un morceau de pain beurré enveloppé dans du papier et on le confiait à la maîtresse, parce qu'en général on avait tellement faim que sinon on le grignotait pendant la matinée au lieu de faire ce qu'on nous disait. Et la maîtresse nous le redonnait à onze heures.

Je n'ai pas beaucoup de souvenirs de mes premiers jours d'école. En fait c'est vers sept ans que j'ai pris comme qui dirait ma place dans la vie. Ma mère partait tôt le matin pour aller faire ses ménages, et comme j'étais l'aînée des filles c'est moi qui devais donner leur petit déjeuner aux enfants. Remarquez, je n'avais pas besoin de faire la cuisine. On ne mangeait jamais d'œufs au bacon et on n'avait jamais entendu parler de céréales ou de choses comme ça. L'hiver c'était du porridge, et l'été juste du pain avec de la margarine et une lichette de confiture si maman en avait. On avait droit à trois tranches, pas plus.

J'ai toujours adoré aller à la boulangerie acheter une miche ronde avec quatre coins sur le dessus (une miche de Coburg*, je crois que ça s'appelait). On se bagarrait pour avoir un coin, parce que ça comptait pour un morceau alors que ça faisait nettement plus qu'une tranche.

Après je préparais le thé ; il était très léger, étant donné qu'on utilisait des débris de thé, ce qu'on trouvait de moins cher dans le commerce ; et puis je débarrassais, je faisais la vaisselle et je partais à l'école.

J'emmenais les deux plus petits à la garderie. Ça coûtait six pence par enfant et par jour, et le déjeuner était compris

---

* Selon la légende, ce pain en forme de couronne doté de quatre coins en relief se serait répandu en Grande-Bretagne après le mariage de la reine Victoria avec le prince Albert de Saxe-Cobourg-Gotha. En réalité il existait bien avant cette date, et doit sans doute son nom à l'un des nombreux boulangers allemands établis à Londres. *(N.d.T.)*

dans le prix. Je les déposais juste avant l'heure de l'école et je les récupérais l'après-midi en sortant.

Le midi je fonçais à la maison, je commençais à faire cuire les pommes de terre et les haricots, je mettais la table – bref, je faisais tout ce que je pouvais pour que ma mère n'ait plus qu'à servir quand elle rentrerait.

En général on mangeait du ragoût, parce que c'était ce qu'il y avait de plus nourrissant, mais parfois maman faisait un pain de viande. C'était drôle, ce pain de viande, quand j'y repense. J'allais à la boucherie et je demandais six pence de « parures de billot ». Vous savez, on ne se souciait pas d'hygiène comme maintenant, et les bouchers avaient devant leur magasin un grand étal en bois où toute la viande était exposée à la vue des passants… et aux mouches ! Quand ils débitaient les rôtis il y avait toujours des morceaux de viande qui restaient tout autour : c'est ça qu'on appelait les « parures de billot ».

J'en achetais donc pour six pence, plus un penny de graisse de bœuf, et avec ma mère faisais un pain de viande absolument délicieux – bien meilleur que ceux que je fais actuellement, alors que je mets pour cinq ou six shillings de viande dedans.

Dès qu'elle avait fini de manger elle se dépêchait de repartir bosser, vu qu'elle n'avait droit qu'à une demi-heure, et c'est moi qui devais faire la vaisselle avant de retourner en classe. L'après-midi, juste après l'école, je récupérais les deux petits à la garderie, je les ramenais à la maison et j'attaquais le rangement et les lits.

Jamais, au grand jamais, je n'ai eu l'impression d'être maltraitée. C'était comme ça, c'est tout. Quand on était l'aînée d'une famille d'ouvriers, on était censée aider.

Naturellement, le soir maman prenait la relève. Elle rentrait vers six heures et elle nous donnait à manger – la même chose qu'au petit déjeuner : du pain avec de la margarine.

Comme j'étais une fille je ne sortais jamais le soir, mes parents étaient très stricts là-dessus. Mais je lisais beaucoup, parce qu'il y avait déjà une bibliothèque gratuite à Hove. Et puis on trouvait toujours des distractions.

Mon grand frère faisait des spectacles de magie ; il était très doué, d'ailleurs. Un jour on nous a donné une lanterne magique avec des plaques – c'étaient des images fixes, bien entendu –, et mon frère s'est mis à inventer des histoires à partir de ça. On ne s'ennuyait jamais le soir. On avait toujours quelque chose à faire.

Contrairement à beaucoup de gens que j'ai rencontrés, à l'école je ne me suis pas fait d'amies pour la vie. Aujourd'hui il serait sûrement facile de dire que mes parents n'étaient pas sociables parce qu'ils ne voulaient pas qu'on ramène des copains à la maison. Mais vous savez, maman avait déjà assez à s'occuper avec ses enfants à elle. Évidemment, je n'ai jamais fait de fête pour mon anniversaire ; c'était inimaginable, des choses comme ça.

Il y avait deux filles, à mon école, c'étaient des copines, mais vous savez ce que c'est quand on est trois : il y en a toujours une de trop, et c'était toujours moi. Je crois que dans leurs familles on abordait certains sujets, la sexualité et tout ça, parce qu'elles avaient une espèce de code à elles qui les faisait hurler de rire, et moi je ne comprenais jamais rien. Je me souviens qu'une fois, j'avais treize ans à ce moment-là, une des deux – Bertha, elle s'appelait – n'a pas voulu venir jouer avec nous, alors je lui ai demandé :

« Pourquoi tu ne viens pas ? Tu ne peux pas courir ? »

Elle m'a répondu :

« Oh, c'est une histoire de cycle. De bicyclette, si tu préfères. Hier j'ai perdu les pédales, alors maintenant je ne peux plus rien faire. »

Et elles sont parties à rire toutes les deux comme des folles.

Mais moi, comme j'avais ma famille, je ne me tracassais pas. Et puis vous savez, on avait aussi la ville pour jouer.

II

Hove, c'était une ville épatante pour les enfants, surtout pour les enfants pauvres. Et ce n'était pas aménagé comme maintenant.

Prenez les pelouses du front de mer, par exemple. Aujourd'hui c'est pour les riches. Il y a un green de golf, un minigolf, des courts de tennis, des jeux de boules. Mais rien pour les enfants. Tandis qu'autrefois les pelouses c'était gratuit, il y avait juste de l'herbe et un abri avec des buissons tout autour, alors pour jouer à cache-cache c'était formidable. On pouvait venir avec son goûter et tout étaler par terre, l'herbe était propre ; et on ne se faisait pas chasser par les gardiens de square.

Dès qu'on sortait de la ville on était à la campagne. De chez nous, il suffisait de marcher quelques minutes et on arrivait aux fermes.

Les fermiers étaient très gentils avec nous. Ils nous laissaient faire notre petit tour, alors on traînait à la porcherie, on grattait le dos des cochons, on faisait « cot cot codec » avec les poules et on regardait traire les vaches. Souvent, la femme du fermier venait nous apporter un verre de limonade.

Il y avait des arbres magnifiques où on pouvait grimper. On aurait dit qu'ils avaient poussé là exprès pour les enfants.

Sur la plage il y avait des spectacles de Pierrot. C'était six pence ou un shilling pour une place assise dans un transat, mais inutile de vous dire qu'on n'avait jamais l'argent, alors on restait debout à l'arrière.

Dans mon souvenir c'étaient de bons spectacles – enfin, il me semble. Pas grossiers ni rien, vu que c'était pour un public familial.

Une dame montait sur scène, une soprano, et elle chantait une chanson d'amour déchirante qui parlait d'un fiancé qu'elle avait eu ; il était parti à cause d'un malentendu et elle espérait de tout son cœur qu'un jour ils seraient réunis. La moitié du public sanglotait, et nous aussi, à l'arrière, on pleurait à chaudes larmes. À l'époque les gens croyaient à ces trucs-là : qu'on pouvait mourir d'amour, se languir, regretter les occasions perdues et tout ça. On n'était pas blasé. Après il y avait un monsieur qui chantait, un baryton. Lui, c'étaient des chansons sur l'amitié, l'Angleterre, et puis *Hands Across The Sea*, une marche militaire américaine.

De nos jours on verrait tout ça comme de la petite bière, mais nous on adorait, et pas seulement nous : tout le monde !

Il y avait aussi les ânes et le monsieur qui s'en occupait. J'ai entendu dire depuis que les gens qui passent beaucoup de temps avec des animaux finissent par leur ressembler, aussi bien physiquement que dans leurs petites manies. Eh bien ce monsieur-là, il ressemblait à ses baudets. Il était vieux, petit, voûté, gris et très poilu. Ce n'est pas juste qu'il avait de la barbe. On aurait dit qu'il avait du poil partout. Je me suis souvent dit que s'il s'était mis à quatre pattes on aurait pu monter sur son dos en croyant être sur un âne.

C'étaient vraiment de pauvres bêtes, ces baudets. On leur donnait sans doute à manger, mais les ânes ça fait toujours pitié sauf quand ils sont très bien soignés, et eux ils n'en avaient pas l'air. Les gosses de riches ne s'asseyaient jamais sur leur dos comme les enfants normaux. Rendez-vous compte, ils auraient pu être contaminés ! Ils montaient à deux dans une petite carriole avec du cuir rouge partout. Ils avaient des nourrices pour s'occuper d'eux, et quand ils arrivaient c'était dans des grands landaus très chics.

Une fois qu'ils étaient dans la petite carriole, il fallait que le propriétaire marche d'un côté et la nourrice de l'autre. Vous n'auriez tout de même pas voulu qu'ils se fassent du mal, ces petits chéris ! Alors que nous, si on attrapait mal aux fesses à force de trotter sur le dos des vieux baudets, ça n'avait aucune importance.

Les gosses de riches n'avaient jamais le droit de jouer avec des enfants du peuple comme nous. Ils pouvaient jouer uniquement avec des enfants aussi riches qu'eux. Ils n'allaient nulle part tout seuls sans leur nourrice. Certains en avaient même deux, une nourrice et une aide-nourrice. Comme les pelouses étaient à tout le monde elles ne pouvaient pas nous chasser, mais si par hasard il y en avait un qui s'approchait de nous sa nurse lui disait :

« Ne va pas par là ! Viens ici ! Viens ici tout de suite ! »

Elles ne les laissaient jamais nous parler.

Remarquez, nous, on avait plutôt du mépris pour eux, parce qu'ils ne pouvaient pas faire les trucs qu'on faisait. Ils n'avaient pas le droit de salir leurs habits. Ils ne pouvaient pas jouer à cache-cache dans les buissons, alors que nous, oui. Ils ne pouvaient pas grimper sur tous les bancs et marcher sur le haut du dossier comme nous. En fait ils ne pouvaient rien faire de vraiment intéressant.

Ce n'était pas de leur faute, mais du coup on ne se mélangeait jamais. Ils jouaient à leurs mignons petits jeux avec des grosses baballes de couleur ; ils faisaient de la trottinette, et les filles poussaient le landau de leur poupée.

Nous on n'avait rien, à part peut-être une vieille balle de tennis, mais c'est fou ce qu'on jouait bien avec trois fois rien.

Peut-être que si on avait eu le droit de se mélanger on serait devenus copains, mais je ne crois pas, parce que depuis toujours on leur inculquait l'idée qu'ils étaient d'une autre classe que nous.

Par exemple, je me souviens d'une fois où je jouais sur la pelouse. Ce jour-là j'avais mis un manteau tout pelucheux qui était à ma grand-mère avant. Une de ces petites filles est venue vers moi et elle a commencé à faire des réflexions sur mon manteau. Sa nourrice lui a fait :

« Il ne faut pas dire des choses comme ça, ma chérie. Tu sais, ce sont de pauvres enfants, leur maman n'a pas d'argent. »

La gamine a répondu :

« Ah, d'accord ! Mais tout de même, elle a une drôle d'allure, non ? Je me demande si Mère n'aurait pas quelque chose à lui donner. »

Ça m'a carrément exaspérée, parce que je m'en fichais, moi, de ce que j'avais sur le dos, et je ne voyais pas ce qu'il y avait de mal à porter le manteau de sa grand-mère. Enfin, même si je me souviens encore de l'incident, à l'époque je ne suis pas restée vexée très longtemps. Il faut dire que j'étais toujours en train de faire quelque chose ou d'attendre quelque chose avec impatience – par exemple le cirque. Tous les ans, il y en avait un qui s'arrêtait à Hove.

III

Le meilleur cirque qui passait par chez nous, c'était celui de Lord George Sanger. Je suppose qu'en fait il s'appelait George Lord et qu'il avait inversé les deux noms, mais nous on croyait que c'était un vrai lord. Il était toujours tellement bien habillé ! On le trouvait splendide avec sa veste en cuir rouge pleine de franges, son immense chapeau de cowboy, sa culotte de cheval et ses bottes toutes brillantes qui montaient en pointe jusqu'au genou, avec une rangée de clous en métal sur le côté. Pour nous, c'était comme ça qu'un lord devait s'habiller, car ce costume était magnifique. On n'avait pas toujours de quoi se payer des places, mais on faisait tout notre possible pour réunir l'argent. Par contre on pouvait toujours aller voir les animaux : les éléphants, les lions et les tigres. Ça, c'était gratuit.

Une année où ils sont venus, je me souviens qu'ils ont annoncé une attraction sensationnelle sur leurs affiches : un homme était projeté par un canon à travers tout le chapiteau et il retombait dans un filet. Tous les soirs, on entendait un énorme « Boum ! » au moment où ils tiraient le canon.

Ça nous donnait encore plus envie d'y aller, mais comme c'était pendant une des périodes de chômage de mon père il ne pouvait pas nous payer l'entrée. Pour les enfants c'était six pence – enfin, pour des places tout au fond. Alors on s'est mis à récolter des sous. On est allés frapper à la porte des gens pour leur demander de nous donner leurs vieux pots de confiture. À la maison on n'en avait pas, des vieux pots. Quand on achetait de la confiture c'était un penny à la fois ; à l'épicerie il y avait des grands bocaux de trois kilos, et on nous la mettait dans une tasse avec une grosse cuillère en bois. J'étais copine avec l'épicier et il me chouchoutait, alors une fois qu'il m'avait servi mon penny de confiture il me donnait toujours la cuillère à lécher. Ce que c'était bon !

Donc on a récolté tous les pots de confiture qu'on a pu et on les a portés chez le chiffonnier. Je crois que c'était un penny les six. Après on est allés ramasser du crottin. On nous en donnait trois pence la brouette. C'était facile, à cause de la charrette municipale. Elle passait tous les jours dans les rues avec un pulvérisateur à l'arrière pour arroser la chaussée. Quand elle arrivait devant chez nous c'était la fin de la tournée, et le cocher entrait dans un café à côté en laissant ses deux chevaux dehors. Je ne sais pas si c'était parce que c'était la fin de la tournée ou parce qu'ils étaient fatigués, mais à ce moment-là ils nous faisaient toujours cadeau d'un gros tas de crottin. Avant d'entrer au café le cocher leur accrochait une musette sur le nez pour qu'ils mangent, et il y avait plein de pigeons qui venaient picorer les petits morceaux qui tombaient par terre. Nous on courait entre les jambes des chevaux pour ramasser le crottin avec une pelle, alors les pigeons s'envolaient et ça faisait sursauter les deux bêtes. Je me demande comment on ne s'est jamais pris un coup de sabot. Ça aurait pu nous tuer.

Parfois aussi on suivait un fourgon de déménagement dans la rue et on attendait qu'il s'arrête pour que les chevaux fassent gentiment leurs besoins. Du coup ça ne prenait pas très longtemps de remplir une brouette.

On était vraiment honnêtes, quand j'y repense. Le crottin, on ne se contentait pas de l'empiler. On l'aplatissait bien avec nos pelles, comme ça les clients en avaient vraiment pour leur argent. On était toujours étonnés, d'ailleurs, que des gens soient prêts à payer pour ça alors qu'il y en avait plein partout.

En vendant des pots de confiture et en ramassant du crottin pendant plusieurs jours, on a réussi à gagner une demi-couronne en tout ; à six pence la place, ça faisait pile le prix de l'entrée pour nous cinq*.

Et puis le grand jour est arrivé et ç'a été un vrai conte de fées. Une jeune fille en collant scintillant est entrée, suivie de quatre ou cinq éléphants. Les éléphants l'ont soulevée avec leur trompe, et puis elle s'est allongée par terre et ils l'ont enjambée.

Après c'était le tour des lions et ils ont rugi bien comme il faut. Pendant le numéro un gars a carrément mis sa tête dans la gueule d'un lion, mais moi je n'ai pas pu regarder.

Le trapèze aérien non plus, je n'ai pas pu regarder.

Mais pour nous le clou du spectacle c'était l'homme-canon. Le soir d'avant, on avait entendu maman dire à papa

---

* Petite révision : 1 shilling = 12 pence ; 1 couronne = 5 shillings. Cinq places à 6 pence font donc bien 2 shillings 6 pence, autrement dit 1/2 couronne. (*N.d.T.*)

32

que, quand le numéro avait tourné en Amérique, un soir le gars n'était pas retombé dans le filet et qu'il s'était cassé le cou. Nous, avec la férocité des enfants, on trouvait que c'était une bonne idée. Et si ça arrivait le soir où on y allait ? Après tout, ça faisait plusieurs fois qu'il réussissait : il était grand temps qu'il ait un accident, non ?

C'était le tout dernier numéro. On l'a vu grimper dans le canon en mettant les jambes en premier. On a entendu le « Boum ! » prévu et il a été éjecté dans un nuage de fumée. Je reconnais que je ne l'ai pas vu traverser le chapiteau d'un bout à l'autre, mais je suppose qu'il l'a fait. Il a atterri dans le filet sain et sauf, tout le monde a beaucoup applaudi et nous aussi. Mais bon, on aurait applaudi tout autant s'il s'était cassé le cou.

Quelle soirée merveilleuse on avait passée ! Cette nuit-là je n'ai pas fermé l'œil ; je repensais à tout ce que j'avais vu.

IV

Une autre distraction qu'on avait, et qui paraît sans doute banale aujourd'hui, c'était le cinéma, mais naturellement ça n'avait rien à voir avec maintenant. Par comparaison, les salles de l'époque étaient vraiment pouilleuses.

Celui qu'on aimait bien, c'était celui de la grand-rue. Les films qui passaient là étaient pleins d'action, et les feuilletons aussi. Il y avait des séances tous les soirs plus le samedi après-midi. Le soir les places étaient à six pence, neuf pence, un shilling ou un shilling trois pence, mais le samedi après-midi pour les enfants c'était trois demi-pence en bas et trois pence au balcon. Tous les enfants riches – enfin, plus riches que nous – prenaient des places au balcon, et ils nous bombardaient de pelures d'orange et de coquilles de noix.

Pour les gamins tenus dans les bras c'était gratuit, alors on portait comme on pouvait les petits de trois ou quatre ans jusqu'au guichet pour qu'ils ne paient pas. Et dès qu'on avait dépassé la caisse on les posait par terre et ils marchaient tout seuls.

On entrait dans la salle au moins une heure avant le début du film, et pendant tout ce temps-là on faisait un potin du diable. Il y avait une dame qui jouait toujours du piano. Elle s'appelait Miss Bottle* – enfin, nous c'est comme ça qu'on l'appelait. C'était une vieille fille entre deux âges ; elle avait les cheveux tirés en arrière et un chignon avec une espèce de brochette passée à travers qui devait être une épingle à chapeau. Elle avait une poitrine carrément énorme. Les femmes ne portaient pas encore de soutiens-gorge rembourrés, alors c'était sûrement sa vraie poitrine.

Environ un quart d'heure avant le moment où elle était censée arriver, on se mettait à taper des pieds en criant : « Miss Bottle ! Miss Bottle ! » Ça devait la flatter, et quand elle faisait son entrée elle avait droit à une ovation fantastique. Même les virtuoses ne devaient pas en avoir de pareilles ! En fait, ça nous était bien égal qu'il y ait de la musique et qu'elle joue du piano. C'est juste que quand elle arrivait on savait que le film allait bientôt commencer.

Pendant tout le temps qu'on passait dans le cinéma, il y avait un raffut infernal. Les bébés pleuraient, les gamins criaient à tue-tête. Mais ce n'était pas grave, c'étaient des films muets. C'est nous qui faisions les dialogues, en fait.

Juste avant que le film commence, le directeur montait sur scène avec un mégaphone et il hurlait :

« Silence ! Silence ! »

Juste après on aurait dit qu'il se mettait à dégouliner de bonté, et il disait en souriant jusqu'aux oreilles :

« Bon, les enfants, cet après-midi vous allez drôlement bien vous amuser. Vous allez voir deux films sensationnels

---

* *Bottle* signifie bien sûr « bouteille », mais aussi « biberon ». (*N.d.T.*)

et je suis sûr que vous allez vous régaler, alors en rentrant à la maison n'oubliez pas de dire à votre papa et à votre maman comme vous vous êtes bien amusés. »

À ce moment-là sa figure changeait, son sourire disparaissait, et il nous regardait d'un air féroce en disant :

« Et occupez-vous des bébés, hein ? Ne laissez pas ces petits sagouins mouiller les sièges ! »

Mais nous on s'en balançait complètement. On tapait des pieds en criant et personne ne faisait attention à lui.

Et puis le grand film commençait, et Miss Bottle jouait du piano tout du long. Quand je pense à ces pianistes, quelle endurance ils avaient ! Pendant les scènes de bagarre elle tapait de toutes ses forces sur les touches en enfonçant la pédale pour que ça fasse le plus de bruit possible. Pendant les scènes d'amour elle jouait des morceaux doux et romantiques, et les gamins sifflaient en mettant les doigts dans leur bouche. En ce temps-là on se fichait pas mal de l'amour !

Le feuilleton, c'était souvent un truc poignant. Pour nous c'était aussi un cauchemar, parce que certaines semaines on n'avait pas les moyens d'y aller. Papa était au chômage et il ne pouvait même pas nous donner les trois demi-pence de l'entrée. Ça arrivait toujours à un moment crucial du feuilleton, par exemple quand l'héroïne était suspendue en haut d'une falaise, ou ficelée sur des rails, ou attachée face à une scie circulaire qui se rapprochait petit à petit. Pile à ce moment-là l'écran affichait : « Rendez-vous la semaine prochaine ! » Combien de fois j'ai traîné aux abords du cinéma, la semaine d'après, en attendant que mes copines sortent et qu'elles me racontent ce qui s'était passé ! Ça ne m'a jamais traversé l'esprit que l'héroïne ne pouvait pas mourir, sinon il n'y aurait plus eu de feuilleton. Je leur posais un tas de questions du style : « Qu'est-ce qui lui est arrivé ? Est-ce qu'elle est morte ? Comment elle a fait pour s'échapper ? » Ah là là, ils m'en causaient du souci, ces feuilletons !

V

Évidemment, les boutiques n'avaient rien à voir avec celles d'aujourd'hui. Il n'y avait pas de supermarchés ni de libres-services. C'étaient surtout des petits commerces familiaux.

Il y avait un genre de grand magasin qui s'appelait le « Thru-penny and Sixpenny Bazaar ». Tout ce qu'ils vendaient coûtait soit trois pence, soit six pence. On pourrait croire qu'à ces prix-là il n'y avait pas beaucoup de choix, mais ils avaient une combine très astucieuse pour contourner le problème : ils séparaient les articles. Par exemple, une bouilloire c'était six pence et le couvercle trois pence mais ils n'étaient pas vendus séparément, alors ça faisait bien six pence et trois pence. Pareil pour les casseroles, les tasses, les soucoupes et ainsi de suite. Malgré tout, pour six pence on pouvait vraiment acheter plein de choses.

Le mont-de-piété tenait une grande place dans la vie des ouvriers. Tous les lundis matin les femmes portaient le costume de leur mari chez « ma tante » pour le mettre en gage et avoir de quoi faire la semaine. Le vendredi soir ou le samedi matin elles allaient le rechercher pour que leur mari puisse le porter le samedi et le dimanche. Et le lundi elles recommençaient. Quand les temps étaient vraiment durs on mettait d'autres affaires en gage, par exemple des draps et des couvertures. On n'en tirait pas grand-chose, mais même un shilling ou deux ça aidait à finir la semaine.

Et puis bien entendu les petits épiciers rendaient drôlement service. Ils étaient toujours prêts à faire crédit. Ma mère m'envoyait à l'épicerie avec un mot disant qu'elle désirait ça, ça et ça et qu'elle paierait à la fin de la semaine. Ils acceptaient, parce que les gens payaient toujours dès qu'ils pouvaient. Presque tout le monde était pauvre et comptait sur le crédit. Les magasins n'étaient peut-être pas aussi attrayants qu'à présent, mais on appréciait sûrement plus ce qu'on mangeait !

Prenez la boulangerie, celle qui faisait le coin de notre rue. Pour nous c'était le plus épatant des magasins. Ils faisaient cuire leur pain eux-mêmes, vous comprenez, alors le matin, en allant à l'école, on respirait la délicieuse odeur en passant devant. Même quand on n'avait pas faim, ça nous faisait saliver tellement ça sentait bon. Ils faisaient des beignets à un demi-penny pièce. Pas ces espèces de trucs qu'on trouve maintenant et où il n'y a que de la pâte. À la première bouchée on se dit : « Tiens, il n'y a pas de confiture », et à la deuxième : « Tiens, il n'y en a plus ! » Ceux-là étaient superbes, gras, bien dorés, enrobés de sucre en poudre et pleins de confiture. Le boulanger en faisait plusieurs fournées par jour. En fin de semaine, quand papa avait été payé, il nous en achetait quelques-uns pour le goûter. Ils étaient meilleurs que tous les gâteaux que j'ai pu manger depuis. Et le pain, donc ! Rien à voir avec celui d'aujourd'hui qui fait comme du coton dans la bouche ; on a beau le mastiquer pendant des heures, on a l'impression d'avaler de la pâte crue. Celui-là, il était aussi bon que du gâteau. Mais évidemment, côté hygiène ce n'était pas terrible : rien n'était enveloppé.

Quand j'étais gamine il y avait un pub pratiquement dans toutes les rues, et dans certaines il y en avait même un à chaque bout.

C'est surtout le samedi soir que les gens buvaient. Cette ambiance qu'il y avait ! Il fallait le voir pour le croire. Et ça s'explique facilement. Vous savez, les patrons d'alors n'étaient vraiment pas commodes. Avec eux c'était « Oui, patron », « Non, patron », et il fallait bosser du matin au soir. Et dur, encore, parce que sinon il y avait une demi-douzaine de gars qui attendaient pour prendre votre place. Mais quand un homme entrait dans un pub il était enfin son propre maître. Oui, à ce moment-là il avait de l'argent dans la poche, même si en principe ça devait lui faire toute la semaine. Alors il se lâchait. Il allait au pub, il exprimait ses opinions et il n'y avait pas de patron pour lui donner des ordres. Il pouvait dire ce qu'il voulait. En général les hommes arrivaient dès l'ouverture et les femmes dès qu'elles avaient couché les gosses. Mais pas mal de femmes emmenaient leurs enfants avec elles et les laissaient dehors, à la porte.

Le samedi soir vers huit heures, c'était la folie à l'intérieur. Tout le monde chantait, dansait. Il y avait toujours de la musique. Un gars jouait de l'accordéon, un autre du banjo ; quelqu'un faisait un numéro de chant. Les hommes juraient à se faire péter les cordes vocales, et souvent les femmes aussi.

Les enfants, eux, ils étaient dehors. Il y en avait dans des landaus et d'autres qui jouaient. Parfois un gamin ouvrait la porte en braillant :

« Maman, tu viens ? Y a le bébé qui pleure ! »

Alors la mère sortait, et soit elle donnait quelque chose au bébé, soit elle talochait toute sa marmaille pour l'avoir fait sortir, et hop, elle y retournait aussi sec. Naturellement, quand l'heure de la fermeture approchait il y avait presque toujours une bagarre générale sur le trottoir. Mais ils se battaient juste avec leurs poings en criant des grossièretés. Ils ne se faisaient pas tomber par terre, ils ne se donnaient pas de coups de pied dans les parties et ils n'utilisaient pas de couteaux ou de bouteilles comme on voit de nos jours.

Il y avait un homme, dans cette rue-là, sa femme ne buvait pas. Quand il sortait du pub, je vous garantis qu'il avait du vent dans les voiles. Arrivé en bas de chez lui il levait la tête vers la fenêtre de sa chambre, et s'il voyait de la lumière il savait qu'elle était couchée, alors il gueulait :

« C'est pas la peine que tu te mettes à pioncer, ma grosse, je vais avoir besoin de toi dans pas longtemps ! »

Pour les ouvriers il n'y avait rien d'autre que le pub comme distraction. Ils n'avaient pas les moyens d'aller au théâtre. Au cinéma, à la rigueur. En fait ils ne dépensaient pas tant que ça au pub, parce que la bière était très forte à l'époque. Quand mon père avait du boulot, le samedi soir il rentrait à l'heure du dîner, et il m'envoyait chercher une demi-pinte de Burton à l'annexe du pub où ils vendaient de la bière à emporter. Mes parents buvaient juste cette demi-pinte à eux deux ; ma mère disait que c'était comme boire du vin, que c'était tellement fort et tellement bon qu'ils n'avaient pas besoin de plus. De nos jours, vous pouvez en descendre des pintes et des pintes, tout ce que ça fait c'est vous remplir le ventre de gaz et de flotte !

VI

On habitait au bord de la mer, et pourtant la plupart du temps on jouait dans la rue. Ça se fait encore un peu, mais à l'époque on jouait à de vrais jeux, et ce qui était formidable c'est qu'on avait toute la chaussée pour nous, pas juste le trottoir. Il faut dire qu'il n'y avait pas beaucoup de circulation.

À Pâques, par exemple, on sautait à la corde dehors. On sortait une longue corde à échafaudages qui faisait toute la largeur de la rue et c'étaient les mères qui tournaient. Tous les enfants qui voulaient pouvaient en profiter, et on était parfois une douzaine à sauter en même temps en chantant : « À la soupe, soupe, soupe, au bouillon, -llon, -llon... »

On jouait aussi aux boutons. Ma mère s'en faisait du mauvais sang, en automne, quand c'était la saison des boutons ! On dessinait un carré à la craie sur le trottoir devant la maison et on lançait les boutons à l'intérieur. Le premier qui réussissait à mettre le sien dans le carré en faisant sortir celui de quelqu'un d'autre gagnait tous les boutons. Moi j'étais complètement nulle à ce jeu-là.

Après venait le temps de la marelle. On dessinait un long rectangle à la craie sur le trottoir et on le divisait en carrés qu'on numérotait de un à douze. On devait d'abord lancer son caillou dans le carré numéro un, sauter sur un pied dans ce carré-là, ramasser le caillou et faire tout le circuit à cloche-pied sans toucher les lignes. Après on lançait son caillou, on sautait et on ramassait le caillou dans le carré numéro deux, on refaisait tout le circuit et ainsi de suite jusqu'à ce qu'on ait lancé son caillou dans tous les carrés. Si on posait le pied par terre ou si on n'arrivait pas à ramasser le caillou, on était éliminé.

Un jeu que tout le monde adorait, c'était les billes. Avec le talon on faisait un trou dans la chaussée à environ deux mètres du caniveau. Il fallait d'abord mettre les billes dans le trou, et après c'était comme pour les boutons. On jouait aussi au cerceau. Ma tante m'avait acheté le plus grand qu'on trouvait dans le commerce, et j'avais une baguette en fer avec un crochet pour le diriger, alors je courais dans les rues en le poussant devant moi. On n'avait pas besoin de faire attention aux voitures, tandis que maintenant, une gamine qui courrait comme ça, elle ne ferait pas de vieux os.

Et puis évidemment on jouait à la toupie. C'était formidable, comme jeu : il suffisait d'enrouler une ficelle autour et après, en tirant dessus d'un coup sec, on pouvait envoyer la toupie à l'autre bout de la rue. Parfois on collait des petits bouts de papier coloriés dessus, comme ça, quand on la lançait, ça faisait un arc-en-ciel-tourbillon.

Plus tard dans la saison, on allait dans les collines ramasser des marrons pour jouer aux *conkers**. Ça ne coûtait rien, et quand on n'avait plus de munitions on pouvait toujours aller en rechercher.

Je ne veux pas non plus vous donner l'impression qu'on passait notre vie à jouer. La plupart du temps il y avait école, et les vacances n'étaient pas aussi longues que maintenant. Mais moi j'aimais bien aller à l'école, parce que j'avais plutôt de bons résultats. Ça ne m'a jamais paru difficile, sauf des matières comme le dessin, le tricot et la couture – qui d'ailleurs ne m'ont pas servi du tout. Ce que je détestais le plus, c'était la couture. Il faut dire qu'on nous faisait faire des choses vraiment moches : des chemises de jour et des culottes bouffantes – les sous-vêtements féminins de l'époque. Et en calicot, en plus ! Les chemises étaient amples, à manches courtes, et elles descendaient jusqu'aux genoux. Les culottes étaient larges et boutonnées par-derrière. Je me demande qui pouvait bien acheter des horreurs pareilles. Je suppose qu'on les donnait à l'hospice ; moi, en tout cas, je n'en ai jamais rapporté à la maison. Il y avait toujours des tas de fronces et il fallait qu'elles soient bien régulières. Ce que j'étais nulle pour ça ! D'abord, je n'ai jamais réussi à me servir d'un dé à coudre ; alors forcément je me piquais les doigts et je mettais des taches de sang sur le tissu. Au début le sous-vêtement était blanc, mais le temps que je l'aie fini il était rouge et noir. Pas étonnant : les cabinets de la cour étaient carrément rudimentaires, et il n'y avait rien pour se

---

* Jeu typiquement britannique opposant deux adversaires munis d'un marron d'Inde troué et attaché au bout d'une ficelle. Chacun à son tour doit essayer de casser le marron de l'autre. *(N.d.T.)*

laver les mains. Alors quand j'allais en couture après la récréation j'avais les mains dégoûtantes.

En chant aussi j'étais nulle. Je me souviens encore du concert de l'école. Il y en avait un tous les ans, et comme j'avais toujours un peu la grosse tête, un jour j'ai voulu présenter quelque chose. La maîtresse m'a dit :

« Tu chantes faux, Margaret, mais je sais ce que tu pourrais faire : tu pourrais raconter une histoire drôle. Je vais te l'écrire et tu n'auras qu'à l'apprendre par cœur. »

C'était l'histoire d'un gars qui entrait dans un restaurant et qui voulait du chou aux lardons, mais il s'emmêlait les pinceaux et finalement il demandait du loup aux chardons. Moi je trouvais ça rigolo. Ma famille aussi. Apparemment ils comprenaient la blague. Mais le jour du spectacle, quand je suis montée sur l'estrade, je me suis mise à la débiter comme un perroquet et je me suis complètement embrouillée dans mes lardons et mes chardons. À la fin j'ai attendu les rires, mais personne n'a ri à part les maîtresses. Elles, elles étaient obligées. C'était horrible. Je n'ai jamais été aussi vexée de ma vie. Je suis devenue rouge comme une tomate et je suis sortie en trombe. Après ça je n'ai plus jamais rien présenté. Ils étaient franchement mal élevés, non ? Moi je trouve qu'ils auraient dû rire, surtout que c'était gratuit.

Mais ce qui était formidable à l'école, c'est qu'on devait apprendre. À mon avis il n'y a rien de plus important que de savoir lire, écrire et compter. C'est de ces trois choses-là qu'on a besoin si on veut travailler et gagner sa vie. Nous, on nous forçait à apprendre, et je pense que les enfants, il faut les forcer. Je ne crois pas aux théories comme quoi « s'ils n'en ont pas envie ça ne leur apportera rien ». Bien sûr que ça leur apportera quelque chose. Nous, notre maîtresse venait nous donner une calotte ou une bonne gifle quand elle nous voyait bayer aux corneilles. Et croyez-moi, quand on sortait de l'école on sortait avec quelque chose. On en savait assez pour se débrouiller dans la vie. Ça ne veut pas dire qu'on avait une idée de ce qu'on ferait. On savait tous que quand on aurait fini l'école il faudrait qu'on fasse quelque chose, mais je ne crois pas qu'on rêvait de faire tel ou tel métier en particulier.

VII

J'ai réussi le concours d'entrée au collège à treize ans. On devait écrire sur sa copie ce qu'on voulait faire comme métier, et moi j'ai mis que je voulais être institutrice. Mes parents sont allés voir la directrice de mon école, mais quand ils ont su que je ne gagnerais pas un sou avant dix-huit ans et que jusque-là ils devraient non seulement me nourrir mais payer mes livres et mes vêtements, ils ont dit qu'ils ne pouvaient pas. En ce temps-là, vous comprenez, il n'y avait pas de bourses d'État.

J'ai été autorisée à quitter l'école parce que j'étais déjà en dernière année, et que si j'étais restée un an de plus j'aurais refait exactement les mêmes choses.

Quand j'y repense, j'aurais bien aimé pouvoir continuer l'école, mais sur le moment, franchement, ça ne m'a pas dérangée d'arrêter. Je n'ai pas trouvé que mes parents étaient durs ; je savais bien que je devais aller bosser et qu'on avait terriblement besoin d'argent. J'avais connu la honte d'être pauvre. Je me rappelle quand j'avais sept ans, c'était au début de la Grande Guerre. Papa n'avait pas encore été appelé, mais personne ne faisait refaire ses peintures : les hommes étaient à l'armée et tout le monde était fauché.

À ce moment-là, la ville de Hove a mis en place la soupe populaire. Ça se passait à Sheridan Terrace, dans un bâtiment en pierre. Il y avait deux marmites sur un poêle à charbon et pour en avoir il fallait faire la queue à midi : c'était le seul moment où ils servaient. Cette soupe, elle était infecte – de la soupe aux pois avec presque rien dedans. Je suis sûre que c'est le genre de cochonnerie qu'on donnait à Oliver Twist. Moi je devais y aller avec un broc de toilette, et maman ne l'a jamais su, mais j'avais honte parce qu'il était blanc avec des fleurs roses. Les autres enfants avaient des brocs en fonte émaillée que je trouvais beaucoup mieux. Et croyez-moi, ce n'était pas évident de marcher après dans la rue avec ce grand machin plein de soupe aux pois en faisant semblant que je n'étais pas allée là-bas pour l'avoir gratuitement et qu'on ne m'avait pas fait l'aumône. Je n'ai jamais dit à maman à quel point ça me faisait honte. De toute façon il n'y avait personne d'autre pour y aller.

Quand mon père a été appelé en 1916, l'allocation militaire qu'on recevait, c'était une vraie misère. Juste de quoi ne pas crever de faim.

Et puis le charbon est devenu rare. Si on avait une gazinière on ne pouvait même pas en toucher vingt-cinq kilos. Alors je devais aller régulièrement à la mairie, toute gamine que j'étais, pour demander un bon. Je jurais mes grands dieux qu'on n'avait pas de gazinière, qu'on n'en avait jamais eu, qu'on faisait toute la cuisine à la cheminée – et tout ça sans me démonter. Étonnez-vous ensuite qu'on devienne malin en grandissant ! Une fois que j'avais le bon, il fallait que j'aille directement au dépôt où arrivaient les trains et que je fasse la queue. C'était l'hiver, il faisait un froid de canard, j'avais l'estomac vide, et après je devais rentrer en poussant le vieux landau où on mettait le charbon. Un jour je me suis évanouie tellement j'étais frigorifiée. Des gens m'ont ramassée et emmenée chez eux. Ils m'ont donné à manger et une pièce de six pence, mais il a quand même fallu que je pousse le landau jusqu'à la maison.

Avec mon père parti, la vie était incroyablement dure. Ma mère se confiait à moi, sa fille aînée. Un jour, je me souviens qu'on n'avait plus rien pour se chauffer et pas d'argent pour acheter du charbon. J'ai dit à maman :

« Tu n'as qu'à décrocher tout ce qui est en bois et on va faire un feu avec. »

Alors elle a enlevé toutes les étagères des murs, elle a même démonté la rampe de l'escalier. Des trucs pareils ça vous endurcit, moi je vous le dis !

Avec les commerçants aussi j'avais pris comme qui dirait des manières d'adulte. Avec le boucher, surtout ; c'était un de mes préférés. J'y allais en fin de semaine et je lui disais :

« Je voudrais le plus gros rôti que vous avez pour un shilling.

— Bon, mais tu as apporté le papier, au moins ?

— Oui, oui, bien sûr. J'ai pris un ticket de bus pour l'emballer. Ça devrait suffire pour un de vos rôtis. »

Un matin sur deux ma mère nous réveillait à six heures, mon frère et moi. Elle nous donnait six pence et une taie d'oreiller, et on allait à la boulangerie Forfar, dans Church Street. Ça n'ouvrait pas avant huit heures, mais plus on arrivait tôt plus on avait du bon pain. Le trajet nous prenait à peu près vingt minutes, alors une fois sur place on poireautait longtemps dehors.

Si on était les premiers de la queue on regardait par la fente de la boîte aux lettres pour voir ce qu'ils avaient cuit ce jour-là. C'étaient le plus souvent des grandes miches plates de pain bis. On appelait ça des pains de vache, parce que ça ressemblait aux bouses qu'on voyait dans les champs – surtout quand quelqu'un avait marché dedans !

Parfois on apercevait un pain aux raisins, et si on réussissait à en avoir un c'était carrément la fête.

En échange de nos six pence, le boulanger remplissait pratiquement la taie d'oreiller.

Le meilleur de tout, c'étaient les petits pains. Quand il nous en mettait on les mangeait sur le chemin du retour et on ne le disait pas à maman. On avait une de ces faims ! On s'était levés à six heures, on avait fait la queue dehors dans le froid, alors pour nous, ces petits pains, c'était le paradis sur Terre.

La meilleure chose qui nous soit arrivée pendant la guerre, à nous et aux gens de notre quartier, c'est quand on nous a donné des soldats à loger.

Ma mère en a eu trois. Un Anglais, un Écossais et un Irlandais. Mais l'Irlandais elle a été obligée de s'en séparer : il faisait vraiment trop de raffut.

Je ne sais pas combien c'était payé, mais j'ai remarqué qu'on vivait mieux. Maman m'a dit que mon père n'était pas emballé par l'idée. Vous comprenez, elle était jolie et lui il était en France à ce moment-là, donc il ne pouvait rien faire.

Ça nous a fait un sacré changement. Du jour au lendemain, tout le monde a eu de nouvelles affaires. Même le colporteur a été payé.

C'était un gars qui faisait du porte-à-porte pour vendre des draps et des taies d'oreiller, des bottes et des chaussures, des trucs comme ça, et il les transportait dans une grande valise. On lui donnait tant par semaine pour les articles qu'on lui prenait, et on les payait un peu plus cher parce qu'il devait attendre son argent. On ne signait pas de contrat, c'était juste écrit dans un cahier. Nous vendre sa marchandise, c'était facile ; tout le monde pouvait lui en acheter. Mais après il s'agissait de trouver les sous, et je vous garantis que c'était une autre histoire. Quand ma mère n'avait pas de quoi payer je me mettais en haut des marches pour guetter le colporteur. Dès que je le voyais arriver je me précipitais à l'intérieur en criant : « Maman, le voilà ! » et elle allait se cacher. Il frappait à la porte et je lui ouvrais en disant : « Maman est sortie. » Il ne me croyait pas, alors il devenait très grossier, mais à part ça qu'est-ce qu'il pouvait faire ? Avec le gars qui venait encaisser le loyer c'était pareil. On n'avait tout bonnement pas l'argent.

Je faisais souvent des cauchemars à cause du loyer. J'avais peur qu'on nous mette dehors. On finissait toujours par payer, mais le problème c'est qu'on accumulait les dettes. Du coup, quand mon père retrouvait du boulot on était fauchés quand même, finalement, parce qu'il fallait qu'on rembourse ce qu'on avait acheté à crédit pendant qu'il était au chômage.

VIII

J'ai commencé à travailler une semaine après avoir quitté l'école. Je faisais le ménage pour un couple de personnes âgées dans une petite maison de plain-pied. La vieille dame était pratiquement invalide : elle était paralysée des jambes et du bassin. Je bossais de sept heures du matin jusqu'à une heure, tous les jours même le dimanche, pour dix shillings par semaine. Je n'étais pas nourrie le midi – c'est bien pour ça qu'ils me faisaient finir à une heure, au moment où ils se mettaient à table –, mais j'avais droit à un petit déjeuner.

À l'époque je n'y pensais pas, mais il était plutôt bizarre, ce petit déjeuner. En fait c'étaient les restes de la veille au soir, et ça pouvait être n'importe quoi : une crème au lait, des macaronis au fromage ou du hachis Parmentier. Mais moi ça m'était bien égal. J'ingurgitais tout ce qu'on me donnait, parce que plus je mangeais là-bas moins ma mère aurait à me nourrir. Mon problème, à ce moment-là, c'est que j'avais tout le temps faim. Je n'avais que treize ans, mais comme j'étais très grande j'avais un appétit incroyable. Et naturellement plus je travaillais plus j'étais affamée. Ma mère, ça la mettait drôlement en colère, ce petit déjeuner. Elle disait que ce n'était pas normal qu'on me donne des trucs pareils, que j'aurais dû avoir des œufs au bacon et pas des vieux rogatons. Mais moi, pourvu que je mange, je me fichais pas mal de ce qu'il y avait dans mon assiette.

Je ne suis pas restée très longtemps à cette place, principalement parce que je me suis mise à avoir des douleurs dans les jambes. Je commençais sûrement à me former. Je me rappelle qu'un matin où j'avais mal j'ai expliqué au monsieur que je ne pouvais plus travailler : mes jambes me faisaient trop souffrir. Il m'a donné un flacon de liniment en me disant de les frictionner avec et que ça allait me faire du bien, vu que c'était un remède pour les chevaux. Ça m'a mise hors de moi. Je pouvais à peine marcher ! Du coup je n'y suis pas retournée.

La première année j'ai fait une douzaine de places en tout. Ces petits boulots de femme de ménage, c'était toujours pareil. Comme j'étais très jeune on me payait au lance-pierre, mais comme en même temps j'avais l'air très costaud on me donnait plein de travail.

Il y a une place où je ne suis restée qu'une semaine. Le boulot consistait à pousser une vieille dame acariâtre dans une chaise roulante. Vu sa façon aristocratique de parler, ç'avait sûrement été une personnalité dans le temps jadis, mais là elle n'avait plus qu'une vieille servante pour s'occuper d'elle et de sa grande maison.

Tous les matins, il fallait que je l'aide à s'installer dans sa chaise roulante. Ce n'était pas une mince affaire, croyez-moi, entre les bonnets, les capes et les bottines à boutons, et pendant tout ce temps-là elle n'arrêtait pas de me chercher des crosses. Une fois qu'elle était bien calée dans sa chaise je la poussais jusqu'aux magasins, et je devais y entrer en disant :

« Mrs Graham est là dehors. Pouvez-vous venir prendre sa commande, s'il vous plaît ? »

Vous imaginez ça, de nos jours, entrer dans une boutique en demandant au vendeur de sortir prendre une commande ? Eh bien elle avait beau être fauchée comme les blés, vu ses manières de duchesse les commerçants sortaient de leur magasin, lui faisaient des tas de courbettes bien obséquieuses, et après ils livraient chez elle ce qu'elle avait commandé.

Elle trouvait à redire à tout ce que je faisais. Soit je ne l'avais pas mise au bon endroit devant la boutique, soit elle avait le soleil dans l'œil, soit je l'avais secouée au retour.

Un matin d'été où il faisait très beau, elle a voulu que je la promène au bord de la mer. On est allées jusqu'à la jetée ouest, à deux kilomètres de chez elle. Après elle a voulu que j'oriente sa chaise pour qu'elle ait le vent dans le dos mais qu'en même temps elle puisse voir les gens. Ce jour-là elle était d'humeur massacrante ; elle n'avait pas arrêté de râler pendant tout le trajet. J'ai essayé de trouver la bonne position, mais au bout de six tentatives ça n'allait toujours pas, alors j'ai laissé tomber. Je n'ai rien dit. Je suis juste partie en la laissant en plan. Je n'ai jamais su ce qui lui était arrivé après, comment elle avait fait pour rentrer chez elle ni rien.

Quand j'ai raconté ça à maman, au début elle ne savait pas quoi en penser, mais quand elle l'a répété à papa il a trouvé ça rigolo, et pendant toute la semaine il n'a pas arrêté de dire :

« Je serais curieux de savoir si la vieille est toujours bloquée à la jetée ouest ! »

Après ça, pour changer du ménage j'ai travaillé dans un magasin de bonbons – le rêve de tous les enfants ! J'avais le droit d'en manger autant que je voulais, mais ça m'a vite écœurée. Si je me suis fait renvoyer, c'est parce que quand mes frères et sœurs venaient me voir avec tous leurs copains ils n'avaient presque pas de sous, mais moi je leur donnais quand même des kilos de bonbons. Alors évidemment, au bout d'un moment la patronne n'y trouvait plus son compte.

La place que j'attendais avec impatience, c'était à la blanchisserie du quartier, mais il fallait avoir quatorze ans pour être embauchée. J'y étais allée à treize ans et demi, en me disant que comme j'étais grande ils allaient me prendre, mais ils m'avaient demandé mon certificat de naissance, alors ça s'était arrêté là.

Dès que j'ai eu mes quatorze ans j'y suis retournée et j'ai été engagée comme trieuse. On m'a mise toute seule dans une pièce où je devais trier le linge du Métropole, le plus grand hôtel de Brighton. J'ai fait ça pendant les six premiers mois. Après j'ai été chargée de donner un coup de main un peu à tout le monde, moitié aux repasseuses et moitié aux blanchisseuses.

Je travaillais de huit heures du matin à six heures du soir pour douze shillings et six pence par semaine. Ce n'était pas cher payé et je n'étais pas nourrie. Mais il y avait une sacrée ambiance, surtout dans la salle de repassage – rien à voir avec les ménages que je faisais avant. Quand on bossait là, à cause du langage et de l'atmosphère on se serait cru dans l'*Enfer* de Dante.

Une des choses que je devais faire, c'était asperger le sol avec un arrosoir. Il n'existait pas de système automatique pour enlever la poussière, et comme on déplaçait constamment les vêtements, à force il y avait une fine couche de poudre blanche par terre. Si par hasard j'aspergeais les pieds des repasseuses au lieu d'arroser le sol, elles se mettaient à jurer comme des poissonnières de la halle. Je n'avais jamais entendu ça, même dans ma rue le samedi soir. Elles racontaient aussi des histoires cochonnes, et quand elles voyaient que je n'y comprenais rien elles étaient pliées de rire.

Je devais avoir une sacrée touche à ce moment-là. C'était l'époque où les filles portaient des bottes jusqu'aux genoux, mais moi mes chaussures montaient juste au-dessus des chevilles, comme les godillots de mon père. J'avais beau avoir seulement quatorze ans, je chaussais déjà du quarante-deux. Le matin il fallait que je fasse attention de ne pas me tromper entre les chaussures de mon père et les miennes. J'avais aussi un pull que ma mère m'avait tricoté, et comme elle était tombée en panne de laine au moment d'attaquer le dos, il n'était pas de la même couleur devant et derrière. Avec mes chaussures, mon pull, mes cheveux tirés en arrière et le goitre que j'avais, je devais ressembler à un dessin de Bozz*.

Quand j'ai eu quinze ans et que j'aurais dû être augmentée d'une demi-couronne, ils m'ont fichue à la porte. Pensez donc, ils n'allaient pas me payer quinze shillings par semaine alors qu'une fille de quatorze ans pouvait faire mon boulot ! Alors voilà : ils ont sauté sur le premier prétexte pour se débarrasser de moi.

---

* Le dessinateur de bande dessinée François Robert Velter (1909-1991) signa dès 1936 ses *Avatars de M. Subito* du pseudonyme de Bozz en hommage à Charles Dickens, qui avait fait paraître en 1836 un recueil de nouvelles intitulé *Esquisses de Boz*. F. R. Velter est surtout célèbre pour avoir créé en 1938 le personnage de Spirou sous le nom de Rob-Vel. *(N.d.T.)*

IX

Quand je suis rentrée de la blanchisserie en disant à ma mère que j'avais été renvoyée, elle a été très embêtée. Je pense qu'elle en avait un peu marre de tous ces boulots différents que j'avais faits depuis que j'avais quitté l'école, alors elle m'a dit :

« Moi je croyais que tu y étais pour de bon, à la blanchisserie. À quatorze ans tu voulais à tout prix y aller, et à quinze ans voilà que tu te fais mettre à la porte. Bon, il n'y a pas trente-six solutions, il va falloir que tu entres en condition et puis c'est tout. »

« Entrer en condition », ça voulait dire devenir domestique et je n'en avais pas du tout envie, et pourtant pas une seconde je n'ai pensé à protester. J'aurais sans doute pu supplier mon père, vu qu'il avait plutôt tendance à me dorloter ; mais chez nous c'était ma mère qui menait la barque, et pour les décisions papa se reposait sur elle. Nous, les enfants, on faisait toujours ce qu'elle disait. C'était comme ça à l'époque : les gosses obéissaient.

Alors j'ai dit : « Bon, d'accord. » Je n'en savais pas tant que ça sur la condition domestique, et ma mère m'a expliqué que c'était un très bon métier, qu'il y avait plein d'avantages, qu'on était bien nourri, bien logé et tout ça, et que l'argent que je toucherais, ça serait mon argent à moi.

Naturellement, comme ça arrive souvent quand on regarde en arrière, elle voyait ses années de service de son point de vue de femme mariée, avec un mari toujours au chômage en hiver, sept enfants et jamais de quoi les nourrir correctement, sans parler de les habiller. Du coup, ces années-là lui apparaissaient comme une période où, au moins, elle avait eu un peu d'argent à elle.

Elle oubliait ce qu'elle nous avait raconté avant : qu'elle était entrée en condition en 1895, à quatorze ans, qu'elle avait dû trimer comme un forçat et que les autres domestiques se moquaient d'elle.

Quand je lui ai rappelé tout ça elle a dit :

« Oui, mais la vie en condition a beaucoup changé depuis : on ne travaille plus autant, on a plus de temps libre, on a le droit de sortir plus souvent et on gagne plus.

— Bon, alors qu'est-ce que je pourrais faire en condition, à ton avis ?

— Écoute, comme tu détestes la couture (ça c'est vrai, j'ai toujours détesté la couture), le seul endroit où tu pourrais aller c'est la cuisine. Quand on est femme de service on doit raccommoder le linge de table, si on est femme de chambre on doit raccommoder le linge de maison, et si on travaille à la nursery on doit raccommoder et même carrément faire les habits des enfants. Mais comme fille de cuisine on n'a pas du tout de couture à faire.

— Bon, alors d'accord. Je serai fille de cuisine. »

Je suis allée à un bureau de placement pour les domes-tiques ; il y en avait à tous les coins de rue en ce temps-là. Les places de fille de cuisine aussi ça courait les rues, parce que c'était tout en bas de l'échelle des gens de maison ; et pour-tant, si on voulait devenir cuisinière et qu'on n'avait pas de quoi se payer des cours, le seul moyen d'apprendre le métier c'était de commencer comme fille de cuisine.

On m'a proposé plusieurs places, et finalement j'en ai choisi une dans Adelaide Crescent, à Hove, parce que ça ne faisait pas trop loin de chez nous. C'est là qu'habitaient le révérend Clydesdale et sa femme. Ma mère est venue avec moi pour l'entretien d'embauche.

Dans Adelaide Crescent les maisons étaient immenses. Pour aller du sous-sol au grenier il y avait bien cent trente marches, et les sous-sols étaient sombres comme des cachots. La partie qui donnait sur la rue, là où il y avait des barreaux aux fenêtres, c'était la salle des domestiques. Quand on était assis dans cette pièce, tout ce qu'on voyait c'étaient les jambes des passants, et quand on était de l'autre côté, c'est-à-dire dans la cuisine, on ne voyait rien du tout à cause d'un jardin d'hiver en saillie juste au-dessus. Il y avait une minuscule fenêtre en haut du mur, mais pour voir dehors on devait grimper sur une échelle. Il fallait laisser la lumière allumée toute la journée.

Adelaide Crescent, c'est une des plus belles rues de Hove. Les maisons étaient de style Regency*, et même maintenant qu'elles ont été transformées en appartements, comme les

---

* Style architectural et décoratif caractéristique des années 1790-1830 en Grande-Bretagne. (N.d.T.)

façades ont été conservées ça ressemble beaucoup à ce que c'était, avec les jardins au milieu. Naturellement, autrefois il n'y avait que les résidents qui avaient la clé et qui pouvaient profiter des jardins – mais bien sûr ça ne s'appliquait pas aux domestiques, ça je vous le certifie !

Ma mère et moi, quand on est arrivées pour l'entretien on s'est présentées à la porte principale de la maison. Pendant tout le temps où j'ai travaillé chez les Clydesdale, c'est bien la seule fois où je suis passée par la grande porte. On nous a fait entrer dans un vestibule qui m'a paru le comble du luxe. Il y avait un beau tapis par terre et un escalier très large entièrement recouvert de moquette – rien à voir avec le petit bout de lino qu'on avait posé chez nous au milieu des marches ! Dans le vestibule il y avait aussi une table en acajou, un portemanteau en acajou, et des miroirs immenses avec des cadres dorés. Pour moi ça respirait tellement la richesse que je me suis dit que les Clydesdale étaient sûrement millionnaires. Je n'avais jamais rien vu de pareil.

C'est un majordome qui nous avait ouvert, et ma mère avait dit que j'étais Margaret Langley et que je venais pour la place de fille de cuisine. Ce majordome, c'était un vrai nabot ; moi qui croyais que les majordomes étaient toujours grands et imposants ! Dans le vestibule on a vu un monsieur assez âgé et la dame qui allait nous recevoir pour l'entretien, et on nous a fait entrer dans une pièce qui était visiblement la salle de jeux des enfants.

C'est ma mère qui a parlé tout le temps, parce que moi j'étais abasourdie : dans cette pièce-là on aurait pu mettre sans problème les trois où je vivais avec ma famille, alors que c'était juste une salle de jeux. Et puis j'étais paralysée par la timidité. Ce que je pouvais être mal à l'aise en ce temps-là, c'était horrible ! Il faut dire que la dame, Mrs Clydesdale, m'examinait de la tête aux pieds comme si on était au marché aux esclaves. Elle avait l'air de soupeser mes capacités.

Ma mère lui a dit que j'avais déjà fait des ménages. Elle n'a pas parlé de la blanchisserie, parce que d'après elle ce n'était pas une référence. Les gens croyaient que les blanchisseries étaient des « antres du vice », comme on disait, parce que les filles qui y travaillaient étaient malpolies.

Mrs Clydesdale a décidé que comme j'étais robuste et en bonne santé je ferais l'affaire. Je serais payée vingt-quatre livres par an et je toucherais mon salaire tous les mois. J'aurais un après-midi plus une soirée de congé par semaine, de quatre heures à dix heures, et un dimanche sur deux aux mêmes heures ; je ne devais jamais rentrer après dix heures, sous aucun prétexte. Il faudrait que j'aie trois robes en tissu imprimé bleu ou vert ; quatre tabliers blancs à bavette et quatre bonnets ; des bas et des chaussures noires à lanière. Je devais toujours dire « Monsieur » et « Madame » à Mr et Mrs Clydesdale quand ils m'adressaient la parole, montrer beaucoup de respect aux domestiques de haut rang et faire tout ce que la cuisinière me dirait.

À chaque fois ma mère a répondu « Oui, Madame » ou « Non, Madame ». Elle a promis de ma part que je ferais tout ça. Moi, plus ça allait plus j'étais démoralisée, et à la fin j'avais l'impression d'être prisonnière.

En sortant je l'ai dit à maman, mais comme elle avait décidé que la place me convenait la question était réglée.

Le problème, c'était l'uniforme. Ma mère a calculé que vu tout ce qu'il fallait m'acheter on ne pourrait pas s'en tirer à moins de deux livres. Je sais bien qu'aujourd'hui ça paraît ridicule, mais pour nous c'était une fortune ; on ne les avait pas, les deux livres. Enfin, ma mère s'est débrouillée pour les emprunter et j'ai eu mon équipement.

Le jour où je devais commencer, elle a sorti la vieille malle en fer-blanc toute cabossée qui lui avait servi pendant ses années de service, et j'ai rangé dedans les quelques affaires que j'avais. À part l'uniforme je n'avais pas grand-chose comme habits. J'ai mis sur moi les plus beaux : un corsage, une jupe, et un manteau qui avait été à ma grand-mère avant.

J'ai demandé à maman :

« Comment on va faire pour transporter la malle jusqu'à Adelaide Crescent ? On va prendre un taxi ? »

Elle m'a répondu :

« Mais, ma parole, tu es folle ! Où est-ce qu'on trouverait l'argent ? Non, ton père va emprunter la brouette. »

Ce qui était prévu, c'est que comme papa travaillait à ce moment-là chez un peintre en bâtiment, il allait charger la malle sur la brouette et la transporter comme ça jusqu'à Adelaide Crescent. On devait faire un sacré convoi, tous les trois : mon père au milieu de la rue avec la brouette, et ma mère et moi à la queue leu leu sur le trottoir ! Quand on est arrivés, papa a descendu la malle au sous-sol.

Pour me dire au revoir ma mère m'a prise dans ses bras, ce qui n'arrivait presque jamais : chez nous on ne montrait pas ses sentiments. Je crois que j'aurais pu hurler tellement j'avais mal. Mes parents ne s'en allaient pourtant pas à des kilomètres, ils vivaient dans la même ville, mais de les voir partir en me laissant dans cette maison étrangère, pour moi c'était atroce. Je pensais : « Oh non, je ne vais quand même pas rester là ! » et pourtant je ne pouvais pas le dire. Je savais très bien qu'il fallait que je travaille, puisque mon père et ma mère ne pouvaient pas me nourrir.

La première personne que j'ai vue, c'est une fille d'à peu près mon âge. Elle m'a dit qu'elle s'appelait Mary et qu'elle était l'aide-femme de chambre.

« Viens ! elle a fait. Je vais t'aider à monter ta malle tout là-haut. »

Tout là-haut, c'était vraiment le cas de le dire ! Je n'aurais jamais cru qu'il pouvait y avoir autant de marches dans une maison.

Depuis le sous-sol il y avait un escalier de service pour les domestiques, comme ça on ne se mélangeait jamais avec « Eux » ; ils ne nous voyaient jamais courir d'un étage à l'autre ni quoi que ce soit. Et bien entendu cet escalier ne ressemblait pas du tout à l'escalier principal : il y avait juste du lino sur celui-là, comme chez nous.

Heureusement que je n'avais pas beaucoup d'affaires, sinon je ne sais vraiment pas comment on aurait fait pour monter la malle jusqu'à la chambre.

Quand on y est enfin arrivées j'ai demandé à Mary :

« Et maintenant, qu'est-ce que je fais ?

– La première chose que tu fais, c'est de mettre tout de suite ton uniforme et de descendre. Et il va falloir que tu fasses quelque chose pour tes cheveux, tu ne peux pas rester comme ça. »

J'avais les cheveux très longs : ce n'était pas encore la mode de se les faire couper. J'avais essayé de me faire un chignon pour venir travailler et maman m'avait donné un coup de main, mais il s'était écroulé parce que je n'avais pas assez d'épingles pour le faire tenir. Mary a dit qu'elle allait m'aider, et elle a tiré tous mes cheveux en arrière ; moi je les avais ramenés vers l'avant pour essayer d'être plus jolie, mais Mary a été catégorique :

« La cuisinière ne te laissera jamais te coiffer comme ça. Quand tu as ton bonnet, il ne faut pas qu'on voie un seul cheveu qui dépasse. »

Donc elle les a tous bien tirés vers l'arrière et elle m'a fait un chignon très serré en utilisant toutes mes épingles plus une douzaine des siennes, qu'elle m'a données. J'avais l'impression d'avoir un coussin d'aiguilles à l'arrière de la tête. Quand je l'ai touché je n'ai senti que des épingles, et quand je me suis regardée dans la glace je me suis trouvée hideuse sans aucun cheveu autour de la figure. J'étais loin de me douter que j'allais être hideuse tout le temps que je travaillerais là, mais bon, un peu plus tôt ou un peu plus tard, quelle différence ?

J'ai enfilé mon uniforme. Il était sacrément moche, et en tant que fille de cuisine je devais le porter du matin au soir : je ne m'habillais pas en noir dans la journée comme celles qui bossaient en haut. C'était un uniforme bleu, pas bleu marine, plutôt entre le bleu marine et le bleu pétrole. J'ai mis par-dessus un grand tablier à bavette avec des bretelles dans le dos qu'on boutonnait à la ceinture, et enfin le bonnet. Ce fichu bonnet, je l'ai toujours détesté, et du jour où je suis devenue cuisinière je n'en ai plus jamais mis. Je me suis drôlement bagarrée avec une de mes patronnes à cause de ça, mais quand j'étais cuisinière il n'était plus question que je porte un bonnet !

Une fois que j'ai été habillée Mary a dit :

« Bon, maintenant on descend à la cuisine. »

Quand on est arrivées en bas, c'était l'heure du thé pour les domestiques. Une aide-femme de chambre y avait droit, mais une fille de cuisine pas forcément.

X

Je crois bien qu'un des moments les plus pénibles ç'a été quand j'ai fait la connaissance de tous les domestiques, et pourtant il n'y en avait pas tant que ça comparé à d'autres maisons où j'ai travaillé après. Il y avait un majordome, une femme de service au lieu d'un valet de pied, une femme de chambre et une aide-femme de chambre, une gouvernante, un jardinier-chauffeur, la cuisinière et moi.

La première chose qu'on m'a montrée, avant même que je m'assoie pour le thé, c'était une liste de tout ce que devait faire la fille de cuisine. Quand je l'ai lue j'ai cru qu'on s'était trompé : il y avait bien du boulot pour six !

La liste commençait par : se lever à cinq heures et demie (six heures le dimanche), descendre au sous-sol, nettoyer les conduits, allumer le feu, passer le fourneau à la mine de plomb – soit dit en passant, pour faire ça on n'avait pas de produit liquide dans une jolie boîte, on avait un vieux morceau tout dur de mine de plomb qu'il fallait mettre dans une soucoupe avec de l'eau avant de se coucher le soir ; comme ça il trempait toute la nuit pour donner une espèce de pâte qu'on pouvait passer sur le fourneau. Moi je ne savais pas tout ça. Le lendemain matin j'ai essayé de me servir du morceau de mine de plomb ; je croyais qu'il fallait frotter le fourneau avec. Personne ne m'avait rien dit. Tout le monde partait du principe que je savais, je me demande bien pourquoi.

Après je devais briquer au papier de verre le pare-feu en acier (qui sans exagérer faisait bien un mètre vingt de long) et les accessoires de cheminée : une énorme pelle, des pincettes et un tisonnier en acier. Je devais aussi astiquer les décorations en cuivre de la porte d'entrée, récurer les marches du perron à la brosse, nettoyer toutes les chaussures et mettre la table du petit déjeuner pour les domestiques.

Tout ça, il fallait que ce soit fait avant huit heures du matin. Et ce que je devais faire pendant le reste de la journée, après le petit déjeuner, ça faisait une de ces listes ! Je n'en avais jamais vu une aussi longue.

Alors entre l'uniforme, le bonnet, mes cheveux et la liste, quand en plus Mary m'a dit : « Viens prendre le thé et faire la connaissance de tout le monde », j'ai vraiment cru qu'il ne pouvait rien m'arriver de pire. J'étais au fond du trou. Je me suis demandé comment ma mère avait pu me faire venir ici en m'assurant que maintenant c'était mieux, que le boulot était moins dur, qu'on avait plus de temps libre et qu'on était mieux considéré.

Je suis donc entrée dans la salle des domestiques, et quand je dis que j'ai fait leur connaissance n'allez pas croire qu'on m'a présentée. Personne ne se donne la peine de présenter une fille de cuisine. Ils m'ont juste regardée comme une bête curieuse. Quelqu'un a dit :

« Elle a l'air assez costaud. »

Et croyez-moi, ça tombait plutôt bien que je sois costaud !

Je me suis assise pour le thé, et je ne sais vraiment pas comment j'ai fait pour manger avec tous ces regards fixés sur moi. Heureusement, mes parents m'avaient appris les bonnes manières à table.

Je n'avais pas encore rencontré la cuisinière parce qu'elle était au cinéma. Elle avait beaucoup plus de temps libre que n'importe qui ; elle pouvait sortir tous les après-midi, du moment qu'elle rentrait à temps pour préparer le dîner. Naturellement, c'était elle que j'avais le plus hâte de rencontrer, vu que c'est avec elle que j'allais passer le plus de temps.

Mary m'avait dit que Mrs McIlroy – une dame écossaise, donc – était très gentille, mais j'attendais de voir. Comme Mary n'était pas sous ses ordres, ce qu'elle pensait ne voulait rien dire.

Après le thé je suis allée jeter un coup d'œil à la cuisine, et ça m'a achevée. Pour le coup, j'avais le moral carrément dans les chaussettes.

Tout un côté de la pièce était occupé par le fourneau, et je suis restée là à le regarder bouche bée. On en avait un à la maison, mais ma mère ne s'en servait jamais pour faire à manger, elle avait une gazinière pour ça. Dans cette cuisine-là il n'y avait pas de gazinière, juste cet énorme fourneau qui allait devenir un cauchemar pour moi, même si je ne le savais pas encore. Il avait un four à chaque bout, un grand et un petit, et il avait été tellement bien briqué à la mine de plomb par la fille de cuisine d'avant qu'on pouvait presque se voir dedans. Quand c'est moi qui l'ai astiqué par la suite il n'était jamais comme ça, je ne sais pas pourquoi. Comme disait la cuisinière, il y a des gens qui savent frotter et d'autres pas. Devant il y avait le pare-feu en acier, et lui aussi il brillait tellement qu'on aurait dit de l'argent.

En face il y avait un buffet avec de très grands placards de rangement en bas et cinq étagères en haut, tout en bois blanc massif. Rien à voir avec le petit buffet qu'on avait chez nous. Celui-là pouvait contenir un service de table complet, et quand je dis un service complet je ne parle pas de ceux qu'on achète maintenant et qui sont en fait des demi-services : cent vingt-six pièces de porcelaine étaient alignées sur les étagères. Sur le bas de buffet, au-dessus des placards, donc, il y avait en plus une énorme soupière, des légumiers et des saucières. Et moi – c'était marqué sur la liste –, il fallait qu'une fois par semaine je sorte toutes ces pièces de vaisselle, que je les lave une par une et que je nettoie le buffet à fond.

Le troisième mur avait deux portes, dont une pour aller à la salle des domestiques. Quand on était en train de manger dans cette pièce-là, ce qui était très rigolo c'était de regarder les jambes des passants dans la rue et d'imaginer la tête qui allait avec. Si on voyait passer une paire de grosses jambes on disait :

« Celle-là, elle a bien cinquante piges. »

Et quelqu'un répondait :

« Oh non ! Celle-là, ou bien elle est courte sur pattes, ou bien elle a une maladie. »

Soit dit en passant, je me suis toujours demandé pourquoi on appelait ça la « salle » des domestiques. Ce n'était pas grand comme une salle, c'était juste une pièce normale. Mais partout où je suis allée la pièce où on pouvait s'asseoir s'appelait la salle des domestiques.

La deuxième porte conduisait à l'office du majordome. Là il y avait deux éviers, un pour laver l'argenterie au savon et l'autre pour la rincer à l'eau claire et laver les verres. Le majordome et la femme de service s'occupaient à eux deux des verres et de toute l'argenterie sauf des couteaux ; ça, c'était le boulot de la fille de cuisine.

Le quatrième mur avait une autre porte qui donnait sur un immense couloir avec un sol en pierre. Ce couloir, il reliait la porte de derrière à la cuisine. Au mur il y avait toute une rangée de sonnettes avec des étiquettes au-dessus pour indiquer d'où ça venait, et chaque fois que j'en entendais une j'étais censée courir à fond de train jusqu'au couloir pour voir laquelle c'était. On avait aussi un système de sifflets. Il fallait retirer du mur une espèce de bonde et siffler dedans vers les différentes pièces du haut pour essayer de choper une bonne et lui dire qu'on la demandait. Quand je ne courais pas comme une dératée la sonnette s'arrêtait avant que j'arrive, si bien que je ne savais pas du tout si ça venait du salon bleu, du salon rose, de la première chambre, de la deuxième, de la cinquième, du grand salon ou de la salle à manger. Dans ces cas-là je revenais à la cuisine en disant :

« Je ne sais pas quelle sonnette c'était. »

Et la cuisinière me répondait :

« Il faut que tu coures plus vite que ça, sinon ça va barder là-haut. »

Mais qu'est-ce que je pouvais y faire ? Quand j'étais en plein milieu d'un travail je ne pouvais pas le laisser tomber comme ça, à la seconde. Au début j'ai eu des tas de problèmes avec ces sonnettes, mais à la fin je maîtrisais la technique, et pour sortir en trombe de la cuisine j'étais championne.

Dans la cuisine elle-même, par terre c'était de la pierre, mais pas des belles dalles brillantes comme on voit maintenant, plutôt des espèces de grosses briques, et il fallait les récurer tous les jours. La table de la cuisine faisait toute la longueur de la pièce ; c'était un gros machin très lourd avec quatre pieds carrés, les pieds les plus énormes que j'aie jamais vus, et à force d'être frottée elle était devenue tellement blanche qu'elle aurait rendu jalouse n'importe quelle poudre à récurer d'aujourd'hui, alors qu'à l'époque on n'avait que du savon et de la soude. C'était la table de la cuisinière, et Mary m'a annoncé que je devais la préparer. Elle m'a demandé :

« Tu sais préparer une table de cuisinière, au moins ? »

J'ai répondu :

« Oui, je sais quels ustensiles il faut pour cuisiner. »

Mais à vrai dire je n'en savais rien du tout.

Ce soir-là vers six heures, quand Mrs McIlroy est arrivée, elle m'a fait l'effet de quelqu'un de très gentil. Elle est venue vers moi et elle m'a même serré la main, ce que personne n'avait fait jusque-là.

C'était une Écossaise d'à peu près cinquante ans, assez petite, grisonnante, avec l'air d'avoir les pieds sur terre, plutôt quelconque physiquement, mais tellement avenante qu'on n'y faisait pas vraiment attention.

Plus tard, quand je l'ai mieux connue, je lui ai dit un jour :

« Mrs McIlroy… »

Le « Mrs », c'était juste une politesse ; en général, même si une cuisinière n'était pas mariée, quand elle avait un certain âge on ne l'appelait pas « Miss » mais « Mrs » – et pas seulement ses patrons, les autres domestiques aussi. Donc je lui ai dit :

« Mrs McIlroy, ça m'étonne que vous ne vous soyez jamais mariée. »

Et j'en ai rajouté, parce que je m'étais aperçue que la flatterie ça payait toujours, surtout vis-à-vis de ses supérieurs :

« C'est vrai, vous êtes tellement charmante ! »

En disant ça, j'ai bien cru que j'allais m'étrangler de rire. Elle m'a répondu :

« Que veux-tu, c'est comme ça. Un jour, j'avais dans les vingt-cinq ans, je me suis regardée dans la glace et je me suis dit : "Ma fille, tu as décidé d'être une petite cuisinière quelconque et tu seras une petite cuisinière quelconque toute ta vie. Tu es petite et quelconque, tu le sais, alors personne ne voudra se marier avec toi, tu le sais aussi." Et la vie m'a donné raison. »

Le premier soir, donc, après s'être présentée elle m'a dit :

« Bon, il va falloir qu'on s'y mette, ma petite fille. Tu veux bien préparer ma table ?

– Oui, oui. »

Et elle est montée dans sa chambre.

Moi, tout ce que j'ai sorti c'est un couteau, une fourchette et une cuillère, la farine, le sel et une passoire. Je croyais qu'elle n'avait pas besoin d'autre chose pour préparer le dîner. Heureusement pour moi, Mary est arrivée à ce moment-là. Elle a piqué un fou rire en m'expliquant que ce n'était pas du tout comme ça qu'il fallait préparer la table de la cuisinière, et puis elle a dit :

« Je vais te montrer avant que Mrs McIlroy revienne. Ce n'est pas qu'elle rouspéterait, mais sûr qu'elle rigolerait en voyant ce que tu as sorti. »

Et elle a commencé à disposer sur la table des couteaux de toutes sortes, de toutes les formes et de toutes les tailles, des couteaux à découper très longs, des petits pour éplucher les fruits, des spatules, certaines recourbées pour gratter l'intérieur des bols, et environ six cuillères en métal, pas le modèle ordinaire, des énormes qui avaient la couleur de l'aluminium.

Sur les plus grandes il y avait les doses de marquées, ça allait de l'once à la cuillère à dessert. Elle a sorti deux tamis, un en crin et un métallique, plus un pour la farine, et aussi un fouet. Bien entendu les fouets électriques n'existaient pas en ce temps-là. En fait, même le modèle avec une petite roue n'existait pas : on battait les œufs à la main avec un bidule en métal. Il y avait aussi deux râpes différentes, une fine pour la noix de muscade et une pour la chapelure ; une grande planche à découper et une petite ; du paprika et du piment de Cayenne, du sel ordinaire, du poivre et du vinaigre. Ça couvrait la moitié de la table. Tout ce matériel devait être sorti deux fois par jour : pour le déjeuner, qui ne comportait pourtant que trois plats, et pour le dîner, qui en comportait cinq ou six.

Quand j'ai vu tous ces ustensiles j'ai dit à Mary :

« Elle ne se sert quand même pas de tout ça ! »

Ele a répliqué :

« Oh, mais tu n'as encore rien vu ! Dans cette maison, dès le début du dîner tu seras en train de courir dans tous les sens pour essuyer certains trucs parce que la cuisinière s'en sera servie une fois et qu'elle en aura encore besoin. Il y en a qu'elle utilise deux ou trois fois par repas. »

Je n'ai pas tardé à m'apercevoir que c'était vrai.

XI

La quantité de nourriture qui entrait dans cette maison me paraissait carrément phénoménale – ce qui était mangé, mais aussi ce qui était gaspillé. Souvent, les Clydesdale se faisaient servir une selle d'agneau entière. C'était fabuleux. Et l'aloyau, donc ! Parfois ils mangeaient uniquement le filet, alors il restait toute la partie du dessus, et ça nous faisait notre dîner. Mais même comme ça on ne pouvait pas tout finir, et on en jetait beaucoup. Quand je pensais à chez moi, où on n'avait pas toujours eu assez à manger, ça me fendait le cœur.

Le laitier passait trois fois par jour : entre quatre heures et demie et cinq heures du matin il déposait le lait, et il revenait à dix heures avec à nouveau du lait plus tout ce qu'on lui avait commandé ; bien entendu il avait toujours de la crème et des œufs avec lui, mais si on voulait du beurre, des gâteaux ou des choses comme ça il revenait vers deux heures de l'après-midi.

Je n'ai jamais vu autant de lait, de crème et d'œufs de ma vie. Dans cette maison la crème arrivait par litres entiers pratiquement tous les jours, même quand le révérend et sa femme ne recevaient pas et qu'il n'y avait qu'eux, leur petite fille et sa gouvernante. Au début que j'y étais, le lait était livré dans un très gros bidon avec une anse. Pas le genre de bidon qu'on voit, ou plutôt qu'on voyait, dans les gares ; là c'était un bidon que le laitier portait à la main. Mais très peu de temps après ça a changé et le lait a été livré dans des bouteilles. C'était beaucoup plus propre, évidemment : les bidons, en général, ils sentaient mauvais.

La plupart des provisions venaient d'un grand magasin de Hove, un genre de Fortnum & Mason*, sauf qu'il fallait être membre pour pouvoir acheter. Ça devait être une sorte de coopérative pour les riches, mais je ne sais pas s'ils touchaient des dividendes.

Ils avaient des rayons pour tout : les fruits et légumes, la boucherie, les gâteaux et l'épicerie.

Mrs Clydesdale descendait vers dix heures et donnait ses menus de la journée à la cuisinière, et si Mrs McIlroy avait besoin de quelque chose qu'elle n'avait pas en réserve, elle téléphonait pour se le faire livrer. C'est tout ce qu'on avait à faire avec les fournisseurs à l'époque : leur téléphoner. En fait, le boucher et le marchand de fruits et légumes venaient prendre la commande quand ils pensaient que la cuisinière savait de quoi elle aurait besoin ce jour-là, et moins d'une demi-heure plus tard ils l'apportaient.

Le poisson, par contre, ce n'était jamais à eux qu'on l'achetait. Il y avait un homme qui venait de la plage avec des

---

* Épicerie de luxe, fondée à Londres en 1707, qui a pour équivalents français les établissements Hédiard et Fauchon. (N.d.T.)

poissons envore vivants dans un seau plein d'eau de mer. Lorsque je devais m'occuper de ces poissons je n'en menais pas large, parce que quand je leur coupais la tête ils sautaient et se tortillaient.

Un jour il a apporté un carrelet géant. Je l'ai posé sur la planche à découper pour lui trancher la tête, mais à ce moment-là il a carrément sauté en l'air, et avec sa nageoire coupante il m'a fait une grosse écorchure sur l'arête du nez. Quand Mary a vu ça elle m'a demandé :

« Ben qu'est-ce qui est arrivé à ton nez ?

– C'est un poisson. Il a essayé de s'envoler et il m'a fait ça. »

Je vous garantis que j'en ai entendu parler un moment, de cette histoire ! Après j'ai changé de méthode. Je prenais le tisonier en acier, un truc bien lourd, et je leur en donnais un bon coup sur la tête. Je n'ai jamais su où était le point sensible chez les poissons, mais comme je faisais ça marchait bien.

Le même pêcheur apportait quelquefois des homards vivants. Je les mettais au garde-manger dans une bassine. Ce garde-manger, ce n'était pas juste un cagibi avec des étagères tout autour : c'était comme une pièce, avec une grosse épaisseur d'ardoise au sol et sur les étagères, pour qu'il y fasse très froid même en été.

Donc je mettais les homards par terre dans une bassine, mais quand j'allais les rechercher en fin de journée, au moment de les faire cuire pour le dîner, ils n'y étaient plus. Ils étaient sortis de la bassine et ils se promenaient. Je devais les ramasser, et pour la peine je me faisais souvent pincer. Je n'ai jamais su par où les attraper pour éviter les pinces.

Je détestais les mettre dans l'eau bouillante. Mrs McIlroy disaient qu'ils mouraient à la seconde où ils touchaient l'eau, mais comment elle pouvait le savoir ? Moi je n'y ai jamais cru ; je suis sûre qu'ils hurlaient de douleur au moment où je les jetais dans la casserole.

Mrs McIlroy n'avait pas vraiment d'« arrangement » avec les fournisseurs, mais n'empêche que quand elle payait les factures du trimestre ils lui faisaient souvent un petit cadeau, et à la fin de l'année elle touchait une commission tout à fait appréciable.

En fait c'était la cuisinière qui choisissait les boutiques, alors quand elle y allait on lui déroulait le tapis rouge. Il faut dire que dans cette maison il n'y avait pas beaucoup de personnel mais que les repas étaient de très bonne qualité. En plus de son salaire, n'importe quelle cuisinière pouvait donc compter sur une prime régulière de la part des commerçants chez qui elle était cliente.

Mais revenons à mon emploi du temps. Je me suis rendu compte que ce que j'avais pris pour le travail de six personnes était en fait celui d'une seule, et qu'à partir de maintenant cette personne c'était moi.

Je me levais à cinq heures et demie, je me traînais péniblement jusqu'au sous-sol et j'attaquais le fourneau. Je devais le nettoyer et le mettre en route. Il fallait aussi que j'allume le feu dans la salle des domestiques.

Après je montais en vitesse faire la porte d'entrée, une porte peinte tout en blanc avec des décorations en cuivre. C'était un boulot vraiment ingrat, surtout en hiver : dès que j'avais fini de l'astiquer et de la faire briller, elle redevenait terne à cause des embruns. Alors le temps que Madame la voie, il y avait forcément quelque chose à redire.

J'avais aussi quatorze marches de pierre très larges à récurer. Et quand je redescendais au sous-sol Mary m'attendait avec toutes les chaussures.

Je me souviens, le premier jour elle m'a fait :

« Carrie (ça, c'était la première femme de chambre) dit qu'elle espère que tu sais faire les chaussures. »

J'ai répondu du tac au tac :

« Évidemment que je sais ! »

Après tout, je les faisais chez moi. Mais je ne savais pas comment « Eux » voulaient que ce soit fait.

Le révérend, lui, il portait des chaussures montantes toute la journée, des noires en semaine et des marron le dimanche. Le soir il mettait des souliers noirs vernis. Madame portait du noir ou du marron, souvent les deux dans la même journée. Et puis il y avait celles de la gouvernante et de la petite Leonora. Je les ai toutes faites, et ma foi j'étais plutôt contente de moi. En tout cas, elles étaient bien brillantes au bout.

Quand Mary est descendue les chercher elle a fait :

« Oh, mais ça ne va pas aller ! Ça ne va pas aller du tout !

— Pourquoi ? Qu'est-ce qu'elles ont ? Moi je trouve que ça va.

— Bon, d'accord, je les monte si tu veux. Mais Carrie va me les balancer à la figure. »

Environ deux minutes plus tard elle est redescendue en disant :

« C'est bien ce que je pensais : ça ne va pas. Tu n'as pas fait les semelles.

— Les semelles ? Je ne savais pas qu'il fallait nettoyer le dessous des chaussures ! »

Enfin bon, j'ai nettoyé les semelles, j'ai redonné un petit coup sur le dessus, et Mary les a remportées là-haut.

Trente secondes plus tard la voilà qui redescend en disant :
« Tu n'as pas fait les lacets.

— Comment ça, je n'ai pas fait les lacets ?

— Tu n'es pas au courant ? Il faut que tu repasses tous les lacets ; tu les enlèves et tu les repasses. »

J'ai cru qu'elle plaisantait.

« Quoi ? Repasser les lacets ?

— Oui. »

En ce temps-là, vous comprenez, ce n'étaient pas des lacets tout fins comme maintenant, ils faisaient souvent un bon centimètre de large. Et ceux de Mrs Clydesdale et de Leonora, ils faisaient largement deux centimètres.

Il a donc fallu que j'enlève les lacets des chaussures et que je les repasse. Bien entendu il n'y avait pas encore de fers électriques, c'étaient juste des fers normaux. Il fallait les faire chauffer à la flamme, et ça prenait pas loin d'un quart d'heure. Jamais de ma vie je n'ai vu faire une chose aussi aberrante.

Je devais aussi nettoyer les couteaux, étant donné qu'à l'époque ils n'étaient pas en inox. Je faisais ça avec une grosse machine ronde : elle avait trois trous où il fallait verser de la poudre à couteaux, une espèce d'émeri en poudre ; après je mettais un couteau dans chaque trou et je tournais la manivelle. Je faisais semblant de jouer de l'orgue de Barbarie, et ça devenait carrément une activité musicale, parce que je chantais en tournant ; à la fin du premier couplet les trois couteaux étaient faits, je les retirais, j'en mettais trois autres, et à la fin de la chanson tous les couteaux brillaient comme des sous neufs.

Après je portais une tasse de thé à Mrs McIlroy et je mettais la table du petit déjeuner dans la salle des domestiques, qui mangeaient à huit heures.

Quand on avait fini, Mrs McIlroy et moi on préparait le petit déjeuner pour là-haut.

Comme la plupart des repas, leur petit déjeuner n'avait rien à voir avec le nôtre. Nous, Mrs Clydesdale trouvait qu'il fallait juste nous nourrir, alors on mangeait du hareng, de la morue, du ragoût et des crèmes au lait, mais rien de tout ça n'atterrissait jamais sur leur table à eux. J'en déduisais que même leurs organes n'étaient pas faits comme les nôtres, puisque ce qui était nourrissant pour nous n'était pas bon pour eux.

Il fallait toujours faire des économies, et pendant toutes mes années en condition j'ai remarqué qu'on commençait toujours par en faire sur le dos des domestiques… et que ça s'arrêtait là.

Là-haut le petit déjeuner était toujours très copieux, qu'ils aient des invités ou pas. Il y avait des œufs au bacon, des saucisses, des rognons, du haddock ou du pilaf de poisson aux œufs durs – et pas un ou deux de ces plats-là, non, tous !

Je ne pouvais pas m'empêcher de penser à mes pauvres parents. Tout ce qu'ils mangeaient le matin, c'était du pain grillé. Et ceux d'en haut, qui ne fichaient jamais rien, on leur servait tout ça ! Je trouvais que la vie était vraiment injuste.

Quand je le disais à Mrs McIlroy elle ne voyait pas où était le problème ; elle acceptait son sort et puis voilà. D'après elle il fallait qu'il y ait des riches et des pauvres.

« Parce que s'il n'y avait pas de riches, elle m'a dit une fois, qu'est-ce qu'on ferait, nous autres ?

– Mais quand même, je lui ai répondu, est-ce que ça ne pourrait pas être un peu mieux réparti, un peu plus équitable ? Ils pourraient avoir un peu moins d'argent et nous un peu plus, non ? Pourquoi vous et moi il faut qu'on travaille dans cette espèce de cachot avec le strict minimum comme confort alors que là-haut ils ont tout ? Et puis n'oubliez pas, Mrs McIlroy, que le vivre et le couvert ça fait partie de notre salaire. C'est censé compléter les deux livres que je touche en argent tous les mois. Alors quand on a un logement comme Mary et moi au grenier, des trucs pas terribles à manger et presque pas de loisirs, vous trouvez que c'est équitable, vous, comme salaire ? »

Déjà à ce moment-là je réfléchissais à tout ça. Ça me venait peut-être de mon père, parce que les inégalités sociales lui faisaient souvent mal au cœur. Ma mère, elle n'y faisait pas autant attention. Du moment qu'elle pouvait boire une bière de temps en temps et nous donner assez à manger, et en été elle pouvait, ça n'avait pas l'air de la déranger plus que ça. Mon père, lui, il en souffrait davantage.

Une fois le petit déjeuner débarrassé, on commençait à préparer le repas de midi.

Selon Mrs McIlroy, le déjeuner était un repas très simple : de la soupe, du poisson, des côtelettes ou une grillade, et un dessert. C'est avec elle que j'ai appris à présenter les plats. Par exemple, quand c'étaient des côtelettes, elle écrasait les pommes de terre en purée et elle en faisait de petites boules un peu plus grosses que des noisettes ; elle les passait dans de l'œuf et de la chapelure, et après elle les disposait en pyramide sur un plat d'argent ; elle mettait les côtelettes debout tout autour avec une petite papillotte à chaque os et du persil entre deux. C'était très appétissant.

Pour nous le repas principal c'était celui de midi, vu que le soir on n'avait que les restes. Et pourtant je voyais bien qu'on n'avait jamais trois plats, seulement de la viande et un dessert. Des choses assez consistantes, mais pas de côtelettes ni de filet de bœuf ni rien de tout ça. Quand c'était du poisson, c'était du hareng ou de la morue. Enfin, il y en avait toujours suffisamment, et comme je n'avais pas été élevée dans le luxe je mangeais toujours ce qu'on me donnait.

XII

Pour ceux d'en haut le repas principal c'était toujours le soir, même quand il n'y avait pas d'invités. Leonora et sa gouvernante mangeaient en général dans une autre pièce que Mr et Mrs Clydesdale, mais le dimanche la petite avait le droit de dîner avec ses parents. Il y avait toujours cinq plats, parfois six.

Ça commençait par une soupe. Mrs McIlroy faisait très bien les consommés. Elle achetait quelques bons os chez le boucher et elle les faisait mijoter toute la journée sur le coin du fourneau dans une casserole où elle avait mis un sachet de mousseline avec des herbes dedans, une carotte, un oignon, plus un rutabaga ou un navet. Vers la fin de l'après-midi elle enlevait le sachet et les légumes et elle mettait des coquilles d'œufs dans le bouillon – pas les œufs eux-mêmes, juste les coquilles – et elle fouettait vigoureusement, ce qui faisait remonter les petits morceaux à la surface. Moi je devais tout écumer, et c'était rudement long. Quand j'en avais retiré autant que je pouvais à la cuillère, il fallait que je prenne du papier spécial et que je le pose tout doucement sur le dessus pour qu'il continue à absorber le gras.

Parfois je devais utiliser plus d'une douzaine de papiers. Après, le consommé était transparent – d'une couleur pâle, un peu dorée, mais transparent.

Parfois c'était de la soupe à la tomate ; pas en boîte, bien sûr, à l'époque on n'en avait pas. Pour la soupe à la tomate on se servait aussi du bouillon ; on avait toujours une marmite de bouillon prête. Quand je suis devenue cuisinière je faisais pareil : tous les os qui restaient quand on avait mangé de la selle d'agneau, du gigot de mouton ou de l'aloyau, et tous les morceaux de légumes qu'on n'avait pas utilisés, on les mettait dans la marmite au bouillon. Pour la soupe à la tomate Mrs McIlroy mettait du beurre dans une casserole (jamais de margarine, tout était au beurre) sur le coin du fourneau pour qu'il fonde tout doucement. Elle le faisait épaissir avec de la farine, elle ajoutait le bouillon, les tomates coupées en deux, et elle mélangeait le tout jusqu'à ce que ça épaississe. Après je devais le filtrer au tamis métallique. Ça aussi c'était long, parce qu'il fallait enlever tous les pépins et toutes les peaux.

Une autre spécialité de Mrs McIlroy, c'était la soupe aux champignons. La préparation était à peu près la même, sauf que les champignons il fallait les filtrer au tamis de crin. Elle disait qu'avec le tamis métallique il restait des petits morceaux ; ils étaient tellement mous qu'ils passaient trop facilement à travers.

Un tamis de crin, ça avait la même forme qu'un tamis métallique, mais au lieu d'être en fer le maillage était en poils très fins ; au toucher ça ressemblait à du crin de cheval, mais ça avait l'air beaucoup plus fin.

À peu près cinq minutes avant de l'envoyer là-haut, Mrs McIlroy ajoutait une bonne cuillère de crème dans la soupière – un gros machin en porcelaine qui avait une louche assortie avec un long manche. Ça me rappelait le proverbe qui dit que si on soupe avec le diable il vaut mieux avoir une longue cuillère. Alors je disais toujours :

« M'est avis qu'ils soupent avec le diable, là-haut, pour avoir une si longue cuillère ! »

S'il en restait un fond Mrs McIlroy me le donnait, parce qu'il n'y en avait pas assez pour qu'on le partage à plusieurs. J'avais toujours faim, et je boulottais tout ce que je pouvais. Elle me disait :

« Tu finiras par t'en lasser, on se lasse de manger à force de travailler dans une cuisine. »

Mais je ne m'en suis jamais lassée. Je crois que c'est parce qu'à la maison on mourait presque de faim quand j'étais gosse. Encore maintenant, je mange tout ce qui traîne.

Le plat suivant, c'était souvent une *entrée**, et Mrs McIlroy préparait parfois un aspic de volaille. Elle faisait sa gelée elle-même, alors que de nos jours on achète ça tout prêt. S'ils avaient mangé du poulet le soir d'avant et qu'il en restait, je le coupais en petits morceaux, et une fois que Mrs McIlroy avait fait sa gelée avec la gélatine, le bouillon et l'assaisonnement elle ajoutait les morceaux de poulet et on mettait le tout à la glacière. On n'avait pas de réfrigérateur, naturellement.

La glacière, c'était une espèce de grande boîte en tôle galvanisée. Tous les matins le livreur de glace nous en apportait un pain que je posais dans un tiroir en haut de la glacière.

---

* En français dans le texte. *(N.d.T.)*

C'est là qu'on mettait tout ce qui devait être réfrigéré. Sinon, dans un garde-manger qui était tout en ardoise ou presque, et au sous-sol par-dessus le marché, il y avait très peu de choses qui se gâtaient. De toute façon on ne cherchait pas à conserver les aliments puisqu'on nous en apportait des frais tous les jours.

Après il y avait le plat de poisson. Du saumon si c'était la saison, ou bien de la limande-sole, parfois un turbot, chacun avec sa sauce : hollandaise, tartare ou mayonnaise. Moi, je devais faire la mayonnaise, et c'était un sacré boulot. J'ai bien cru que je n'y arriverais jamais. D'abord je mettais un jaune d'œuf dans un bol, j'ajoutais de l'huile d'olive, une goutte à la fois, juste une goutte, et je battais, je battais, je battais, jusqu'à ce que ça fasse une belle mixture jaune bien épaisse, un peu comme de la crème pâtissière. Mais si j'essayais d'aller vite et que je versais trop d'huile à la fois, elle retombait ; alors je devais la jeter et tout recommencer. Qu'est-ce que j'ai pu jeter comme mayonnaise au début !

Après il y avait le plat de résistance. Quelquefois c'était un rôti de bœuf ; s'ils avaient des invités ça pouvait être une selle de mouton entière, ou juste un gigot d'agneau.

Mrs McIlroy réussissait un magnifique glaçage. Je n'ai jamais su exactement comment elle faisait. Maintenant ça s'achète en pot, mais elle, elle le préparait elle-même à partir d'une espèce de caramel. Ça fondait en prenant une belle couleur dorée, et elle l'étalait sur le gigot ou la selle avant de l'envoyer là-haut. C'était vraiment superbe.

Et puis il y avait le dessert. Ça pouvait être n'importe quoi, mais c'était presque toujours froid : une mousse au chocolat, qu'on préparait avec du chocolat râpé, des œufs et du sucre en poudre ; ou bien des fruits frais avec un nappage de sucre qu'on avait fait réduire en sirop ; ou alors une compote d'oranges, ou une compote de bananes ; en tout cas pas forcément un plat salé, parce que le révérend n'aimait pas trop ça, même si ça lui arrivait de manger des canapés aux sardines ou aux anchois*.

Après il y avait le fromage et le café.

Ça, c'était leur dîner à eux.

Nous, ce qu'on mangeait le soir c'étaient les restes de la veille, ou alors un gratin de macaronis, ou des toasts au fromage. Ce n'était pas la faute de Mrs McIlroy ; elle n'avait pas le droit de nous donner plus. Certaines des bonnes râlaient sacrément, en disant qu'elles n'avaient jamais assez à manger. Moi je ne râlais pas, mais je trouvais que ce n'était pas juste.

Là-haut ils ne dînaient jamais avant huit heures du soir, mais moi je devais avoir tout préparé pour Mrs McIlroy avant six heures, et pas seulement sa table, vu qu'avec elle il fallait que tout soit fait à la main. Par exemple, quand elle faisait un soufflé au fromage (ils adoraient ça), elle utilisait du parmesan parce que c'est plus fin et plus léger qu'un fromage ordinaire. Maintenant, bien entendu, on trouve du parmesan tout râpé dans le commerce, mais en ce temps-là ça s'achetait en morceaux. Je peux vous dire que c'était dur comme du caillou, et en plus je devais le frotter du côté le plus fin de la râpe. Ça me prenait un temps fou, et au début je me râpais les doigts en même temps.

Si elle avait prévu une sauce au raifort, il fallait aussi le râper à la main, et râper du raifort c'est bien pire que

---

* Vers la fin d'un dîner anglais traditionnel, on servait autrefois des amuse-gueules salés ou épicés censés stimuler la digestion. (N.d.T.)

d'éplucher des oignons. Ça me faisait pleurer à chaudes larmes, et j'appréhendais ce travail-là. Si elle avait l'intention de servir des épinards à la crème je devais les passer au tamis – encore une longue corvée !

Le pire de tout, c'était quand il y avait du pain de viande au menu. Je devais d'abord passer le bœuf cru – en général du filet – au hachoir. Ça, déjà, ce n'était pas évident. Mais ensuite il fallait que je le passe encore cru au tamis métallique, alors je vous laisse imaginer le temps que ça me prenait. La première fois j'ai cru que ce n'était pas possible, et puis je me suis aperçue que si, à condition d'y passer beaucoup de temps.

Après on mélangeait le bœuf haché avec des herbes et un jaune d'œuf, on le tassait bien dans une mousseline et on le mettait à cuire à feu doux dans un peu de bouillon pendant vingt minutes, pas plus. Comme ça, quand on coupait la viande elle était encore plus ou moins crue, mais elle était tellement fine, après le passage au tamis, qu'au goût on avait l'impression qu'elle avait cuit jusqu'à ce qu'elle soit tendre. C'était délicieux, mais ça demandait beaucoup de boulot.

Avec le gibier on servait des chips. Maintenant tout le monde achète des chips en sachets, mais en ce temps-là il fallait les faire à la main. D'abord on épluchait les pommes de terre. Après on prenait un torchon propre qu'on étalait bien sur la table et on coupait les pommes de terre en rondelles tellement fines que quand on les tenait en l'air on pouvait voir au travers. On aurait dit des bulles d'air. Il fallait poser chaque rondelle séparément sur le torchon et les recouvrir avec un autre torchon jusqu'à ce qu'elles soient sèches. Alors on faisait fondre de la matière grasse – du saindoux, pas de la sauce de rôti, sinon les chips auraient été trop foncées. Soit dit en passant, on n'achetait pas notre saindoux en demi-livres ; c'étaient des pains entiers qui faisaient environ la taille d'un ballon de rugby et qui avaient à peu près la même forme. Bref, on en faisait fondre un morceau dans une poêle à frire très profonde, et quand ça bouillait en dégageant une fumée bleue on jetait les chips dedans, une par une, parce que si on en mettait deux en même temps elles restaient collées, et après, impossible de les séparer. À peine on avait jeté la dernière que la première était déjà cuite, alors entre le moment où on les mettait dans la poêle et celui où on les repêchait, c'était la course. Si on les laissait une minute de trop, au lieu d'avoir des chips bien dorées on avait des espèces de copeaux marron foncé et durs comme du bois.

Quand ma mère me demandait si j'avais appris beaucoup de choses en cuisine je lui répondais : « Non, maman, je n'ai pas le temps », mais je crois qu'en fait j'absorbais des connaissances sans m'en apercevoir, parce que quand je me suis retrouvée cuisinière j'ai été sidérée de voir tout ce que je savais faire.

XIII

Mr Clydesdale avait un jardinier-chauffeur et une voiture à lui, mais deux matins par semaine un taxi de louage venait le chercher à la porte. Le vieux canasson qui était entre les brancards, il avait l'air tout juste bon pour l'abattoir, et le cocher, un homme d'un certain âge, s'appelait Ambrose Datchet.

Quand il me parlait (c'est-à-dire pas très souvent, étant donné qu'il discutait surtout avec la cuisinière), cet Ambrose Datchet me racontait qu'il avait été jardinier dans une grande maison, une maison beaucoup plus grande que toutes celles que ma mère et moi on a connues. Là-bas il y avait deux régisseurs, deux chefs cuisiniers, sept valets de pied, six femmes de chambre et plus de vingt-huit jardiniers dont lui. Il avait commencé comme page, mais il n'aimait pas travailler à l'intérieur, et quand il avait vu que les valets devaient toujours être en uniforme, avec des gants blancs et même une perruque, il avait dit qu'il ne pourrait pas supporter cette vie-là, alors on l'avait mis à l'extérieur et il était devenu jardinier.

Je l'entendais quand il racontait à Mrs McIlroy tout ce qui se passait dans ce grand château. J'adorais l'écouter. Vous savez ce que c'est : quand on entend quelque chose qu'on n'est pas censé entendre, on trouve ça épatant ! D'après cet Ambrose Datchet, donc, il se passait des choses absolument choquantes dans cette maison, et bizarrement ça ne concernait pas tellement les bonnes. Ça se passait plutôt entre les valets de pied ou les régisseurs d'une part et les gens d'en haut d'autre part – et pas seulement les maîtres de maison, les invités aussi. Un jour j'ai entendu Mrs McIlroy s'écrier :

« Non, pas Madame la duchesse, tout de même ! »

Et Ambrose Datchet a répondu :

« Je l'ai vu de mes yeux.

– Quoi, avec elle ? a fait Mrs McIlroy.

– Avec elle et aussi avec lui. C'était un très beau jeune homme. »

D'après ce que j'ai compris, c'était un valet de pied qui avait une liaison à la fois avec le maître et avec la maîtresse de maison.

Remarquez, pour voir autant de choses de ses yeux, Ambrose Datchet devait en avoir derrière la tête, des yeux, parce que si je ne l'ai pas entendu dire cent fois : « Je l'ai vu de mes yeux », je ne l'ai jamais entendu !

Je me souviens d'une histoire qu'il m'a racontée un jour. C'était une fille de la campagne qui venait d'entrer en condition, c'était sa toute première place, et la dame lui avait dit :

« Elsie, le matin je prends mon petit déjeuner à huit heures. »

Et Elsie avait répondu :

« Oh, ce n'est pas grave, Madame. Si je ne suis pas descendue, ne m'attendez pas. »

Quand Ambrose Datchet revenait de ses sorties avec Mr Clydesdale il avait le droit de venir à la cuisine. En été il buvait un verre de limonade et en hiver une tasse de cacao. Il s'asseyait là, et il taillait une bavette avec Mrs McIlroy et parfois avec Mr Wade, le majordome.

Juste avant de s'en aller il traversait la cuisine pour aller dans l'espèce de cour qu'il y avait derrière. Au début je croyais qu'il allait papoter avec le jardinier-chauffeur de la maison, mais quand il revenait Mrs McIlroy lui disait :

« Alors, Ambrose, on est allé serrer la main de son meilleur ami ? »

Je ne comprenais pas du tout pourquoi ils rigolaient, mais étant donné qu'ils me regardaient je devenais rouge comme une tomate. Après, une fois que j'ai eu l'explication, moi aussi je rigolais. Mrs McIlroy avait l'air un peu collet monté, comme ça, mais en fait pour les blagues elle n'était pas la dernière.

Presque tous les matins Mrs Clydesdale sortait faire sa promenade de santé, et quand elle rentrait je n'en menais pas large, parce qu'à ce moment-là elle inspectait la porte d'entrée. Le cuivre qu'il y avait sur cette porte, c'était une horreur, croyez-moi. La poignée était toute tarabiscotée, alors le produit se mettait dans les creux ; il y avait un énorme heurtoir en forme de gargouille avec plein de petits trucs en relief, plus une grande boîte aux lettres, et le seuil aussi était entièrement en cuivre. Parfois, les matins où il faisait vraiment froid, j'attrapais des engelures, alors je fignolais un peu moins. Il me semblait que ça ne se voyait pas, mais en général Mrs Clydesdale trouvait quelque chose à redire.

Si j'entendais la sonnette deux minutes après son retour, je savais pour quoi c'était. La femme de service descendait en disant :

« Madame fait dire qu'elle désire parler à Langley (ça, c'était moi) dans le petit salon. »

Rien que de penser qu'il fallait que je monte j'avais les jambes en coton, parce que je savais ce qu'elle allait me dire ; c'était forcément à propos de la porte d'entrée. Elle commençait par faire une remarque ambiguë du style :

« Langley, qu'est-il donc arrivé à la porte d'entrée ce matin ? »

Ça pouvait vouloir dire soit qu'elle était impeccable, soit qu'elle n'avait pas été très bien astiquée, mais moi je savais parfaitement où elle voulait en venir. Elle continuait :

« Langley, vous êtes ici dans une bonne maison, vous êtes bien nourrie, vous disposez d'un logement confortable et vous apprenez un métier. J'exige en retour que le travail soit bien fait. »

À ce moment-là j'étais déjà en larmes tellement je me sentais humiliée. J'avais tout juste quinze ans à l'époque. Avec le temps je me suis endurcie, et plus tard, lorsque j'avais droit à ce genre de réflexions, ça ne me faisait plus ni chaud ni froid.

Quand je redescendais, même Mrs McIlroy prenait mon parti. Elle me disait :

« Ne t'en fais pas, va ! Dis-toi qu'ils font leurs besoins exactement comme nous. »

Je ne voyais pas le rapport, et eux au moins ils pouvaient faire leurs besoins confortablement. Nous, tout ce qu'on avait c'étaient des cabinets au sous-sol, et ils étaient fréquentés par toutes sortes de bestioles, des araignées velues, des cafards et un tas d'autres insectes.

Mary partageait la chambre du grenier avec moi, et elle se réveillait souvent la nuit pour aller aux cabinets. Comme elle avait peur de descendre toute seule elle me réveillait pour que je vienne avec elle. On descendait sur la pointe des pieds, en essayant de ne pas faire craquer les marches, comme si on était en faute. D'ailleurs je suis sûre que Mrs Clydesdale aurait trouvé qu'on était en faute ; elle aurait dit que les domestiques devaient faire leurs besoins aussi régulièrement que tout le reste et ne pas aller aux cabinets la nuit.

Un matin où Mr et Mrs Clydesdale étaient sortis, Mr Wade est descendu demander à Mrs McIlroy si elle pouvait se passer de moi un moment.

Mrs McIlroy et Mr Wade étaient plutôt copains, même si Mrs McIlroy pensait depuis toujours que Mr Wade avait un secret. Du reste, quelques mois après mon arrivée, un soir il est rentré soûl comme un cochon, et quand on l'a trouvé il avait mis un des costumes du révérend. Il a été flanqué à la porte immédiatement. Dans sa chambre, derrière l'office du majordome, on a découvert que son placard était plein de bouteilles de whisky vides. C'était peut-être ça, son secret.

Bref, ce matin-là, quand Mr Wade est descendu demander à Mrs McIlroy si elle pouvait se passer de moi, elle lui a demandé pourquoi.

« Pour voir les sucreurs de fraises de dix heures.

– Les sucreurs de fraises de dix heures ?

– Oui.

– Bon, je peux me passer d'elle une demi-heure. »

Alors on est montés au rez-de-chaussée, on a ouvert la porte d'entrée et on a regardé.

Sur toute la longueur d'Adelaide Crescent on a vu des voitures et des chauffeurs en uniforme très élégants. Ils portaient des hauts-de-chausses, des bottes toutes brillantes, une casquette à visière et des gants blancs. Certains uniformes étaient gris, d'autres verts ou bleus. Les chauffeurs se tenaient au garde-à-vous à côté des voitures, prêts pour quand leurs patrons sortiraient de chez eux.

À dix heures tapantes, la rue s'est animée tout d'un coup. Ça a commencé à deux maisons de la nôtre. La porte s'est ouverte et un vieux monsieur est sorti. Le majordome l'a aidé à descendre les marches, et puis la vieille dame est sortie au bras de la femme de chambre ; l'aide-femme de chambre suivait avec un tabouret et un petit chien de manchon qui avait l'air horriblement vieux. Les domestiques les ont installés dans la voiture, ils ont mis le tabouret sous les pieds du vieux monsieur et déposé gentiment le chien sur les genoux de la vieille dame. Le chauffeur s'est penché à l'intérieur, il les a soigneusement enveloppés tous les deux dans un plaid pour les protéger du vent – et hop, les voilà partis. La même scène s'est reproduite tout le long de la rue. C'étaient eux, les sucreurs de fraises de dix heures.

Après ça Mr Wade a dit qu'il allait me faire visiter la maison, parce que depuis plusieurs mois que j'étais là comme fille de cuisine je n'avais rien vu à part l'escalier de service. Tout ce que j'avais fait, c'était l'aller-retour entre le sous-sol et le grenier.

Ce que c'était beau, chez eux, par rapport à chez nous ! Il y avait des tapis magnifiques partout, des tapis turcs et chinois très épais et de toutes les couleurs ; il y en avait dans le petit salon, dans le grand salon, dans la salle à manger et dans les chambres. Et puis des fauteuils trapus, d'immenses rideaux en beau velours, des lits superbes avec des matelas tellement épais que la princesse du conte* n'aurait jamais senti le petit pois si elle avait couché dessus. Tout ça respirait le calme et le confort.

J'ai pensé à notre chambre à nous, où il faisait une chaleur tropicale en été et un froid de canard en hiver, au point que quand on laissait de l'eau dans nos brocs le soir il y avait une couche de glace sur le dessus le lendemain, et on devait la casser pour se laver. On ne pouvait même pas prendre un bain confortablement : on n'avait qu'une baignoire sabot. Pour la remplir il fallait se coltiner toute l'eau depuis la salle de bains, deux étages au-dessous, et quand on voulait la vider il fallait redescendre tout jusqu'à la dernière goutte aux cabinets. Et puis dans une baignoire sabot je ne savais jamais comment me mettre : carrément dedans, avec les fesses en bas et les genoux sous le menton, ou assise avec les jambes à l'extérieur ? D'une façon comme d'une autre, j'étais frigorifiée.

J'ai aussi pensé à la salle des domestiques ; c'était notre salon, en fait. Là-haut il y avait des lampes, de magnifiques lampes de lecture avec de beaux abat-jour. Nous, tout ce qu'on avait comme lumière dans notre salle c'était une ampoule, une seule, avec un abat-jour en porcelaine blanche. Il y avait un vieux lino marron par terre et de méchantes chaises en osier toutes déformées ; à une époque elles avaient

---

* Allusion à un conte de Hans Christian Andersen intitulé *La Princesse au petit pois* et publié en 1835. Une jeune fille inconnue se prétend princesse. Pour s'en assurer, on la fait dormir sur vingt matelas et vingt édredons sous lesquels on a glissé un petit pois. Au matin elle se plaint d'avoir des bleus partout et c'est la preuve qu'elle disait vrai, car seule une princesse peut avoir la peau aussi délicate ! *(N.d.T.)*

garni leur jardin d'hiver, mais maintenant même pour ça ils les trouvaient trop moches. Les murs étaient peints en marron brillant jusqu'à mi-hauteur et en vert jaunâtre délavé au-dessus, des couleurs carrément déprimantes. Il y avait des barreaux aux fenêtres et une seule table avec une vieille nappe. Voilà, c'était ça notre salon.

Mary et moi on avait la chambre la moins bien, c'est vrai, vu qu'on était tout en bas de l'échelle des domestiques, mais même celle de Mrs McIlroy était meublée avec des vieux machins que les patrons avaient mis au rebut. Son lit, il avait servi à Leonora à un moment ou à un autre et ils ne le trouvaient plus assez bien pour elle. Les petits tapis, c'étaient leurs anciennes descentes de lit. On pouvait regarder n'importe où, la différence était flagrante. Si au moins ils avaient essayé de nous mettre quelques objets neufs ! Pourquoi il fallait toujours qu'on hérite de leurs cochonneries ?

Une chose que je détestais vraiment, c'était quand le jardinier-chauffeur avait son jour de congé et que je devais sortir l'horrible petit chien de Mrs Clydesdale. C'était un carlin femelle, et elle était tellement grosse, à force de s'empiffrer, qu'on aurait dit un cube sur pattes. Elle s'appelait Elaine, mais je ne suis pas sûre que Lancelot aurait eu le béguin pour cette Elaine-là ! Je la promenais d'un bout à l'autre d'Adelaide Crescent, et naturellement elle traînait autour des arbres. Tous les garçons de courses – il y en avait des centaines en ce temps-là – me sifflaient au passage en disant :

« Alors, on sort son singe ? Et ton orgue, tu l'as oublié ? »
Mon Dieu que j'avais horreur de ce boulot-là !

XIV

Pendant mes premiers mois dans cette place, j'ai fait sottise sur sottise. Je me souviens surtout d'une fois où j'étais en train de briquer la porte d'entrée – j'étais un peu en retard ce jour-là – quand le livreur de journaux est passé. Juste comme je m'apprêtais à les poser sur la table du vestibule, Mrs Clydesdale est descendue ; alors je suis allée vers elle et je lui ai tendu les journaux. Elle m'a regardée comme si j'étais quelque chose de pas tout à fait humain. Elle n'a pas prononcé un mot, elle est juste restée là à me regarder. Elle avait visiblement du mal à croire que quelqu'un comme moi pouvait marcher et respirer. Je me suis dit : « Qu'est-ce qu'il y a ? J'ai mon bonnet, mon tablier, mes bas noirs, mes chaussures… » Je n'arrivais pas à trouver ce qui n'allait pas. Finalement elle a articulé :

« Langley, vous ne devez jamais, jamais, vous m'entendez, sous aucun prétexte, me tendre quoi que ce soit avec vos mains ; toujours sur un plateau d'argent. Vous devriez le savoir. Votre mère a pourtant été en condition. Elle ne vous a donc rien appris ? »

Je me suis mise à pleurer à gros sanglots. Pour moi c'était horrible qu'une personne me trouve tellement inférieure à elle que je ne pouvais même pas lui tendre quelque chose à la main sans l'avoir d'abord posé sur un plateau d'argent.

J'étais si malheureuse que j'avais envie de rentrer chez moi ; c'était la goutte d'eau qui faisait déborder le vase. Je me disais que je n'allais pas pouvoir supporter ce boulot. Je crois bien que je n'ai jamais eu autant de chagrin. Mais je savais que je ne pouvais pas retourner chez mes parents. Ils n'avaient que trois pièces dans la moitié d'une maison, deux au rez-de-chaussée et une à l'étage, et depuis que j'étais entrée en condition le père de ma mère était mort, alors ma grand-mère avait été obligée de venir vivre avec eux. Donc maintenant il n'y avait plus de place. Je n'en ai même pas parlé à ma mère. Ça m'aurait servi à quoi de les rendre malheureux aussi ? De toute manière je crois qu'elle m'aurait juste dit de ne pas faire attention, et elle aurait eu raison. C'était la seule solution si on voulait garder un peu de dignité : ne pas faire attention.

Pour nous, aller à la messe n'était pas une obligation, mais nos patrons partaient du principe qu'on devait y aller au moins une fois le dimanche, de préférence en fin d'après-midi. Ça dérangeait moins leur petit confort qu'on y aille l'après-midi. Un jour le révérend m'a demandé si j'avais fait ma confirmation et j'ai dit que non, alors il a voulu savoir pourquoi. J'ai répondu :

« Ma mère ne s'en est pas occupée, elle ne m'en a jamais parlé, et maintenant que j'ai quinze ans je trouve que ça ne vaut pas la peine de se tracasser pour ça. »

Après tout je ne vois pas ce que ça pouvait bien faire que j'aie fait ma confirmation ou pas pour être fille de cuisine ;

franchement, ça ne changeait rien pour mon travail. Mais bien sûr le révérend se souciait énormément de ma religion et de ma moralité.

En fait, pendant toute ma vie en condition j'ai constaté que les patrons se souciaient toujours énormément de notre bien-être moral. Ils se fichaient pas mal de notre bien-être physique. Pourvu qu'on soit capable de bosser, ça leur était bien égal qu'on ait mal au dos, au ventre ou ailleurs, mais tout ce qui avait à voir avec notre moralité, ils trouvaient que ça les regardait. C'est ce qu'ils appelaient « prendre soin des domestiques », s'intéresser à ceux d'en bas. Ça ne les dérangeait pas qu'on fasse de grosses journées, qu'on manque de liberté et qu'on soit mal payé ; du moment qu'on travaillait bien et qu'on savait que c'était le Bon Dieu qui avait tout organisé pour que nous on soit tout en bas à trimer et qu'eux ils vivent dans le confort et le luxe, ça leur convenait parfaitement. Quand le révérend disait, à la fin de la prière du matin : « Et maintenant, remercions le Seigneur pour tous Ses bienfaits », je trouvais ça franchement déplacé ; je me disais que ça devait lui prendre drôlement plus de temps qu'à nous !

En bas, on se moquait sans arrêt du révérend, mais à l'époque la plupart des blagues me passaient au-dessus de la tête. C'était sans doute à cause de mes parents : les histoires cochonnes et tout ça, chez moi on ne connaissait pas. Je me souviens, un jour où je lavais les légumes, c'étaient des poireaux et des pommes de terre cette fois-là, une des bonnes a regardé ce que je faisais et elle a dit :

« Si tu veux une belle purée, faut souffler dans le poireau ! »

Tout le monde a éclaté de rire, et moi je n'ai pas compris pourquoi.

Elles causaient tout le temps du révérend et des huit filles qu'il avait eues avec sa première femme. Elles faisaient la comparaison avec les prêtres catholiques qui n'ont pas le droit de se marier ; elles se demandaient comment il pouvait monter en chaire pour parler du péché de chair – en faisant plein d'autres allusions qui m'échappaient complètement. Je n'étais pas naïve ; je me rendais bien compte que pour un homme d'Église, qui est censé parler de la vie spirituelle et de l'autre monde, avoir une famille aussi nombreuse ce n'était pas très… convenable, disons – même si huit enfants ça ne faisait pas tant que ça, en ce temps-là. Mais comme c'était un homme d'Église, qu'il s'était remarié en espérant avoir un fils, un héritier, et qu'en fait il s'était retrouvé avec une fille de plus, on ne pouvait pas s'empêcher de rigoler. On trouvait que c'était rudement bien fait pour lui. Maintenant je sais que moi j'aurais laissé tomber, après huit enfants et tout ce que ça suppose !

Un peu plus tard j'ai compris de quoi les bonnes parlaient, et naturellement je me suis mise à rajouter mon grain de sel. De ma part c'était de la lâcheté : je me prêtais à beaucoup de choses qui en fait ne me plaisaient pas. Mais si je n'étais pas entrée dans leur jeu elles m'auraient prise pour une bêcheuse, et il fallait bien que je travaille avec elles. Pas seulement que je travaille, mais que je *vive* avec elles : c'est tout juste si on ne dormait pas dans le même lit ! Alors je m'arrangeais pour rester en bons termes avec mes collègues. Elles étaient toute ma vie, vous comprenez ?

XV

Je suis restée un an chez les Clydesdale, et puis j'ai décidé de tenter ma chance à Londres. J'avais toujours entendu dire que c'était une ville formidable et que là-bas on pouvait faire fortune. Je ne croyais pas que les rues étaient pavées d'or ou ce genre de bobards, évidemment, mais qu'il y avait plus de possibilités à Londres que dans une petite ville de province, ça oui, je le croyais.

Quand j'en ai parlé chez moi, mes parents ont eu l'air consternés ; on aurait cru que je venais de leur annoncer mon départ pour Tombouctou. Ma mère s'est souvenue aussitôt d'un article du journal qui racontait que toutes les jeunes filles disparaissaient dès qu'elles arrivaient à Londres et qu'on n'entendait plus jamais parler d'elles. Elle a dit qu'on savait bien que « ces femmes » – elle voulait dire les prostituées, bien sûr – étaient au départ des jeunes filles innocentes qui étaient allées à Londres avec la même idée que moi et qui s'étaient fait piéger par des promesses d'argent facile et de luxe. Je me rappelle que j'ai répondu :

« Oh, ne t'inquiète pas, maman, quand je serai à un coin de rue je dirai que j'attends le bus et puis c'est tout. »

Ça n'a pas consolé ma mère. Mon père, lui, il ne faisait jamais tellement d'histoires pour quoi que ce soit. Je ne sais pas pourquoi ma mère en faisait autant ; je n'étais pas d'une beauté renversante, tous les garçons n'allaient pas décider au premier coup d'œil de m'enlever pour décorer leur harem ! Je suppose qu'elle voyait ça comme un éclatement de la famille.

En tout cas, malgré toutes ses protestations et ses pronostics, j'ai décidé que j'en avais marre de vivre à Hove, alors j'ai acheté le *Morning Post* et j'ai répondu à une petite annonce pour une place de fille de cuisine à Thurloe Square, dans le quartier de Knightsbridge, à Londres.

Le salaire était meilleur que ce que j'avais touché jusque-là : quatre livres de plus par an. Je sais bien qu'aujourd'hui ça ne paraît pas beaucoup, mais à l'époque c'était une somme.

Ma mère voulait venir à Londres avec moi.

« Tu vas te perdre, tu ne vas pas trouver.

– Mais maman, j'ai une langue, j'ai des bras, je sais parler, je sais marcher, et puis il y a des bus, des métros. »

Je n'avais jamais mis les pieds à Londres et je ne connaissais personne là-bas, mais j'ai décrété :

« Maintenant que j'ai seize ans, je vais me débrouiller toute seule. »

Ça m'a donné un sacré sentiment de supériorité sur mes frères et sœurs, surtout sur mon grand frère, parce que les grands frères, ça veut toujours dominer.

Au début, j'ai été effrayée par la taille et le standing des maisons de Thurloe Square. Et l'entretien avec la maîtresse de maison, Mrs Cutler, m'a intimidée encore plus que la maison. Quand je lui ai dit que je m'appelais Margaret Langley, j'ai bien vu qu'elle trouvait ça tout à fait déplacé pour une fille de cuisine. C'était un genre de nom pour faire de la scène, pas pour travailler au sous-sol. Manifestement elle trouvait que j'aurais dû m'appeler Elsie Smith ou Mary Jones. D'habitude les filles de cuisine avaient des noms comme ça. Margaret Langley, ça faisait frivole.

Ça, c'était la bête noire de tous les patrons. Ils avaient toujours peur qu'on soit frivole. Les femmes de service nous racontaient souvent que quand c'était le « jour » de ces dames, une fois par mois, en servant les invités elles les entendaient parler de leurs domestiques. C'était un de leurs sujets de conversation favoris. Elles disaient :

« Eh oui, j'ai dû m'en défaire. Elle était frivole. »

Si on se maquillait, même un tout petit peu, on était frivole. De toute façon ce n'était pas tellement à la mode, mais si on se maquillait un peu, ou si on se faisait friser les cheveux, ou si on portait des bas de soie de couleur – des bas de soie marron, ça allait, mais si on mettait des bas de couleur, je veux dire même pendant nos congés, pas pour travailler –, c'est qu'on était frivole ; et les filles frivoles, n'est-ce pas, ça finit toujours mal.

Je n'ai jamais compris pourquoi, et d'ailleurs je ne comprends toujours pas. Pour nous, les filles du soi-disant populo, mal finir ça voulait dire se retrouver enceintes. Mais à mon avis on était bien les dernières à en avoir envie : on n'avait pas les moyens d'élever un bébé, et il n'y avait pas de foyers où on aurait pu aller. Si on avait un enfant hors mariage on était rejetée de partout. Alors pourquoi ceux d'en haut nous croyaient si pressées de faire des fredaines, je me le demande. Peut-être qu'en leur for intérieur ils savaient que notre vie était sacrément monotone ; donc ils se disaient que si un gars nous invitait à sortir, il pouvait demander n'importe quoi en échange, de toute façon pour nous ça serait une aubaine.

Je sais que moi je n'aurais jamais osé faire des fredaines – pas parce que je n'en avais pas envie, mais parce que j'avais bien trop peur. Je n'avais pas la moindre idée de ce qu'on pouvait faire au juste avec un garçon sans qu'il y ait des suites, si vous voyez ce que je veux dire. Je devais donc rester sur le « droit chemin », comme on disait, parce que si je m'en écartais je ne savais pas où ça me mènerait.

Malgré mon nom, ce jour-là mon chemin me menait vers Mrs Cutler. J'avais l'impression qu'elle m'étouffait, que toute la pièce m'étouffait. Il y avait du velours partout ; c'était la mode à cette époque-là. Les rideaux du salon étaient en velours marron foncé, le canapé et les deux fauteuils étaient tapissés de velours marron foncé, les cadres des tableaux étaient bordés de velours et Mrs Cutler portait un corsage de velours pourpre. Elle me rappelait la reine Victoria, qui n'était pas non plus du genre rigolote. Pour elle la vie c'était une chose grave, une chose qu'on ne devait pas prendre à la légère.

Je n'étais pas le type de fille que Mrs Cutler recherchait ; en fait elle cherchait une Londonienne. Mais elle a quand même dû se dire que je ferais l'affaire puisqu'elle m'a embauchée. Je crois que si j'ai décroché la place, c'est parce que j'avais l'air robuste et en bonne santé – et du reste ça ne m'a pas été inutile, croyez-moi !

En arrivant là-bas je me suis aperçue que leur fille vivait chez eux avec ses trois enfants, à qui naturellement il fallait une nourrice, mais aussi une aide-nourrice et des repas spéciaux. Après ça, plus jamais je n'ai choisi une maison où il y avait des nourrices et des enfants, et où ils devaient prendre leurs repas séparément dans la nursery – plus jamais.

La nourrice descendait nous voir au sous-sol en se donnant de grands airs de patronne pour nous dire ce que les enfants et elle désiraient. Il y avait toujours de l'animosité entre la cuisine et la nursery, ça avait toujours été comme ça. La femme de service, la femme de chambre et la cuisinière disaient que la nourrice et l'aide-nourrice se croyaient supérieures à elles, et c'était ma foi vrai.

Elles étaient comme qui dirait à mi-chemin entre nous et les gens d'en haut, et à mon avis ça leur posait pas mal de problèmes. Elles passaient plus de temps que nous avec les gens d'en haut ; elles amenaient les enfants voir leurs parents le soir avant qu'ils aillent se coucher et elles s'asseyaient au salon avec « Eux », mais évidemment elles n'étaient pas des leurs pour autant. Et quand elles venaient au sous-sol elles n'étaient pas des nôtres non plus, parce qu'on croyait qu'elles étaient amies avec « Eux » et qu'elles allaient répéter là-haut tout ce qu'on dirait sur « Eux ». En fait elles ne l'auraient sans doute pas fait, mais nous c'est ce qu'il nous semblait.

Bien entendu ça mettait toujours la cuisinière en rogne quand la nourrice venait à la cuisine, parce que la cuisine, c'était *son* territoire. Il n'y avait que la maîtresse de maison qui avait le droit d'y entrer, et encore une seule fois, le matin, pour donner ses instructions. Alors quand la nourrice venait lui demander ce qu'il y avait au menu, déjà ça mettait la cuisinière en pétard, mais si en plus la nourrice lui demandait quelque chose d'autre pour les enfants, alors là elle lui volait carrément dans les plumes !

À Thurloe Square la cuisinière s'appelait Mrs Bowchard, et c'était une sacrée vieille rosse. Comme autres domestiques il y avait : la fille de cuisine, c'est-à-dire moi ; pas de major-dome ni de valet de pied (ils n'aimaient pas trop avoir des domestiques hommes dans cette maison, à part un valet pour Mr Cutler) mais une première femme de service et une aide-femme de service à la place ; une première femme de chambre et une aide-femme de chambre ; la nourrice et l'aide-nourrice ; un chauffeur, un jardinier et un aide-jardinier. Ça ne faisait pas beaucoup de personnel pour une maison aussi grande, mais comme par rapport à maintenant on faisait chacune le travail de deux, on peut dire qu'il y avait à peu près six personnes pour faire tourner la maison – je ne compte pas la nourrice.

La cuisinière était hargneuse comme c'est pas possible. Quand j'y repense, je me dis que c'était peut-être à cause du défilé de filles de cuisine qui arrivaient et repartaient sans arrêt. C'est vrai qu'elles ne restaient jamais bien longtemps. Il faut dire que ce n'était pas difficile à trouver comme boulot. De nos jours, naturellement, on vous déroule le tapis rouge et tout ça, mais même à l'époque on ne se bousculait pas pour cette place. Le problème avec les filles de cuisine, d'après tous ceux qui n'étaient pas fille de cuisine, c'est qu'elles passaient leur temps à flirter avec les fournisseurs.

Vous trouvez peut-être que ma vie ressemblait à une tragédie, et pourtant on ne peut pas dire ça. Je travaillais vraiment dur et j'étais souvent triste, mais à quinze ou seize ans on n'est pas triste en permanence. Comme toutes les filles de cuisine je flirtais avec les fournisseurs, et plus particulièrement avec les garçons de courses. Ces gars-là, c'était une des attractions touristiques de Londres. Il fallait les voir circuler dans les rues à vélo, avec un chargement haut comme une tour, en sifflotant tous les airs à la mode ! Et ils étaient drôlement effrontés.

Les filles de cuisine aussi étaient effrontées, et Mrs Bowchard était hargneuse comme pas possible à cause de leur défilé continuel, de leur effronterie et de leurs flirts. Pour la peine, elle faisait de ma vie un enfer. Elle était toujours à me critiquer et à rouspéter après moi. Pas parce que j'étais moins capable que celles d'avant, juste parce que j'étais jeune. Et cette maladie-là, je vous garantis qu'elle a fait de son mieux pour m'en guérir. Au bout d'une journée avec elle, je me sentais nettement moins jeune.

Ce qu'il y avait aussi avec Mrs Bowchard, c'est qu'elle souffrait d'un mal inconnu de la médecine qui s'appelait « mes pauv' jambes ». À cause de « mes pauv' jambes », il y avait tout un tas de choses qu'elle ne pouvait pas faire ; « mes pauv' jambes » l'empêchaient de monter l'escalier pour aller dormir au grenier comme tout le monde, donc elle devait coucher au sous-sol. « Mes pauv' jambes » lui interdisaient de faire quelque chose que quelqu'un d'autre pouvait faire à sa place, par exemple s'asseoir pour lacer ses chaussures, alors c'était toujours à moi de m'y coller. M'accroupir le matin pour lui mettre et lui lacer ses chaussures, m'accroupir le soir pour lui délacer et lui enlever ses chaussures – il n'y avait rien que je détestais plus. Ce n'était peut-être pas plus dégradant que de servir les autres domestiques à table, mais j'avais l'impresion d'être un des petits cireurs de chaussures de Dickens. Ça ne faisait pas partie de mon boulot, mais bon, comme j'étais sous les ordres de la cuisinière il valait mieux que je fasse ce qu'elle disait, sinon elle m'aurait mené la vie encore plus dure.

Mrs Bowchard avait un chat. C'était un énorme bestiau noir et blanc, ce qu'on appelle généralement un beau chat. Elle l'avait baptisé « Monsieur le comte », et moi je vous laisse deviner comment je l'appelais. Je n'ai jamais beaucoup aimé les animaux, mais lui je le haïssais carrément. Il avait l'air tellement méprisant, ce « Monsieur le comte » ! Remarquez, personnellement je trouve que tous les chats ont l'air méprisants ; ils vous regardent toujours comme si vous étiez de la crotte. Par contre, je reconnais que c'était un animal très intelligent. Il couchait dans la chambre de la cuisinière, sous son lit, et tous les matins sans faute, à sept heures moins le quart, quand le réveil avait fini de sonner, il sortait de sous son lit, il allait à la porte et il faisait cliqueter la clenche avec sa patte. C'était sa façon de dire à Mrs Bowchard qu'elle devait se lever et lui ouvrir. Une fois dehors il parcourait tranquillement le couloir, il entrait dans la cuisine et il restait là à me fixer. Il ne bougeait pas, il restait juste là jusqu'à ce que je le regarde ; c'était sa façon de me dire que je devais porter à Mrs Bowchard un broc d'eau chaude et une tasse de thé. Ça m'horripilait. Je lui disais :

« Ça m'étonne que la vieille ne t'ait pas fait un mot, comme ça tu me l'aurais apporté dans ta gueule. Allez, dégage ! »

Mais c'est qu'il ne voulait pas s'en aller, vous savez ! Si je le poussais du pied jusqu'à la porte, il restait là jusqu'à ce que je sorte de la cuisine avec le broc d'eau chaude et la tasse de thé. À l'époque je n'aurais pas dit ça, mais il était vraiment très futé.

Deux fois par semaine on nous livrait une tête de morue pour lui, et c'est moi qui devais la faire cuire et enlever toutes les arêtes. Pendant ce temps-là Mrs Bowchard restait assise à regarder son chat d'un air complètement gâteux en me disant :

« Et enlève bien toutes les arêtes, hein ? Il ne faudrait pas que Monsieur le comte avale une arête, hein non ? »

J'étais verte de rage. Mais bon, je le faisais ; après je lui en mettais un peu par terre, et vous savez quoi ? Parfois cette sale bête reniflait juste un peu la morue et s'en allait, la queue et le nez en l'air. Évidemment, s'il faisait ça à un moment où sa maîtresse n'était pas là je le chassais encore plus loin avec le bout de ma chaussure. Mais il est devenu tellement malin que quand j'étais toute seule il ne venait même pas voir le poisson ni le renifler. Ah ça, pour être malin il était malin !

Mrs Cutler recevait beaucoup. Deux ou trois fois par semaine il y avait un dîner pour au moins douze personnes, quelquefois plus, et avec tous les plats à préparer je n'avais pas le temps de faire la vaisselle entre deux. Dès qu'un plat était parti je me précipitais pour préparer les assiettes suivantes, ce qui fait qu'à la fin du repas je me retrouvais avec un tas de vaisselle inimaginable : les casseroles, les plats, les assiettes, pas l'argenterie parce que ça et les verres c'étaient les femmes de service qui s'en occupaient, mais tout le reste c'était à moi de le laver. Il y avait des piles et des piles de vaisselle dans l'évier, sur la paillasse, et aussi par terre dans la pièce sombre et humide qui servait d'arrière-cuisine.

Les éviers étaient en ciment gris foncé et pas très profonds. Ils étaient poreux, rien à voir avec ceux d'aujourd'hui en faïence vernissée ou en inox, alors au bout d'un moment ils étaient comme qui dirait saturés d'eau sale et ils puaient comme c'est pas permis. Cette vaisselle, c'était vraiment ce qu'on appellerait aujourd'hui une corvée ménagère. Une fois que j'avais fini, et ça me prenait pas mal de temps, il fallait encore que je mette la table pour les domestiques et que je fasse leur vaisselle après.

Mr Cutler, c'était très rare que j'aie affaire à lui. Pour moi c'était un genre de fantôme qui ne faisait que passer. Il ne descendait jamais à la cuisine, et même si ça lui était venu à l'esprit, pour rien au monde il ne l'aurait fait. C'était une grosse légume à la City. Je ne suis pas spécialiste de ces métiers bizarres qui vous imposent de partir le matin vers dix heures et de rentrer chez vous vers quatre heures de l'après-midi, mais à mon avis ce n'était pas un truc trop fatigant. Il ne sortait jamais sans son parapluie. Un jour où Mrs Bowchard était plutôt de bonne humeur par rapport à d'habitude, je lui ai demandé ce que Mr Cutler faisait et elle m'a répondu :

« Qu'est-ce que j'en sais ? Que dalle, sûrement ! »

N'empêche, je crois que c'était une grosse légume à la City.

Comme je vous le disais, on avait rarement affaire à lui. Par contre son valet le voyait souvent, évidemment. Moi j'aurais cru qu'un valet c'était un genre de grand manitou dans une maison. En fait, je ne sais pas si c'était toujours comme ça, mais celui-là était drôlement efféminé. Peut-être que c'est la nature de leur travail qui veut ça ; mais bon, quand on y réfléchit, servir comme valet ce n'est pas tellement féminin comme boulot. Ou alors c'est parce qu'en condition ils sont toujours avec des femmes ? En tout cas, nous on se comportait avec lui comme avec une collègue. De toute manière je ne me serais pas mise en quatre pour un valet : je ne voulais pas me marier avec un domestique. En plus il avait l'air rudement vieux. Je suppose qu'il avait dans les quarante-cinq ans, mais comme j'en avais seulement quinze ou seize je trouvais qu'un homme de quarante-cinq ans c'était un grand-père. Moi, je ne m'intéressais qu'à ce qui pouvait devenir une relation durable. En ce temps-là, je passais ma vie à essayer de trouver le bon fiancé. Et comme j'éliminais d'entrée de jeu les domestiques, je n'ai jamais fait très attention au valet.

Il en avait autant à mon service, comme on dit. La cuisinière, par contre, elle était aux petits soins pour lui. Elle l'aimait vraiment bien. Mais personne ne le traitait comme un homme. On parlait et on blaguait toutes avec lui comme avec une femme. Il avait les mains tellement molles et la voix tellement douce qu'on n'aurait jamais dit un homme. Moi, il me faisait plutôt penser à une méduse. Je ne prétends pas qu'il ne pouvait pas faire d'enfants, naturellement ; je suppose que physiquement il avait tout ce qu'il faut. Mais on ne pouvait pas l'imaginer en train d'essayer. Du reste, à quarante-cinq ans il n'était pas marié. Peut-être qu'il n'avait jamais voulu se marier, je n'en sais rien. En y repensant, je me dis qu'il était peut-être homosexuel, mais ce qui est sûr c'est qu'on n'avait jamais entendu ce mot-là. On savait vaguement qu'il y avait des hommes qui « allaient avec des hommes », comme on disait à l'époque, mais de toute façon je n'y connaissais rien, et je crois que c'était à peu près pareil pour tout le monde. Si ça se passait dans notre entourage c'était vraiment en cachette, et personne ne parlait de ce genre de choses. D'ailleurs, si quelqu'un avait prononcé ce mot-là, je n'aurais même pas su ce que ça voulait dire !

Le cagibi aux chaussures, c'était le domaine de la fille de cuisine, et j'y passais beaucoup de temps au milieu des couteaux et des chaussures. Mais au moins, dans cette maison-là personne n'avait jamais eu l'idée de repasser les lacets.

Quand j'avais parlé à Mrs Bowchard de mettre le fer à chauffer, elle m'avait fait :

« Repasser les lacets ? Mais de quoi tu parles ?

— Eh bien, dans la dernière place où j'étais, il fallait que j'enlève les lacets et que je les repasse.

— Je n'ai jamais entendu une ânerie pareille. Ici, pas question ! Et si ça ne leur plaît pas, tu n'auras qu'à leur dire d'enlever leurs foutus lacets et de les repasser eux-mêmes. »

Elle m'avait drôlement soutenue cette fois-là.

Bref, pour moi le cagibi aux chaussures c'était un vrai refuge ; là-dedans j'étais à l'abri des ordres de cette vieille rosse de cuisinière. Elle n'y allait jamais parce que c'était très bas de plafond et plein de toiles d'araignées. Moi je m'amusais à les faire tomber, juste pour le plaisir de les voir revenues le lendemain matin.

Vous allez rire : je crois que maintenant les araignées ne tissent plus comme avant. Autrefois elles tendaient leurs toiles d'un mur à l'autre, et elles dessinaient des motifs très compliqués. Si Robert Bruce avait été dans ce cagibi, pour lui ç'aurait été Noël : il n'aurait pas su quelle araignée choisir pour apprendre comment on repart à zéro* !

---

* Selon la légende, Robert Bruce (1274-1329), champion de l'indépendance écossaise, se serait réfugié dans une grotte au cours d'une période de découragement. Là, il observa longuement une araignée et fut inspiré par sa persévérance. Il décida alors de reprendre les armes, vainquit les Anglais et régna sur l'Écosse de 1306 à sa mort. (N.d.T.)

Le matin, je passais une heure à nettoyer les chaussures, et je les faisais briller comme des sous neufs. J'étais devenue experte à ce boulot-là, j'ai même été félicitée pour ça dans cette maison. Pourtant je me sentais un peu comme Cendrillon dans ce cagibi aux chaussures, avec mon tablier de grosse toile, à penser à tout ce que j'avais envie de faire. Oh, je n'espérais pas voir un Prince charmant débarquer avec une pantoufle de verre, ça sûrement pas. D'ailleurs, quand on chausse du quarante-deux, on ne peut pas espérer que le Prince charmant se balade avec une pantoufle de cette taille, n'est-ce pas ?

XVI

Mrs Bowchard avait une sœur à Londres qui était aussi cuisinière ; cette sœur était mariée avec un majordome et ils travaillaient tous les deux dans la même maison. Moi je trouvais ça épouvantable de se marier et de continuer à bosser comme cuisinière et majordome dans la même maison.

Ce n'est pas comme quand on est cuisinière quelque part et qu'on s'offre de temps en temps une partie de jambes en l'air avec le majordome. Si c'est votre mari, ce n'est pas pareil. Faire la chose avec son légitime, c'est tout de suite moins drôle, non ? Enfin, je me trompe peut-être, mais j'ai connu des cuisinières qui s'en payaient de bonnes tranches avec les majordomes. Alors je trouvais ça bizarre d'en épouser un et de rester en condition avec lui toute sa vie. Vous parlez d'un couple harmonieux !

La sœur de Mrs Bowchard et son mari travaillaient pour un certain Lord Tartempion, j'ai oublié son nom, et ils prenaient leur soirée de congé le même jour. Bien obligés, sinon ils n'auraient jamais eu de temps libre ensemble.

Ce jour-là, ils venaient voir Mrs Bowchard. Ça devait drôlement les dépayser ! En fait ils ne sortaient jamais de leur condition ; ils devaient avoir ça dans le sang, à force. Vous imaginez, vous, avoir seulement une soirée de libre par semaine et un dimanche sur deux, et venir les passer dans un autre sous-sol pour manger avec une autre cuisinière ? Moi, si je n'avais rien trouvé de mieux à faire pendant mes congés, je me serais tiré une balle.

Une fois que Mrs Bowchard avait préparé le dîner, elle se retirait avec ses deux invités et le valet, et il fallait que je les serve dans sa chambre avant de servir les autres dans la salle des domestiques. Je vous laisse imaginer la scène : les filles étaient drôlement en pétard, elles rouspétaient parce que leur repas était en retard, mais qu'est-ce que j'y pouvais, moi ? Hiérarchiquement, les invités étaient au-dessus des femmes de service et des femmes de chambre.

Le beau-frère de Mrs Bowchard, Mr Moffat, était un type énorme avec une grosse bedaine et un double menton. Il riait beaucoup, le plus souvent à ses propres plaisanteries. Son rire démarrait tout en bas de son ventre et escaladait ses bourrelets de graisse jusqu'à son double menton, qui se mettait à tressauter en même temps que tout le reste. Je trouvais ça fascinant.

Il parlait tout le temps de son travail, de l'*importance* de son travail. Il disait sans arrêt des phrases du genre : « J'ai dit à Monsieur le duc », « J'ai déclaré à Monsieur le duc », « Monsieur le duc m'a consulté »… Franchement, si on l'écoutait un bout de temps on avait l'impression que Monsieur le duc ne pouvait rien faire, ne pouvait prendre aucune décision, sans demander à Mr Moffat ce qu'il en pensait.

Quand il était un peu pompette à cause du porto et des cigares – le porto et les cigares de Mr Cutler, soit dit en passant –, il devenait très gamin, comme qui dirait coquin. Je trouvais ça complètement déplacé de la part d'un homme de son gabarit et de son âge, et aussi par rapport à sa soi-disant dignité. Quand il était comme ça et que j'étais en train de les servir, il demandait à Mrs Bowchard :

« Alors, sommes-nous en bonne voie ? (Là il parlait de moi.) Apprenons-nous tout ce que nous pouvons en cuisine ? N'oublions pas que pour gagner le cœur d'un homme il faut parler à son estomac ! »

Je lui répliquais en mon for intérieur : « Eh ben dis donc, s'il fallait que je cherche ton cœur, à toi, sûr que je me perdrais ! » Après avoir dit ça il s'offrait une bonne pinte de rire et toute sa chair tremblotait à nouveau comme de la gélatine. Mrs Bowchard, qui n'avait pas non plus craché sur le porto de Mr Cutler, ça se voyait à son teint, répondait :

« Oui, ma foi, par rapport à d'autres filles de cuisine Margaret n'est pas trop maladroite. »

Si Mr Moffat était plus pompette que d'habitude, il s'adressait même directement à moi. Quel honneur il me faisait là ! Rendez-vous compte, un majordome qui travaillait pour un lord, qui était consulté par un lord, et qui s'adressait directement à une fille de cuisine ! Si ça se trouve il s'attendait à ce que je lui fasse des courbettes. Il me demandait :

« Alors, ma fille, vous vous plaisez ici ? »

Moi je ne pouvais rien dire, avec Mrs Bowchard assise juste là. J'aurais bien aimé lui répondre : « C'est la place la plus pourrie que j'ai jamais eue », mais je n'osais pas.

C'est drôle, non, quand on y pense, que je n'aie pas osé. Vous en voyez, vous, aujourd'hui, des filles de seize ans qui ont peur de dire quoi que ce soit ? De nos jours, elles feraient aussitôt demi-tour en disant : « Allez vous faire voir ! »

Moi je ne répondais pas, et il continuait :

« Est-ce que vous avez un petit ami ? Moi, à votre âge, j'en pinçais drôlement pour les filles. J'étais valet de pied, et je peux vous dire que pour les baisers et les mamours à l'office je n'étais pas le dernier ! »

Quand je montais me coucher le soir, comme Gladys avait entendu son rire tonitruant elle me demandait :

« De quoi il a parlé, le gros patapouf ?

— Il m'a raconté que dans sa jeunesse il tombait toutes les filles à l'office.

— En ben dis donc, s'il avait la même bedaine que maintenant, ça devait valoir le coup d'œil ! »

Et rien que de l'imaginer en pleine action, on piquait une de ces crises de rire !

Mrs Moffat était une femme douce et docile – ce qui était plutôt indiqué si on était mariée avec Mr Moffat. Je me suis souvent demandé si elle était pareille avec sa fille de cuisine. En tout cas, pour elle tout ce que disait Mr Moffat était parole d'Évangile. Son petit nom à lui je ne sais pas ce que c'était, mais elle ne l'employait jamais pour parler de lui. Elle disait toujours : « Comme Mr Moffat en a informé Monsieur le duc », « Quand Mr Moffat était au service de Madame Unetelle » ou « Mr Moffat a dit à John »… (John, c'était un des valets de pied.) Elle nous servait sans arrêt des Mr Moffat par-ci et des Mr Moffat par-là. Toute sa vie tournait autour de Mr Moffat. Sa personnalité, si elle en avait une – mais bon, elle devait bien en avoir eu une au départ pour séduire Mr Moffat, à moins qu'elle l'ait séduit par sa cuisine –, sa personnalité à elle, donc, était comme qui dirait engloutie par sa personnalité à lui, et du coup, même s'ils venaient tous les deux dîner avec Mrs Bowchard, c'était comme s'il n'y avait qu'une personne : Mr Moffat.

Quand je faisais le service je commençais par lui, je lui servais le porto en premier et tout ça. C'était lui le grand manitou. On aurait dit que le prestige de la classe pour laquelle il bossait déteignait sur lui. Je crois que c'est de ça qu'on parle quand on dit que certains domestiques vivent à travers leurs patrons.

Pour Mr Moffat c'était le cas : il s'identifiait complètement à Monsieur le duc. Quand Monsieur le duc dînait à l'extérieur Mr Moffat dînait à l'extérieur, parce qu'il imaginait tout ce que faisait Monsieur le duc. Quand on présentait Monsieur le duc à des membres de la noblesse on leur présentait aussi Mr Moffat. Je m'en rendais bien compte, parce qu'il nous racontait en détail des trucs qu'il ne pouvait pas savoir, vu qu'il n'assistait pas aux réceptions. Naturellement, c'était le genre de domestique que les patrons préféraient, car si on adoptait entièrement la personnalité de ses employeurs c'est là qu'ils pouvaient tirer de nous le maximum. À mon avis, c'est pour ça que je n'ai jamais été une très bonne employée : pour moi, ils étaient juste un moyen d'atteindre mon but. À l'époque c'était un moyen de gagner ma vie, et mon but c'était de quitter la condition domestique dès que je pourrais.

À force de vivre les uns sur les autres, les domestiques se disputaient souvent. On ne peut pas enfermer des femmes, et c'est peut-être vrai aussi pour les hommes, sans qu'il y ait des mots d'échangés – et pas n'importe quels mots ! Mais même si on se disputait souvent entre nous, face à ceux d'en haut on se serrait toujours les coudes.

On les appelait toujours « Eux ». « Eux », c'était l'ennemi. C'étaient « Eux » qui nous donnaient trop de travail, « Eux » qui ne nous payaient pas assez, et pour « Eux » les domestiques étaient une race à part, un mal nécessaire.

On était d'ailleurs leur principal sujet de conversation. D'après les femmes de service, qui descendaient nous le raconter, ils disaient des trucs du genre :

« Vous savez, si j'habitais une petite maison à la campagne je ne m'embêterais pas à avoir des domestiques ; pour moi c'est un fléau, ni plus ni moins. Ils se disputent, ils réclament toujours plus d'argent, ils n'ont pas envie de travailler et ils ne font pas les choses comme on voudrait. Mais que voulez-vous, j'ai un rang à tenir, alors je suis bien obligée d'avoir des gens de maison. »

Mrs Cutler, c'est sûr qu'elle nous considérait comme un mal nécessaire, et c'est pour ça que dans cette maison on était toujours solidaires contre « Eux ». « Eux », là-haut, ils pensaient que les domestiques ne devaient jamais tomber malades, ni être trop bien habillés, ni avoir une opinion différente de la leur. Après tout il était parfaitement évident, n'est-ce pas, que si on n'était allée à l'école que jusqu'à treize ou quatorze ans on avait des connaissances très limitées par rapport à « Eux ». Alors si on devait absolument avoir des opinions, on n'avait qu'à adopter les leurs : ils en savaient tellement plus que nous !

Selon « Eux », les domestiques n'étaient pas capables d'apprécier les bonnes choses ni le confort ; il fallait donc les nourrir très simplement, les faire travailler et manger dans des cachots, les loger dans des chambres nues et glaciales.

Et puis à quoi ça aurait servi de dépenser de l'argent pour rendre la vie plus facile et plus confortable à des individus ingrats qui se fichaient pas mal de ce que vous faisiez pour eux ? Remarquez, ils n'essayaient jamais de nous offrir de bonnes conditions de travail et de nous donner des chambres agréables pour voir si on s'en ficherait moins. Non, ça ne valait pas la peine de dépenser de l'argent pour les domestiques parce que, peu importe ce que vous faisiez pour eux, de toute façon ils ne restaient jamais. Au bout du compte, « Eux » seuls avaient besoin de luxe, « Eux » seuls pouvaient faire honneur à une bonne table et bavarder avec esprit. Vous comprenez, il faut bien qu'une partie de la société puisse danser avec grâce et bavarder avec esprit, et une personne qui travaille dur ne peut pas faire ça. Moralité : rendez la vie de vos employés encore plus dure, comme ça ils auront encore moins envie de bavarder.

Mais si « Eux » avaient entendu les bavardages que les femmes de service rapportaient de là-haut, ils se seraient aperçus que, derrière nos visages sans expression et nos manières respectueuses, il y avait du mépris et de la dérision.

XVII

Mr Cutler aimait beaucoup la chasse. Il avait vécu quelques années en Afrique, et à voir les trophées accrochés partout dans la maison il avait dû passer beaucoup de temps à chasser.

Les murs du vestibule étaient carrément tapissés de cornes de ceci et de cornes de cela – je ne sais pas quels animaux c'étaient. Tout ce que je sais, c'est que certaines étaient recourbées et les autres toutes droites, et que c'est moi qui devais les épousseter en grimpant sur un tabouret.

Ici, en Angleterre, il n'y avait pas ce genre d'animaux, évidemment, alors Mr Cutler chassait des oiseaux. J'ai fini par en avoir par-dessus la tête des grouses, des faisans et des perdrix. Ils étaient envoyés le plus rapidement possible de là où il chassait et on les suspendait jusqu'à ce qu'ils soient faisandés – et quand je dis faisandés, vous pouvez me croire.

Ils étaient accrochés à une tringle métallique dans le couloir du sous-sol, et souvent quand j'arrivais le matin il n'y avait plus que la tête d'accrochée ; le corps était par terre, à cause des vers qui s'y étaient mis. À ce moment-là on estimait que la bête était assez faisandée pour être servie au dîner.

C'était à moi de la plumer, en faisant bien attention de ne pas abîmer la peau, et de la vider. C'était vraiment écœurant, comme boulot. Ça puait, mais ça puait !

Quand la cuisinière préparait le faisan elle gardait la tête avec toutes ses plumes, et aussi les grandes plumes de la queue, et l'oiseau était présenté à table avec la tête à un bout du plat et les plumes de la queue à l'opposé.

Un autre boulot qui me répugnait, c'était de vider les lièvres tués par Mr Cutler. On aurait dit qu'ils étaient pleins de sang. Ma parole, ça devait être des espèces de vampires ! Quand il faisait froid ils restaient suspendus au moins quinze jours, et il fallait une sacrée poigne pour les dépiauter.

J'essayais de le faire d'un seul geste, parce que ces trucs-là, les peaux de lapins et de lièvres, c'était mon argent de poche. Pour une peau enlevée d'un seul coup et pas du tout abîmée, le chiffonnier me donnait neuf pence.

La cuisinière ne voulait jamais que je passe les lièvres à l'eau. Il fallait que je les nettoie avec du papier. D'après elle, si on lavait le gibier ça lui enlevait toute sa saveur. D'ailleurs elle n'aimait pas qu'on lave quoi que ce soit, elle disait toujours que le goût partait dans l'évier.

Mrs Bowchard adorait faire du civet de lièvre à cause du porto : on en envoyait toujours à la cuisine les jours de civet. La femme de service en apportait deux grands verres du salon, mais il n'y en avait qu'un qui servait pour la sauce. L'autre, c'est Mrs Bowchard qui l'éclusait. Elle essayait de faire ça en cachette, pour que je ne puisse pas dire après qu'elle en avait bu, mais je la surveillais du coin de l'œil. Il y avait un verre pour le civet et un verre pour le gosier de

Mrs Bowchard. Si elle s'apercevait que je l'avais vue elle disait :

« Bah, c'est le privilège de la cuisinière. Toutes les cuisinières font ça. »

C'était sans doute vrai ; je me rappelle l'avoir fait plus tard.

Malgré tout Mrs Bowchard était une très bonne cuisinière, et la cuisine en ce temps-là c'était vraiment quelque chose, parce qu'on avait tous les ingrédients qu'on voulait. Ce n'était pas du tout comme pendant la guerre, où on vous expliquait comment faire un gâteau sans œufs et sans matière grasse avec du vinaigre et du saindoux. En fin de compte c'était le truc le plus dégoûtant qu'on ait jamais mangé, et ceux qui croyaient le contraire se faisaient avoir.

Encore maintenant, quand on voit une recette économique et qu'on vous dit que c'est pareil que l'original, c'est peut-être vrai pour ceux qui n'ont jamais goûté l'original, mais sinon on sent drôlement bien la différence. C'est comme quand on utilise de la margarine à la place du beurre, la peau du lait à la place de la crème fraîche, des bas morceaux de viande à la place du filet ou du saumon surgelé à la place du frais. Ça n'a pas du tout le même goût.

La nourriture de l'époque était délicieuse parce qu'elle était toujours fraîche ; même les bouchers et les poissonniers n'avaient pas de congélateurs. Ils avaient une chambre froide, mais ils ne congelaient pas les aliments, alors tout ce qu'on mangeait était frais et goûteux.

De nos jours on ne sait plus quoi inventer pour redonner aux aliments le goût qu'ils ont perdu à cause de la congélation. Mais ce n'est pas possible ; personne ne pourra jamais me faire croire ça. Enfin, si on n'a rien connu d'autre, évidemment, on ne fait pas la différence.

Aujourd'hui, quand les gens parlent de leur boulot il est toujours question d'« avantages en nature ». Comme je vous l'ai dit, les cuisinières en avaient de la part des fournisseurs avec qui elles travaillaient. Moi j'aurais cru que les vêtements dont les patrons ne voulaient plus finissaient par atterrir au sous-sol, mais pas du tout. Ils n'avaient pas envie de nous les donner, parce qu'ils n'auraient pas aimé qu'on les porte tant qu'on vivait chez eux, et bien entendu ils ne voulaient pas qu'on s'en aille pour pouvoir les porter ailleurs. Ils préféraient les donner à des œuvres de bienfaisance.

Tous ces gens faisaient partie d'associations caritatives, et ils siégeaient à pas mal de comités. Si on lisait les journaux on apprenait que Lady Machin et Mrs Chose tenaient un stand à telle ou telle vente de charité.

Mrs Cutler en avait un pour les filles perdues, et Mrs Bowchard faisait régulièrement des gâteaux pour son stand. Mrs Cutler tenait absolument à aider les filles perdues, mais de loin. Comme beaucoup de gens, elle pouvait être généreuse à condition de ne pas être impliquée personnellement. Leurs vieux habits, c'est à ce genre d'institutions qu'ils les envoyaient.

Je me souviens qu'une fois la première femme de service a été très contrariée à cause d'un beau manteau à col de fourrure que Mrs Cutler avait depuis plusieurs années. Elle savait que la patronne allait bientôt s'en débarrasser, et elle était sûre d'en hériter, parce qu'elle avait glissé quelques allusions qui semblaient avoir eu de l'effet – mais finalement non, il a été emballé et envoyé à une œuvre de charité.

Ils ne nous faisaient vraiment pas beaucoup de cadeaux. À Noël par exemple ils nous donnaient du tissu pour qu'on fasse nous-mêmes nos tabliers avec ; leurs cadeaux, c'étaient toujours des machins moches et utiles.

J'avais beau avoir fait un tas d'histoires pour aller à Londres, pendant les deux ans que j'ai passés à Thurloe Square je n'ai pas vu grand-chose de la ville. J'étais toujours trop fatiguée pour faire du tourisme. Pourtant, avant de venir j'avais lu un bouquin sur le vieux Londres, sur les maisons où avaient vécu des gens comme Carlyle, Wells et Dickens, et je m'étais dit que ce serait épatant de m'y balader et de pouvoir raconter après que j'y étais allée, moi qui avais toujours raffolé d'histoire et de culture en général.

Mais j'étais toujours trop crevée. La seule chose qui me faisait envie c'était d'aller au cinéma ; là on était assis dans le noir, et ça ne faisait rien si on ne s'était pas mise sur son trente et un.

Quand c'était mon jour de congé j'allais au cinéma le plus proche pour vivre des histoires d'amour par procuration. Ça me demandait beaucoup moins d'énergie. Je me disais souvent que même si un homme fantastique débarquait dans ma vie je ne saurais pas quoi en faire. Je n'aurais pas la force.

Un dimanche sur deux j'avais ma soirée de congé en même temps que Gladys, et on allait se balader du côté de Hyde Park.

Gladys avait un an de plus que moi et elle avait toujours vécu à Londres. Sa famille habitait à Stepney, dans la proche banlieue, et elle avait huit frères et dix sœurs. Elle avait du mal à se souvenir de sa mère autrement qu'avec un bébé dans les bras. Elle me racontait des choses horribles sur Stepney, comment ils vivaient les uns sur les autres, les punaises dans les lits, la saleté, les ivrognes et les bagarres du samedi soir. J'adorais quand elle me racontait tout ça, mais je n'aurais pas aimé y vivre !

Gladys disait que son père buvait comme un trou, et que pratiquement tous les soirs il rentrait soûl comme un cochon et incapable de rien faire. Moi, je me disais qu'il y avait au moins une chose qu'il était capable de faire, sinon sa femme n'aurait pas eu dix-neuf enfants !

Gladys n'était pas du tout ce qu'on appelle une belle fille, et moi non plus d'ailleurs, mais elle, elle était très gaie et très débrouillarde. Bien obligée, je suppose, quand on vient d'un quartier comme Stepney, qu'on a une flopée de frères et sœurs et un père qui boit. Elle avait appris à encaisser les coups du sort avec le sourire. Elle ne se faisait jamais avoir, et elle me donnait plein de bons conseils. Par exemple elle me disait :

« Si tu rencontres un garçon, ne lui dis jamais, mais alors jamais, que tu es en condition. Sinon il va te traiter de bonniche et il ne voudra plus de toi.

– Mais alors qu'est-ce que je dis ?

– Oh, tu n'as qu'à lui dire n'importe quoi, que tu bosses dans un magasin, ou à l'usine.

– Bah, pourtant les ouvrières ne sont pas mieux que nous.

– Pour les garçons, si. Pour eux n'importe quelle domestique c'est une bonniche, et ça ne les intéresse pas. Rien que le fait qu'on ne soit pas souvent libres, ça suffit pour qu'ils mettent les voiles. »

Je suivais toutes ses instructions à la lettre, mais je ne voyais pas bien ce que ça changeait, étant donné que les seuls gars qu'on rencontrait c'étaient des soldats de la caserne de Knightsbridge.

Ils n'avaient jamais un sou en poche – en tout cas, aucun n'a jamais dépensé un sou pour nous. Tout ce qu'on faisait, c'était se promener pendant des heures et des heures dans le parc ou écouter les orateurs qui haranguaient la foule à Marble Arch. Comme il fallait qu'on soit rentrées à dix heures pile, on ne jouait pas les prolongations au moment des adieux. Les garçons faisaient beaucoup de réflexions idiotes, nous on gloussait beaucoup, il y avait quelques baisers d'échangés et on se promettait de se retrouver la semaine suivante à la même heure, mais Gladys et moi on n'avait pas l'intention de sortir tout le temps avec des cavaliers aussi fauchés. Faire le tour de Hyde Park pendant des heures avec des soldats qui ne nous payaient jamais rien, ça n'était pas vraiment l'idée qu'on se faisait de l'amour.

Toutes les deux, on dévorait les magazines féminins. Il y était souvent question d'une héroïne pauvre et solitaire qui finissait par épouser un gars aussi beau que Rudolph Valentino ou un genre de Rothschild plein aux as. Naturellement, malgré son éducation la jeune fille avait toujours un visage à l'ovale parfait et de beaux yeux violets ; nous non, mais ça ne nous empêchait pas de rêver qu'on était belles et qu'un jour notre prince viendrait.

Gladys avait beaucoup d'imagination. Peut-être qu'à Stepney c'est la seule façon de tenir le coup. Elle était capable de donner à tous les gars qu'elle rencontrait une flopée de détails sur le boulot qu'elle s'était inventé. Moi, ce n'était pas la peine que je me vante de faire autre chose qu'un travail physique ; j'avais toujours les mains rouges et écorchées, alors ça se serait vu. C'était obligé qu'elles soient comme ça, mes mains. Il n'y avait pas de gants en caoutchouc à l'époque, ou s'il y en avait, en tout cas les filles de cuisine n'en mettaient pas. Et les crèmes protectrices, inutile de vous dire que ça n'existait pas encore. De toute façon, même si j'en avais mis, une fois que j'avais récuré les marches de l'entrée, astiqué le cuivre de la porte et fait toute la vaisselle avec de l'eau pleine de soude, le résultat aurait été exactement le même.

Je crois qu'un des trucs que je détestais le plus, c'était nettoyer les marches de l'entrée à la pierre à récurer. De nos jours, si on veut récurer les marches, et ça ne se fait plus beaucoup, on achète du produit en poudre, mais autrefois il fallait frotter les marches de toutes ses forces avec une espèce de gros galet. Alors moi j'étais là, avec mon tablier de toile et le derrière en l'air, et les garçons de courses me lançaient des réflexions grivoises au passage. Au début j'ai essayé de me mettre en bas pour faire les marches du haut, mais je n'y arrivais pas, je basculais vers l'avant. Il fallait les faire de haut en bas.

Une autre de mes bêtes noires, c'était le nettoyage des casseroles en cuivre. Elles se salissaient à chaque fois qu'on s'en servait. Après chaque repas tout le brillant était parti et elles étaient à nouveau ternes. On les nettoyait avec un horrible mélange de sable, de sel, de vinaigre et d'un peu de farine, et on le faisait à mains nues. On ne pouvait pas utiliser de chiffon, sinon on n'appuyait pas assez fort ; il fallait enfoncer la main dans la boîte où on avait fait la mixture et frotter l'extérieur du récipient avec. C'était dégoûtant, et je devais faire ça tous les matins. Remarquez, une fois qu'elles étaient astiquées ça faisait joli, toutes ces casseroles accrochées au mur de la cuisine ; ça allait de la plus minuscule, qui ne contenait pas plus d'une tasse à thé, jusqu'à la plus énorme où on pouvait mettre trois Christmas

puddings côte à côte. Et il y avait aussi une grande poissonnière. Parfois j'en avais tellement marre que j'aurais voulu
qu'ils aient tous une intoxication à cause du cuivre. C'est ce
qu'on me répétait sans arrêt, que si je ne récurais pas tout ça
comme il faut ils seraient intoxiqués. Au moins, si c'était
arrivé, ils auraient peut-être changé de casseroles !

Ils ont fini par le faire, à ce que j'ai entendu dire plus tard,
parce que la nouvelle fille de cuisine refusait catégorique-
ment de les nettoyer. Je me demande souvent ce qui se serait
passé si moi j'avais refusé. Je suppose qu'ils m'auraient tout
bonnement fichue à la porte.

Au bout d'un an dans cette place c'est moi qui ai donné
mon préavis, et ç'a été très éprouvant pour mes nerfs. Naturellement, je devais le dire en premier à Mrs Bowchard, la
cuisinière, et comme je m'y attendais elle m'a servi tout un
sermon sur l'ingratitude des jeunes en général et des filles de
cuisine en particulier :

« Alors voilà, on s'échine à les former, et tout ça pour
quoi ? Dès qu'elles vous ont soutiré tout ce que vous savez,
elles s'en vont voir ailleurs ! »

Et elle a continué comme ça un bon moment en me fusil-
lant du regard.

Tout ça, c'était mensonge et compagnie. Elle ne m'avait
appris à faire aucune de ses spécialités, les choses que j'aurais
vraiment voulu savoir. Les plats ordinaires, on peut les
trouver dans un livre de cuisine, mais une bonne cuisinière
a toujours ses propres recettes, avec ce petit quelque chose
qui n'est pas dans les livres. Je lui avais demandé je ne sais
combien de fois pourquoi telle chose avait tel goût ou pourquoi ceci se transformait en cela, mais elle ne me répondait
jamais. Elle disait :

« Ça, c'est le secret du chef ! »

Et c'était drôlement injuste, parce que quand on est fille de cuisine on se tape le boulot le plus dur, on travaille plus que tout le monde, on sert même les domestiques, en espérant qu'un jour on aura la meilleure place, celle de cuisinière. Alors on se décarcasse pour la cuisinière, justement, et ce serait quand même la moindre des choses qu'elle vous renvoie la balle et qu'elle vous aide, non ?

Enfin, revenons à mon préavis. Après la corvée avec Mrs Bowchard il fallait que j'aille voir Madame, naturellement. À mon avis elles ne valaient pas mieux l'une que l'autre : pour moi c'étaient toutes les deux des harpies et elles me terrifiaient. Mais quand on voulait voir Madame et qu'on n'était que fille de cuisine, c'était toute une histoire. Il fallait d'abord prier la femme de service de prier Madame de bien vouloir vous accorder quelques minutes, et tout ça sur un ton qui montrait qu'on savait à quel point le temps de Madame était précieux.

Pendant l'année que j'avais passée dans cette maison je n'avais pas dû voir Madame plus d'une douzaine de fois, parce que quand Mrs Bowchard savait qu'elle devait descendre à la cuisine et que je n'étais vraiment pas présentable, ce qui évidemment arrivait souvent, elle me faisait sortir jusqu'à ce que la patronne soit partie. Personne ne semblait faire le rapprochement entre le fait que je n'étais pas présentable et le fait que la cuisine était propre, la table d'un blanc immaculé et les casseroles en cuivre rutilantes. Bref, comme je disais donc, je n'avais vu Madame qu'une douzaine de fois, et encore, ces fois-là je ne crois pas qu'elle m'avait vue. En tout cas elle avait fait comme si j'étais transparente.

131

Bref, par l'entremise de la femme de service Madame m'a accordé une audience pour le lendemain à dix heures et je lui ai dit que je partais. Bien entendu, elle a voulu savoir pourquoi :

« N'êtes-vous pas heureuse ici ? »

Elle m'a demandé ça d'un ton un peu fâché qui voulait dire : « Comment peut-on travailler chez moi et ne pas être heureuse ? »

Elle a ajouté que je ne trouverais nulle part une meilleure place et qu'elle était sûre que j'avais appris beaucoup de choses. J'ai répondu que le travail était trop dur et les journées trop longues. Eh bien, à ma grande surprise, elle a dit qu'elle allait me faire aider, que si je restais elle embaucherait un homme à tout faire pour me donner un coup de main. J'aurais quand même préféré partir, mais j'étais tellement sidérée que quelqu'un veuille vraiment de moi que les bras m'en sont tombés. Je me suis retrouvée en train de dire que j'étais d'accord pour rester, et même que j'aimais bien ce boulot.

Franchement, je devais être folle à lier. Mais, vous comprenez, personne ne m'avait jamais demandé de rester avant, sauf un gars, une fois, et lui je savais très bien pourquoi il voulait que je reste.

Même Mrs Bowchard, cette vieille rosse, a pris un air un peu moins sévère quand je lui ai annoncé que Madame m'avait demandé de rester. Elle a voulu savoir si j'avais eu une augmentation. Je parie que si j'avais dit oui, dès le lendemain elle allait en réclamer une. J'ai répondu :

« Non, je n'ai pas eu d'augmentation, mais je vais avoir un homme à tout faire pour me donner un coup de main. »

Évidemment, il a fallu qu'elle dise :

« Ah là là, les gamines de maintenant, ce n'est plus ce que c'était ! C'est qu'il faut vous bichonner, à présent ! Enfin, c'est toujours mieux que d'avoir à former une nouvelle. Je préfère que tu restes plutôt que de tout recommencer à zéro. Mais bon, à part ça toutes les filles de cuisine se valent. »

Et elle a continué sur ce ton un bon moment. Mais j'avais déjà entendu tout ça, alors je n'ai pas fait attention.

En tout cas, à partir de ce moment-là il y a un homme à tout faire qui est venu tous les matins sauf le dimanche. On l'appelait le vieux Tom. Il avait sûrement un nom de famille, mais nous on l'appelait toujours le vieux Tom. Il arrivait à six heures, il travaillait une heure et demie, et je ne peux pas vous dire quelle bénédiction c'était pour moi de ne plus avoir à sortir pour faire les marches du perron. Lui, ça lui était égal. Personne ne lance de remarques grivoises à un homme qui frotte par terre avec le derrière en l'air. Il faisait toutes les chaussures et il rentrait aussi le charbon. C'était tout simplement le paradis. Je suis restée encore un an dans cette place parce que le travail était devenu beaucoup moins dur. C'est bien simple : ça me paraissait trop beau pour être vrai !

XVIII

Dans la maison tout continuait à peu près comme avant. C'était le même train-train, avec les « jours » de Madame et les dîners qui venaient rompre la monotonie.

Les « jours » ne me concernaient pas vraiment, au niveau du travail, je veux dire, mais ça m'intéressait. Toutes ces dames avaient leur « jour ». Celui de Mrs Cutler tombait le premier jeudi de chaque mois, et c'était un défilé permanent de trois heures et demie à cinq heures environ. Il y avait surtout des femmes, mais aussi quelques messieurs, et tous ces gens ne faisaient que passer. Ils entraient, disaient « Comment allez-vous ? », buvaient une tasse de thé et repartaient aussitôt, sans doute pour faire une apparition au « jour » de quelqu'un d'autre. Je suppose que c'était leur façon à eux de rester dans le coup.

Mais celles qui trimaient pour rester dans le coup, c'étaient les femmes de service, et je peux vous dire qu'elles maudissaient les invités de tout leur cœur, parce que c'étaient elles qui se tapaient tout le boulot : elles devaient couper des montagnes de tranches de pain très fines, les beurrer et les tartiner d'une pâte d'anchois baptisée « Gentleman's Relish* ». Je ne sais pas si on en trouve encore, ni pourquoi ça s'appelait comme ça. Moi je trouvais cette chose infecte, beaucoup trop salée. J'imagine que c'était fait pour donner soif à ces messieurs, en prévision des apéritifs qu'ils prenaient en général vers cinq heures et demie.

Madame était toujours à l'affût de nouvelles idées pour son « jour », et elle tannait la cuisinière et les femmes de service avec ça. Il fallait comme qui dirait faire mieux que les voisins. Je suppose que pour le bal des débutantes ils le font toujours – essayer d'avoir le dernier groupe à la mode et tout ça.

Mais bon, ça ne me concernait pas vraiment, pas comme les dîners. Ces soirs-là, même si ça me donnait beaucoup de travail en plus, même si ça mettait Mrs Bowchard de mauvaise humeur, il y avait toujours une atmosphère de fête. À la cuisine ça se sentait, mais c'est là-haut que ça se voyait.

J'essayais toujours de monter jeter un coup d'œil dans la salle à manger avant le dîner. Sur la table il y avait une nappe de dentelle splendide, un héritage de famille. Elle était entièrement faite à la main, et vous imaginez sa taille, pour couvrir toute la table de la salle à manger avec ses deux rallonges ! C'était la nappe la plus magnifique que j'aie jamais vue. Au centre il y avait un surtout en cristal, et toute l'argenterie était de style georgien**. Avec tout ça plus les

---

* C'est-à-dire « Régal du Gentleman » ou « Condiment du Gentleman », l'appellation anglaise jouant sur ces deux sens du mot *relish*. *(N.d.T.)*
** C'est-à-dire caractéristique de la période (1714-1830) couvrant les règnes des quatre premiers rois de Grande-Bretagne prénommés George (dynastie de Hanovre). *(N.d.T.)*

deux chandeliers en argent, quand les bougies étaient allumées on se serait cru dans une scène des *Mille et Une Nuits*.

Je trouve vraiment que lorsqu'on mettait une nappe, même si elle n'était pas en dentelle mais en tissu damassé blanc, la table avait une autre allure qu'avec tous ces napperons de bric et de broc qu'on voit maintenant.

Mrs Bowchard n'était jamais un modèle d'amabilité, mais alors, les jours où Mrs Cutler recevait à dîner, elle devenait carrément horrible. Elle dégageait une telle sévérité qu'on ne pouvait pas l'approcher. On aurait dit qu'elle faisait à manger en même temps pour Buckingham Palace et pour un régiment de la Garde royale. Ça ne me facilitait pas la tâche, c'est le moins qu'on puisse dire. Mais le plus intéressant, dans ces dîners, c'étaient les chauffeurs des invités ; ils passaient toute la soirée avec nous, dans la salle des domestiques, pendant que leurs patrons étaient en haut.

Vous n'imaginez pas l'excitation qu'il y avait dans l'air ces soirs-là. Il faut dire qu'on était six ou sept femmes et qu'on ne parlait pratiquement jamais à un homme ; notre féminité était tellement refoulée qu'on était des espèces d'eunuques au féminin. Et là, tout à coup, on s'apercevait qu'on avait un sexe, qu'on était bien des femmes. Alors on se poudrait le nez, on relevait nos cheveux, on resserrait nos ceintures. Il fallait avoir la taille fine en ce temps-là : on ne portait pas de robes droites. La poitrine ressortait, le postérieur ressortait, alors si en plus on resserrait sa ceinture on avait l'air d'un sablier, mais bon, c'était la mode. Même Flora, la première femme de service, et Annie, la première femme de chambre, elles avaient plus de quarante ans et elles s'étaient résignées au célibat, mais ces soirs-là elles jouaient les jeunes filles. La salle des domestiques attirait les femmes comme un aimant ; même la couturière et l'aide-nourrice trouvaient généralement un prétexte pour venir. Et tout ça à cause de ces chauffeurs en uniforme.

Dans la vie c'était certainement une bande de gars tout ce qu'il y a d'ordinaires. C'est comme les soldats pendant la guerre : ils étaient tous tellement beaux quand ils se baladaient en uniforme ! Mais si on les croisait habillés en civil, une fois sur deux on n'aurait sûrement pas changé de trottoir pour aller leur parler, surtout quand c'étaient des Américains.

Gladys et moi on les trouvait sensationnels, ces chauffeurs, et on n'en revenait pas de pouvoir parler à des vrais hommes en leggings. Pour nous, c'était tout bonnement fantastique.

L'uniforme, ça n'avantage pas du tout les femmes, c'est triste mais c'est la vérité : ça ne fait qu'accentuer leurs bourrelets mal placés. Par contre, l'homme le plus insignifiant a tout de suite l'air plus mâle en uniforme. Peut-être que c'est prévu pour exhiber ses attributs (mais non, je ne suis pas vulgaire !), je veux dire pour mettre en valeur sa virilité.

Naturellement, les chauffeurs étaient ravis d'être le centre d'intérêt. Quel homme ne serait pas ravi d'avoir autour de lui cinq ou six femmes en train de papillonner, de lui offrir sans arrêt des biscuits, du thé, et de boire ses paroles bouche bée ? Les hommes sont très sensibles à la flatterie. Même un gars moche comme un pou, si on lui dit qu'il n'est pas si mal, il le croit. On peut leur faire gober tout ce qu'on veut : ils croient n'importe quoi. Il suffit de les regarder dans les yeux en ayant l'air de penser ce qu'on dit. J'ai essayé, alors je sais de quoi je parle !

Les chauffeurs racontaient toujours des histoires salées sur les aristos. Tous ceux d'en haut, on les appelait des aristos. Au bout d'un moment on savait tout sur leurs patrons : le bon, le mauvais et le croustillant. Ils nous parlaient de leurs liaisons. Ces messieurs avaient souvent ce qu'on appelait un « nid d'amour », un appartement où ils avaient installé une femme, et ils s'y faisaient conduire en voiture. Ce que les chauffeurs savaient vraiment s'arrêtait là, puisqu'ils n'entraient jamais dans l'appartement. Mais à les entendre on aurait cru qu'ils avaient été de la fête. Ils employaient le « nous » de majesté, comme le beau-frère de Mrs Bowchard, et ils nous faisaient profiter de tous les détails de la parade amoureuse. Même s'ils ne pouvaient pas les connaître, ce n'était pas très difficile à deviner, je suppose !

En fait certains d'entre eux étaient chauffeurs-valets, et leurs patrons les considéraient sans doute comme des sortes de confidents. Ils savaient qu'il n'y avait aucune chance pour qu'ils discutent un jour d'égal à égal avec quelqu'un d'important, et de se confier ça devait soulager leur conscience – enfin, s'ils en avaient une. De toute façon, les hommes aiment bien parler de ce genre de choses.

Moi-même, il m'est arrivé de travailler pour un monsieur qui avait un pied-à-terre au bord de la mer. Et quand le reste de la famille était à Londres il faisait souvent un saut à Brighton pour visiter son petit nid d'amour.

Les gens trouvaient ça normal de la part d'un homme. Par contre, si une femme en faisait autant c'était scandaleux. C'est vraiment injuste, la vie, non ? Nous, on ne pourrait pas installer un homme dans un nid d'amour, et pourtant on pourrait très bien en avoir envie. C'est comme pour les quartiers chauds, tenez. Pourquoi les hommes ont tous les privilèges sur le plan sexuel ? Après tout, certaines femmes ne sont pas comblées par leur mari. Je trouve qu'il devrait exister des endroits pour elles, où il y aurait des hommes qui auraient passé un examen médical et qui seraient prêts à leur rendre service pour une petite somme. Le sexe féminin est vraiment défavorisé, et dans tous les domaines.

Pour revenir aux chauffeurs, vous trouvez peut-être qu'ils n'auraient pas dû avoir ce type de conversation, mais c'était toujours comme ça avec les domestiques de haut rang. Leur vie personnelle était tellement inintéressante qu'ils devaient tout vivre par procuration. Leur vie sexuelle, leur vie sociale, tout.

En parlant de ce genre de trucs devant leurs domestiques, nos employeurs s'exposaient sans arrêt au chantage. Mais en ce temps-là on n'aurait pas su comment s'y prendre. C'est venu quand les gens ont eu plus d'instruction, quand il y a eu une plus grande liberté de la presse. Nous, il nous semblait que tout ce que faisaient ceux d'en haut, même si ça provoquait des scandales, des potins et des moqueries, ça faisait partie de leurs privilèges. Pas parce qu'ils valaient mieux que nous, mais parce qu'ils étaient riches, et que ça ne servait à rien d'être riche si on ne pouvait pas s'écarter de la norme.

Il n'y avait pas longtemps que j'avais rempilé chez Mrs Cutler quand il est arrivé une chose qui me reste en mémoire comme si c'était une scène de mélodrame victorien : on s'est aperçu qu'Agnes, l'aide-femme de service, allait avoir un bébé.

Maintenant les choses ont rudement changé ; les patrons veulent tellement garder leurs domestiques que, s'ils s'aperçoivent que leur bonne est enceinte, je suis sûre qu'ils lui disent :

« Oui, bon, ce n'est pas de chance. Mais surtout, revenez quand vous aurez accouché, hein ? »

On voit des petites annonces avec « enfant accepté ». C'est comme s'ils disaient :

« Vous êtes fille mère ? Pas de problème, on est prêts à prendre l'enfant aussi ! »

Mais autrefois on était flanquée à la porte, virée sans un sou, et la plupart du temps rejetée par sa famille. Il ne vous restait plus que le trottoir ou l'hospice.

Gladys et moi on partageait une chambre avec Agnes. Je l'avais vue vomir le matin en se levant, mais je n'avais pas fait le rapprochement avec la grossesse. Je croyais juste qu'elle avait des crises de foie. Je trouvais quand même bizarre que ça la prenne dès qu'elle posait le pied par terre et que le reste de la journée elle aille bien, mais bon, je mettais ça sur le compte de la digestion.

Au bout de quelque temps, Gladys, qui en savait beaucoup plus que moi sur la question, lui a demandé carrément si elle était enceinte. « Enceinte », quel mot terrifiant pour nous ! Agnes a répondu que oui, et elle nous a suppliées de ne rien dire. Comme ça ne faisait pas longtemps, ça ne se voyait pas encore.

Mais les vêtements de l'époque n'étaient pas prévus pour cacher le ventre. La taille était marquée par une ceinture, alors ce n'était pas facile. Je voulais aider Agnes de tout mon cœur, mais je n'avais aucune idée de ce qu'il fallait faire. C'était Gladys la moins ignorante de nous trois, et elle a fait tout ce qu'elle a pu.

Elle a acheté des pastilles à la menthe pouliot, censées être très efficaces pour faire passer le bébé, des pilules laxatives et de la quinine. Le seul résultat, c'est que le lendemain Agnes a passé la moitié de la journée aux cabinets. Après, sur les instructions de Gladys, on s'est mises à trimbaler de l'eau chaude dans l'escalier pour remplir la baignoire sabot ; on versait dedans des pots entiers de moutarde, jusqu'à ce que l'eau soit toute jaune. Ça aussi c'était censé être efficace, les bains à la moutarde. Peut-être que ça aurait marché si Agnes avait pu se tremper dedans jusqu'à la taille, mais comme elle ne pouvait pas… Ensuite elle a essayé de porter tout ce qu'elle trouvait de lourd. Elle passait son jour de congé au parc, à grimper sur les bancs et à sauter par terre. Ça a l'air amusant, comme ça, mais pour elle c'était affreux. Elle a essayé en déplaçant des meubles. Elle soulevait un gros fauteuil et elle le transportait d'un bout à l'autre de la pièce. Mais ça n'a rien donné.

Évidemment, elle n'a pas pu le cacher éternellement à Mrs Cutler, et un beau jour elle a été priée de quitter la maison à la fin de la semaine.

Ce que ça a dû être pour la pauvre Agnes, c'est impossible à imaginer aujourd'hui. Gladys et moi on était franchement désolées pour elle, mais vous savez, c'est comme quand on va voir une personne mourante à l'hôpital : on est quand même bien content que ce ne soit pas nous. Eh bien Gladys et moi c'était pareil : on la plaignait, Agnes, mais on était soulagées de ne pas être à sa place.

Madame lui a donc dit de partir à la fin de la semaine, et pourtant elle lui a donné un mois de salaire. Ça m'a confirmée dans les soupçons que j'avais sur l'identité du père. Agnes ne voulait pas dire qui c'était. Qu'elle ne le dise pas à Madame, ça me paraissait normal, mais même à Gladys et moi elle ne voulait pas le dire alors que je savais qu'elle savait, vu qu'elle n'était pas du genre à sortir avec le premier venu.

À mon avis ça ne pouvait être que le neveu de Mrs Cutler. Il était très jeune, pas beaucoup plus de vingt ans, je pense, et très beau garçon. Il avait une voix tellement sensuelle que rien que de l'entendre dire bonjour ça vous donnait des idées. Ça vous envoyait des frissons de la tête aux pieds. Si je le soupçonnais, c'est parce que je l'avais croisé plusieurs fois dans l'escalier de service, c'est-à-dire *notre* escalier, alors qu'il n'avait pas le droit d'y être. Il m'avait dit bonjour de sa belle voix sensuelle. Certains Américains ont ce genre de voix, je m'en suis aperçue depuis.

À mon avis Mrs Cutler se faisait du mauvais sang parce qu'elle savait que c'était lui, ou qu'elle en était presque sûre. Elle nous a posé des tas de questions, à Gladys et à moi, et on a dit qu'on ne savait pas, mais elle ne nous a pas crues.

Elle avait beau penser que le responsable était de sa famille et tout, j'ai quand même eu droit à un sermon interminable sur les méfaits d'une conduite dévergondée. Selon elle, un jeune homme comme il faut n'aurait jamais proposé ça à une fille qu'il espérait épouser. Vous avez déjà entendu une ânerie pareille, vous ? Ça fait partie des choses qu'ils proposent toujours, oui ! Qu'ils aient ou non l'intention de se marier avec vous, les hommes aiment bien tester la marchandise avant, croyez-moi ; personnellement, je ne suis jamais sortie avec un homme qui ne le propose pas. Et Mrs Cutler a ajouté que jamais une jeune fille convenable ne laisserait un homme profiter d'elle.

Ça, c'était encore une réflexion idiote : comme il y avait beaucoup plus de filles que de garçons, si on avait un petit ami qu'on aimait vraiment bien et qu'il le proposait, ça paraissait la seule façon de le garder. C'était vraiment difficile de refuser si on ne voulait pas se retrouver sans fiancé alors qu'on rêvait de quitter le service domestique – et on en rêvait presque toutes. Qu'est-ce qu'elle pouvait bien savoir, Mrs Cutler, de nos sentiments à nous, les gens du sous-sol ? Les seules raisons pour lesquelles les filles comme moi ne s'écartaient pas du « droit chemin », c'étaient l'ignorance et la peur. L'ignorance de ce qu'il fallait faire pour ne pas tomber enceinte et la peur d'attraper une maladie. On nous rabâchait qu'il suffisait d'aller avec un garçon pour choper une maladie vénérienne. S'il y a tant de jeunes qui s'en écartent maintenant, du droit chemin, c'est bien parce que ces deux peurs-là ont disparu, non ? La maladie on sait la guérir, et le bébé quelqu'un s'en occupera si on décide de le garder. Quoique maintenant on soit plutôt incitée à s'en débarrasser avant.

Mais Agnes n'était ni comme Gladys ni comme moi. Gladys venait d'une famille très nombreuse, elle avait eu une vie très dure et elle avait les pieds sur terre. Moi j'avais seulement peur de ce qui pouvait m'arriver, et j'étais ignorante. Je savais grosso modo comment on faisait les enfants, mais je ne savais pas jusqu'où on pouvait aller sans en avoir. Agnes, elle était douce, naïve, très sentimentale ; d'ailleurs, quand elle allait au cinéma elle revenait avec la tête pleine de rêves.

Je me rappelle qu'elle avait le béguin pour un acteur au sourire ravageur. Quand Gladys et moi on l'avait vu dans un film, j'avais dit à Gladys :

« Qu'est-ce qu'il a de belles dents ! »

Et elle m'avait répondu :

« Oui, et je parie qu'il en a d'autres à la maison ! »

On avait tellement rigolé qu'on s'était fait sortir du cinéma. Mais pour la pauvre Agnes ce gars-là c'était comme qui dirait un dieu.

Alors vous imaginez, si c'était le neveu de Mrs Cutler, avec cette voix incroyable qu'il avait, il devait savoir y faire avec les filles. Il a dû donner l'impression à Agnes qu'elle était quelqu'un d'exceptionnel, pas juste une aide-femme de service sans un sou et sans avenir. En plus c'était une beauté, Agnes, et naturelle avec ça, elle n'utilisait jamais d'artifices. Je vois très bien comment elle a pu se laisser séduire. Et il lui faisait des cadeaux, je le sais parce qu'elle avait des dessous en soie. Elle disait que ça lui venait de sa famille, mais à mon avis ce n'était pas possible.

D'accord, c'était peut-être quelqu'un d'autre, mais moi je suis presque sûre que c'était lui, et Mrs Cutler aussi. Sinon qu'est-ce qu'il serait venu faire dans l'escalier de service ? Il ne menait qu'aux chambres de bonnes, cet escalier-là !

Pour revenir à l'ignorance, à la peur et au droit chemin, tout ce qui concernait la sexualité, les gens voyaient ça comme un péché, comme un truc dégoûtant. Même dans les couples mariés, quelquefois ça se passait mal à cause de ça.

Je me souviens qu'environ un an après mon mariage j'ai croisé par hasard une fille que j'avais connue en condition ; on est allées dans un salon de thé pour parler du passé et elle m'a dit qu'elle était mariée depuis cinq ans. Mais quand je lui ai demandé si elle avait des enfants elle s'est écriée :

« Oh là là ! Ce que je peux détester ce côté-là du mariage ! Même quand George m'embrasse je ne supporte pas, parce que je sais très bien que c'est à "ça" qu'il veut en venir. »

Elle n'appelait jamais la chose par son nom, elle disait toujours « ça ». Je lui ai fait remarquer que sa mère n'était sûrement pas de cet avis puisqu'elle avait eu douze enfants – oui, douze ! Elle m'a répondu :

« Oh, mais c'était mon père, il ne la laissait jamais tranquille. Même quand elle était en train d'étendre le linge il s'amenait tout doucement par-derrière, et en plein jour, par-dessus le marché ! »

J'en suis tombée à la renverse. Et j'ai ri, mais ri ! Son « et en plein jour, par-dessus le marché », c'était trop drôle ! Et quand je lui ai dit : « Eh bien, ça lui faisait une chouette récréation les jours de lessive », ça l'a tellement choquée qu'elle est sortie d'un air outré et que j'ai dû finir mon thé toute seule. Mais je n'avais vraiment pas pu m'empêcher d'éclater de rire. Ça m'a fait une chouette récréation, à moi aussi.

Jusque-là j'ai dit pas mal de choses qui peuvent vous donner à penser que j'enviais la vie d'autres gens, mais ce n'est pas le cas. La plupart du temps c'étaient l'inégalité et l'injustice qui me heurtaient. Pourtant il y avait bel et bien une personne dont j'étais à la fois envieuse et jalouse. C'était Mademoiselle Susan, l'aînée des petits-enfants de Mrs Cutler. Elle n'avait que deux ans de moins que moi, mais sa vie était tellement différente de la mienne ! Elle était aussi grande que moi et elle avait à peu près la même couleur de cheveux, mais franchement la ressemblance s'arrêtait là, parce que Mademoiselle Susan était tout ce que je n'étais pas, et elle avait tout ce que je n'avais pas. Elle avait des tonnes de vêtements, un cheval, un court de tennis. Elle parlait français, elle jouait du piano et elle chantait bien. J'étais jalouse de sa vie et de tout ce qu'elle savait faire. Pas tout le temps. Mais quand elle descendait à la cuisine demander quelque chose et que j'étais à l'évier en train de laver des casseroles, les mains dans la cuvette d'eau grasse, les cheveux raides comme des baguettes, avec mon tablier de grosse toile, et qu'elle, elle arrivait en sautillant, tirée à quatre épingles, pour demander de sa voix distinguée quelque chose que je devais immédiatement aller chercher à toute vitesse pour elle, il aurait fallu que je sois surhumaine pour ne pas l'envier. On lui faisait absolument tout : l'aide-nourrice lui brossait les cheveux, on lui préparait son bain, on mettait même le dentifrice sur sa brosse à dents.

Parfois elle avait un message pour la cuisinière, et vous auriez vu Mrs Bowchard, elle était tout sourires avec elle. C'étaient des : « Oh oui, Mademoiselle Susan », « Non, Mademoiselle Susan », « Certainement, Mademoiselle Susan ». Et une fois qu'elle était partie Mrs Bowchard me disait :

« Mon Dieu qu'elle est belle ! C'est un régal pour les yeux, un vrai rayon de soleil ! »

Je crois bien que ça me faisait mal. Une fois, j'ai eu l'audace de répondre :

« S'il fallait qu'elle bosse ici ne serait-ce qu'une semaine, elle ne ressemblerait sûrement pas autant à un rayon de soleil. »

Mrs Bowchard s'est mise en colère après moi. Elle m'a dit :

« Tu es juste jalouse comme un pou parce qu'il n'y a aucune chance pour que tu sois comme elle un jour. Même si tu étais riche tu ne serais pas aussi jolie qu'elle, et tu n'aurais pas d'aussi bonnes manières. »

Je ne crois pas que j'en voulais vraiment à Mademoiselle Susan de sa position sociale, c'est juste que quand elle entrait dans la cuisine le contraste me sautait à la figure. Et puis vous comprenez, elle ne me parlait jamais, elle ne faisait même pas attention à moi. Elle aurait quand même pu, non ? J'étais une jeune fille comme elle, à peu près de son âge. Alors du coup je la trouvais bêcheuse. Mais peut-être que c'était de la délicatesse de sa part, parce qu'elle avait remarqué à quel point nos vies étaient différentes. Si ça se trouve j'étais injuste avec elle, maintenant que j'y pense.

XIX

Noël quand j'étais en condition, ça n'avait rien à voir avec les Noëls à la maison. Je me souviens de l'excitation qu'il y avait chez nous malgré le manque d'argent. On était tellement excités qu'on se réveillait de bonne heure, et on se précipitait dans la chambre des parents pour voir nos cadeaux et nos souliers. On n'avait pas de dinde ni de sapin, mais on riait beaucoup et on avait toujours assez à manger.

Noël chez Mrs Cutler, c'était tout un machin très officiel et très compliqué. Il y avait un grand sapin décoré par la nounou dans la salle à manger.

Le jour de Noël, après le petit déjeuner, tous les domestiques devaient se mettre en rang d'oignons dans le hall. Comme j'étais tout en bas de l'échelle, j'étais la dernière de la queue. Après on devait défiler dans la salle à manger devant toute la famille : Mr et Mrs Cutler, leur fille et leurs petits-enfants. Pour la circonstance ils s'étaient tous accroché sur la figure des sourires et des mines de travailleurs sociaux. Les enfants nous regardaient comme si on venait d'un autre monde. Et pour eux c'est sûrement ça qu'on était : une sous-espèce vivant sous terre. Ça me rappelait les actualités où on voyait des Noirs défiler. Je racontais sans arrêt des blagues à Gladys pour essayer de la faire rigoler, mais on ne pouvait pas vraiment rire tellement c'était solennel. Vous parlez d'un Noël ! Quand on arrivait près du sapin, les enfants nous tendaient un paquet qu'on prenait avec respect en marmonnant : « Merci, Monsieur Charles », « Merci Mademoiselle Susan ». Ce que je pouvais détester ça !

Après on devait se présenter devant Monsieur et Madame et ils nous donnaient une enveloppe avec de l'argent ; moi j'avais une livre et Mrs Bowchard cinq. Les cadeaux, c'était toujours quelque chose d'utile : des coupons de tissu imprimé, des tabliers, des bas noirs – pas en soie, naturellement, ils ne nous donnaient jamais rien de frivole –, des bas noirs en laine. Moi j'aurais tellement voulu certains des trucs qu'ils avaient : des dessous en soie, du parfum, des bijoux... Pourquoi ils ne pouvaient pas nous offrir quelque chose comme ça ? Pourquoi il fallait toujours qu'on ait des cadeaux raisonnables ? À mon avis, s'ils nous donnaient des uniformes c'est parce qu'ils savaient très bien qu'on n'avait pas de quoi en acheter avec nos salaires de misère. Et puis, si on avait eu du parfum ou de la soie, on se serait forcément mal conduites, n'est-ce pas ? C'est pour ça que je détestais cet étalage de bienveillance, toute cette comédie pour faire croire que nous aussi on s'amusait bien à Noël.

En fait on travaillait comme des forçats, vu qu'on devait se coltiner leurs dîners et toutes les autres réceptions qui se passaient là-haut. D'accord, on avait un arbre de Noël dans notre salle et c'est eux qui l'avaient payé, mais c'est tout ; c'était à nous de le décorer avec des guirlandes, des cloches et tout ça, et ils ne mettaient pas leurs cadeaux sous le sapin. Il fallait qu'on passe devant eux en file indienne pour recevoir leurs aumônes. Voilà ce que c'était Noël chez eux.

Et c'était toujours comme ça, partout où j'ai été en condition : un machin très officiel et très compliqué avec beaucoup de réceptions pour eux et pas grand-chose pour nous. Je crois que dans les très grandes maisons ils organisaient un bal des domestiques comme à Buckingham Palace, mais pour ce que j'en sais ce n'était jamais à Noël, c'était toujours bien plus tard.

Environ deux mois après Noël on attaquait le nettoyage de printemps. C'était un boulot énorme et ça durait un mois. En ce temps-là on faisait le nettoyage de printemps avec rien, je veux dire sans aspirateur, sans appareils ménagers, sans détergents modernes – rien. Maintenant ça ne se fait plus, le nettoyage de printemps, les gens gardent leur maison propre toute l'année et puis voilà.

Pendant ce mois-là je me levais à cinq heures tous les matins et je bossais jusqu'à huit heures du soir. Et après ça il fallait encore que je serve le dîner des domestiques. On faisait tous les mêmes heures, mais évidemment je me souviens surtout des miennes : c'étaient les miennes qui me fatiguaient, pas les leurs ! Le soir je me traînais jusqu'à mon lit, et j'étais trop crevée pour me laver. Vous trouvez sûrement ça dégoûtant, mais je voudrais bien vous y voir ; après une journée de grand ménage de cinq heures du matin à huit heures du soir dans une vieille maison avec une cheminée à charbon dans toutes les pièces, vous aussi vous seriez crevé !

La première chose que je devais faire, c'était frotter par terre tout le sous-sol avec un mélange de savon et de sable. Ce n'étaient pas des pavés tout brillants comme on voit aujourd'hui devant les maisons ou dans les cuisines. C'était de la pierre, et elle était pleine de petits trous. Toute la saleté se mettait là, dans les petits trous, et pour l'enlever il fallait que je frotte le sol à la brosse avec ce mélange de savon et de sable. Toutes les casseroles en fer et en cuivre, je devais les récurer à l'extérieur encore plus que d'habitude, et l'énorme pare-feu en acier, je devais le briquer jusqu'à ce qu'il soit comme neuf. Il fallait que je lave toute la vaisselle de porcelaine, et il y en avait assez pour ouvrir un magasin. Les grandes tables de cuisine, les chaises et le buffet, je devais les frotter à la brosse jusqu'à ce que le bois soit blanc. À force, j'avais les mains en sang et les ongles en dents de scie.

À l'étage c'était plus facile pour les femmes de chambre et les femmes de service, elles n'avaient pas à frotter autant. Le pire, là-haut, c'étaient les tapis. Et puis en ce temps-là les gens avaient des centaines de bibelots en porcelaine, et il fallait tous les laver.

Le nettoyage de l'argenterie, c'était aussi un sacré boulot. Dans cette maison, et dans à peu près toutes celles du même genre, elle était entreposée dans un coffre-fort, et on devait y ranger les ustensiles de cuisine en argent tous les soirs. Le coffre-fort, c'était une espèce de pièce qui donnait sur la salle à manger, avec une porte cachée derrière un paravent. On pouvait carrément entrer dedans. Il y avait des services à thé – pas un service, plusieurs –, des services à café, des chandeliers, des centres de table et des plateaux d'argent. On aurait dit la caverne d'Ali Baba. Pour nettoyer l'argenterie on utilisait le même rouge à polir que les bijoutiers, pas une de ces pâtes blanches en pot qu'on trouve maintenant, et après il fallait astiquer à la peau de chamois et à la brosse. C'était très long, parce qu'il ne fallait surtout pas qu'il reste du produit dans les petites fentes.

Malgré toutes les heures qu'on faisait pendant le nettoyage de printemps, on n'était pas payées plus, mais comme récompense Mrs Cutler nous offrait des places de théâtre. La moitié du personnel y allait une semaine et l'autre moitié la semaine suivante. Je me rappelle que le dernier spectacle que j'ai vu c'était une comédie. Mais je n'ai pas vraiment pu apprécier parce qu'on était à des places chères, au milieu des riches, et j'avais l'impression que tout le monde avait les yeux rivés sur mon manteau noir élimé et mes gants de coton noir – que je n'osais pas enlever parce que mes mains étaient toutes rouges et tout irritées. Je me souviens qu'après la cuisinière m'a demandé :

« Alors, tu t'es bien amusée ?

– Ouais, c'était pas mal.

– En tout cas, demain matin n'oublie pas de remercier Madame pour la soirée qu'elle t'a donnée.

– Oui, eh bien moi, Madame ne m'a pas remerciée pour tout le travail en plus que j'ai fait. »

C'était très osé de ma part, et j'ai bien cru que la cuisinière allait s'étouffer de rage. Elle m'a dit :

« Tu es ici pour travailler, et si le boulot ne te plaît pas on peut très facilement te trouver une remplaçante. »

De toute façon, à ce moment-là ça faisait bientôt trois ans que j'étais fille de cuisine, et après trois ans tout en bas de l'échelle et au salaire le plus bas j'estimais que je pouvais passer pour une cuisinière expérimentée. Je savais au moins faire cuire les légumes, préparer les sauces, et il me semblait avoir appris deux ou trois autres choses au passage.

J'ai donc épluché les journaux, et finalement je suis tombée sur une petite annonce : « Recherche bonne cuisinière pour cuisine familiale. » C'était à Kensington. Alors j'ai écrit, mais dans ma lettre je me suis donné deux ans de plus, parce que si je disais mon âge j'étais sûre qu'ils ne m'embaucheraient pas. Ils trouveraient que dix-huit ans c'était trop jeune pour une cuisinière. J'ai reçu une réponse : j'étais convoquée pour un entretien.

Le jour prévu je me suis présentée avec pas mal d'appréhension, parce que quand même entre fille de cuisine et cuisinière il y a un sacré fossé. J'ai eu droit à l'interrogatoire habituel. Madame m'a tout de suite demandé :

« Quel âge avez-vous ?

– Vingt ans.

– Est-ce que vous habitez à Londres ? Est-ce que le travail vous fait peur ? »

Alors ça, pour une question idiote c'était une question idiote ! « Est-ce que le travail vous fait peur ? » Je connais plein de gens à qui le travail ne fait pas peur mais qui n'aiment pas ça. Elle aurait aussi bien pu me demander : « Est-ce que vous aimez travailler ? » Ç'aurait été tout aussi idiot. Moi, l'idée que je me faisais du paradis, à l'époque, c'était un endroit où on n'avait rien à faire à part s'asseoir ici ou là en jouant vaguement de la harpe.

Cette dame avait un titre : elle s'appelait Lady Gibbons. Mais j'ai tout de suite vu que ce n'était pas une aristocrate. Elle m'a dit qu'ils étaient une famille de trois personnes : elle-même, Sir Walter Gibbons et leur fils, et elle a enchaîné.

« Quel salaire demandez-vous ? »

Là, j'ai entendu une voix qui ne ressemblait pas à la mienne répondre :

« Quarante livres.

– Quarante livres ! »

À son ton, on aurait cru que je demandais la lune. Après elle a fait une pause. Elle espérait peut-être que j'allais en profiter pour changer d'avis. Au lieu de ça, j'ai continué :

« Oui, et je veux une journée entière de congé par mois. »

Sa figure s'est allongée un peu plus, et elle a fait :

« Si je vous donne une journée entière de congé par mois, la femme de chambre et la femme de service vont en vouloir une aussi. »

Je n'ai pas répondu. Je suis restée assise là sans rien dire.

J'ai souvent constaté que c'était ça la meilleure défense, me taire, ne pas répondre ; comme ça, même s'ils sentaient que je n'étais pas d'accord avec eux, ils voyaient que je savais rester à ma place et que je ne me permettais pas de discuter avec mes supérieurs. En général c'était payant. Et puis les domestiques étaient encore faciles à trouver, mais tout de même il commençait à y avoir des bruits de contestation à propos des gages et des conditions de travail, alors c'était moins facile pour les patrons de nous donner un salaire de misère et pour ainsi dire pas de congés.

J'ai eu la place. Et les quarante livres par an. Et la journée entière de congé par mois.

Pour la deuxième fois, il a fallu que je donne mon préavis à Mrs Cutler, et ça c'était plutôt embêtant. Cette fois, rien ne pourrait me persuader de rester, et elle ne pourrait pas me proposer d'augmentation, sinon tous les autres domestiques en réclameraient une. J'ai encore dû passer par tout le rituel pour obtenir une audience ; ma parole, elle se prenait pour un membre de la famille royale ! Elle a eu droit à sa dose de flatterie et j'ai eu droit à mon petit sermon. Enfin, ç'aurait pu être bien pire.

Une qui a été désagréable, par contre, c'est Mrs Bowchard. Elle n'avait rien contre moi personnellement, c'est juste qu'elle n'aimait pas les filles de cuisine ; en fait, ce qu'elle n'aimait pas c'est qu'on soit beaucoup plus jeune qu'elle. Pendant tout mon mois de préavis, elle n'a pas arrêté de me lancer des piques sur mes capacités en cuisine. Elle me posait des questions du style :

« Et s'ils te demandent de faire tel ou tel plat, comment tu feras ? »

Je ne pouvais pas savoir comment je ferais, vu que je n'avais jamais eu l'occasion d'apprendre, alors je répondais :

« Je regarderai dans un livre.

— Mais on ne cuisine pas avec un livre, Meg, on apprend en cuisinant.

— Peut-être, mais il faut bien commencer un jour.

— Pfff, moi je n'ai pas commencé à dix-huit ans. J'en avais vingt-cinq quand j'ai estimé que j'en étais peut-être capable.

— Oui, mais les temps changent.

— Pour Lady Gibbons ce n'est vraiment pas de chance. Tout ce que tu sais faire, c'est les légumes ! »

Et elle repartait pour un tour, sur le thème « pourvu qu'ils n'aient pas de problème de digestion ». Bref, elle me cherchait des crosses sans arrêt.

Et puis bien entendu il a fallu que je nettoie tout à fond, comme ça, quand la nouvelle fille de cuisine arriverait, tout serait impeccable. Je savais exactement comment Mrs Bowchard serait avec elle. Devant la nouvelle elle me couvrirait d'éloges, du genre :

« Ah, quand c'était Margaret ! Elle était vraiment bien, elle, elle faisait ceci et cela, et patati et patata. »

Le pire, ç'a été les quinze derniers jours, mais comme je savais que je m'en allais je ne me suis pas mis martel en tête, et je suis restée aussi aimable que je pouvais.

La seule que je regrettais de quitter, c'était Gladys. Elle et moi, on avait été comme les deux doigts de la main ; elle venait d'une famille aussi pauvre que la mienne et elle ne faisait pas de châteaux en Espagne. On s'était vraiment bien entendues.

Moi, en tout cas, je me suis juré que si un jour j'étais assez bonne cuisinière pour avoir une fille de cuisine, jamais je ne serais aussi infecte avec elle que Mrs Bowchard l'avait été avec moi.

XX

Quand je suis arrivée chez Lady Gibbons j'étais très confiante, à défaut d'être très savante.

Mon premier choc, ç'a été quand je suis allée à la salle des domestiques. Là j'ai fait la connaissance de la femme de chambre, Jessica, mais je n'ai pas vu de femme de service. Jessica m'a expliqué qu'il y avait un défilé permanent de femmes de chambre et de femmes de service, que personne ne restait longtemps à cause du caractère de Lady Gibbons :

« C'est un vrai chameau. Grippe-sou comme c'est pas permis, avec des yeux de lynx et un nez de vieux renard. »

Je me suis dit : « Allons bon, je me suis trouvé une place épatante, on dirait. » J'ai demandé à Jessica :

« Ça veut dire quoi, un nez de vieux renard ?

– Ça veut dire que si tu as laissé le feu s'éteindre et que tu te sers de la gazinière, elle se pointe en haut de l'escalier et elle hurle : "Est-ce que vous vous servez de la gazinière ?" Elle le sent. Voilà ce que ça veut dire. »

Dès le lendemain j'ai pu me rendre compte à quel point Lady Gibbons était radin. Je venais d'une maison où la cuisinière n'avait qu'à téléphoner chaque fois qu'elle avait besoin de quelque chose ; où on utilisait tous les jours des quantités énormes de lait, de crème, de beurre et d'œufs ; où le caviar et le foie gras faisaient partie de l'ordinaire, et où on jetait tous les restes dans le seau à ordures.

Ce premier matin, donc, Lady Gibbons est descendue à la cuisine, elle est entrée dans le garde-manger et elle a passé en revue toute la nourriture. Jamais je n'ai vu quelqu'un d'autre faire ça, ni avant ni depuis. Elle a inspecté le pot où on mettait le pain rassis, elle a même compté les croûtons. Elle a regardé dans la boîte de farine, dans le bac à légumes, dans la glacière, et à la fin elle a compté les œufs. J'étais sidérée. J'imaginais la tête de Mrs Bowchard si Mrs Cutler avait fait ça. Elle ne serait pas restée cinq minutes, elle aurait donné son congé immédiatement !

Le choc suivant, c'est quand elle m'a dit que c'était elle qui s'occupait de toutes les commandes et qu'à chaque fois que j'aurais besoin de quelque chose il faudrait que je passe par elle. Elle avait un placard à provisions au sous-sol, elle me donnait ce que je demandais au compte-gouttes, et après elle verrouillait le placard. Jamais elle ne m'a donné la clé.

La confiture, par exemple, elle la prenait avec une louche dans un gros bocal de trois kilos, et à la voir on aurait cru que c'était de l'or en poudre. Pareil avec le thé et le reste : elle m'en donnait juste la quantité nécessaire pour la journée. Remarquez, d'un sens, pour moi c'était peut-être mieux, vu que je n'avais aucune expérience ; je n'aurais pas su quoi commander, et gérer les provisions ça m'aurait fait un souci de plus.

Il faut dire que, comme j'avais été embauchée pour faire de la cuisine familiale, je n'avais pas de fille de cuisine. Et il n'y avait pas non plus tout le personnel que j'avais connu avant. À part moi il y avait seulement un chauffeur, une femme de chambre et une femme de service – et le plus souvent une seule sur les deux, je vous l'ai dit.

Lady Gibbons voulait que je porte un bonnet, mais moi ça ne me plaisait pas. J'ai toujours vu ça comme un signe de servitude. Je sais bien que les nurses en portent un, mais elles ce n'est pas pareil, ne me demandez pas pourquoi. De toute façon ce bonnet était affreux, alors je ne le mettais jamais. Lady Gibbons n'était pas contente, mais qu'est-ce qu'elle pouvait y faire ?

Le matin, la femme de service montait à l'étage pour aider la femme de chambre à faire les lits, et Lady Gibbons m'a demandé si je voulais bien répondre à la porte pendant ce temps-là. Et comme mes robes imprimées avaient des manches courtes qui m'arrivaient seulement aux coudes, un matin elle s'est pointée avec un bonnet et des espèces de brassards en coton blanc pour couvrir les avant-bras, et elle m'a dit :

« Tenez, je vous ai apporté ça ; j'ai pensé que vous seriez plus à l'aise pour aller répondre à la porte. »

En fait elle n'avait pas du tout pensé que je serais plus à l'aise ; c'est elle qui aurait été nettement plus à l'aise si je les avais mis. Alors j'ai répondu :

« Oui, merci, Milady. »

Il fallait toujours qu'on l'appelle « Milady » ; pas « Madame », vous pensez bien, elle avait un titre ! Donc j'ai répondu : « Oui, merci, Milady » et j'ai fourré les machins dans un tiroir. Je ne les ai jamais utilisés, et elle ne m'en a jamais reparlé. Elle connaissait les règles – des règles qui n'étaient pas écrites noir sur blanc mais qui existaient quand même –, et elle savait très bien qu'elle n'avait aucun moyen de m'obliger à porter son fichu bonnet et ses brassards.

Quand j'ai commencé à cuisiner, je me suis aperçue que c'était vrai ce que disait Mrs Bowchard : suivre une recette dans un livre ça ne suffit pas, et même l'expérience ça ne suffit pas ; il faut avoir une sorte d'instinct, et apparemment je n'en avais pas beaucoup à l'époque.

Un plat qui m'a donné du fil à retordre, c'est les paupiettes de bœuf. J'avais regardé Mrs Bowchard quand elle en faisait. Elle prenait du filet de bœuf de première qualité, elle le coupait en tranches très fines et elle mettait un peu de hachis de veau sur chaque tranche. Après elle les roulait, elle les attachait avec de la ficelle très fine, et elle les mettait à cuire à la cocotte. Une fois les paupiettes cuites, on enlève la ficelle et on sert. C'est vraiment délicieux. Lady Gibbons adorait le bœuf salé, et elle aimait bien en manger en ragoût le dimanche, par exemple, avec des carottes et des oignons. C'était un plat très économique, et quand il était froid elle me demandait de faire des paupiettes avec. Sauf que quand on coupe une tranche de bœuf salé froid et qu'on la roule elle se fendille de partout, alors je faisais des petits paquets que j'attachais en mettant de la ficelle dans tous les sens. Naturellement, après la cuisson je n'arrivais pas à enlever la ficelle, elle était pour ainsi dire incrustée dans la viande, alors j'envoyais les paupiettes à table telles quelles. Quand les trois assiettes redescendaient, il restait tous les petits bouts de ficelle sur le bord, on aurait dit des reproches.

Je ne me décourageais pas pour autant. J'étais gaie comme un pinson en ce temps-là. C'est drôle, mais moins on en sait en cuisine, plus on se sent compétente. C'est seulement quand on sait cuisiner qu'on se fait du mouron s'il y a quelque chose qui cloche. Quand on ne sait pas, on ne sait pas que ça cloche. Moi, plus j'avais d'expérience, plus je me faisais du mouron. Quand un plat n'était pas formidable je m'en rendais vite compte. Mais bon, je ne pouvais pas vraiment espérer concocter des plats formidables chez Lady Gibbons : même la meilleure cuisinière du monde ne peut pas faire de merveilles avec des ingrédients de mauvaise qualité.

Si j'étais aussi gaie, c'est parce que je n'étais plus fille de cuisine mais cuisinière. La différence de statut qu'il y a entre les deux, il faut avoir été en condition pour la comprendre. Quand on est fille de cuisine on n'est personne, on n'est rien, personne ne vous écoute, on est même la bonniche des autres domestiques. D'accord, quand on est cuisinière dans une maison où il n'y a que deux autres bonnes on n'est pas non plus Dieu le Père, mais je n'en demandais pas tant. Je ne voulais pas être au-dessus de tout le monde, je voulais juste qu'il n'y ait pas continuellement quelqu'un après moi.

Lady Gibbons était un vieux chameau, c'est vrai, mais en général je ne la voyais que le matin, quand elle descendait à la cuisine donner ses instructions. Il lui arrivait de rouspéter contre moi. Au bout de ma première semaine, par exemple, elle a regardé la table de la cuisine et elle a fait :

« Dites donc, cette table est en train de devenir affreusement jaune.

– Ah bon ? Ça doit être la couleur du bois, Milady.

– Alors il a dû changer de couleur depuis que vous êtes là. »

Mais ça n'a pas douché ma bonne humeur.

J'étais là depuis plusieurs semaines quand Jessica, la femme de chambre, est partie. La nouvelle femme de service, Olive, n'avait que quinze ans. Une femme de service de quinze ans, vous vous rendez compte ? Même les aides-femmes de service sont souvent plus vieilles que ça ! Lady Gibbons embauchait généralement des bonnes très jeunes et elle disait qu'elle les formait. En fait, si elle faisait ça c'était pour pouvoir les payer beaucoup moins, et aussi parce qu'elle s'était fait une telle réputation chez les gens de maison qu'elle n'arrivait plus à avoir personne d'expérimenté.

Olive était une fille de la campagne. Elle venait d'un petit village paumé à cinq kilomètres de la première gare ou du premier arrêt de bus. Elle était belle, mais belle ! Elle avait des yeux magnifiques, des cheveux noirs ravissants, et un caractère très calme. Pour travailler chez Lady Gibbons, il valait mieux ! Elle et moi, on est devenues amies pour la vie.

Sir Walter, le mari de « Milady », ne parlait pas beaucoup ; il avait toujours l'air de rêver à sa gloire d'autrefois et il ne voyait pas ce qui se passait autour de lui. Il avait eu un poste important à l'étranger, je ne sais pas quoi au juste. Peut-être dans la Compagnie des Indes orientales ; il avait le teint foncé, ça c'est sûr. Parfois Lady Gibbons se lançait dans des explications du style : « Quand Sir Walter dînait avec le maharadjah… » C'est pour ça que je me disais qu'il avait dû avoir un poste important.

J'avais aussi l'impression que son mariage avec Lady Gibbons avait été l'erreur de sa vie, et que socialement ça l'avait sacrément fait plonger. Il faut dire qu'elle parlait comme une poissonnière, on aurait dit qu'elle n'avait aucune éducation. En fait, *Le Déclin et la chute* de Gibbon*, c'était elle !

---

* Allusion à l'œuvre de l'historien Edward Gibbon (1737-1794) intitulée *Histoire du déclin et de la chute de l'Empire romain. (N.d.T.)*

Les seuls moments où il se dégelait un peu, c'était aux repas. Un jour, Olive m'a raconté qu'il avait fait une remarque comme quoi les bonnes cuisinières étaient une espèce en voie de disparition, ce qui prouve qu'il avait de l'humour. Et ça valait mieux, quand j'y repense, vu les plats que je servais parfois… Je me souviens d'un autre exemple. Le monte-plats était dans la cuisine, et pour atteindre l'étage il traversait le plancher de la salle à manger. Du coup, de là-haut on entendait les bruits de la cuisine. Ce soir-là je n'avais pas arrêté de chanter gaiement en envoyant les plats, et manifestement Sir Walter n'en pouvait plus ; à un moment il s'est penché par l'ouverture du monte-plats et il a crié :

« Vous ne chanteriez pas *God Save the King* maintenant, qu'on en finisse avec ce concert* ? »

Ils avaient beau n'être que trois dans cette famille, le travail n'était pas facile pour autant. Là encore je devais me lever tôt pour allumer le fourneau, parce qu'il fallait qu'il chauffe un certain temps avant que Sir Walter puisse prendre son bain. Après je devais préparer un petit déjeuner très matinal, vers sept heures et demie, pour le fils qui partait travailler. Ensuite il y avait le nôtre à huit heures, et celui de Sir Walter et Lady Gibbons à neuf heures. Et avant qu'elle descende à dix heures pour donner ses instructions il fallait que j'aie non seulement briqué la cuisine et l'arrière-cuisine mais aussi rangé la salle des domestiques et le garde-manger, parce qu'elle inspectait tout.

---

* En Grande-Bretagne, l'hymne national est souvent joué à la fin des concerts. (*N.d.T.*)

La femme de service avait une tonne de choses à faire, surtout l'hiver, quand il fallait allumer toutes les cheminées qui marchaient au charbon. Elle devait se coltiner des seaux de charbon du sous-sol au rez-de-chaussée pour l'âtre de la salle à manger, et jusqu'au premier étage pour celui du salon. Et il fallait aussi une flambée dans la salle du petit déjeuner. Ces trois feux devaient être allumés tous les matins à huit heures, et elle n'avait droit qu'à un demi-fagot de petit bois par cheminée. Certains jours elle y arrivait les doigts dans le nez, mais quand le vent ne soufflait pas dans la bonne direction ils refusaient de démarrer. Ces jours-là elle courait du haut en bas de l'escalier une tasse de paraffine à la main, et sur ses joues les larmes se mélangeaient à la suie.

De ce point de vue-là, la femme de chambre avait de la chance : les Gibbons étaient tellement radins qu'ils ne faisaient jamais allumer de feu dans les chambres.

Ils avaient une habitude bizarre que je n'ai jamais vue ailleurs : ils utilisaient une bassinoire. En fait, à l'époque on n'en trouvait déjà plus depuis longtemps, mais Lady Gibbons en avait deux. Il y en avait une accrochée dans le vestibule comme décoration, mais l'autre on la remplissait tous les soirs avec des braises du fourneau et on la passait sur les lits. Je trouvais que nous, on était drôlement mieux loties : les soirs d'hiver je mettais des briques dans le four et on les glissait dans nos lits avec un morceau de flanelle autour. Croyez-moi, on avait sûrement plus chaud avec nos briques qu'eux avec leur bassinoire !

Il y avait une seule chambre au grenier, et je la partageais avec Olive. J'aurais pu avoir la chambre de l'étage en dessous, mais je la laissais à la femme de chambre parce que je voulais être le plus loin possible d'« Eux ». Lady Gibbons trouvait très curieux que la cuisinière partage : normalement elle avait une chambre à elle, et c'étaient la femme de chambre et la femme de service qui partageaient. Mais moi je préférais le grenier.

Mes congés, c'était tous les dimanches après-midi et un après-midi en semaine, plus la journée entière une fois par mois que j'avais réclamée. Olive avait un dimanche sur deux seulement, mais quand c'était possible on allait ensemble à un thé dansant ce jour-là. Ne croyez pas que ces bals étaient du genre frénétique ou quoi que ce soit ; aujourd'hui ils le seraient sûrement, mais à l'époque c'était tout à fait innocent comme distraction. En général on y allait en couple ; si on y allait avec une fille, on risquait de se retrouver à danser avec elle tout l'après-midi.

Mais bien entendu on avait l'espoir de s'y trouver un petit ami. C'était la seule véritable occasion qu'on avait de rencontrer quelqu'un. Si on allait au cinéma, par exemple, et qu'un gars s'asseyait à côté de nous et commençait à nous draguer, naturellement on s'attendait au pire. De toute façon, dans le noir on voyait à peine à quoi il ressemblait, et pour discuter c'était moyennement pratique. Moi, quand un homme me draguait, en général je m'apercevais après qu'il était aussi beau que le monstre de Frankenstein et aussi raffiné qu'un valet de ferme, alors je ne m'y risquais pas trop. Mais à un thé dansant on pouvait observer les garçons, et s'il y en avait un qui nous plaisait on pouvait sortir le grand jeu pour essayer de le séduire Et croyez-moi, quand on sortait le grand jeu on sortait le grand jeu !

Vous comprenez, je voulais absolument me marier. Je ne voulais pas rester vieille fille. Les gens d'alors étaient très méprisants avec celles qui « n'arrivaient pas à se caser ». Ça voulait dire qu'elles n'avaient vraiment rien pour elles. Maintenant il y a des femmes célibataires qui ont tout le sexe et toute la sécurité qu'elles veulent. Simplement elles refusent d'être avec le même homme toute leur vie, et je ne leur jette pas la pierre, loin de là. Mais moi j'avais besoin d'un homme pour subvenir à mes besoins. Je ne me voyais pas rester cuisinière jusqu'à la fin de mes jours, alors je voulais qu'il y en ait un qui me prenne en charge définitivement.

Olive, non seulement elle était ravissante mais elle dansait incroyablement bien, beaucoup mieux que moi, et elle était tellement jolie qu'elle avait toujours une ribambelle de cavaliers. Et si elle avait autant de succès, c'est parce qu'elle avait confiance en elle.

Elle avait passé son enfance à la campagne et elle était toujours allée aux bals de son village. Les parents y emmenaient leurs enfants, même les tout petits, alors ils apprenaient à danser de bonne heure et ils avaient confiance en eux. Moi, je ne savais pas du tout danser. Je n'arrivais jamais à suivre mon partenaire. Comme j'étais d'un tempérament plutôt agressif, je voulais toujours diriger au lieu de le laisser faire.

Le seul atout que j'avais c'était la conversation, et sur une piste de danse ce n'est pas terrible, comme atout. Les hommes ne vont pas au bal pour discuter, ils y vont pour danser et voir qui ils pourraient bien ramener après. En fait ma conversation ne me rendait pas service, au contraire, même, parce que je ne parlais pas de choses normales. En principe ça donne :

LE GARÇON : Vous venez souvent ici ?

LA FILLE : Oui, assez souvent.

LE GARÇON : Elle est chouette, la piste, hein ?

166

LA FILLE : Oh oui, le parquet est très souple.

LE GARÇON : Et l'orchestre, il est bath, non ?

LA FILLE : Oui, il joue vraiment bien en rythme.

Moi, au lieu de ça, je parlais à mes cavaliers de l'histoire de Londres, ou bien je leur demandais s'ils avaient lu Dickens. Ils devaient me prendre pour une hurluberlue. Dickens, ils n'en avaient jamais entendu parler, alors ils ne risquaient pas d'en avoir lu !

Je commençais déjà à me gaver de culture ; même à ce moment-là je trouvais toujours le temps de lire – des bouquins intéressants, je veux dire.

Parfois j'essayais de parler de Joseph Conrad, parce qu'il a écrit des bouquins qui peuvent plaire aux garçons. Mais ils n'en avaient jamais lu non plus, et ils me laissaient tomber comme une vieille chaussette.

Olive, par contre, elle était expressive et sentimentale ; elle levait vers eux des yeux tendres et elle répondait toujours ce qu'il fallait quand il fallait. Et en plus elle dansait bien.

Je me suis rendu compte que quand deux filles se baladent ensemble il y en a toujours une plus séduisante que l'autre ; pour Olive et moi c'était comme ça, elle était nettement plus jolie que moi, et quand on se trouvait deux copains c'était pareil : il y en avait un beau et un moche. Si ça se trouve, c'est comme ça que la nature rétablit l'équilibre.

Olive, elle sortait tout droit de sa campagne et elle n'avait que quinze ans, mais les garçons lui tournaient autour comme des mouches autour d'un pot de miel. Il faut dire qu'elle savait comment leur parler, les tenir comme qui dirait en haleine, et ça c'est tout un art.

Moi, naturellement, je me récupérais le plus vilain. Parfois il n'était pas trop mal et je me disais : « Ah, cette fois ça y

167

est. » La semaine suivante c'était un gars au menton fuyant avec rien dans le ciboulot, alors je passais juste la soirée avec lui et je laissais tomber.

On a beau avoir envie de se marier, il faut quand même faire attention. Si on n'apprécie déjà pas la compagnie d'un gars au menton fuyant avec rien dans le ciboulot pendant quelques heures, on ne peut pas en vouloir comme vis-à-vis à table tous les jours de sa vie, pas vrai ? Olive me disait toujours :

« Tu es trop exigeante. Qu'est-ce que ça peut faire ? Tu n'as qu'à garder celui-là jusqu'à ce que tu en trouves un autre.

— Mais je ne pourrai pas en trouver un autre si je sors tout le temps avec celui-là !

— Mais si, bien sûr que tu pourras ! »

Elle, elle pouvait. Comme je disais, c'est tout un art, et moi je n'ai jamais été très douée pour la sociabilité et tout ça. Quand je me plaignais de mon cavalier elle me disait :

« Faute de grives, on mange des merles ! »

Enfin bon, à dix-huit ans on ne risque jamais trop la disette. Et plus tard, quand finalement j'ai trouvé un mari, il était plutôt beau garçon, ma foi.

Olive a pourtant dû avoir des tas d'occasions, mais elle n'a jamais fait la même bêtise qu'Agnes. Apparemment elle avait la tête sur les épaules. Ça aussi, je crois que c'est parce qu'elle avait vécu à la campagne.

Elle avait passé son enfance à Ripe, un village du Sussex. Avec l'accent cockney, ça ressemble à une atteinte aux bonnes mœurs, ce nom* ! Bref, ce n'était pas comme maintenant

---

* C'est ainsi, en effet, que dans les quartiers populaires de Londres on prononce le mot *rape*, « viol ». *(N.d.T.)*

dans les villages, les jeunes ne cherchaient pas à partir à la première occasion. Ils avaient une vie sociale, et elle tournait autour de la salle des fêtes.

Les gens emmenaient leurs enfants à toutes les festivités, ce qui fait que très tôt les filles et les garçons étaient mélangés. C'est pour ça que, contrairement à moi, Olive n'était jamais mal à l'aise avec les hommes. C'est bien joli de dire que les gars de la campagne sont des péquenots, n'empêche qu'un garçon c'est un garçon et qu'un homme c'est un homme, qu'il soit de la ville ou de la campagne.

Il y a aussi autre chose : dans un village, si on s'écarte du droit chemin tout le monde est au courant, et du coup on fait un peu attention où on met les pieds. Mais en cas de faux pas on n'est pas non plus rejeté comme en ville. Là-bas les gens sont beaucoup plus proches de la nature, alors ils savent que quand un garçon et une fille sont ensemble il peut se passer des choses. Notez bien que si ça arrive les parents de la fille, et même du garçon, trouvent normal qu'il l'épouse. Olive m'a raconté que beaucoup de filles se mariaient en blanc alors qu'elles étaient déjà enceintes. En fait, quand elles ne l'étaient pas certains les trouvaient un peu bêcheuses, parce qu'un enfant c'est un don de Dieu, peu importe comment il a été fabriqué. En plus les villageois sont en contact avec des animaux qui se reproduisent sans arrêt. Et puis de toute façon il n'y a pas grand-chose d'autre à faire, et il y a tellement d'occasions ! Je veux dire : si on se promène sur un sentier, qu'il n'y a pas de réverbères et qu'il fait tout noir... C'est l'occasion qui fait le larron, comme dit le proverbe !

En ville ce n'est pas du tout la même chose : c'est très impersonnel, on n'a pas souvent la chance de sortir en famille et on n'apprend pas à connaître les garçons. Si on tombe enceinte d'un homme il peut passer entre les mailles du filet, et on se retrouve avec un bébé sur les bras et une réputation de marie-couche-toi-là.

Une fois je suis allée passer quelques jours à Ripe avec Olive. Tout à l'heure j'ai parlé des avantages du village sur le plan social, mais je peux vous dire que vivre en ville n'avait pas que des inconvénients. D'abord, le village se trouvait à cinq kilomètres de l'arrêt de bus le plus proche, alors j'ai dû marcher plus d'une heure en me coltinant mes bagages. Il n'y avait ni eau courante, ni gaz, ni électricité, juste des lampes à huile pour le soir, et on se lavait dans une cuvette en émail posée sur un tas de briques avec un trou ; on versait l'eau dans le trou et elle tombait directement par terre, en vous éclaboussant les pieds si on ne se reculait pas – moi je me suis fait avoir, la première fois. L'eau, on la tirait du puits qui était dans le jardin. Il n'y avait ni treuil ni corde pour la remonter, il fallait se mettre à genoux par terre et plonger le seau dedans. Elle grouillait de petits trucs qui se tortillaient comme des têtards. Olive m'a dit que de toute façon ils étaient bouillis avant qu'on les avale en même temps que le thé, mais moi je me serais très bien passée de têtards bouillis. Et tout ce qu'on mangeait avait le goût de fumée. Forcément, sa mère avait seulement une cheminée pour faire la cuisine.

J'ai partagé un lit avec Olive, un lit drôlement douillet, avec un de ces matelas de plumes qu'on a juste à secouer. J'ai trouvé que comme confort c'était le fin du fin. Mais juste au-dessus de nos têtes il y avait des grattements à vous donner la chair de poule, et ça n'arrêtait pas. J'ai demandé à Olive ce que c'était et elle a dit :

« Oh, ça ? C'est juste un rat dans les combles. »

Juste un rat dans les combles ! J'étais à deux doigts de la crise cardiaque. Je l'ai suppliée d'aller fouiller le grenier et de le chasser, mais elle a répondu :

« Ne t'inquiète pas, il ne sort jamais. Il a son nid là-haut. »

J'ai bien failli tomber dans les pommes.

Les sanitaires étaient sacrément rudimentaires. Ils étaient installés tout au bout de l'allée du jardin, et croyez-moi ça valait mieux. De l'extérieur c'était un petit endroit charmant, couvert de rosiers grimpants, mais quand on entrait à l'intérieur, punaise ! C'était un de ces horribles trucs qu'il fallait vider et enterrer régulièrement. Et il y avait un siège à deux trous, le modèle « Tristan et Iseut », pour les amoureux qui ne supportent pas d'être séparés – autant dire pour les cœurs qui battent à l'unisson ! En fait on risquait déjà l'asphyxie quand une seule personne y était allée. Mais deux, je ne crois pas qu'ils en seraient sortis vivants.

Malgré tout c'était la maison d'Olive, et elle y était heureuse.

Les citadins disent que dans les villages tout le monde est au courant de vos affaires. C'est vrai, bien entendu, mais on est aussi au courant des affaires des autres ; du coup ça fait une communauté très soudée, et à mon sens c'est une bonne chose. Moi j'habite en ville, et je serais bien incapable de vous dire comment s'appellent les gens à deux ou trois maisons de chez moi. Personne ne se parle, et le plus grand compliment qu'on puisse faire à une femme, c'est de dire qu'elle est discrète et réservée. Mais bon, ce genre d'attitude, c'est la meilleure façon de devenir une vieille fille discrète et réservée, vous ne trouvez pas ?

XXI

Avec le temps Lady Gibbons est devenue de plus en plus désagréable. Vu les allusions qu'elle faisait, je crois que ça n'allait pas fort côté finances et que Sir Walter avait fait de mauvais placements. Si ça se trouve, c'est pour ça qu'elle était aussi radin : parce qu'ils étaient vraiment justes.

Au moment de Noël, j'ai dû faire cuire une dinde et je l'ai complètement ratée. Je ne m'en sortais pas avec ce fourneau. Il était toujours soit trop chaud, soit pas assez. Cette fois je l'avais trop fait chauffer, et la dinde a brûlé. Je l'ai grattée comme j'ai pu avec la râpe à muscade, j'ai recouvert les parties les plus brûlées avec de la chapelure, et je l'ai envoyée à table en croisant les doigts. Je m'attendais à entendre Sir Walter exploser de rage par le monte-plats, mais rien. Silence. Quand Olive est redescendue, je lui ai demandé :

« Il n'a rien dit ?

– Rien du tout.

– Et elle ?

172

– Euh… elle, elle a un peu changé de couleur, elle a tourné la dinde pour la regarder sous toutes les coutures, mais personne n'a rien dit. »

Au bout de deux ou trois jours, comme Lady Gibbons n'en avait toujours pas parlé, j'ai commencé à croire que ça avait peut-être été, finalement.

Mais le matin du quatrième jour, comme ça, sans prévenir, elle m'a demandé :

« Qu'est-ce qui s'est passé avec la dinde ?

– La dinde, Milady ?

– Oui, la dinde.

– Eh bien, en fait elle a un peu brûlé.

– Un peu brûlé ? C'était un vrai tas de charbon, vous voulez dire ! Quand Sir Walter a voulu la découper, elle s'est tout bonnement écroulée.

– Ah, ça, c'est le signe qu'elle était tendre.

– Non, ce n'est pas le signe qu'elle était tendre, votre dinde. Quel dommage que nous ne soyons pas tous végétariens : il n'y a que les légumes que vous savez faire cuire !

– Justement, Milady, il y a quelque chose dont je voulais vous parler. »

Quand j'ai dit ça j'ai remarqué qu'elle pâlissait ; elle a cru que j'allais lui donner mon congé, et manifestement ça n'aurait pas fait son affaire. Mieux valait tout de même des plats carbonisés que pas de plats du tout.

« Voilà : j'ai pensé que je pourrais prendre quelques cours de cuisine l'après-midi. »

J'y avais réellement pensé, et l'histoire de la dinde a comme qui dirait emporté le morceau. Vous comprenez, ça avait été mon échec le plus cuisant, et après tout c'est vrai que ça coûte cher, une dinde, alors j'avais cette pauvre bête sur la conscience.

« C'est une très bonne idée », elle a dit, et sa figure a commencé à se décrisper et à reprendre des couleurs.

Et puis aussitôt sa mâchoire s'est contractée, et elle a ajouté :

« Mais vous devrez les payer de votre poche, bien sûr. »

Chassez le naturel, il revient au galop !

J'ai fait des recherches, et je me suis décidée pour un établissement baptisé « Haute École de cuisine continentale de Léon ». Extérieurement c'était un bâtiment très imposant ; après coup je me suis aperçue que l'école n'en occupait qu'une toute petite partie, une seule grande pièce, à vrai dire, et en très mauvais état. Mais les cours n'étaient pas chers, deux shillings six pence en groupe et cinq shillings pour les cours particuliers. J'ai commencé par m'inscrire aux séances de groupe.

Monsieur Léon était un homme entre deux âges avec les cheveux en broussaille et une grande toque de chef par-dessus. Il avait vraiment l'air professionnel et c'était un bon cuisinier, il n'y a pas à dire. Il nous a appris à faire des plats sensationnels avec trois fois rien. Ça, ça plaisait à Lady Gibbons.

Par exemple, il nous a montré comment faire de la pâte feuilletée. Elle montait comme je n'ai jamais vu une pâte monter, et pourtant il utilisait de la margarine. Remarquez, il ne nous faisait jamais goûter, et ce n'était sans doute pas plus mal.

Pendant tout le cours il n'arrêtait pas d'employer des mots typiquement français du style « *Voilà* », « *Comme ci comme ça* », « *Oui, oui* ». Moi je ne savais même pas ce que ça voulait dire, mais comme je trouvais que ça ressemblait vraiment à du français je ne me méfiais pas.

Quand j'ai pris mon premier cours particulier, j'ai dû contourner sa table pour m'approcher de ses deux gazinières et des ustensiles qui se trouvaient tout autour. Punaise ! De toute ma vie je n'ai jamais vu une horreur pareille. Il y avait des piles de casseroles avec des morceaux de nourriture qui devaient macérer dedans depuis une éternité ; à mon avis, si on avait connu la pénicilline à l'époque, on en aurait eu assez pour soigner tout un hôpital ! Les poêles étaient collées aux gazinières par la graisse figée et ça puait, mais ça puait ! C'est ça qui m'a achevée. J'ai fait :

« Monsieur Léon, c'est trop dégueulasse ! »

Et j'ai tourné de l'œil. Je suis tombée dans les pommes par terre, carrément.

Quand je me suis réveillée monsieur Léon était penché sur moi et il me faisait boire une goutte de cognac. Lui, il en a bien éclusé un demi-verre. Il était en train de me parler, et il n'avait plus du tout l'accent français. Je lui ai dit :

« Monsieur Léon, vous n'êtes pas plus français que moi.

– 'videmment que non », il a répondu.

Et sous l'effet du cognac il s'est mis à me faire plein de confidences :

« J'ai fait mon régiment comme cantinier en France pendant la guerre. C'est là que j'ai appris les rudiments. Après j'ai déserté. J'avais une fiancée là-bas, d'ailleurs on s'est mariés. Et puis bon, après elle m'a quitté, mais j'avais appris les ficelles du métier. Alors je suis rentré en Angleterre et j'ai monté cette affaire.

– Et votre vrai nom, c'est quoi ?

175

– Percy Taylor. Comment vouliez-vous que je lance une "École de cuisine continentale de Percy Taylor" ? Je n'aurais pas eu une seule élève. Alors je me suis appelé Léon et je me suis mis à employer des mots français que j'avais appris là-bas. J'en connaissais beaucoup plus avant, mais maintenant je les ai oubliés. »

Je me suis dit en moi-même : « Oui, et la cuisine française aussi tu l'as sûrement oubliée. » Bref, après ça je n'y suis plus retournée. Lady Gibbons a dû se contenter de la cuisine *à la Margaret**.

S'il y avait bien une chose qu'elles ne supportaient pas, elle et la plupart de ses semblables, c'était qu'on casse des trucs. Pour les domestiques, la casse ça fait partie des risques du métier, surtout quand on a beaucoup de vaisselle à faire. Mais aucune de mes patronnes ne voulait l'admettre, Lady Gibbons encore moins que les autres. Quand je faisais tomber quelque chose, c'était toujours pareil :

« Qu'est-ce que c'est, cette fois ? »

Et dès que je lui avais dit ce que c'était elle s'écriait : « Oh non, pas ça ! » comme si « ça » était ce qu'elle avait de plus cher au monde. En fait c'est très curieux : pendant toutes mes années de service, j'ai remarqué qu'on pouvait casser n'importe quoi, de toute façon c'était toujours un objet auquel Madame « tenait particulièrement », ou qui « coûtait les yeux de la tête » ; c'était « un héritage de famille », c'était « irremplaçable », ou bien ça avait une « valeur sentimentale » ; ce n'était jamais une bricole qu'on pouvait acheter dans n'importe quel magasin. Ça me faisait penser à un

* En français dans le texte. (*N.d.T.*)

déménageur qui avait cassé une assiette en emballant de la vaisselle. La propriétaire s'était écriée :

« Oh, mon Dieu, cette assiette avait plus de cent ans ! »

Et le gars lui avait répondu :

« Cent ans ! Ben dites donc, elle avait largement fait son temps, non ? »

Un matin, Lady Gibbons est venue nous annoncer que la famille s'apprêtait à passer deux mois à la campagne, quelque part dans le Yorkshire, et qu'ils allaient fermer la maison. Elle a dit qu'elle avait trouvé une autre place pour Olive chez une amie à elle. J'ai été surprise qu'Olive la laisse lui trouver une place. Moi, je n'aurais jamais voulu travailler pour une amie de Lady Gibbons, parce que bien souvent les gens ont des amis qui leur ressemblent bigrement. Elle a dit qu'elle m'emmenait avec eux, et que comme il y avait déjà une cuisinière là-bas je ferais fonction de femme de service.

Et tout ça sans le moindre « si ça ne vous fait rien », sans me demander si ça me dérangeait de changer de boulot ou d'aller dans le Yorkshire. Non mais, elle me prenait pour quoi, au juste ? Pour un meuble qu'elle pouvait déplacer comme elle voulait ? Ma décision était prise : pour rien au monde je n'irais dans le Yorkshire, même si elle doublait mes gages. Pas comme femme de service. J'aurais été trop mal à l'aise. Je souffrais déjà le martyre rien que d'entrer dans la pièce où ils étaient, alors s'il avait fallu que je les serve à table !

Quand je lui ai dit que je ne voulais pas quitter Londres, elle a dit que l'endroit où ils allaient se trouvait en pleine nature, dans un endroit magnifique. Elle ne pouvait pas le savoir, mais pour moi ça réglait définitivement la question :

j'avais eu ma dose de campagne quand j'étais allée chez Olive.

Je me représentais très bien le Yorkshire. J'imaginais un endroit en plein milieu des landes et moi coincée là-bas avec mes patrons bien-aimés. De toute façon je détestais la campagne. À mon sens, une fois qu'on a vu une vache ou un arbre, on les a tous vus. Une vache ça a quatre pattes, un arbre ça a des branches, mais à part ça qu'est-ce qu'ils font ? Moi ce que j'aime c'est la conversation, les gens, les choses qui bougent et qui sont utiles.

Quand cette chère Lady Gibbons a compris que j'étais déterminée à ne pas aller dans le Yorkshire, elle a voulu me trouver un remplacement : elle voulait rentrer dans ses frais, vous comprenez ? Sinon elle devrait me donner deux mois entiers de vacances payées, et ça, rien que d'y penser ça la rendait malade. Moi je lui ai dit :

« Écoutez, Milady, je suis vraiment désolée, mais je n'aime pas les remplacements. Je veux bien le faire, mais si le poste me convient j'aurai envie de le garder, alors il ne faudra pas compter sur moi à votre retour. »

Ça a suffi. Je savais très bien qu'elle ne me laisserait pas partir.

Elle n'a rien répondu sur le moment ; il fallait qu'elle fasse comme si la décision venait d'elle. Mais le lendemain elle est venue me dire que Sir Walter et elle avaient pensé que vu les circonstances il valait mieux ne pas fermer la maison et que je pouvais rester pour la surveiller. Je pourrais y loger si je voulais. Elle me paierait mes gages plus cinq shillings par semaine pour la nourriture. C'était impeccable. J'allais avoir deux mois de congés payés – un truc inouï ! J'étais au septième ciel.

Bizarrement, après son retour je ne suis restée que quatre mois. Je m'étais peut-être trop bien habituée à ne pas travailler dans cette maison. J'ai donné mon préavis, en disant que d'après le docteur ce n'était pas bon pour ma santé de vivre dans un sous-sol sombre avec la lumière allumée toute la journée.

Quand on donnait son préavis, on essayait toujours de donner l'impression qu'on était désolée de partir ; il fallait faire semblant, à cause du certificat. On ne pouvait pas trouver un autre boulot si on n'avait pas un bon certificat. Aujourd'hui, naturellement, les gens font des faux. Moi, si j'avais su faire ça, je ne m'en serais pas privée. C'était complètement aberrant que les patrons se fient à l'avis de la dernière personne pour qui on avait travaillé. Elle pouvait très bien essayer de vous nuire parce qu'elle vous en voulait d'être partie. Si les gens étaient foncièrement honnêtes, qu'ils vous aiment ou pas ils vous donneraient un bon certificat du moment que vous le méritez, mais les gens ne sont pas comme ça, c'est tout.

Je ne sais pas si Lady Gibbons a gobé mon histoire ; en tout cas elle m'a fait un très bon certificat. Elle ne me couvrait pas d'éloges, mais elle disait que j'étais honnête, travailleuse et bonne cuisinière. Que demander de plus ?

XXII

Après avoir quitté Lady Gibbons j'ai décidé d'essayer les remplacements, pour changer. Je me disais que comme ça je ne resterais pas longtemps dans chaque place, que je ferais un maximum de maisons en un minimum de temps et qu'à la fin j'aurais plein d'expérience. Vous savez, c'est rare que deux personnes voient la cuisine de la même façon. Il y en a qui aiment les plats recherchés, d'autres les plats tout simples ; certaines sont exigeantes sur le sucré, d'autres sur le salé. Donc je croyais qu'en ayant pas mal de postes différents j'aurais vite fait d'apprendre beaucoup de choses.

Ça ne s'est pas du tout passé comme ça. Je me suis aperçue que si des gens cherchaient une remplaçante par petite annonce c'était en général parce que aucune cuisinière digne de ce nom n'aurait accepté une place fixe chez eux. Le premier remplacement que j'ai fait, c'était dans les Stanley Gardens, à Notting Hill.

Dernièrement, le secteur est devenu célèbre à cause d'une histoire de meurtre. À l'époque où j'y étais, c'était un quartier de grandes maisons victoriennes plutôt moches et déjà délabrées.

Les gens pour qui je travaillais étaient juifs et ils s'appelaient Mr et Mrs Bernard. Ce n'étaient pas des juifs orthodoxes : ils ne mangeaient pas de porc, mais ils n'observaient pas toutes ces règles comme mettre à part les couverts, le linge et les ustensiles qu'on utilise pour le lait. Plus tard j'ai bossé pour deux autres familles juives très généreuses, mais on ne pouvait vraiment pas dire ça de Mr et Mrs Bernard. Eux, ils étaient carrément radins ; Lady Gibbons, à côté, c'était la déesse de l'abondance ! Enfin, ils étaient tout de même plus faciles à vivre qu'elle.

Par exemple, dans ma chambre et dans celles de la femme de chambre et de la femme de service, comme meubles il y avait vraiment le strict minimum. Les lits étaient tout sauf rembourrés, et comme couvertures on avait des rideaux pelucheux avec tous les pompons encore accrochés. Les miens étaient verts, et ceux de mes collègues rouges. La courtepointe avait été coupée en deux, alors d'un côté il y avait une frange et de l'autre, celui qui était contre le mur, juste un ourlet. On avait une seule chaise, et dans un coin de quoi accrocher ses habits, pas une armoire, juste quelques crochets avec un rideau qu'on tirait devant. Et puis une table de toilette ; comme la mienne avait un pied cassé, on l'avait remplacé par une pile de livres.

Mrs Bernard faisait de la phlébite ; elle se plaignait sans arrêt et montrait sa jambe à tout le monde. Moi, ça m'horripilait. Le soir, quand je montais me coucher, j'essayais de ne pas faire de bruit dans l'escalier, parce que si elle m'entendait passer devant sa chambre elle criait :

« Qui est-ce ? Ah, c'est vous, venez là. »

Alors je devais entrer et contempler son horrible jambe étendue sur le lit, et je peux vous dire que ce n'était pas ragoûtant comme spectacle : elle était toute gonflée, on aurait dit une poche de graisse. J'aurais dû compatir, c'était sûrement douloureux et Mrs Bernard avait réellement du mal à se déplacer. Mais je n'y arrivais pas, parce qu'elle faisait constamment étalage de ses malheurs. En plus sa chambre était luxueuse, et quand je la comparais aux nôtres ça me mettait carrément en rogne. Elle passait toutes ses journées au lit à manger des chocolats en exhibant sa jambe. Je crois bien qu'elle avait fini par en être fière. En tout cas, elle trouvait que ça faisait partie de notre boulot de nous apitoyer sur son sort.

La dernière chose qu'Edna, la femme de service, devait faire le soir, c'était de lui monter un petit pain bis et une plaquette de beurre au cas où elle aurait faim pendant la nuit. Si elle ne le mangeait pas, elle le renvoyait à la cuisine et c'était pour nous. Mais jamais je ne m'en serais servie, pour la bonne raison que ce pain et ce beurre avaient passé la nuit sur sa chaise percée. Vous parlez d'une hygiène !

Mr Bernard était un vieux monsieur à l'air bienveillant, mais c'était juste une façade. On dit que la beauté ce n'est qu'une question d'apparence, mais croyez-moi c'est vrai aussi pour la bienveillance. Si Mrs Bernard ne pouvait pas descendre à la cuisine pour donner ses instructions, c'est Mr Bernard qui descendait. Il essayait toujours de m'attirer dans un coin, dans le garde-manger ou dans l'arrière-cuisine, il mettait la main sur mon bras ou sur mon épaule (d'ailleurs il avait les doigts crochus comme un voleur) et il disait :

« Qu'allons-nous trouver comme menu ? »

Je me demande bien où il comptait le trouver, son menu. Et après, pendant que j'écrivais, il se penchait par-dessus mon épaule. Ses petites avances ne m'auraient pas dérangée si pour la peine il m'avait offert une paire de bas ou une boîte de chocolats, par exemple, mais jamais il ne m'a rien donné. Je sais bien qu'il voulait juste me caresser le cou, mais bon, est-ce qu'on est censée trouver ça agréable de la part d'un vieillard ?

C'est lui qui faisait les courses, et tous les matins il allait au marché de Portobello. Si on voulait faire une salade composée il rapportait une laitue et une betterave, ou une laitue et des tomates. Jamais rien d'autre. Pour faire une salade composée, je vous demande un peu ! Il disait que ça laissait le champ libre à mon imagination. Mais enfin, même avec de l'imagination il faut quelques ingrédients de base, non ? Je ne pouvais pas faire de miracles. Ça m'étonne qu'il n'ait pas descendu l'eau à la cuisine pour voir si je ne pourrais pas la changer en vin…

Le problème, c'est qu'ils n'avaient pas les moyens d'avoir trois bonnes, alors que pour entretenir une maison de cette taille-là il en aurait fallu *au moins* trois. Tel que ça fonctionnait, rien n'était jamais fait comme il aurait fallu. Tout avait l'air vieux et râpé, sauf dans sa chambre à elle et le salon.

Dans la cuisine il y avait un lino élimé, des chaises en osier tout avachies et un fourneau qui datait de Mathusalem. Tous les ustensiles étaient archi-usés, les balais et les brosses perdaient leurs poils sans arrêt et rien n'était jamais remplacé. Pas étonnant qu'ils aient dû recruter des domestiques temporaires par petites annonces. Ils savaient très bien qu'ils n'en garderaient aucune.

J'y suis restée trois mois, et tout le bénéfice que j'en ai retiré, c'est d'avoir inventé là ma fameuse entrée au hareng fumé. C'est arrivé d'une façon assez rigolote. Un matin on a mangé du hareng fumé au petit déjeuner, et Mrs Bernard, qui prenait toujours son petit déjeuner au lit, n'a pas mangé le sien. Quand Edna a redescendu le plateau, j'ai jeté le hareng dans le seau à ordures sous l'évier. Mais quand Mr Bernard est venu me donner ses instructions il m'a dit :

« Madame voudrait que vous lui fassiez une entrée pour le dîner avec le hareng qu'elle a laissé au petit déjeuner. »

J'ai cru que mon cœur s'arrêtait. Je n'ai pas osé dire que je l'avais jeté, parce que ça leur aurait gâché la journée à tous les deux, et je ne voyais pas pourquoi je devrais gâcher la journée de quelqu'un à cause d'un hareng. Alors j'ai répondu :

« Très bien, Monsieur, pas de problème. »

Aussitôt qu'il a eu le dos tourné je me suis précipitée sur le seau à ordures pour repêcher le hareng. Il était couvert de feuilles de thé et d'autres détritus, alors je l'ai rincé sous le robinet. Mais j'avais une vaisselle en cours à ce moment-là, et manque de pot, en le rinçant je l'ai fait tomber dans ma bassine. Je l'ai donc repêché et rincé en vitesse encore une fois en le reniflant sans arrêt pour voir si l'odeur de savon s'en allait. Au bout d'un moment il m'a semblé que ça y était. Le problème, après, c'était de savoir quoi en faire pour être sûre que ça n'ait pas le goût de savon. J'ai enlevé toute la chair du hareng, je l'ai bien broyée au pilon dans le mortier, et j'ai utilisé cette bonne vieille sauce diable d'Escoffier, une sauce toute prête épatante pour camoufler le goût de quelque chose. J'ai présenté la chose avec un accompagnement et une jolie décoration, et à ma grande surprise Mrs Bernard a envoyé la femme de service me féliciter :

« Dites à la cuisinière que c'est l'entrée la plus délicieuse que nous ayons jamais mangée. »

Je me suis dit : « Tu vois, ma fille, quand tu veux qu'un truc ait vraiment du goût, commence par lui faire faire un petit séjour dans le seau à ordures. »

Vous vous doutez bien qu'au bout de pas longtemps j'avais appris tout ce que je pouvais apprendre dans cette maison, alors je suis partie.

Ma place suivante, c'était à Chelsea, chez des gens qui s'appelaient Lord et Lady Downhall. Entre eux et les Bernard, la différence était incroyable. C'étaient les gens les plus prévenants et les plus aimables que j'aie rencontrés depuis que j'étais en condition. Malheureusement, eux cherchaient vraiment une remplaçante. Leur cuisinière était à l'hôpital et elle ne devait rester absente que trois mois. Ils étaient tellement gentils, tellement simples dans leurs relations avec nous, que pour la première fois depuis mes débuts comme domestique je n'avais plus le sentiment qu'on était une race à part et qu'entre ceux d'en haut et nous il y avait un fossé infranchissable.

Les Downhall nous parlaient exactement comme ils auraient parlé à des gens de leur monde.

Par exemple, ils nous appelaient tous par nos prénoms. Moi, c'était la première fois que j'étais dans une maison où « Eux » m'appelaient par mon prénom.

Et vous auriez vu la salle des domestiques ! Je n'aurais jamais cru ça possible. Elle était meublée confortablement et décorée dans des couleurs assorties. On avait des fauteuils moelleux, un tapis par terre, un lampadaire et d'autres petites lampes tout autour, des tableaux et des bibelots. On voyait que c'étaient des objets achetés spécialement pour nous, pas des vieux machins mis au rebut. Des objets vraiment assortis, pas un bric-à-brac de cochonneries venant aussi bien du jardin d'hiver que du salon ou de la salle à manger. La pièce était tellement accueillante que quand on avait un peu de temps libre on sentait qu'on pouvait vraiment se détendre, même si la journée n'était pas finie.

Chaque chambre avait une couleur, et la mienne c'était le vert. J'avais un tapis vert, un édredon vert, des couvertures vertes avec une bande de satin tout autour et, incroyable mais vrai, une lampe de chevet et une table.

Ils faisaient tout pour qu'on sente qu'ils se souciaient vraiment de nous. Tous les domestiques de Lady Downhall étaient à son service depuis des années, et aucun n'avait l'intention de s'en aller.

Comme je l'ai déjà dit, si j'étais là, c'est que sa propre cuisinière était à l'hôpital. Et à sa sortie elle devait partir pour un mois de convalescence aux frais de Lady Downhall. On allait s'occuper d'elle pendant tout un mois ! Des choses comme ça, je ne savais même pas que ça existait.

Et pour leur anniversaire tous les domestiques recevaient de beaux cadeaux : pas des robes en tissu imprimé, des bas noirs, des bonnets ou des trucs comme ça, non, de vrais cadeaux. Des choses qu'on n'aurait pas eu l'idée de s'acheter nous-mêmes. Tenez, juste pour vous montrer comme ils étaient généreux : mon anniversaire tombait six semaines après mon arrivée là-bas, et même moi j'ai eu un cadeau. Je ne l'avais pas dit à Lady Downhall ; elle a dû chercher la date elle-même, et elle m'a offert de magnifiques dessous en soie, le genre de choses que je n'avais jamais pu me payer. J'étais là depuis seulement six semaines, elle savait que je ne restais que trois mois, mais pour elle ça ne changeait rien.

Peut-être que c'étaient de vrais aristocrates. Leur nom était très ancien, je crois.

Lord Downhall avait été un personnage important en Inde, comme beaucoup de mes patrons. Il avait dû être une grosse légume là-bas. Je n'ai jamais réussi à savoir ce qu'il avait fait ni quel titre il avait. Il était très grand, un mètre quatre-vingt-dix, il avait une allure très aristocratique, et on aurait dit que ses yeux pouvaient voir en vous.

Je me souviens de la première fois que je l'ai rencontré. Je l'ai croisé par hasard dans l'escalier, et il s'est arrêté pour me demander :

« Êtes-vous notre nouvelle cuisinière ?

— Oui, Monsieur, j'ai répondu en devenant rouge écarlate.

— Eh bien j'espère que vous serez heureuse ici. Vous verrez, c'est une maison très heureuse. »

Et il avait raison. La femme de service m'a dit :

« Tu verrais, à Noël, on s'amuse drôlement bien ! On a notre sapin à nous avec nos cadeaux tout autour. Pas besoin de monter là-haut, de défiler devant eux et tout le tralala pour les récupérer. Ils les mettent là pendant la nuit. Et puis en janvier on peut aller une fois au théâtre, celui qu'on veut, et on n'est pas obligées d'y aller ensemble, si on veut on peut emmener un ami. »

Ça ne m'étonnait pas que Lady Downhall n'ait jamais de problèmes avec son personnel. Là-bas les domestiques aimaient vraiment leurs patrons. Si on m'avait dit ça avant j'aurais répondu : « Alors là, mon œil ! On ne peut pas aimer ses employeurs. On bosse pour eux, on fait de son mieux parce qu'on est payé pour ça et qu'on aime le travail bien fait, mais les aimer, ça, ce n'est pas possible. »

En plus j'étais payée quatre livres par mois. Vous savez, leur pauvre cuisinière, je ne lui voulais pas de mal, mais je ne pouvais pas m'empêcher d'espérer qu'il y aurait des complications et qu'elle serait absente, mettons... un an environ. C'est affreux d'être comme ça, je sais bien, mais j'étais tellement heureuse là-bas !

Et c'était si agréable quand Lady Downhall descendait à la cuisine le matin. Elle disait gentiment :

« Bonjour, Margaret. Avez-vous une suggestion pour le déjeuner ? »

Ou bien :

« Margaret, étant donné que nous avons beaucoup de monde à dîner ce soir, nous prendrons un repas froid ce midi. Cela vous laissera plus de temps pour préparer la réception. »

Vous voyez, elle avait des égards pour nous – et c'était si rare !

Du coup j'avais à cœur de cuisiner au moins aussi bien, et même mieux, que je ne l'avais fait jusque-là. Une de mes spécialités, c'étaient les soufflés. J'en faisais de sensationnels, sucrés ou salés ; j'avais du doigté en ce temps-là ! En général, avec les fourneaux de l'époque ça ne donnait pas grand-chose. Soit ils chauffaient trop, et le soufflé gonflait à toute vitesse alors que le milieu n'était pas cuit, soit il ne levait pas du tout. Je m'étais tellement bagarrée avec les fourneaux que j'en étais arrivée à les détester comme si c'étaient mes pires ennemis. Mais là j'avais une gazinière, alors tout allait bien.

Tous les soirs, avant de m'endormir, je me plongeais dans le livre de cuisine de Mrs Beeton*. C'était celui qu'on utilisait toutes en ce temps-là. Je choisissais une recette, je l'étudiais bien à fond, comme ça le lendemain, quand Mrs Downhall me demandait si j'avais une suggestion, je pouvais proposer ce plat d'un ton un peu désinvolte, comme si je l'avais souvent préparé. Je le mettais au point en imagination jusqu'à ce qu'il soit parfait – enfin, dans ma tête, pas toujours sur la table ! Mais ça, ça arrive à toutes les cuisinières. On prévoit des trucs qui ne donnent pas forcément le résultat qu'on espérait.

Lady Downhall appréciait toutes mes suggestions, et une fois elle m'a même dit :

« Vous savez, j'ai vraiment beaucoup d'affection pour cette chère Aggie (leur vraie cuisinière), elle est chez nous depuis des années et elle a commencé comme fille de cuisine chez ma mère, mais c'est très agréable de changer, de goûter toutes ces choses différentes que vous savez faire. »

Elle était loin de se douter que j'avais passé une bonne partie de la nuit à les potasser !

Lady Downhall adorait aller au Caledonian Market, le marché aux puces de Camden Town, un quartier du nord de Londres. Elle aimait s'y balader en regardant les antiquités – du moins, c'est comme ça que les vendeurs les appelaient : de *véritables* antiquités. On y allait à tour de rôle avec elle, et moi je trouvais ça très amusant. Le chauffeur amenait la

* Isabella Mary Beeton (1836-1865) est l'auteur d'un manuel de gestion ménagère intitulé *Mrs Beeton's Book of Household Management* contenant essentiellement des recettes de cuisine ; ce fut dès sa publication un best-seller en Grande-Bretagne, où il a été maintes fois réédité. *(N.d.T.)*

voiture à la porte vers dix heures, et je m'asseyais devant avec lui.

Il était très bel homme, mais je ne pouvais pas tellement en profiter parce que si on rigolait trop ou quoi que ce soit, Lady Downhall pouvait s'en apercevoir. De toute façon, beau ou pas, ça ne pouvait pas aller bien loin vu qu'il était déjà pris. Il était marié et père de deux enfants.

On faisait le tour du marché en se promenant et Lady Downhall choisissait tous les articles qui lui plaisaient et qui lui paraissaient de bonne qualité. Elle ne marchandait jamais elle-même : elle disait que dès qu'elle ouvrait la bouche elle vendait la mèche. Elle voulait dire par là que quand c'était elle qui demandait le prix les marchands devinaient qu'elle était riche et ils augmentaient leurs tarifs. Alors si elle voyait quelque chose qui lui faisait envie, elle envoyait la personne qui l'accompagnait demander le prix et marchander.

Je me souviens qu'une fois, pendant qu'elle cherchait un objet pour elle, je me suis baladée pour voir s'il n'y avait pas un objet qui me plairait à moi, et j'ai remarqué sur un étal un très beau pot bleu avec une anse de chaque côté. Je me suis dit que ce serait parfait pour l'aspidistra de ma mère – tout le monde avait un aspidistra à l'époque. Je me suis donc approchée du vendeur d'un air nonchalant – enfin, c'est ce que je croyais. Mais eux ils le savent très bien quand vous avez repéré quelque chose, ils ne sont pas nés de la dernière pluie. Bref, je regardais tout sauf ce pot, et je me trouvais drôlement futée. Au bout d'un moment je lui ai demandé :

« C'est combien, le pot bleu, là ?

– Pour vous, ce sera dix shillings. »

J'ai répliqué du tac au tac :

« Et pour les autres c'est une demi-couronne, je suppose ? Je vous en donne cinq shillings.

— Cinq shillings, vous voulez rire ? Et de toute façon, c'est pour quoi faire ? »

Je lui ai expliqué que c'était pour l'aspidistra de ma mère. Il a dit :

« En voilà une bonne idée ! Et quand elle aura fini de s'en servir pour sa plante, elle pourra toujours casser une des anses et le fourrer sous son lit. Deux pots pour le prix d'un, ça vaut largement dix shillings, non ? »

Je suis devenue rouge comme une tomate, je me suis sauvée en vitesse, et plus jamais je ne me suis approchée de ce stand.

XXIII

Ces trois mois ont passé beaucoup trop vite à mon goût, et ensuite, peut-être grisée par mon succès chez Lady Down-hall, j'ai décidé de faire un autre remplacement.

J'ai trouvé une place près de la gare Victoria, dans une de ces grandes maisons à la façade triste et délabrée qui ont l'intérieur parfaitement assorti. Une de ces maisons qui ont l'air de dire : « Je suis là pour toujours. »

C'était encore un endroit où on était mal logés et mal nourris. Pour la première et dernière fois de ma vie j'ai couché sur la paille – je vous jure ! Le matelas était vraiment en paille et il était juste posé sur des lattes, sans ressorts ni rien d'élastique. Quand je bougeais la nuit ça faisait le même bruit qu'un cheval qui se retourne dans son box. Même chez mes parents c'était mieux : on avait des matelas de bourre qu'on pouvait secouer pour les rendre confortables.

La première nuit je n'ai pas fermé l'œil, et en me levant j'étais bien décidée à me plaindre du lit. Mais quand ma patronne – Mrs Hunter-Jones, elle s'appelait (Hunter-Jones avec un trait d'union, pour qu'on prononce toujours les deux ensemble) – quand donc elle a fait son entrée sur le coup de dix heures, elle m'a tellement intimidée que toutes mes résolutions se sont envolées d'un seul coup. Je n'ai pas eu le cran de dire quoi que ce soit. C'est terrible d'être aussi lâche, mais rien que de la regarder ça m'a tuée. Je me suis consolée en me disant que je n'étais pas condamnée à rester là toute ma vie, que c'était juste un remplacement, et j'ai immédiatement décidé que je ne jouerais pas les prolongations.

La femme de chambre et la femme de service étaient là depuis deux ans, mais comme elles avaient soixante-trois et soixante-cinq ans, ce n'était pas évident pour elles de se placer ailleurs. Les conditions de travail s'amélioraient un tout petit peu pour les domestiques, pas parce que les employeurs étaient brusquement devenus plus humains, mais parce que maintenant il y avait plus de métiers accessibles aux femmes, et vous pensez bien que si elles pouvaient choisir autre chose elles ne s'en privaient pas. Du coup il y avait un peu de concurrence, et ça obligeait les patrons à offrir de meilleures conditions de travail. Mais pour des femmes de soixante-trois et soixante-cinq ans, il n'y avait pas d'autre solution que de rester domestiques.

Les deux pauvres vieilles en question, après toutes ces années de célibat, toutes ces années à bosser chez les autres, elles avaient les mains tordues, la figure anguleuse et le caractère à l'avenant. L'aspect de ces deux spécimens desséchés de l'espèce féminine, plus celui de la redoutable Mrs Hunter-Jones, m'ont persuadée de partir à la première occasion. Vous comprenez, je pensais tout le temps au mariage, c'était mon objectif principal dans la vie, et à chaque nouvelle place je me disais que j'allais peut-être rencontrer quelqu'un ; un des fournisseurs me plairait peut-être, et hop, l'affaire serait dans le sac !

Mais je me suis tout de suite rendu compte que chez les Hunter-Jones c'était raté de ce point de vue-là, et que pour ce qui était d'accumuler de l'expérience ça ne marcherait pas non plus, étant donné qu'ils ne recevaient jamais et que chez eux on mangeait non seulement peu mais mal. Alors sans le plaisir de cuisiner, sans autre compagnie que celle de deux faces de carême et dans une maison aussi animée qu'un cimetière, je vous laisse imaginer le cafard que j'avais.

Même quand on a une maîtresse désagréable, si les autres bonnes sont jeunes et gaies on peut rigoler ensemble, ne serait-ce qu'en disant du mal de « celle d'en haut ». On faisait souvent une espèce de psychanalyse de cuisine de nos patrons. Ça n'avait pas grand-chose à voir avec Freud, mais je suis sûre qu'on en savait plus sur leur vie sexuelle que tout ce que lui aurait pu découvrir !

De toute façon, même si mes deux sacs d'os avaient été capables d'en parler, dans le cas de Mrs Hunter-Jones il n'y avait rien à dire sur le sujet. Je suis pratiquement sûre que la pauvre chérie n'avait jamais fait la chose. Elle n'avait pas d'enfants, et il suffisait de regarder son mari. Si vous voulez mon avis, pour elle c'était juste un trophée, et pour l'usage qu'elle en avait elle aurait aussi bien pu l'accrocher au mur avec les autres têtes empaillées.

Dans cette maison, non seulement je n'avais personne à qui parler mais je n'avais nulle part où m'asseoir pour me reposer. Il n'y avait même pas de salle des domestiques. Tout ce que je pouvais faire, c'était rester assise dans la cuisine entre la chaudière, la gazinière, la table et le buffet. C'est comme ça que je me suis mise à sortir le soir.

J'avais une amie qui habitait à seulement dix minutes à pied et qui était en condition aussi ; j'allais la voir vers huit heures et demie, et j'étais toujours rentrée pour dix heures. Ça ne faisait de mal à personne, mais ça ne plaisait pas aux deux vieilles chouettes. J'avais beau savoir qu'elles étaient aigries, je ne pensais quand même pas qu'elles iraient se plaindre, vu que pour elles finalement ça ne changeait rien. Mais comme elles ne pouvaient pas sortir, elles ne voyaient pas pourquoi moi je pourrais.

Alors au bout de quelques soirs elles l'ont dit à Mrs Hunter-Jones, et ça lui a fait un choc. Elle n'avait jamais entendu parler d'une domestique qui sortait en dehors des moments prévus dans son contrat. J'ai eu droit à un sermon interminable, et elle a exigé de savoir pourquoi je voulais sortir le soir.

« Mais enfin ! elle a fait. Vous êtes libre tous les dimanches soir plus un autre soir dans la semaine !

– Oui, Madame, mais quand j'ai fini mon travail je n'ai pas d'endroit confortable pour m'asseoir.

– Et alors ? Les autres cuisinières s'asseyaient bien dans la cuisine, pourquoi pas vous ? En tout cas, vous n'avez absolument pas le droit de sortir quand bon vous semble. »

J'ai beaucoup réfléchi à tout ça, et aux deux pauvres vieilles. Malgré tout je n'arrivais pas à les détester : je voyais bien qu'elles étaient malheureuses.

Leurs petits noms, c'était Violet et Lily. Ça leur allait sûrement très bien quarante ans plus tôt, mais ça ne collait plus du tout avec l'allure et le caractère qu'elles avaient maintenant.

Une des rares fois où on a discuté ensemble comme des copines, elles m'ont raconté qu'elles avaient travaillé pas moins de vingt-cinq ans, une comme femme de chambre et l'autre comme femme de service, chez une veuve riche et sans enfants. D'après Lily et Violet, cette dame leur avait promis que si elles restaient à son service jusqu'à sa mort elle leur laisserait une rente suffisante pour qu'elles puissent prendre leur retraite et s'installer ensemble dans un appartement. Moi, pour tout vous dire, je trouvais qu'elles avaient été drôlement gourdes de ne pas demander à voir une preuve. Enfin bref, quand la vieille dame est morte il s'est avéré qu'elle n'avait pas fait de testament, et tout l'argent est allé à son parent le plus proche, à savoir son neveu. Lui, il a vendu la maison, et tout ce que les pauvres Lily et Violet ont eu c'est trois mois de salaire – et encore, le neveu trouvait que c'était très généreux de sa part, puisque rien ne précisait qu'il devait leur donner quoi que ce soit.

Vous vous rendez compte, bosser vingt-cinq ans dans la même maison en s'imaginant qu'on va toucher le gros lot à la fin, et se retrouver à la porte avec trois mois de salaire ! Pas étonnant que ça les ait rendues odieuses.

Remarquez, ça arrivait souvent, ce genre de choses. C'était une façon de garder ses domestiques quand on vieillissait. Mais ces deux-là avaient été carrément idiotes de faire confiance comme ça à leur patronne. Moi, à leur place, je n'aurais pas cru un mot de ce qu'elle disait !

Le problème, c'est qu'elles étaient persuadées que cette dame leur avait bel et bien laissé quelque chose et que c'était le neveu qui avait piqué le magot. J'ai eu beau essayer de leur expliquer comment ça se passait avec les testaments, les notaires et tout, elles n'ont jamais voulu me croire. Il faut dire que ce n'est jamais agréable d'admettre qu'on s'est fait avoir... Enfin, ça m'a aidée à comprendre pourquoi elles étaient aussi hargneuses.

Mrs Hunter-Jones n'allait rien leur laisser non plus, ça crevait les yeux. Déjà qu'elle les sous-payait parce qu'elle savait très bien qu'elles auraient du mal à retrouver du boulot ailleurs…

Malgré tout, je n'avais pas l'impression que si je restais je pourrais adoucir leur sort ; tout ce que ça ferait, c'est trois mécontentes au lieu de deux. Alors j'ai donné mon congé à Mrs Hunter-Jones. Après il a fallu que je fasse mon mois de préavis, et ça n'a pas été une partie de plaisir. C'est long, un mois, quand les gens sont désagréables avec vous, et les deux vieilles, quand bien même je ne leur rendais pas la vie plus difficile, ça leur restait en travers de la gorge que je puisse partir, que j'aie un avenir, alors qu'elles, elles n'en avaient pas. Elles avaient seulement un passé, et il n'avait pas été tellement folichon…

Moi, c'était surtout pour mon certificat que je me faisais du souci. Quelque chose me disait que Mrs Hunter-Jones n'allait pas m'en faire un bon, alors que j'avais une excellente recommandation de Lady Downhall en arrivant chez elle. J'ai essayé de lui demander un certificat écrit pour pouvoir lire ce qu'elle pensait de moi ; comme ça j'aurais peut-être pu y faire quelque chose. Mais elle m'a dit qu'il n'en était pas question.

Du coup je n'en menais pas large quand j'ai donné le numéro de téléphone de Mrs Hunter-Jones à ma – peut-être – future patronne. Je savais qu'elles ne pourraient pas se rencontrer puisque j'avais décidé de travailler à Brighton pendant quelque temps. Comme ça, au moins, j'étais sûre qu'elles n'allaient pas jacasser sur mon dos pendant des heures.

La place que je lorgnais, c'était dans The Drive, une avenue vraiment splendide à l'époque. J'ai eu un entretien avec une dame, une certaine Mrs Bishop. J'ai bien insisté sur le fait que je n'avais fait qu'un remplacement chez Mrs Hunter-Jones, mais elle a répondu qu'elle allait l'appeler et que si je voulais bien repasser le lendemain elle me donnerait son verdict.

Quand je suis arrivée elle m'a dit :

« Quelle personne singulière que votre ancienne patronne ! Lorsque je lui ai téléphoné pour avoir des renseignements, elle m'a déclaré : "Voyez-vous, je pense que Margaret Langley saurait cuisiner s'il lui arrivait d'être là, mais comme elle trouve naturel de sortir matin, midi et soir, elle n'a jamais le temps." »

Un rapport comme ça, normalement, c'était accablant ; mais il se trouve que Mrs Bishop avait une vie assez particulière et qu'elle avait du mal à recruter et à garder des gens de maison. Du coup, malgré les efforts de Mrs Hunter-Jones, elle m'a engagée comme cuisinière avec un salaire de cinquante-deux livres par an. C'était rudement bien payé, d'autant que ce n'était pas un remplacement mais une place fixe.

Vous trouvez peut-être que je radote un peu avec cette histoire de certificat, mais vous n'imaginez pas à quel point c'était important en ce temps-là. Nos patrons avaient toujours peur qu'on leur pique des trucs ou qu'on travaille « de l'intérieur » pour une bande de voleurs, alors ils voulaient avoir un maximum d'informations sur nous. Remarquez, eux ils ne nous fournissaient jamais de certificat. Pourtant, je trouvais qu'on aurait eu le droit de savoir si on allait trimer comme un forçat, s'ils se couchaient tard, s'ils étaient pingres et égoïstes, s'ils allaient nous traiter comme de la crotte – mais rien de tout ça. Eux, par contre, ils voulaient tout savoir sur nous. Et si on n'avait pas eu un bon certificat de son dernier employeur, ce n'était même pas la peine d'expliquer qu'on était en condition depuis l'âge de quinze ans, qu'il y avait beaucoup d'autres gens à qui ils pouvaient s'adresser, et que si ce certificat-là n'était pas bon c'était parce que la dernière fois on avait osé protester contre les conditions de travail. Ils ne voulaient pas entendre ce genre de choses. Pour eux c'était du bolchevisme. « Quoi ? Le bas peuple oserait-il critiquer les classes supérieures ? » Pensez donc, une fille comme moi, d'origine aussi misérable, comme ils disaient, devait être bien contente de travailler dans une grande maison chauffée où on lui donnait à manger. Pour ceux d'en haut, n'importe quel foyer valait mieux que celui où on avait passé son enfance. Si on s'était plainte de ne pas avoir telle ou telle chose dans sa dernière place, c'était de l'insubordination : en fait c'était forcément mieux que ce qu'on avait connu avant. Et que des domestiques puissent avoir la prétention de s'élever au-dessus du sous-sol, alors là, pour eux c'était carrément impensable !

Même Lady Downhall était un peu comme ça. Je lui ai demandé un jour si je pouvais emprunter un livre de sa bibliothèque, et je vois encore son air étonné. Elle m'a répondu :

« Oui, bien sûr, Margaret. »

Mais elle a ajouté :

« À vrai dire, je ne savais pas que vous lisiez. »

Ils savaient qu'on respirait, qu'on dormait et qu'on travaillait, mais qu'on lisait, ça, ils ne savaient pas. Comme si une chose pareille dépassait l'entendement. Ils croyaient que quand on avait du temps pour nous on le passait à bayer aux corneilles ou à feuilleter des magazines féminins. Je les imaginais assez bien en train de me dénoncer à leurs amis :

« Margaret est une bonne cuisinière, mais malheureusement elle lit. Des livres, figurez-vous. »

XXIV

Les Bishop avaient une grande maison individuelle de quatre étages, avec le sous-sol habituel pour les domestiques plus un escalier de service.

Quelqu'un comme Mrs Bishop, je ne savais absolument pas que ça existait. J'étais habituée à ce que les gens d'en haut soient d'une respectabilité à toute épreuve, du moins en apparence, alors avec elle ça m'a fait un sacré changement. Elle était d'origine italienne et elle avait presque soixante ans, mais elle se maquillait tellement qu'elle en paraissait trente, et de dos c'est l'âge qu'on lui aurait donné. Elle avait une espèce de couche d'émail sur la figure, je ne sais pas exactement ce que c'était, mais ça l'empêchait de rire franchement ; elle pouvait juste glousser un peu, sinon ça risquait de se craqueler. En fait elle ne bougeait jamais les muscles du visage. Elle se faisait aussi teindre les cheveux, et comme les produits n'étaient pas aussi perfectionnés qu'aujourd'hui la teinte n'était jamais la même d'une fois sur l'autre, et ça lui faisait une espèce de patchwork de plusieurs couleurs sur la tête.

La première fois que je l'ai vue, je n'ai pas arrêté de la regarder, je ne pouvais pas m'en empêcher. Elle avait une silhouette de jeune fille, et c'était vraiment inhabituel à l'époque. Les gens ne faisaient pas attention à leur poids et personne n'aurait eu l'idée de faire un régime. Ils s'enfilaient allègrement leurs trois plats au déjeuner plus cinq ou six au dîner tous les jours, et au diable la ligne ! Elle avait une voix rauque très sensuelle. D'ailleurs, le jour de l'entretien j'avais cru qu'elle avait une angine. Elle était très fière de sa voix. Elle disait :

« Vous savez, j'ai exactement la même que Tallulah Bankhead. »

Tallulah Bankhead était une actrice américaine qui faisait fureur à ce moment-là.

En plus de la maison, les Bishop avaient un appartement à Londres où ils logeaient du mardi après-midi au vendredi après-midi. Ça voulait dire qu'on avait du temps libre dans la semaine, mais jamais le week-end. C'est pour ça que Madame avait du mal à trouver des domestiques : elles aimaient bien avoir leurs congés en fin de semaine, surtout si elles « fréquentaient ». Moi ça ne me dérangeait pas : je n'avais pas encore de fiancé.

Du vendredi soir au lundi matin la maison était pleine à craquer ; parmi les invités il y avait quelques jeunes hommes d'affaires, mais surtout des parasites du monde du théâtre et du cinéma. Pas un seul n'était « de la haute », mais c'étaient toujours des jeunes gens d'un tas de nationalités différentes. Mrs Bishop adorait les jeunes gens. Nous, on n'avait jamais une minute à nous le week-end, mais ça m'était complètement égal ; au moins c'était vivant, même si je vivais par procuration.

Dans cette maison un tantinet bizarre, pour que Mrs Bishop me donne ses instructions il fallait que je monte la voir pendant qu'elle prenait son bain. Au début j'étais horrifiée parce que je n'avais jamais vu quelqu'un tout nu, même une femme. Et puis en fait, croyez-moi si vous voulez, au bout de deux ou trois semaines j'y étais habituée, et je m'asseyais sur le bord de la baignoire pendant qu'elle me disait ce qu'elle voulait.

Un matin, à dix heures, je suis montée à la salle de bains. C'était devenu une habitude, alors je frappais à la porte et j'entrais sans attendre la réponse. Mais ce matin-là, horreur ! Au lieu de voir un corps tout blanc et tout mince allongé dans l'eau, j'en ai vu un énorme, noir et poilu, debout dans la baignoire – un Italien. C'était la première fois de ma vie que je voyais ce genre d'appendice grandeur nature, et après y avoir jeté un coup d'œil j'ai bien compris pourquoi Adam s'était dépêché d'aller cueillir une feuille de figuier ! J'en aurais fait autant si je m'étais aperçue que j'avais un outil pareil. Ça m'a fait un de ces chocs ! J'ai mis à peu près une semaine à m'en remettre. Lui, par contre, ça ne l'a pas dérangé que je le voie. Il a dit à Madame qu'il allait descendre à la cuisine pour s'excuser, mais il ne l'a pas fait, Dieu merci ! Après l'avoir vu tout nu je n'aurais pas pu le voir habillé. J'aurais visualisé le truc tout le temps.

Je me souviens que les autres filles voulaient connaître tous les détails. Elles me disaient : « Je parie que tu es sortie en courant », ou alors : « Je parie que tu t'es bien rincé l'œil. » Une chose est sûre : à partir de ce moment-là je ne suis plus jamais entrée sans frapper et sans attendre d'être absolument certaine que c'était bien ma patronne qui répondait.

Les jeunes gens, c'était toute sa vie, à Mrs Bishop. Si c'est vrai ce qu'on dit, que la vie commence à quarante ans, elle a dû en baver pendant vingt ans. Remarquez, elle n'était pas vilaine, elle était bien maquillée et on laissait toujours les stores à moitié fermés. La lumière tamisée, ça aide.

Parfois elle se disputait avec ces jeunes gens, quelque chose de gratiné, et je savais que le lendemain matin, quand j'irais la voir, j'aurais droit à une séance de larmes. Elle me chantait toujours le même refrain, j'ai bien dû l'entendre une douzaine de fois :

« Vous savez, Margaret, je sortais directement du couvent quand on m'a mariée, j'avais dix-sept ans et je n'avais jamais vu Mr Bishop avant de me retrouver devant l'autel avec lui. Je n'ai pas vécu quand j'étais jeune, on m'a mariée à un homme qui avait dix ans de plus que moi, je n'ai rien vu du monde, rien, et désormais il est trop tard. »

Moi, évidemment, j'étais censée opiner du bonnet. Ce qu'elle voulait, ce n'était pas mon opinion, c'était que je compatisse. Personnellement je ne trouvais pas qu'elle avait fait une si mauvaise affaire : elle avait une belle maison, des domestiques, des bijoux, des loisirs… Si ça, ce n'était pas la vie, c'était rudement bien imité ! Moi, en tout cas, pour vivre comme elle, je me serais mariée avec le diable sans problème !

Mr Bishop n'était pas du tout du même acabit. Je crois qu'il était d'origine allemande et qu'il avait changé de nom pendant la guerre. Il était d'un caractère très calme. Naturellement, ils menaient des vies complètement séparées ; elle dormait au deuxième étage et lui au troisième, et ils ne partageaient pas grand-chose. Ils allaient à Londres ensemble et ils revenaient ensemble, mais quand je les ai connus ils ne vivaient plus comme mari et femme, c'était fini.

Lui, je l'aimais bien. Il avait vraiment le sens de l'humour. Quand ils étaient à Londres c'est nous qui tenions la maison, alors on utilisait leur salon, on passait tous leurs disques, et moi j'essayais de jouer des airs au piano en tapant comme une sourde. Un jour où ils rentraient, je me suis coincé la main dans le porte-bagages de la voiture et j'ai failli me casser le pouce. Il a fallu m'emmener chez le médecin pour qu'il me mette un bandage. Le lendemain, quand j'ai croisé Mr Bishop il m'a demandé :

« Alors, comment va votre pouce ?

— Oh, ça va, Monsieur, j'ai répondu. C'est juste un peu gênant pour travailler.

— Oui, et un peu gênant aussi pour jouer du piano, sans doute ? »

Quelqu'un avait dû lui rapporter ce qu'on faisait quand ils n'étaient pas là, mais il m'a dit ça en me faisant un clin d'œil. En fait ça lui était égal.

Il faut dire que c'était de la roupie de sansonnet par rapport à ce qu'il devait supporter de la part de Mrs Bishop. Là-dessus aussi il fermait les yeux. J'ai entendu dire qu'elle avait tenté ou fait semblant de se suicider deux fois en avalant des médicaments ou quelque chose comme ça, et qu'un de leurs fils était en liberté conditionnelle en Australie ; ils lui envoyaient deux livres par semaine pour son entretien. Je crois qu'il avait fait un chèque en imitant la signature de son père. Mr Bishop avait donc déjà eu son compte de problèmes, et il ne tenait pas à en avoir d'autres.

Ces patrons-là n'étaient pas ce qu'on appelle des aristo-crates, naturellement, mais chez eux c'était vivant, vous comprenez. Assez souvent, quand elle recevait des amis italiens, Mrs Bishop descendait à la cuisine et me demandait si ça ne me dérangeait pas qu'ils viennent préparer des plats de chez eux. Ça ne me dérangeait pas, vu que c'étaient presque toujours des jeunes. Remarquez, ils mettaient une sacrée pagaille et ils laissaient la cuisine dégoûtante ; ça ne leur serait pas venu à l'idée de faire la vaisselle. Mais je les regardais faire et j'essayais de retenir un maximum de choses. Voilà : je ne pouvais pas dire que je travaillais pour des « gens de la haute », mais je m'en fichais éperdument. J'avais mon argent à moi, une vie gaie, amusante, et pour moi c'était le plus important.

Un de ces jeunes Italiens a été le chouchou de Madame pendant plus longtemps que tous les autres. Il n'était pas italien pour rien, croyez-moi. Il se promenait avec un petit singe sur l'épaule, et ça me terrifiait. Mrs Bishop lui donnait de l'argent ; c'était ce qu'on appelle un gigolo. Il avait vingt-cinq ans à tout casser, et elle, du fait qu'elle en avait soixante, elle ne devait pas lui donner grand-chose d'autre. Alors s'il pouvait s'offrir une petite récréation avec une jeune bonne il ne se gênait pas. Il descendait à la cuisine avec son sale singe sur l'épaule et il essayait d'engager la conversation. Au début il parlait des repas et tout ça, et au bout d'un moment il demandait :

« Est-ce que vous avez un fiancé ? »

Ensuite il faisait le tour de la table petit à petit pour se rapprocher de moi, et moi je m'éloignais au fur et à mesure, parce que je ne savais pas ce qu'il voulait au juste, mais je me doutais bien que ses intentions n'étaient pas honnêtes. Il n'est jamais arrivé à ses fins avec moi. Ça ne valait pas la peine que je perde mon temps avec ce genre de gars, il fallait que je garde toute mon énergie pour séduire des hommes « possibles », ceux dont les intentions étaient peut-être honnêtes.

L'autre jour, j'ai lu dans le journal qu'actuellement, en Angleterre, parmi les jeunes de seize à vingt et un ans il y a cinquante-six mille garçons de plus que de filles*. Ça m'a fait bondir, parce qu'à l'époque à Brighton on était cinq filles pour un garçon, alors je vous laisse imaginer comment il fallait se battre pour en choper un et le garder ! Nous, en plus, on n'était jamais libres le week-end, le seul moment où les garçons avaient de l'argent. Quand on en rencontrait, de toute façon ils étaient fauchés comme les blés. Et si on disait qu'on était en condition c'était toujours la même histoire, on les voyait changer de tête. Les plus malpolis disaient : « Ouh là là, des bonniches ! » et ils décampaient aussitôt en nous plantant là.

Je me rappelle un soir où Hilda et moi on est allées danser. Hilda, c'était la femme de service, et elle faisait toujours croire à ses cavaliers qu'elle était secrétaire. Ce soir-là on est tombées sur deux officiers de marine. Croyez-moi, il n'y a pas plus prétentieux que les officiers de la Royal Navy. Je ne sais pas quel grade ils avaient, sans doute le plus bas qu'on pouvait avoir en étant officier. Du reste ils étaient aussi radins que prétentieux : ils nous ont ramenées en bus, on n'a pas eu droit au taxi. Moi, je ne prétendais jamais être autre chose que cuisinière, parce que je me retrouvais toujours à leur préparer un petit souper. Je me disais que c'était peut-être comme ça que je séduirais un homme : en parlant à son estomac. On les faisait entrer dans la cuisine ; on n'était pas

* Rappelons que ce livre est paru en 1968. *(N.d.T.)*

207

censées faire ça, mais bon, il fallait bien compenser le fait qu'on n'était pas libres le week-end.

Ce soir-là on venait d'arriver, et Hilda était montée aux toilettes. Son officier s'est approché de moi et il m'a dit :

« Elle n'est pas secrétaire. »

Moi, pour la couvrir, j'ai répondu :

« Si elle le dit, c'est que c'est vrai.

– Non, je suis sûr qu'elle n'est pas secrétaire, elle est femme de service.

– Comment vous le savez ?

– Je l'ai emmenée dans la pièce avec un évier, là (il parlait de l'office), et avant que j'aie pu la toucher elle avait lavé les couverts. »

Vous comprenez, elle n'avait pas réfléchi : elle avait tellement l'habitude de ne jamais laisser traîner les couverts sales qu'elle les avait lavés, c'était comme un réflexe chez elle. Évidemment, une secrétaire n'aurait jamais fait ça. Remarquez, si l'officier avait été un gentleman il n'en aurait pas parlé non plus. En tout cas la pauvre Hilda n'est jamais entrée dans la marine.

Ce qui ne l'empêchait pas d'avoir envie de s'en sortir.

Pour moi, finalement, la vie là-bas n'était pas trop dure, il y avait un homme à tout faire qui s'occupait de la chaudière, des marches du perron et des chaussures. Le sol de la cuisine était épatant : c'étaient des tommettes rouges, et pour les nettoyer il suffisait de passer un linge humide. Il y avait l'énorme buffet habituel, mais comme il avait des vitres la vaisselle ne prenait pas la poussière. Et on avait un téléphone dans la cuisine.

Après mon séjour chez Mrs Hunter-Jones, ç'a été un plaisir de pouvoir cuisiner des pavés de saumon ou du civet de lièvre, de faire de la vraie mayonnaise et pas de la sauce blanche ! On servait du filet de bœuf, de la selle d'agneau ; ça me donnait l'occasion de m'exercer et d'apprendre la cuisine.

J'étais devenue assez experte dans mon domaine, et j'avais rudement bien fait de ne pas choisir un autre métier, par exemple femme de service. J'ai servi à table une seule fois, et ça m'a suffi. Un soir où Mrs Bishop recevait à dîner, Hilda est tombée malade et elle n'a pas pu servir. Mrs Bishop a déboulé à la cuisine pour me demander si je pouvais venir donner un coup de main entre deux. La femme de chambre était chargée de ce qu'il fallait servir avec deux couverts, et moi je devais faire passer les légumes. Je savais d'avance que j'allais être horriblement mal à l'aise. Je m'imaginais déjà en train d'arriver de la cuisine rouge comme une pivoine à cause de la chaleur, et dans ma robe imprimée par-dessus le marché. Quand je suis entrée dans la salle à manger Mrs Bishop a annoncé à toute l'assemblée :

« Voici ma cuisinière. »

Du coup tout le monde m'a regardée avec de grands yeux, évidemment, et ça n'a rien arrangé ; je me faisais l'effet d'une bête curieuse. Comme accompagnement, il y avait entre autres de minuscules pommes de terre nouvelles présentées dans un légumier, lui-même posé sur un plateau d'argent ; elles étaient très appétissantes avec leur sauce au beurre de menthe, et elles étaient drôlement chaudes. La première invitée que je devais servir était une Française très séduisante. J'avais tellement le trac que ma main s'est mise à trembler comme une feuille ; du coup le légumier a glissé du plateau, et toutes ces petites billes de pomme de terre se sont renversées sur le devant de sa robe et sur ses genoux. Elle a sauté sur ses pieds en prononçant tout un tas de mots français que je n'ai pas compris. Et puis j'ai vu qu'une des pommes de terre s'était logée dans son décolleté, alors j'ai voulu l'enlever avec la cuillère de service. Mais cette idiote n'arrêtait pas de bouger – en fait ça devait la brûler –, ce qui fait qu'au lieu de l'enlever je l'ai écrasée contre sa poitrine. Elle m'a arraché la cuillère de la main en criant : « *Coshon !* *Coshon !* » une bonne demi-douzaine de fois. On se serait cru dans *Oliver Twist*, sauf que lui, il en redemandait*. Je me suis sauvée à la cuisine sans demander mon reste.

Environ une semaine plus tard, quand il m'a semblé que l'ébullition était retombée, j'ai demandé à Mrs Bishop ce que ça voulait dire, « *coshon* ». Je croyais que c'était un truc épouvantable. Elle m'a répondu :

« Oh, c'est juste un mot français qui veut dire quelque chose comme *zut* en anglais. »

Quelques années plus tard j'ai cherché dans un dictionnaire de français. J'ai découvert que ça s'écrivait C.O.C.H.O.N.N.E. et que l'invitée m'avait traitée de dégoûtante. Ça m'était bien égal. Après tout, c'est elle qui s'était pris les pommes de terre, pas moi !

Quelquefois Mr Bishop revenait de Londres pendant la semaine. Il avait sûrement une petite amie quelque part à Brighton ; on ne l'a jamais vue, mais c'est ce qu'on a toujours supposé. Il téléphonait systématiquement avant pour nous prévenir qu'il arrivait, comme ça il était sûr de ne pas nous surprendre dans une situation embarrassante. Si

---

* Allusion à la célèbre scène du roman de Charles Dickens où Oliver Twist répète : « J'en veux encore » (du porridge à l'eau) au milieu d'une assemblée pétrifiée et incrédule. *(N.d.T.)*

jamais il dînait à la maison ce n'était pas un souci, il voulait toujours la même chose : de la soupe d'abattis de volaille (des abattis on en avait forcément, vu qu'il y avait toujours des poulets en réserve), des sprats grillés et des pieds de porc en ragoût – même qu'il les mangeait avec les doigts et qu'il suçait les os. Il prenait le même repas à chaque fois. C'était ça qu'il aimait, alors il ne voulait rien d'autre.

Si on avait prévu d'aller danser on n'avait pas besoin d'annuler puisque c'était censé être nos jours de congé. On se répartissait le travail entre nous, la femme de chambre, la femme de service et moi. Pendant que l'une s'occupait du dîner de Mr Bishop les autres se préparaient pour sortir, et du coup il voyait parfois une personne différente à chaque plat. Hilda lui servait sa soupe d'abattis de volaille et se dépêchait d'aller se changer, la femme de chambre lui apportait ses sprats grillés et repartait en trombe, et moi je montais quatre à quatre avec ses pieds de porc. Ça n'a jamais eu l'air de le déranger.

J'étais dans cette place depuis plusieurs mois quand j'ai découvert qu'il n'était pas tout à fait normal. S'il était seul à la maison, il sonnait toujours de sa chambre vers onze heures et demie, une fois qu'on était couchées. Ça sonnait là-haut, sur le palier de nos chambres, et Hilda ou Iris, la femme de chambre, enfilaient un peignoir et descendaient le voir. Il leur demandait de lui apporter un whisky avec de l'eau de Seltz, ou bien une cruche d'eau, ou même un livre qu'il avait laissé dans la bibliothèque. Un soir j'ai demandé à Hilda :

« Pourquoi il attend toujours qu'on soit couchées pour sonner ? »

Elle m'a répondu :

« C'est parce qu'il aime nous voir avec nos bigoudis. »

Moi, étonnée, j'ai fait :

« Comment ça ?

– Il aime nous voir avec nos bigoudis », elle a répété.

En ce temps-là on n'avait pas des rouleaux comme maintenant, c'étaient des tout petits bigoudis en métal, et on en mettait tous les soirs parce que c'était la mode d'avoir plein de frisettes, et plus ça faisait du volume mieux c'était.

« Tu plaisantes, là, ou quoi ?

– Non, non, je te jure que c'est vrai.

– Et alors, qu'est-ce qu'il fait une fois que vous êtes là avec vos bigoudis ?

– En fait, pas grand-chose. Il nous demande d'enlever notre résille et il tripote les bigoudis dans nos cheveux. »

Je n'arrivais pas à y croire tellement je trouvais ça idiot.

« Et c'est tout ? Il touche seulement vos bigoudis ?

– Oui, c'est tout. Et dans ces moments-là il est content comme pas deux. »

Donc elle s'asseyait sur le bord de son lit, il caressait ses bigoudis, et c'est tout. Sur le coup ça m'a paru une façon très bizarre de se faire plaisir, et aujourd'hui encore je trouve ça aberrant. Non mais vous avez déjà vu ça, vous, un homme qui a envie de voir les femmes en bigoudis, et de caresser leurs bigoudis, en plus ? Enfin, pour Hilda et Iris c'était une bonne affaire : à chaque fois il leur donnait des produits de beauté, une boîte de chocolats ou des bas.

J'aurais pu en avoir aussi si j'avais voulu. Il se fichait pas mal de qui répondait à la sonnette du moment que c'était une femme en robe de chambre et en bigoudis, mais jamais je n'y serais allée. Ce n'est pas que ça m'aurait dérangée qu'il me voie avec mes bigoudis ; un jeune homme, non, je n'aurais jamais voulu, parce que là je pouvais faire une croix sur une histoire d'amour et un foyer possibles ; mais avec lui, ça n'avait pas d'importance. Non, si je ne voulais pas y aller, c'est parce que c'était encore une preuve de l'infériorité des domestiques. Vous comprenez, ça ne lui serait jamais venu à l'esprit de demander à des invitées s'il pouvait caresser leurs bigoudis. Mais les bonnes, pensez donc, elles devaient être bien contentes puisqu'elles avaient un cadeau à chaque fois ! Hilda et Iris n'étaient pas d'accord avec moi là-dessus. Elles disaient :

« Et alors, qu'est-ce que ça peut faire ? Ça ne nous fait pas de mal, et en plus ça nous rapporte ! »

Moi j'ai essayé de leur faire comprendre mon point de vue, parce que malgré tout elles avaient envie de s'en sortir, même si ça ne les menait nulle part. Mais Iris a répondu :

« Et puis quoi, on est bien des domestiques, non ? Alors si on nous donne quelque chose sans qu'on ait rien à faire, c'est toujours ça de pris. »

Quant à Hilda, elle a dit :

« Moi, j'adore quand je sers à table et que Mr Bishop est là à faire des grands discours aux invités. Souvent, j'ai envie de lui mettre un bigoudi dans son assiette ! »

De toute ma vie je n'ai jamais entendu parler d'une manie aussi bizarre que cette histoire de bigoudis. Je me demande d'où ça lui venait. De son enfance, sans doute. Sa mère devait en mettre, ou quelque chose dans ce goût-là.

XXV

À peu près à cette période-là, j'ai bien cru que j'avais mis la main sur le bon fiancé. Vous l'avez sûrement compris, ce n'était pas une mince affaire, vu que les candidats ne se bousculaient pas. Celui-là était laveur de carreaux, et quand il venait laver les carreaux je l'invitais à la cuisine. Je lui offrais une tasse de thé et des gâteaux que j'avais faits moi-même, j'arrangeais ma tenue et je me décarcassais pour lui faire bonne impression. On dit que pour séduire un homme il faut parler à son estomac, mais croyez-moi ce n'est pas toujours facile, il y a des estomacs drôlement durs d'oreille !

Bref, ce gars s'appelait George et il m'invitait à sortir depuis trois mois. Trois mois, vous vous rendez compte ? Pour moi c'était une éternité, en tout cas bien assez pour que je l'envisage comme mari. Mais il avait des défauts, et le pire c'était la radinerie. Il était pingre que c'en était insupportable.

Quand on allait au cinéma il achetait cent grammes de chocolats, soi-disant pour moi pendant la séance, mais il les gardait à la main, ou sur ses genoux, et il les gobait tranquillement jusqu'au dernier. J'ai vite compris. Dès qu'on était assis je me mettais à piocher dedans moi aussi, et au bout de trois minutes il n'y avait plus de chocolats ; on jetait le sachet sous les sièges et on se préparait à regarder le film.

Une autre de ses radineries, la plus grave, c'est qu'il passait devant tous les pubs sans s'arrêter. En ce temps-là on ne pouvait pas entrer dans un pub toute seule, ni même avec une copine, sinon après on avait mauvaise réputation. Tout le monde vous prenait pour une fille facile. Ça n'avait rien à voir avec le fait qu'on ait envie de boire un verre plutôt qu'une tasse de thé. C'est juste que ça ne se faisait pas.

Mon père et ma mère aimaient bien aller boire une bière le soir. Ils ne buvaient pas beaucoup, peut-être deux demis chacun. La bière était forte à l'époque, et beaucoup moins chère du fait qu'elle était forte. Si vous buviez deux demis ça vous faisait de l'effet ; de nos jours, on peut boire à se faire éclater la panse et rentrer chez soi avec le moral dans les chaussettes. Quand mes parents avaient envie d'aller au pub ils m'emmenaient avec eux. La première fois j'avais quatorze ans, et normalement je n'avais pas le droit, mais comme j'ai toujours été très grande je faisais plus que mon âge. Au début je buvais de la limonade, après je suis passée au panaché et de là à la bière, et c'est comme ça que j'ai pris l'habitude d'aller au pub. Ce n'était pas tellement pour la bière, c'était pour l'ambiance.

C'est qu'en ce temps-là il y en avait, de l'ambiance, dans les pubs ! Alors qu'aujourd'hui, entre un pub et la morgue, vous voyez une différence, vous ? Personne ne parle à personne, il n'y a pas de vie, pas d'animation. Surtout maintenant qu'ils sont tous transformés en bars à cocktails, en lounges et tout ça. L'autre jour on est allés dans un pub et il y avait un gars qui fredonnait tout seul. Il avait un peu bu mais il ne faisait rien de mal, il était juste un peu gai. Le gérant est venu deux fois lui dire d'arrêter, et la troisième fois ils l'ont mis dehors. On n'est pas censé s'amuser dans les pubs, apparemment.

Celui où j'allais avec mes parents le samedi soir avant d'entrer en condition, il était tellement bourré de monde qu'on devait rester debout en tenant son verre contre soi, mais on s'y sentait drôlement bien ; il y avait de l'ambiance, de la vie, quoi ! C'est comme ça que j'ai commencé à boire, parce que j'aimais l'ambiance, et ça me plaît toujours. Je préfère aller boire un verre dans un pub que d'aller n'importe où ailleurs. Heureusement, mon mari est comme moi. (Oui, j'en ai dégotté un, finalement !) Alors si on a de l'argent on fait la noce, sinon on boit juste une bière ou deux.

À part l'ambiance, j'avais une autre raison d'en vouloir à George de ne pas m'emmener au pub : c'était les effets de l'alcool. En général je me sentais amoureuse quand j'avais un peu bu, et c'était pareil pour n'importe quel garçon. Un type moche comme un pou, que je n'aurais même pas regardé si j'avais été à jeun, après une ou deux bières je le trouvais aussi beau que Rudolph Valentino. Remarquez, il fallait que je fasse attention à ne pas boire trop, il y avait une limite, ça devait être juste assez pour qu'ils m'embrassent, qu'ils soient aux petits soins pour moi et qu'ils se disent que la prochaine fois ils pourraient sûrement aller un peu plus loin, mais je ne voulais pas qu'ils se jettent sur moi comme des malades la première fois qu'ils me ramenaient chez moi. Après tout, une fille n'a jamais qu'un petit capital, n'est-ce pas, alors si elle se met à le distribuer à tout un chacun, qu'est-ce qu'elle aura de particulier à offrir à son mari quand il débarquera ? Enfin bref, ce George, chaque fois qu'on passait devant un pub il me demandait :

« Tu veux boire quelque chose ? »

Et moi je répondais :

« Si tu veux. »

Et lui :

« C'est comme tu veux. »

Et moi :

« Non, c'est comme tu veux toi. »

À ce moment-là on avait dépassé le pub et c'était fichu. Je ne voulais pas paraître en avoir trop envie parce que j'avais des vues sur lui comme mari : je ne voulais pas qu'il croie que je ne pensais qu'à me précipiter dans tous les pubs venus.

On est donc sortis régulièrement encore quelque temps, mais comme on ne faisait qu'aller au cinéma aux places les moins chères, manger cent grammes de chocolats à nous deux, et qu'on n'allait jamais au pub, au bout d'un mois ou deux j'ai décidé, à contrecœur malgré tout, de mettre une croix sur George. Je me suis dit que si un homme ne m'offrait déjà pas grand-chose avant le mariage, il y avait peu de chances qu'il le fasse après. Et que s'il ne m'emmenait jamais au pub quand on était déjà dehors, il ne quitterait jamais le coin du feu pour y aller.

Maintenant, quand j'y repense, je sais bien que si j'ai fait des efforts pour garder ce gars-là, si je me suis donné tant de mal, c'est uniquement parce qu'il y avait très peu de choix. À vrai dire, il était plutôt minable, George : il était plus petit que moi et il n'avait aucune conversation. Il faisait des maquettes, vous savez, des maquettes d'avions. Il m'avait dit qu'il en avait une collection sensationnelle. Vous imaginez tous ces vieux nids à poussière ? Non seulement on ne peut rien en faire mais ça prend toute la place. Je parie que celle qui a hérité de George elle le maudit maintenant, lui et ses fichus avions ! Mais vous auriez vu comment je faisais semblant de m'y intéresser. Je lui disais :

« Pas possible, tu sais vraiment faire des maquettes ? Qu'est-ce que j'aimerais en voir une ! »

Et quand il m'en a apporté une je me suis extasiée, alors qu'en fait je m'en fichais comme de ma première chemise. On était obligées de mentir aux hommes pour leur faire croire qu'on s'intéressait à eux, et tout ça parce qu'il y avait tellement peu de choix. Les filles d'aujourd'hui, si elles n'aiment pas ce que fait un gars, ou si sa tête ne leur revient pas, elles l'envoient balader. Mais à cette époque-là ça ne risquait pas !

Naturellement il y avait quelques vieux – il y en a toujours, on dirait, et ils vous expliquent qu'ils sont jeunes puisqu'ils se sentent jeunes. Tant mieux pour eux, mais s'ils ont l'air d'avoir quatre-vingt-dix ans ce n'est quand même pas pareil ! Et puis certains ne se sentent pas si bien que ça…

Je suis restée un an chez Mrs Bishop. Après, je me suis dit qu'il fallait vraiment que je trouve une place dans une maison où il y aurait beaucoup de domestiques et où je pourrais avoir une fille de cuisine. Donc j'ai répondu à une annonce dans le *Morning Post* pour retourner à Londres.

La maison se trouvait dans Montpelier Square, à Knights-bridge. C'étaient des Hollandais, des banquiers très riches, très sérieux et très respectables. Lui, il ressemblait exacte-ment à l'idée que je me faisais d'un banquier hollandais : il avait une grosse bedaine avec une chaîne de montre dorée en travers.

C'est dans cette maison que j'ai vu évoluer les conditions de vie des domestiques. Dans d'autres j'avais remarqué ce qui était sans doute les débuts, mais là j'ai constaté un changement complet. Là, on faisait vraiment partie de la maison.

En comptant la femme de chambre de Madame on était sept domestiques, et chacun avait sa chambre. Très confortable, la chambre, et en plus on tenait compte de nos goûts. On m'a demandé si je voulais qu'on change quelque chose, si j'avais assez de draps et de couvertures, si je désirais plus de lampes... On voyait qu'ils avaient vraiment besoin de nous et qu'ils appréciaient qu'on soit là.

La cuisine était équipée de tous les appareils ménagers qui existaient à l'époque, et même si elle était encore au sous-sol elle était claire et spacieuse ; les murs étaient peints en blanc, pas en marron jusqu'à la moitié et en vert au-dessus. L'évier de l'arrière-cuisine était en émail blanc, pas en ciment, et les casseroles étaient en aluminium ; ça faisait un sacré changement par rapport à la fonte ou au cuivre !

Tout avait été acheté spécialement pour le personnel, rien à voir avec les cochonneries du genre « ça suffira bien pour le sous-sol ». Ils nous fournissaient gratuitement tous nos uniformes, alors que jusque-là j'avais toujours dû acheter les miens. La femme de service, la femme de chambre et la fille de cuisine avaient des robes à rayures, et elles choisissaient la couleur qu'elles voulaient, n'importe laquelle, rose, vert, bleu... En tant que cuisinière je pouvais choisir la couleur et le style de ma tenue, et on m'a présenté plusieurs modèles. C'est fou ce que ça avait changé !

Madame était très stricte et tout devait être impeccable – mais bon, elle nous payait pour ça. Les repas devaient être servis pile à l'heure et tous les plats parfaitement cuits. Mais j'estimais qu'elle avait le droit d'être exigeante. Elle avait montré qu'elle avait de la considération pour nous. Après, c'était à nous de montrer qu'on en avait pour eux.

Elle établissait certains des menus elle-même et j'étais chargée des autres. Je n'avais pas l'habitude de prévoir tout un repas, et au début j'ai fait des bêtises, forcément. Il y avait tellement de choses que je n'avais jamais faites, ni même vu faire ! Mais je pouvais compter sur cette bonne vieille Mrs Beeton. À mon avis, elle n'a jamais déçu personne : elle donnait toutes les recettes possibles et imaginables. Je sais bien que maintenant ça faire rire les gens, sa façon de dire : « Prenez une douzaine d'œufs et un demi-litre de crème », mais je vous jure qu'en ce temps-là on prenait vraiment une douzaine d'œufs et un demi-litre de crème !

Avoir une fille de cuisine ça m'aidait, naturellement, mais moi je n'ai pas été tellement à la hauteur : je me souvenais trop bien de l'époque horrible où j'étais à sa place, et où je m'étais juré que je ne serais jamais aussi dure que Mrs Bowchard quand je serais cuisinière. Mais je me suis aperçue que c'était vrai, ce que disait cette vieille rosse : une fille de cuisine, il faut toujours être derrière.

Celle que j'avais avec moi dans cette maison, si on ne l'asticotait pas sans arrêt elle ne fichait rien, et moi je n'étais pas assez sévère. Comme je n'avais jamais eu quelqu'un sous mes ordres, je n'arrivais pas à faire preuve d'autorité. Je lui demandais quelque chose, et si elle mettait trop longtemps je finissais par le faire moi-même. Vous parlez d'une formation pour une jeune fille ! Mais je ne pouvais tout simplement pas être sans arrêt après elle, lui dire qu'elle n'était bonne à rien, qu'il fallait qu'elle se secoue – bref, être infecte avec elle. D'une part ce n'était pas dans mon caractère, et d'autre part ça me paraissait plus rapide de faire les choses moi-même. Mais ce n'était pas un bon apprentissage. Je crois que j'ai manqué à mes devoirs envers elle.

Madame, elle, n'a pas manqué à ses devoirs envers moi. Au début, j'ai eu du mal à croire qu'elle s'intéressait réellement à nous. Vous comprenez, après toutes ces années où j'avais été mal logée et mal nourrie, j'étais persuadée qu'il faudrait au moins une révolution, et une sanglante, pour améliorer les conditions de travail des gens de maison. Et puis, au bout de quelques semaines, je me suis rendu compte que Madame voulait vraiment qu'on soit contents de travailler chez elle. Pas parce qu'elle avait une tendresse particulière pour le bas peuple, non : parce qu'elle pensait que si le personnel était satisfait la maison serait bien tenue – et elle avait parfaitement raison. Quand les domestiques se sentent exploités, ils peuvent rendre la vie dure à leurs patrons de plein de façons différentes : ils peuvent traîner pour répondre quand on les sonne, prendre un air renfrogné, avoir une attitude insolente même sans rien dire et causer pas mal de petites tracasseries pour se venger de ne pas être assez payés. Dans cette maison-là, ils ne faisaient rien de tout ça. Comme je l'ai dit, Madame n'avait pas d'affection pour nous, mais ce n'était pas son affection qu'on voulait. Ce qu'on voulait, on l'avait : être bien payés et faire du bon boulot en échange.

À cette place je suis devenue très compétente en cuisine, et je sais que ce que je faisais était apprécié – pas seulement par ceux d'en haut mais aussi par le personnel, et surtout par le majordome, Mr Kite.

Il avait environ cinquante ans et il était en condition depuis l'âge de treize ans ; il avait commencé comme page et il avait gravi les échelons. Sa première place, c'était dans un château où il y avait six valets de pied, deux régisseurs, deux servantes rien que pour la distillerie, six femmes de chambre, un chef cuisinier, un sous-chef, quatre aides-cuisiniers et quatorze jardiniers – autrement dit un personnel énorme. Les domestiques qui travaillaient à l'extérieur logeaient dans des petites chaumières sur le domaine, mais ceux qui bossaient à l'intérieur avaient tout le haut de la maison pour eux. Notez, il y avait une séparation stricte entre les hommes et les femmes, et si un gars se faisait pincer dans le quartier des femmes une fois qu'elles étaient couchées, il était renvoyé aussi sec, et sans certificat.

J'ai demandé à Mr Kite comment c'était de travailler là-bas, et il m'a répondu :

« C'étaient de vrais aristocrates.

– Mais en quoi ils étaient différents de nos patrons d'ici, par exemple ?

– Eh bien, en fait, ils étaient tellement au-dessus de leurs gens qu'ils ne les *voyaient* pas, tout bonnement. Je me souviens d'un soir où je servais à table – je venais de passer valet de pied à ce moment-là. Ces dames s'étaient retirées et on faisait circuler le porto. Ces messieurs parlaient d'un scandale qui touchait un membre de la famille royale, et ils ajoutaient tous leur grain de sel à la rumeur. Un des invités a remarqué : "Dites donc, il ne faudrait pas qu'on nous entende !" Et le maître de maison a répondu : "Comment pourrait-on nous entendre ? Nous sommes seuls ici." À ce moment-là on était trois valets de pied dans la pièce, mais il faut croire qu'on était invisibles. Voilà à quel point ils étaient au-dessus de nous : pour eux on n'était pas là, tout simplement. »

S'il y avait une chose que j'enviais à ceux d'en haut, c'était leur façon de parler. Qu'est-ce que j'aurais aimé causer d'une voix distinguée comme eux ! Un jour, j'ai dit à Mr Kite :

« Vous savez, si on parlait comme eux on pourrait entrer au Ritz sans un sou en poche : dès qu'on ouvrirait la bouche les serveurs se précipiteraient pour nous montrer une table ; alors que là, si on se pointait même avec cinquante livres et qu'on demandait une table, la seule chose qu'ils nous montreraient c'est la porte ! »

Mais Mr Kite était un peu rasoir ; comme ça arrive souvent, à force de fréquenter les gens d'en haut il leur ressemblait par certains côtés. Il sortait des banalités comme si c'étaient des perles de sagesse. Et ça lui plaisait vraiment d'être majordome. Il disait régulièrement :

« Je n'échangerais ma place avec personne, il n'y a pas de honte à faire un travail honnête. »

Je ne sais pas ce qu'il voulait dire par « travail *honnête* » ; il y a plein de choses malhonnêtes qu'on peut faire, mais le travail n'en fait sûrement pas partie ! Il disait aussi :

« Un homme n'a besoin que de deux choses dans la vie : le confort et l'amour. »

Madame lui fournissait le confort, et je me suis souvent posé la question de savoir si je devais lui fournir l'amour. Il ne me l'a jamais demandé, remarquez, mais bon, grâce à la proximité et à ma cuisine il aurait sûrement fini par le faire si je m'étais mis en tête d'en faire mon mari. Mais ç'aurait voulu dire rester domestique toute ma vie, et pour moi c'était hors de question.

Enfin bref, c'est à ce moment-là que j'ai réalisé mon ambition de toujours : j'ai quitté cette place pour me marier, et ç'a été mon dernier emploi fixe comme domestique.

XXVI

En repensant à l'époque où j'étais en condition, je me suis souvent demandé pourquoi c'était aussi mal considéré, pourquoi on nous collait toujours l'étiquette méprisante de « bonniche ». Peut-être que c'était à cause du caractère intime de notre boulot, je me suis souvent dit ça, que c'était le fait qu'on serve nos maîtres comme des esclaves et qu'on leur donne pratiquement la becquée alors qu'ils auraient très bien pu se débrouiller tout seuls. Par certains côtés, c'est vrai qu'on n'était pas beaucoup mieux lotis que des serfs ; toute notre vie était régie par nos patrons : c'étaient eux qui décidaient de nos heures de travail, des habits qu'on portait – en tout cas de ceux qu'on mettait pour travailler, et en partie aussi de ceux qu'on mettait pour sortir. Même notre temps libre, déjà qu'on n'en avait pas beaucoup, il était gâché par l'idée qu'il fallait qu'on soit rentrées « pas plus tard que dix heures ». On n'avait aucune liberté. C'est peut-être pour ça qu'on nous regardait de haut, nous et notre boulot : parce qu'on avait comme qui dirait des rapports de servitude avec nos patrons.

Eux, ils prétendaient toujours qu'ils nous donnaient une formation et que ça nous servirait quand on partirait pour se marier et fonder une famille. Moi, quand je suis partie, je savais préparer un dîner de sept plats sophistiqués et j'avais un énorme complexe d'infériorité. Je ne peux pas dire que ces deux choses m'aient tellement servi une fois que j'ai été mariée !

Mon mari était laitier, il gagnait trois livres cinq shillings par semaine et là-dessus il me donnait trois livres, alors vous imaginez comme ça m'aidait de savoir préparer un repas de sept plats ! Il a fallu que je désapprenne en vitesse toute la cuisine compliquée que je faisais avant et que je me rabatte sur celle que faisait ma mère quand j'étais petite, et ça m'a carrément fait passer le plaisir de cuisiner.

Remarquez, au début de mon mariage je faisais beaucoup de plats recherchés parce que je croyais que ça plairait à mon homme. Je me donnais beaucoup de mal et j'utilisais des morceaux de viande moins chers, naturellement. Ça me demandait un boulot monstre, et à la fin du repas mon mari disait :

« Ce n'était pas mauvais, ma grande, mais j'aurais autant aimé un fish and chips. »

Inutile de vous dire que j'ai vite modéré mes ardeurs !

Eh oui, n'importe quel art demande à être reconnu. Tous ces gens qui peignent, qui sculptent ou qui écrivent des livres, ils veulent avoir un public, c'est pour ça qu'ils le font, non ? Eh bien c'est pareil quand on est cuisinière. On a besoin de quelqu'un qui savoure, pas de quelqu'un qui dit juste : « Ouais, c'est pas mauvais. »

Bref, j'ai rapidement fait un sort au complexe du dîner-de-sept-plats, mais le complexe d'infériorité, j'ai mis beaucoup plus longtemps à m'en débarrasser. Ce n'était pourtant pas faute d'essayer. On parlait déjà beaucoup de psychiatrie, de psychologie et de tous ces machins-là, et il y avait une quantité de livres qui paraissaient sur « Comment ne pas rougir » et « Que faire quand on a un complexe d'infériorité ». Alors j'en ai acheté un, histoire de voir ce que je pourrais bien faire pour le mien. Non seulement j'ai lu des bouquins sur le sujet, mais je suis allée à des cours, et là j'ai découvert que le complexe existe sous deux formes : soit on est timide, soit on est agressif. Moi, c'était la deuxième forme que j'avais. Je vous garantis que ce n'est pas un trait de caractère engageant, et que pour « Se faire des amis et influencer les autres » ce n'est pas l'idéal. Quand on n'est ni riche ni jolie et qu'on est très agressive, on se fait très peu d'amis et on n'influence absolument personne. Je suis arrivée à la conclusion que l'agressivité ne servait à rien si on n'avait pas en plus la beauté ou le pouvoir. Comme je n'avais hélas ni l'une ni l'autre, j'aurais dû faire preuve de bon sens et me résigner à être une espèce de ménagère opprimée, une de ces nombreuses femmes qui voudraient faire quelque chose et qui ne s'en donnent jamais les moyens.

En plus des livres, j'avais droit aux conseils de tout le monde. C'est fou le nombre de gens qui sont toujours prêts à vous abreuver de conseils, vous ne trouvez pas ? C'était soit : « Il te faut des enfants », soit : « Il faut que tu fasses des études », soit : « Ce qu'il faudrait, c'est que tu voyages. » Alors bon, comme la première de ces recommandations était la plus facile à suivre, j'ai décidé de faire ça. Et c'est vrai que ça m'a bien occupée puisque j'ai eu trois enfants en cinq ans. Trois garçons. À la fin, j'étais habituée !

Je me souviens que le dernier s'est annoncé un dimanche. D'ailleurs mes trois enfants sont nés un dimanche, je ne sais

pas si ça veut dire quelque chose… Mon mari est allé chercher la sage-femme, et comme elle s'apprêtait à aller à la
messe elle n'a pas apprécié – ma parole, elle croyait que
j'avais choisi l'heure de la naissance ou quoi ? En tout cas, de
voir sa mine revêche ça ne m'a pas aidée – déjà qu'un accou-
chement ce n'est pas une partie de plaisir, même quand tout
se passe bien… Au moment où le bébé est né, elle s'est
écriée :

« Ah, dommage ! C'est encore un garçon ! »

J'ai répondu du tac au tac :

« Je me fiche pas mal que ce soit un affreux macaque du
moment que c'est enfin fini ! »

Elle m'a regardée d'un air très choqué et elle m'a fait :

« Vous savez, je considère chaque enfant que je mets au
monde comme une fleur envoyée du ciel pour être plantée
en terre. »

Ça lui allait bien de dire ça ! Elle n'avait jamais rien fait
pousser, vu qu'elle était vieille fille ! Du coup j'ai répliqué :

« Mais il y a des terres trop dures pour les petites graines,
pas vrai ? »

J'avais une vision très prosaïque de la chose, parce que
dans la rue où j'avais habité étant gamine la plupart des
enfants étaient le résultat de la nouba du samedi soir. On les
appelait les « enfants de la bière ».

Lorsqu'on a décidé de se marier, Albert et moi, vous
pensez bien que j'ai voulu quitter mon boulot tout de suite.
Rappelez-vous, pendant toutes mes années en condition je
m'étais dit que pour m'en échapper aussi vite que possible
il fallait que je me marie, alors dès que la date a été fixée j'ai
donné mon préavis.

Cette fois j'avais une raison parfaitement légitime de le faire, et Madame a été très aimable avec moi. C'est drôle, si on partait pour aller travailler ailleurs, ça ne leur plaisait jamais trop, à nos patrons, mais si c'était pour se marier, alors là, pas de problème. C'était non seulement acceptable, mais respectable.

Pourtant, quand on essayait de se trouver un fiancé, pour eux ce n'était pas respectable, et ils dénigraient toutes les relations qu'on pouvait avoir. On était censées trouver un mari dans les choux, apparemment. Leurs filles, elles, c'étaient des « débutantes », elles pouvaient rencontrer des jeunes gens à des bals officiels, à des soirées dansantes ou à des fêtes privées, mais quand une domestique avait un petit ami on disait que c'était un « galant ». C'est méprisant comme mot, je trouve : on imagine une femme qui rôde en cachette dans des ruelles bien sombres avec n'importe quel gars qui s'intéresse à elle. Pourquoi ça ? Pourquoi on ne devrait pas être amoureuse quand on est domestique, alors qu'eux ils ont inventé toute cette affaire de débutantes pour que leurs filles rencontrent des jeunes gens ? Ils auraient pu dire :

« S'il y a un jeune homme qui vous intéresse, vous pouvez l'inviter dans la salle des domestiques après votre travail. »

Mais non, il fallait qu'on grimpe en cachette l'escalier extérieur du sous-sol pour aller le retrouver au coin de la rue sous un prétexte quelconque, par exemple aller poster une lettre. Et quand on revenait de notre soirée de congé on ne pouvait pas rester en haut de l'escalier avec lui ni l'inviter à descendre pour lui dire bonne nuit. Ce n'était pas un jeune homme, c'était un « galant ». On aurait dit que, pour ceux d'en haut, si on plaisait à un individu de sexe masculin c'était forcément mal.

Albert et moi, on a décidé de se marier à la mairie. On n'était pas très riches et on se fichait un peu des cérémonies et des tralalas, alors on a fait simple. J'ai eu droit à toutes les questions rituelles, du style : « Tu te maries pour ne plus être domestique, c'est ça ? » Ou bien : « Est-ce que tu es vraiment amoureuse ? » Je n'étais pas follement amoureuse d'Albert mais je l'aimais beaucoup, et je trouvais que c'était une bonne base pour construire un couple.

Étant donné que mon mari ne gagnait que trois livres cinq par semaine et que là-dessus il m'en donnait trois, vous vous demandez peut-être pourquoi je ne travaillais pas à l'extérieur. C'est tout simplement qu'à l'époque ça ne se faisait pas. Les ouvriers mariés ne supportaient pas l'idée que leur femme soit obligée de travailler en dehors de leur foyer. Pour eux ça dévalorisait le mari, ça voulait dire qu'il n'était pas capable de subvenir aux besoins de sa femme. S'il était au chômage ce n'était pas pareil, évidemment. Là, elle était obligée.

Au début on a habité à Chelsea, et dans le logement à côté de chez nous il y avait une femme qui était mariée avec un Russe. Mrs Balkonsky, elle s'appelait – et le prénom de son mari c'était Boris, naturellement. Elle avait cinq enfants et pas beaucoup plus d'argent que moi pour les nourrir. C'était une modiste sensationnelle, et elle aurait pu continuer son activité chez elle, ça aurait fait un complément de salaire pour la famille. Mais son mari était tellement contre le fait qu'elle travaille, ou qu'elle gagne de l'argent en plus de ce qu'il lui donnait, qu'il n'a jamais voulu.

Moi, personnellement, je n'avais pas envie de travailler pour les autres. Je ne m'ennuyais jamais ; au contraire, j'étais bien contente de ne rien avoir à faire pendant quelque temps. J'avais beau défendre les droits des femmes, je n'étais pas féministe à ce point-là. Je revendiquais mon indépendance pour tout ce qui concernait la maison, et je n'étais absolument pas soumise à mon mari. Je trouvais qu'il en avait largement pour son argent sur tous les plans : au niveau physique, au niveau de la maison, au niveau des relations sociales aussi, et je ne me sentais pas du tout redevable vis-à-vis de lui.

De toute façon, le seul travail pour lequel j'étais vraiment qualifiée c'était la cuisine, et pour faire ça il aurait fallu que je sorte le soir, que je prépare des dîners. Mais à mon avis, si la femme bosse le soir, ce n'est pas très bon pour le couple.

Moi je voulais réussir mon mariage, de la même façon que je voulais réussir d'autres choses dans la vie. Et j'avais passé tellement d'années à vouloir quitter la condition de domestique qu'il m'a fallu beaucoup de temps pour m'apercevoir que la vie au foyer ne me suffisait pas. Mais à ce moment-là j'avais déjà trois enfants, alors les autres aspirations que j'avais, j'ai dû les mettre au placard en attendant. S'occuper de trois enfants c'est un boulot à plein temps, pour moi en tout cas, parce que j'étais une mère au sens fort du terme – enfin, je crois.

Comme j'ai dit, juste après notre mariage on a habité à Chelsea, qui nous semblait être le meilleur quartier de Londres. On payait quinze shillings par semaine pour un studio avec une cuisine minuscule. C'est là qu'on a eu notre premier enfant. Mais quand la famille s'est agrandie, une pièce avec une cuisine ça ne suffisait plus, évidemment, alors on a déménagé. On a habité successivement à Willesden, Harlesden et Kilburn, des quartiers tristes et miteux.

Au bout de cinq ans de mariage j'avais trois enfants, donc, et comme à ce moment-là Albert était encore laitier on commençait à être un peu justes financièrement.

Un jour, je suis sortie faire des courses et je suis tombée sur une de mes anciennes collègues. Elle m'a dit que les gens pour qui elle travaillait étaient dans tous leurs états : leur cuisinière n'était pas là et ils devaient recevoir du monde à dîner. Elle m'a demandé :

« Pourquoi tu ne viendrais pas le préparer, leur dîner ?

– Oh là là, je ne saurais plus ! Ça fait des années que je n'ai pas fait ce genre de cuisine.

– Mais ça va revenir en un clin d'œil, ça ne s'oublie pas, ces trucs-là. Pourquoi tu n'essaies pas ? »

En rentrant à la maison j'en ai parlé à Albert. Je lui ai dit que ça me rapporterait entre dix shillings et une guinée* à chaque fois, et que pour les enfants ça serait rudement utile. Alors il a accepté, et j'y suis allée.

Je me suis plutôt bien débrouillée, d'ailleurs, et à la fin la maîtresse de maison est descendue me voir à la cuisine pour me demander si j'aimerais qu'elle me recommande à ses amies. J'ai dit oui. Après ça, des gens qu'elle connaissait m'ont écrit de temps en temps pour me demander si je pouvais venir faire à dîner chez eux ; quelquefois pour six personnes, quelquefois plus, ça pouvait aller jusqu'à douze personnes, et dans ce cas-là ils commandaient aussi des plats à l'extérieur. Pour un petit dîner j'étais payée une

---

* Une guinée valait à l'époque 21 shillings, autrement dit 1,05 livre. (N.d.T.)

demi-guinée, mais un repas élaboré pouvait me rapporter deux guinées, et quand on pense que mon mari ne gagnait qu'à peu près quatre livres par semaine, deux guinées c'était sacrément bien payé. Et ça me plaisait bien, ces petites expéditions. En dehors de l'argent, ça me permettait de voir à quel point la vie en condition avait évolué. Les patrons étaient tellement différents, tellement gentils ! Ils faisaient sans arrêt des allers et retours à la cuisine et ils me parlaient d'égal à égal. Pour les gens de maison, c'est fou ce que les choses avaient changé !

XXVII

On a vécu comme ça, plutôt agréablement, jusqu'en 1942, et puis mon mari a été mobilisé. Il a été enrôlé dans la Royal Air Force, et du coup j'ai décidé de retourner habiter à Hove.

Comme je ne voulais pas rester à Londres pendant la guerre avec mes trois petits garçons, j'ai écrit à mes parents pour voir s'ils pouvaient me trouver une maison. C'était très facile à ce moment-là, car beaucoup de gens avaient quitté Hove à cause des raids éclairs. Mes parents m'en ont trouvé une de six pièces pour une livre par semaine. C'était formidable : pour la première fois depuis qu'on était mariés on avait une maison. Le plus grand logement qu'on avait eu jusque-là, c'était un trois pièces avec des toilettes communes.

Je me souviens d'un appartement qu'on a eu à Kilburn ; il fallait descendre au rez-de-chaussée et traverser la cuisine d'un locataire pour aller aux cabinets. Cet homme a passé tout l'été à faire de la chaise longue juste devant la porte des toilettes, et j'étais très gênée quand je devais lui demander de se pousser. Je crois bien que c'est là que j'ai été constipée pour la première fois !

Je me disais que tout ça était à moi, et j'étais comme un coq en pâte. Je vous laisse imaginer de quoi nos affaires avaient l'air là-dedans, vu qu'on avait seulement de quoi meubler trois pièces. Il fallait les répartir dans toute la maison, alors dans chaque chambre il y avait juste un lit et rien par terre, mais ça m'était complètement égal.

Pour les trois garçons ça s'est bien passé à Hove. Au début ils sont tous allés à la même école primaire, et après ils ont réussi l'examen d'entrée au collège. Pour moi ç'a été une joie énorme, mais en même temps ça m'a causé des soucis terribles. Comme je devais m'occuper toute seule des trois garçons je ne pouvais pas travailler à l'extérieur, et l'allocation militaire que je touchais était sacrément maigre.

J'ai écrit je ne sais combien de lettres aux services de l'éducation avant de recevoir enfin un supplément. Mais même comme ça j'avais beaucoup de mal à joindre les deux bouts, et quand Albert avait une promotion (à la fin il était caporal) on n'y gagnait rien, parce que chaque fois qu'il était augmenté le gouvernement diminuait mon allocation d'autant. Du coup, ça ne l'encourageait pas à essayer de monter en grade.

Je ne pouvais plus faire moi-même les vêtements des garçons. Pour des filles j'aurais pu, mais les garçons, il faut qu'ils soient tous habillés pareil. On ne peut pas les envoyer à l'école avec des habits faits maison.

Je me souviens d'un épisode affreux, la seule fois de ma vie où j'ai été obligée de demander la charité. Les garçons n'avaient qu'une paire de chaussures chacun. Quand mon mari était à la maison il les rafistolait, mais à ce moment-là il était à l'étranger. Je ne savais pas à qui m'adresser pour les faire réparer, donc je suis allée à l'Association de bienfaisance des soldats, marins et aviateurs, et ils m'ont envoyée à la mairie. C'était horrible, je vous assure. Je crois qu'il fallait avoir une peau de rhinocéros pour leur demander quoi que ce soit. Certaines personnes avaient l'habitude d'y aller pour plein de choses, et ça ne leur faisait ni chaud ni froid. Mais moi c'était la première fois que je demandais quelque chose, alors quand je suis entrée j'étais terriblement nerveuse et rouge comme une tomate. J'avais l'impression d'être une pauvresse.

« Pourquoi vous voulez des chaussures pour vos enfants ? Ils n'en ont pas, des chaussures ?

— Si, mais une paire seulement.

— Et pourquoi vous ne les faites pas réparer ?

— Je peux les faire réparer, mais pendant ce temps-là ils ne pourront pas aller à l'école ; ils n'en ont pas de rechange. »

Après cet interrogatoire, ils m'ont renvoyée à l'Association des soldats, marins et aviateurs. Une fois sur place j'ai expliqué :

« Là-bas ils ont dit que c'était de votre ressort.

— Mais non, ce n'est pas à nous de fournir des chaussures. Retournez à la mairie et recommencez depuis le début. »

J'y suis retournée, j'ai à nouveau suivi toute la procédure, et là, à contrecœur, ils m'ont donné des formulaires. Ils ne donnaient pas d'argent, ils ne donnaient pas de chaussures, ils donnaient des formulaires avec lesquels on devait aller dans un magasin spécial à Hove.

Là je n'ai pas pu avoir de chaussures, seulement des godillots, ces gros machins bien reconnaissables que les œuvres de charité distribuaient. Mes fils n'en avaient jamais

porté avant. Je n'ai pas trop cherché à savoir s'ils en souf-
fraient ; j'en avais tellement honte moi-même que je ne leur
ai jamais demandé ce qu'ils ressentaient, mais c'était sûrement dur pour eux d'aller à l'école avec ces godillots : tout le
monde savait d'où ils venaient.

Quand mes fils sont allés au collège, c'était encore payant,
alors évidemment les familles des autres garçons étaient
beaucoup plus riches que nous. La plupart étaient allés dans
des écoles primaires privées et leurs parents leur donnaient
de l'argent. Certains avaient une livre d'argent de poche par
semaine. Une livre par semaine, vous vous rendez compte !
Moi je ne pouvais même pas donner un shilling* aux miens.
Je me souviens d'un petit souci que j'ai eu avec un de mes fils
(il avait dessiné une moustache sur la photo du directeur) ;
ce jour-là le directeur m'a assurée qu'ils ne se sentaient pas
inférieurs parce qu'ils étaient pauvres, que tout ça c'étaient
des balivernes. Il a ajouté :

« Moi je suis parti de rien. Si j'ai pu aller au collège, c'est
uniquement grâce à une bourse, et je n'avais que six pence
d'argent de poche par semaine. »

Mais les temps avaient changé. On leur donnait plus,
maintenant, aux enfants.

Dans la même veine, si on gagnait moins de cinq livres par
semaine on avait droit à des repas gratuits. L'ennui, c'est que
personne d'autre dans leurs classes n'y avait droit, et qu'au
début de chaque trimestre le maître disait :

« Levez-vous, ceux qui veulent des tickets repas. »

Je vous laisse imaginer ce qu'on peut ressentir quand on
est le seul de sa classe que ses parents n'ont pas les moyens

* C'est-à-dire vingt fois moins. (N.d.T.)

de nourrir. Ça doit être affreux. Moi-même je ne m'en rendais pas bien compte à l'époque. Si j'avais su tout ça, je n'aurais pas cherché à mettre mes enfants au collège. Certainement pas. Enfin bon, comme je savais à l'avance quel maître ils auraient, je lui écrivais en le priant de ne pas demander tout haut en classe : « Qui a besoin de manger gratuitement à l'école ? » Je dois dire qu'ils en ont tenu compte, et qu'après ils ne l'ont plus fait.

Je n'avais pas saisi non plus l'importance du sport. Le cricket, par exemple. Je ne pouvais pas leur acheter des tenues spéciales pour le cricket. Pour le foot je leur avais fait des shorts, mais quand il y avait un match à l'extérieur je n'avais pas de quoi payer le déplacement. Je me disais que ce n'était pas grave, qu'ils recevaient une bonne éducation et que c'était le principal. Mais les autres choses étaient importantes aussi.

Je crois que parfois on a trop d'ambition. On veut que ses enfants soient instruits, alors on les envoie dans un autre milieu social et ils ne peuvent pas s'intégrer. En fait les gens ont l'instinct grégaire, comme les animaux. Il suffit qu'il y en ait un de différent, et tous les autres lui tombent dessus.

XXVIII

C'est à cause de tous ces problèmes que j'ai décidé de retravailler, et j'ai choisi de faire des ménages. La cuisine, il ne fallait pas y compter ; pendant la guerre il n'y avait pas beaucoup de travail pour les cuisinières. Donc ça ne pouvait être que des ménages. C'était très mal payé : au début je ne gagnais que dix pence de l'heure. Ça paraît incroyable aujourd'hui, quand on y pense. Je suppose que tout le monde touchait la même chose, sinon j'aurais demandé plus, c'est sûr.

Je travaillais chez un pasteur, et d'ailleurs c'était un sacré boulot. Vous savez comment c'est dans les presbytères : il y a le jour des boy-scouts, le jour des éclaireuses, le jour de l'Association des femmes, celui de l'Union des mères, et bien sûr ces vieux presbytères ne sont pas conçus pour économiser la main-d'œuvre. Ils ont été construits à une époque où les gens avaient une flopée de domestiques. Pourtant j'aimais bien bosser là-bas. Le salaire était maigre mais j'avais des avantages en nature, par exemple des restes de nourriture ; et puis quand il y avait une vente de charité la femme du pasteur me laissait toujours choisir tout ce que je voulais avant. Elle me disait :

« Mettez juste une petite pièce et servez-vous. »

J'ai récupéré comme ça pas mal de costumes et de chandails tout à fait corrects pour mes fils avant l'arrivée de la foule.

Je suis restée au presbytère pendant quelque temps, et puis un jour j'ai bavardé avec une amie qui faisait aussi des ménages et elle m'a dit qu'elle gagnait un shilling trois pence de l'heure ; le tarif avait augmenté de cinq pence en peu de temps. Et comme je faisais ce boulot uniquement pour l'argent, j'ai commencé à chercher une autre place.

La première chose qui m'a sidérée, c'est le changement que j'ai trouvé après toutes ces années. Dans des maisons qui avaient été luxueuses et qui employaient avant une ribambelle de domestiques, il n'y avait plus du tout de personnel ; juste une femme de ménage quelques heures par jour. La plupart des beaux objets avaient disparu ; leurs propriétaires avaient été obligés de les vendre pour payer leurs impôts.

C'étaient surtout des dames très âgées, et elles acceptaient cette baisse de standing avec pas mal de cran. Quelques-unes me parlaient de leur situation d'autrefois et des biens qu'elles avaient perdus. Je me souviens d'une maison où je travaillais deux matinées par semaine. Tout ce qui restait de leur argenterie, c'était un grand plateau où on pouvait mettre tout un service à thé, et un jour où j'étais en train de l'astiquer Mrs Jackson, une très vieille dame, m'a dit :

« Ah, Margaret, quand le service à thé était disposé sur ce plateau et que le majordome l'apportait au salon, c'était l'image même de la sécurité. Nous n'imaginions pas que les choses allaient changer. »

Je ne pouvais pas m'empêcher d'être désolée pour ces femmes, même si par rapport à ce que je gagnais elles étaient encore plutôt à l'aise. C'est sûrement beaucoup plus dur d'être pauvre quand on a longtemps roulé sur l'or que quand on a toujours été fauché ; et puis en arriver à devoir faire soi-même presque tout son ménage quand on est aussi âgée… C'est plus facile de s'y mettre quand on est jeune, on est plus résistante.

Remarquez, ce qui était drôle, c'est qu'elles avaient beau ne plus pouvoir se payer que des femmes de journée, malgré tout certaines avaient gardé leurs manières autoritaires. Elles se plaignaient amèrement que la vie était sordide ; elles aimaient beaucoup dire ça, que tout était « sordide ». Leur phrase favorite, c'était : « Maintenant les ouvriers singent leurs supérieurs » (les supérieurs en question étant elles-mêmes, évidemment) et aussi : « Le pays est gouverné par une bande de moins que rien, et tout part à vau-l'eau. »

Une des dames pour qui je travaillais s'appelait Mrs Rutherford-Smith. Un jour elle m'a dit :

« Margaret, vous travaillez très bien et je vous apprécie, mais tout de même vous avez un défaut. J'espère que vous ne serez pas vexée que je vous le dise. Vous ne m'appelez jamais "Madame". »

Et elle a ajouté :

« Vous savez, Margaret, si je m'adressais à la reine je lui dirais "Madame". »

J'aurais bien voulu lui répondre : « Oui, mais il n'y en a qu'une, de reine, alors que des Mrs Smith, il y en a à tous les coins de rue ! »

Ce qui leur manquait beaucoup, à Mrs Rutherford et aux autres dames comme elle, c'étaient toutes ces petites attentions auxquelles elles avaient eu droit autrefois. Elles regrettaient le temps où on ôtait son chapeau sur leur passage, où les commerçants leur parlaient avec déférence, où elles étaient servies par des domestiques stylés.

Les personnes chez qui je faisais des ménages étaient en général vieilles et seules, et j'étais souvent leur unique contact avec l'extérieur. Ça me paraissait bizarre, étant donné que la plupart vivaient en appartement : je croyais que quand on habitait dans un immeuble on faisait partie d'une sorte de microcosme. Mais pas du tout. J'ai bossé dans une demi-douzaine d'immeubles comme ça et je n'ai jamais vu personne entrer ou sortir. Apparemment tout le monde était cloîtré dans sa petite cellule. Ces vieilles dames habitaient là par nécessité, parce que c'était facile à entretenir, mais elles étaient très seules.

Quelques-unes prenaient les choses avec philosophie et discutaient avec moi d'égale à égale, mais certaines avaient l'impression de me faire une énorme faveur en s'asseyant à côté de moi comme si j'étais de leur monde. Celles-là trouvaient aussi très bizarre qu'une femme de ménage ait ne serait-ce qu'une once d'intelligence.

J'ai travaillé pour une certaine Mrs Swob. En fait je ne devrais pas l'appeler comme ça : son nom s'écrivait Schwab, elle le prononçait « Swayb » et c'est comme ça qu'elle voulait que tout le monde fasse, mais la plupart des gens disaient « Swob* », ce qui avait le don de l'exaspérer.

---

* Cette dame trouvait sans doute que *swob* ressemblait trop à *swab*, qui signifie entre autres « serpillière ». *(N.d.T.)*

La maison de cette Mrs Schwab était pleine d'antiquités – de vieux nids à poussière, si vous voulez mon avis. Elle avait notamment quelques miroirs ronds avec des cadres dorés à volutes, et le jour où j'ai fait tomber un morceau de cadre ça n'a pas eu l'air de lui plaire. Elle m'a fait :

« Il faut traiter les objets mieux que ça, Margaret. N'aimez-vous pas les beaux objets ?

– Non, Mrs Schwab. Je suis plutôt d'accord avec G. K. Chesterton* quand il parle de la malfaisance des objets inanimés. Je les trouve malfaisants à cause de tout ce temps que je passe à les épousseter, à les astiquer et à les nettoyer. Ce vase-là, par exemple, vous dites qu'il vaut cent livres, mais s'il tombait par terre ça ne ferait jamais que trois ou quatre morceaux de porcelaine sans valeur. »

Ça lui a coupé le sifflet pendant quelques secondes, et puis elle a dit :

« Je ne savais pas que vous lisiez, Margaret. Moi-même je lis beaucoup, naturellement. »

Ça, c'était bien elle : si vous faisiez quelque chose, elle le faisait aussi, mais à la puissance dix.

Un jour où je parlais de films, elle m'a sorti :

« Oh, moi, j'aurais pu être une star de cinéma. J'aurais bien aimé, mais à l'époque je sortais avec l'homme qui devait devenir mon mari, et lui ne voulait pas. Tout le monde a été extrêmement déçu. »

---

* L'écrivain britannique Gilbert Keith Chesterton (1874-1936) fut notamment journaliste, poète, biographe (*Charles Dickens*, 1906) et penseur politique (*Plaidoyer pour une propriété anticapitaliste*, 1927). Il s'illustra également dans le genre policier (*Les Enquêtes du père Brown*, 1911-1935). (*N.d.T.*)

Le nombre de salades qu'elle me servait, c'était incroyable – et elle n'y allait pas de main morte ! Moi je prenais mon air impressionné, il fallait bien. Je bossais pour elle, j'avais besoin de son argent, et si ça n'avait pas été elle ç'aurait été quelqu'un d'autre. Ce genre de personne vous emploie pour avoir un public captif sous la main. Et puis bon, pendant que je l'écoutais je ne travaillais pas !

Cette Mme Schwab avait une habitude exaspérante. Chaque fois que j'allais chez elle, elle me disait :

« Margaret, quand vous nettoierez la salle de bains, n'oubliez pas de faire les coins. »

Je vous garantis que ça ne lui a rien rapporté. À partir de là je n'ai plus utilisé la brosse à pavés, je passais juste un peu de produit par terre.

La goutte d'eau qui a fait déborder le vase, ç'a été le balayage du balcon. Un matin elle m'a fait :

« Non, non, ne balayez pas la poussière de ce côté-ci, balayez-la de l'autre côté. »

Vous avez déjà entendu une ânerie pareille, vous ? J'ai ramassé mon salaire et je suis partie. Je n'ai pas eu le courage de lui dire que je ne reviendrais pas, parce que je savais qu'elle allait me balancer des injures ; mon instinct me disait que c'était son genre. Je lui ai écrit une lettre très classe – du moins il me semble – où je lui disais qu'il était « vraisemblablement aussi irritant pour elle d'avoir éternellement à me dire comment procéder qu'exaspérant pour moi d'avoir à écouter ses conseils ».

Quand on travaillait à la journée on n'avait pas à s'en faire pour le certificat. Il suffisait de dire qu'on n'avait jamais bossé à l'extérieur, ou que nos derniers employeurs étaient morts. Du reste, c'était mon cas : tous les gens pour qui j'avais travaillé les derniers temps avaient rendu l'âme. Je ne sais pas s'il y avait un rapport de cause à effet entre les deux, mais bon, c'était comme ça.

XXIX

Mon fils cadet allait encore au collège et mon aîné se préparait à entrer à l'université quand je me suis aperçue qu'en dehors de la météo il n'y avait aucun sujet dont on pouvait parler ensemble. En rentrant à la maison ils discutaient d'histoire, d'astronomie, de français, de plein de choses comme ça, et quelquefois j'étais complètement perdue. Je n'avais jamais essayé de me hisser au niveau de qui que ce soit, mais j'ai décidé de faire ce que je pourrais pour rester au niveau de mes fils.

Au début, j'ai pensé prendre des cours par correspondance. Mais, même sans parler de la dépense, quand on suit des cours par correspondance on est tout seul ; si on n'a pas envie de travailler il n'y a personne pour vous dire de vous y mettre, et comme on ne peut se comparer à personne on ne fait pas attention au temps qu'on met.

Et puis un jour le prof d'histoire d'un de mes fils m'a parlé d'une série de conférences pour le grand public données par un enseignant d'Oxford, le professeur Bruce. Ce n'était pas cher, un shilling la conférence, je crois, et même moins si on s'inscrivait pour toute la série, c'est-à-dire vingt-quatre. Je me suis inscrite pour toute la série.

Ces conférences m'ont passionnée. Il devait être vraiment génial, ce professeur, parce que c'était le soir de sept heures et demie à neuf heures et demie, avec une pause-café au milieu, et pourtant on continuait souvent à discuter jusqu'à onze heures, et je n'étais pas chez moi avant onze heures et demie. Mon mari me disait :

« Je me demande bien ce que tu apprends, pour rentrer aussi tard. »

Mais moi, franchement, ça m'a ouvert les yeux. J'avais toujours cru que l'histoire c'était une discipline aride, une succession de dates et tout ça.

Après j'ai pris des cours du soir en philosophie, en histoire et en littérature. Le seul sujet auquel je n'ai vraiment rien compris, c'est la philosophie métaphysique. Vous savez ce que c'est quand on est débutant : on prend un peu des poses. On n'a pas envie de choisir les mêmes matières que tout le monde, on veut pouvoir sortir un nom bien ronflant. C'est comme ça que je me suis inscrite en philosophie métaphysique.

Je n'ai jamais su de quoi ça parlait. Tout ce que j'ai compris, c'est que ça avait à voir avec l'hédonisme ou quelque chose comme ça. Au bout de six soirées j'ai décidé que ce n'était pas pour moi. Mais c'est le seul cours que je n'ai pas suivi jusqu'au bout.

Vous vous demandez peut-être où tout ça m'a menée. Eh bien j'ai eu mon brevet à cinquante-huit ans, et actuellement je prépare le bac, que j'espère obtenir prochainement*. Les gens me disent qu'ils ne comprennent pas pourquoi je fais ça.

Moi je crois que ça vient de mon enfance. La vie, ça forme un tout, non ? J'aimais l'école, j'ai réussi l'examen d'entrée au collège, mais je n'ai pas pu y aller parce que c'était trop cher et je suis entrée en condition. Ça m'a frustrée, et toute cette frustration s'est manifestée dans mon attitude vis-à-vis du sort des domestiques. Si j'avais fait un autre métier, je pense que j'aurais milité activement contre leurs conditions de travail.

Quand je me suis mariée, j'ai eu des enfants et je suis devenue mère à plein temps. Et puis, quand je n'ai plus eu besoin de m'occuper d'eux, l'envie d'étudier est revenue.

Les gens me disent : « Il faut croire que tu t'ennuyais », mais en fait ça ne s'est pas produit tout d'un coup. C'est quelque chose d'enraciné en soi, et même si ça prend dix, vingt ou quarante ans, on finit par être capable de réaliser le désir qu'on avait depuis le début.

Est-ce que j'aurais été plus heureuse si j'avais pu faire ce que je voulais quand j'étais jeune ? C'est possible. Je ne suis pas de ceux qui prétendent que quand on est pauvre ça a quelque chose de merveilleux. Moi, j'adorerais être riche. Je ne vois pas ce qu'il y a de formidable à être pauvre, à ne pas avoir les bons vêtements, à ne pas pouvoir aller dans les chouettes endroits. Je n'envie pas spécialement les gens riches, mais je ne les blâme pas non plus. Ils se cramponnent à leur argent, et à leur place j'en ferais autant. Ceux qui disent que les riches devraient partager racontent vraiment

---

* Margaret a effectivement obtenu l'équivalent britannique du baccalauréat en 1969. *(N.d.T.)*

n'importe quoi ; ils pensent ça parce qu'ils n'ont pas d'argent. Moi, si j'en avais, je ne le partagerais certainement pas.

Quand je repense à ce que je vous ai dit, j'ai l'impression que vous devez me trouver drôlement amère par rapport à ma vie de domestique. L'amertume est présente, c'est vrai, parce que c'était ce sentiment-là qui dominait chez moi à l'époque. Et les anecdotes que je vous ai racontées, c'est ce qui me reste en mémoire aujourd'hui.

Je sais que tout ça est fini, bien fini. Ça n'existe plus, maintenant, ce genre de choses. Mais je pense qu'il ne faut pas oublier que ça a existé.

Et puis il y avait quand même de bons moments, et j'ai vraiment bien profité de la vie. Souvenez-vous que je n'avais pas été habituée à beaucoup de liberté !

Vivre en condition, ça donne un aperçu, voire des idées, sur ce que ça peut être qu'une vie meilleure. On pense à la façon dont nos employeurs vivaient, et peut-être qu'incon-sciemment on essaie de les imiter. Les bonnes manières, ce n'est peut-être pas très important, mais ça aide à faire son chemin dans la vie, malgré tout.

Alors non, même si je vous ai donné cette impression, je ne ressens pas d'amertume par rapport au fait que j'ai dû être domestique. Je me demande souvent ce qui serait arrivé si j'avais pu réaliser mon ambition et devenir institutrice, mais aujourd'hui je suis heureuse. Et comme le champ de mes connaissances et de mes lectures s'élargit, l'avenir s'annonce radieux !

Composition et mise en pages : FACOMPO, LISIEUX

 IMPRIM'VERT®

Achevé d'imprimer
en mars 2013
par Corlet imprimeur
14110 Condé-sur-Noireau

Dépôt légal : mars 2013
N° d'imprimeur : 153929
Imprimé en France